THE CONSTITUTION OF INDONESIA

For decades, Indonesia's 1945 Constitution, the se[c] e
modern world, was used as an apologia by regimes. A bare-bones text originally inte[r] it did little beyond establish basic s' presidency. It did not offer citizens r[e] hese weaknesses were ruthlessly exploited [b] egime that President Soeharto headed from 1966 [to] 1998. The (first ever) amendments of the Constitution, w[hich beg]an the following year and were completed in 2002, changed all this. Enlarging and rethinking the Constitution, they ushered in a liberal democratic system based around human rights, an open society and separation of powers. These reforms also created a Constitutional Court that has provided Indonesia's first judicial forum for serious debate on the interpretation and application of the Constitution, as well as its first significant and easily-accessible body of detailed and reasoned judgments. Today, Indonesian constitutional law is rich, sophisticated and complex. This book surveys this remarkable constitutional transition, assessing the implementation of Indonesia's new constitutional model and identifying its weaknesses. After covering key institutions exercising executive, legislative and judicial powers, the book focuses on current constitutional debates, ranging from human rights to decentralisation, religious freedom and control of the economy.

Constitutional Systems of the World
General Editors: Peter Leyland and Andrew Harding
Associate Editors: Benjamin L Berger and Grégoire Webber

In the era of globalisation, issues of constitutional law and good governance are being seen increasingly as vital issues in all types of society. Since the end of the Cold War, there have been dramatic developments in democratic and legal reform, and post-conflict societies are also in the throes of reconstructing their governance systems. Even societies already firmly based on constitutional governance and the rule of law have undergone constitutional change and experimentation with new forms of governance; and their constitutional systems are increasingly subjected to comparative analysis and transplantation. Constitutional texts for practically every country in the world are now easily available on the internet. However, texts which enable one to understand the true context, purposes, interpretation and incidents of a constitutional system are much harder to locate, and are often extremely detailed and descriptive. This series seeks to provide scholars and students with accessible introductions to the constitutional systems of the world, supplying both a road map for the novice and, at the same time, a deeper understanding of the key historical, political and legal events which have shaped the constitutional landscape of each country. Each book in this series deals with a single country, or a group of countries with a common constitutional history, and each author is an expert in their field.

Published volumes

The Constitution of the United Kingdom
The Constitution of the United States
The Constitution of Vietnam
The Constitution of South Africa
The Constitution of Japan
The Constitution of Germany
The Constitution of Finland
The Constitution of Australia
The Constitution of the Republic of Austria
The Constitution of the Russian Federation
The Constitutional System of Thailand

Link to series website

http://www.hartpub.co.uk/series/csw

The Constitution of Indonesia

A Contextual Analysis

Simon Butt and Tim Lindsey

•HART•
PUBLISHING

OXFORD AND PORTLAND, OREGON
2012

Published in the United Kingdom by Hart Publishing Ltd
16C Worcester Place, Oxford, OX1 2JW
Telephone: +44 (0)1865 517530
Fax: +44 (0)1865 510710
E-mail: mail@hartpub.co.uk
Website: http://www.hartpub.co.uk

Published in North America (US and Canada) by
Hart Publishing
c/o International Specialized Book Services
920 NE 58th Avenue, Suite 300
Portland, OR 97213-3786
USA
Tel: +1 503 287 3093 or toll-free: (1) 800 944 6190
Fax: +1 503 280 8832
E-mail: orders@isbs.com
Website: http://www.isbs.com

British Library Cataloguing in Publication Data
Data Available

ISBN: 978-1-84946-018-7

Typeset by Hope Services Ltd, Abingdon
Printed and bound in Great Britain by
TJ International Ltd, Padstow, Cornwall

For our parents:
from Tim for Jenny and Paul, and Simon
for Marion and Peter

Preface

Before 1998, discussions about Indonesian constitutional law were usually dominated by efforts to explain why there was so little of it. Under Soeharto, the Constitution was used as an apologia by an authoritarian regime that saw the text as accountable to it, and not vice versa. In many respects this was exactly what its framer, Professor Soepomo, intended, as we show in Chapter 1. If we had tried to write this book then, it would have been a slim document indeed – just like the original Constitution itself, the second-shortest in the modern world.

Since 1998, and, in particular, since the Fourth Amendment of the Constitution in 2002, this has all changed, and the long shadow of Soepomo has faded. Today, Indonesian constitutional law is rich, sophisticated and complex – and there is lots of it, just like the lengthy new amended Constitution. The open multi-party and liberal democratic polity built from the ruins of the repressive New Order dictatorship has an enthusiasm for vigorous argument that has ensured this, and has made this book possible.

The new Constitutional Court has been central to this process. It has provided both Indonesia's first public forum for serious debate on the interpretation and application of the Constitution, and its first significant and easily-accessible body of detailed and reasoned judgments. This book is therefore to a great extent an account of the jurisprudence of that court. We are grateful to its founding Chief Justice, Professor Jimly Asshiddiqie, for his key role in establishing the practices and culture of this innovative and influential institution, and for his generous personal support for our own research, both jointly and separately.

We also wish to thank Indonesia's leading advocate of rule of law and constitutionalism, Professor Adnan Buyung Nasution. It is to his credit that many of the unlikely dreams he pursued over many decades as a legal aid lawyer, dissident activist and scholar of constitutionalism have now been realised. In his more recent roles as defence counsel and a member of the Presidential Advisory Team (*Wantimpres*) he has continued to nurture the growth of seeds planted decades ago. We are grateful to Abang Buyung for his commitment to constitutional scholarship in

Indonesia, and for his friendship and support for our work on Indonesian law, over nearly three decades.

Thanks go also to the many other Indonesian lawyers and scholars who have generously given us the benefit of their thoughts on Indonesian constitutional law, in what the euphemism describes as 'full and frank discussions'. These include another long-standing and indefatigable champion of the *negara hukum*, Dr Todung Mulya Lubis, as well as Professor Bagir Manan, Dr Denny Indrayana, Professor Satya Arinanto, Dr Arskal Salim and Dr Susi Dwi Harijanti. Professors MB Hooker and Virginia Hooker have also greatly guided our thinking on Indonesia and law.

Special thanks must go to Arjuna Dibley, researcher at the Asian Law Centre at the University of Melbourne and a law student at the Australian National University. He played a central role in the research for, and drafting of, this book. Thorough and reliable, it has been a great pleasure to work with Arjuna. Any errors are undoubtedly ours!

Tim also thanks Julia Suryakusuma, *provokator tercinta*, for inspirational discussions during the drafting of this book. His thanks go as well to the Asian Law Centre and Centre for Islamic Law and Society at the Melbourne Law School (especially Kathryn Taylor, Tessa Shaw, Tom Bray and Helen Pausacker), for providing supportive institutional bases for the research and drafting of this book. Simon likewise thanks his wife Angela for her encouragement, as well as Sydney Law School and his colleagues at the Centre for Asian and Pacific Law for their support for this project. Research for the book was funded in part by Tim's Federation Fellowship ('Islam and Modernity: Syari'ah, Terrorism and Governance in South-East Asia') and in part by Simon's Australian Research Council Post-Doctoral Fellowship (project No DP110104287). We are both grateful to Hart Publishing, and especially Professors Andrew Harding and Peter Leyland, for inviting us to write it.

Finally, we have both written for many years on Indonesian law and politics, jointly and independently. We have drawn from some of these previous publications in different places in this book and acknowledge this in the footnotes.

Tim Lindsey and Simon Butt
17 August 2011

Contents

Terminology

For simplicity, 'Law' has been preferred to 'Act', or 'Basic Law', in translating the terms *undang-undang* and *undang-undang pokok*, and 'Interim Emergency Law' for *peraturan pengganti undang-undang*. We have also simplified the titles of legal instruments by not translating *nomor* (number) and *tahun* (year).

For convenience, the term 'Article' (*pasal*) is taken to cover sub-articles, paragraphs, etc. 'Elucidation' has been preferred to 'explanatory memorandum' for *penjelasan*.

Indonesian judicial decisions are usually referred to by case numbers and not by the names of the parties. We provide these case numbers in notes but for convenience have also developed short titles for cases we discuss.

Laws passed in 2009 led Indonesian government Departments to revert to the title 'Ministry'. Depending on the context, both terms are used but, for convenience, 'Ministry' is generally preferred.

Kabupaten, the next administrative division below the provincial level, is usually translated as 'Regency' or 'District'. Largely rural, *kabupaten* are equivalent in status to cities. We have preferred 'County' as the nearest English-language equivalent.

The modern Indonesian standard orthography as determined by the Indonesian Ministry of Education since 17 August 1972 is used for all Indonesian words except where *ejaan lama* (old spelling) is used in quotation. In the case of names, the spelling used by the person named has been preferred where it is known, thus 'Soeharto' rather than 'Suharto'.

As at 27 July 2011, 1,000 Indonesian Rupiah were worth US$00.12.

Acronyms and Abbreviations

ADB	Asian Development Bank
ASEAN	Association of South East Asian Nations
Bawaslu	Badan Pengawas Pemilihan Umum – Election Supervisory Board
BPP	Bilangan Pembagi Pemilu – Vote Division Number
BPUPKI	Badan Penyelidik Usaha-usaha Persiapan Kemerdekaan Indonesia – Investigatory Body for the Preparation of Indonesian Independence
CSR	Corporate Social Responsibility
DOM	Daerah Operasi Militer – Military Operations Zone
DPD	Dewan Perwakilan Daerah – Regional Representative Assembly
DPR	Dewan Perwakilan Rakyat – People's Representative Assembly
DPRA	Dewan Perwakilan Rakyat Aceh – Aceh People's Representative Assembly
DPRD	Dewan Perwakilan Rakyat Daerah – Regional People's Representative Assemblies
FPI	Front Pembela Islam – Islamic Defender's Front
GAM	Gerakan Aceh Merdeka – Free Aceh Movement
GBHN	Garis-Garis Besar Haluan Negara – Broad Guidelines of State Policy
Golkar	Golongan Karya – Functional Groups
Hanura	Partai Hati Nurani Rakyat – People's Conscience Party
ICIP	International Centre for Islam and Pluralism
ICW	Indonesia Corruption Watch
ILO	International Labour Organization
IMF	International Monetary Fund
JAI	Jemaat Ahmadiyah Indonesia
KADIN	Kamar Dagang dan Industri Indonesia – Indonesian Chamber of Commerce
KK	Kartu Keluarga – Family Card
KLI	Komando Laskar Islam – Islamic Militia Command

KPK	Komisi Pemberantasan Korupsi – Corruption Eradication Commission
KPKPN	Komisi Pemeriksa Kekayaan Penyelenggara Negara- Public Official Asset Investigation Commission
KPU	Komisi Pemilihan Umum – General Electoral Commission
KTP	Kartu Tanda Penduduk – Identity Card
KUHP	Kitab Undang-Undang Hukum Pidana – Criminal Code
KUHAP	Kitab Undang-Undang Hukum Acara Pidana – Criminal Procedure Code
LBH	Lembaga Bantuan Hukum – Indonesian Legal Aid Institute
LeIP	Lembaga Kajian dan Advokasi untuk Independensi Peradilan – Institute of Advocacy and Study for an Independent Judiciary
Migas	Minyak dan Gas Bumi – Oil And Natural Gas
MK	Mahkamah Konstitusi – Constitutional Court
MOHA	Ministry of Home Affairs
Monas	Monumen Nasional – National Monument
MPR	Majelis Permusyawaratan Rakyat – People's Consultative Assembly
MPU	Majelis Permusyawaratan Ulama – Consultative Assembly of Ulama
MRP	Majelis Rakyat Papua – Papuan People's Assembly
MUI	Majelis Ulama Indonesia – Indonesian Ulama Council
NGO	Non-governmental organisation
NKRI	Negara Kesatuan Republic Indonesia – Unitary Republic of Indonesia
OPM	Organisasi Papua Merdeka – Free Papua Movement
PAN	Partai Amanat Nasional – National Mandate Party
Pansus	Panitia Khusus – Special Committee
PDI	Partai Demokrasi Indonesia – Indonesian Democracy Party
PDI-P	Partai Demokrasi Indonesia – Perjuangan – Indonesian Democracy Party – Struggle
Perda	Peraturan Daerah – Regional Regulations

Perpu	Peraturan Pengganti Undang-Undang – 'Regulations in Lieu of Statute', or Interim Emergency Law
PKB	Partai Kebangkitan Bangsa – National Awakening Party
PKI	Partai Komunis Indonesia – Indonesian Communist Party
PKS	Partai Keadilan Sejahtera – Prosperous Justice Party
PLN	Perusahan Listrik Negara – State Electricity Company
PPP	Partai Persatuan Pembangunan – United Development Party
Prolegnas	Program Legislasi Nasional – National Legislation Programme
PSHK	Pusat Studi Hukum dan Kebijakan – Centre for the Study of Law and Public Policy
RIS/RUSI	Republik Indonesia Serikat – United States of Indonesia
SBSI	Serikat Buruh Sejahtera Indonesia – Prosperous Workers Union of Indonesia
SBY	President Susilo Bambang Yudhoyono
UDHR	Universal Declaration of Human Rights
UN	United Nations
US	United States
Wantimpres	Dewan Pertimbangan Presiden – Presidential Advisory Council

Glossary

(Hukum) Adat	Traditional custom/customary law
Asas Kekeluargaan	Family Principle
Azas Tunggal	Sole Foundation
Badan Usaha Milik Negara	State-Owned Legal Enterprise
Bupati	Regent (head of a *kabupaten* or county)
Dasar Negara	Basis of the State – Grundnorm
Democracy Terpimpin	Guided Democracy, led by former President Soekarno (1945–1966)
Dwifungsi	Dual function (of the military)
Ekonomi Keraykatan	People's Economy
Fraksi	Faction (political)
Fiqh	Islamic jurisprudence
Hak	Right
Hukum revolusi	Revolutionary law
Instruksi Presiden	Presidential Instruction
Integralistic Staatsidee	Integralist State Idea
Interpelasi	Interpolation
Istimewa	Special
Jaksa	Public Prosecutor
Kabupaten	County or Regency, region below the level of province, headed by a *bupati*
Kasasi	Cassation – a form of appeal heard by the Supreme Court
Katolik	Roman Catholic Christianity
Kawasan khusus	Special area
Kecamatan	Sub-district
Kekeluargaan	Familiness
Kepala Daerah	Regional Head
Kepala Desa	Village Head
Kepercayaan	Beliefs
Keputusan	Decision
Keputusan Menteri	Ministerial Decision
Keputusan Presiden	Presidential Decision

Ketuhanan yang Maha Esa	Belief in Almighty God
Konstituante	Constituent Assembly
Kota	City
Kristen	Protestant Christianity
Lex specialis derogat lex generalis	A specialist law prevails over a law of a general nature (if they conflict)
Lex posteriori derogat lex priori	A more recently-enacted law prevails over an earlier law (if they conflict)
Machtsstaat	State based on power
Mahkamah Agung	Supreme Court
Mahkamah Syar'iyah	Syariah Court (Aceh)
Majelis Kehormatan Mahkamah Konstitusi	Constitutional Court Honour Council
Maklumat	A form of Presidential Decree
Negara Hukum	Law State
New Order	Regime led by former President Soeharto (1966–1998)
Otonomi Daerah	Regional Autonomy
Otonomi Khusus	Special Autonomy
Pancasila	The Five Principles – Indonesia's state philosophy
Partai Demokrat	Democratic Party
Pembangunan	Economic Development
Pemuda	Youth
Pengadilan Agama	Religious Court
Pengadilan Hak Asasi Manusia	Human Rights Court
Pengadilan Hubungan Industrial	Industrial Relations Court
Pengadilan Militer	Military Court
Pengadilan Niaga	Commercial Court
Pengadilan Pajak	Taxation Court
Pengadilan Perikanan	Fishery Court
Pengadilan Tata Usaha Negara	Administrative Court
Pengadilan Tinggi Agama/ Militer/Tata Usaha Negara/Umum	High Religious/Military/Administrative/ General Courts

Pengadilan Tipikor	Pengadilan Tindak Pidana Korupsi – Anti-corruption Court
Pengadilan Umum	General Courts
Pengadilan Utama Militer	Supreme Military Court
Peninjauan kembali	Reconsideration, a re-opening and review of a 'final' case by the Supreme Court
Penodaan	Dishonouring
Peraturan	Regulation
Peraturan Daerah (Perda)	Regional Regulation
Peraturan Desa	Village Regulation
Peraturan Menteri	Ministerial Regulation
Peraturan Pemerintah	Government Regulation
Persatuan Indonesia	The Unity of Indonesia
Piagam Jakarta	Jakarta Charter
Praperadilan	Pre-trial hearing
Propinsi	Province
Qanun	Regional Regulation of the Province of Aceh
Rakyat	The People
Rechtsstaat	Law State
Reformasi	Reformation
Satu Atap	One Roof
Sementara	Temporary
Sesat	Deviant (of religious belief)
Shari'ah	Islamic law
Sidang Istimewa	Special Session
Sila	Principle
Sisa suara	Surplus votes
Suara terbanyak	Majority vote
Surat Edaran	Circular Letter
Trias politika	Political triad – separation of powers
Tujuh kata	Seven words (reference to the *Piagam Jakarta*)
Ulama	Islamic scholars
Undang-undang	Statute
Undang-Undang Dasar	The Constitution
Volksgeist	The spirit of the people, the essence of a nation
Walikota	Mayor

Table of Constitutional Court Cases

Table of Legislation

DECREES OF THE MPR (KETETAPAN)

NATIONAL GOVERNMENT REGULATIONS (PERATURAN) AND DECISIONS (KEPUTUSAN)

COURT REGULATIONS (PERATURAN)

1

Indonesia's Constitutions

Introduction – Integralism in Indonesian Constitutional Thought – The Pancasila – The Pancasila and Integralism – The Persistence of Liberal Democratic Ideas – Dismantling Integralism – The Reinvention of the Pancasila – Conclusion

INTRODUCTION

INDONESIA'S *UNDANG-UNDANG DASAR*, or Constitution, of 1945 was an interim measure intended to allow the swift establishment of the government of a new independent Indonesian republic. It was hastily drafted in an atmosphere of chaos at the end of World War II. In this chapter we consider the consquences of this, beginning with a brief history of Indonesia's three constitutions before identifying key debates influencing Indonesian constitutional thinking – all of which were raging as the tumultuous events of 1945 unfolded.

Occupying Japanese forces had facilitated the establishment of an Investigating Body for Preparatory Work for Indonesian Independence (*Badan Penyelidik Usaha Persiapan Kemerdekaan Indonesia*) in March 1945 and then the Preparatory Committee for Indonesian Independence (*Panitia Persiapan Kemerdekaan Indonesia*) on 7 August, the day after the bombing of Hiroshima.[1] The nationalist leaders who comprised these bodies, many of whom who had been jailed or exiled under Dutch colonial rule, foresaw military conflict with The Netherlands. As the Japanese

---

[1] MC Ricklefs, *A History Of Modern Indonesia Since C. 1300*, 4th edn (Stanford, CA, Stanford University Press, 2008) 245–46. Some material in this chapter draws from T Lindsey, *Islam, Law and the State in Indonesia: Vol I – Indonesia* (London, IB Tauris, 2012) Ch 2; T Lindsey, 'Constitutional Reform in Indonesia: Muddling towards Democracy' in T Lindsey (ed), *Indonesia: Law and Society* (Sydney, Federation Press, 2008).

surrendered to the victorious Allies on 15 August, Indonesians rightly expected their former rulers would soon return to reclaim the empire in the East Indies that they had ruled for centuries, and which had hugely enriched The Netherlands, making it a major mercantile power in the eighteenth and nineteenth centuries. The members of the Investigating Body and the Committee were therefore concerned to establish an independent state within the former colonial boundaries as quickly as possible.

Outside these meetings, many Indonesians were fighting each other over what to do next and what sort of state to establish. Most had only nationalist sentiment in common. Some were reviving old political organisations or establishing new ones; others had seized weapons from the Japanese and formed militias. The leaders at the Investigating Body meeting reflected these divisions, representing a range of conflicting ideological positions.

The short and skeletal Constitution of 1945 produced by the Investigating Body was more like notes for a constitution than a comprehensive basis for a new state. It was, in fact, described by its drafters as a provisional, temporary or 'lightning' constitution for the emergency conditions that then prevailed.[2] They intended it to be replaced by a more detailed and considered document as soon as conditions allowed. Despite this, their constitution has been in force in Indonesia for all but the decade from 1949 to 1959. In that period, two other constitutions were applied, products of the United Nations (UN) sponsored agreement that recognised Indonesian independence in 1949. Despite being one of the shortest constitutions in the world,[3] and being initially intended as only a stop-gap measure, the 1945 Constitution was not amended until 1999.

For much of the four years that followed the declaration of Independence on 17 August 1945 Indonesians fought against the returning Dutch, as their leaders had expected. A hard-fought, if intermittent, guerrilla campaign was sustained by poorly-equipped militias of *pemuda* (youths) led by a small corps of soldiers once trained by the

---

[2] S Bahar, NH Sinaga, and A Kusuma, *Risalah Sidang Badan Penyelidik Usaha-usaha Persiapan Kemerdekaan Indonesia (BPUPKI), dan Panitia Persiapan Kemerdekaan Indonesia (PPKI), 28 Mei 1945–22 Agustus 1945* (Jakarta, Sekretariat Negara Republik Indonesia, 1992).

[3] Only the interim Constitution of the Kingdom of Thailand of 1959 was shorter: S Soemantri, *Prosedur dan Sistem Perubahan Konstitusi* (Alumni, Bandung, 1979).

Japanese and the Dutch colonial armies. The *pemuda* were supported in their armed struggle by the astute diplomacy of politicians such as President Soekarno, his vice-president, Mohammad Hatta, and the Prime Minister, Sutan Syahrir. These leaders had learnt both their craft and the value of persistence in long years of protest, exile and imprisonment under the Dutch.

Eventually, popular opinion in the West – and, in particular, the United States – turned, and the Dutch colonial claim to the Indies became politically unacceptable. Post-war reconstruction aid to The Netherlands was soon at stake and repeated efforts were made to negotiate a settlement under the auspices of the UN, through the 'good offices' of America, Australia and Belgium, who acted as facilitators of talks, despite continued hostilities. Peace was not achieved until the Round Table Conference of 1949, when the Dutch finally accepted they had lost their colonies in the East Indies (with the exception of Papua, which they held until October 1962).[4]

The Dutch transfer of sovereignty took place on 27 December 1949. It was not made to the unitary Republic of Indonesia, however, but to a federation, the United States of Indonesia (*Republik Indonesia Serikat*, RIS or RUSI), of which the Republic was but one of 16 member states. Its constitution was federal, bicameral, parliamentary and liberal democratic. Regarded by Indonesian nationalists as a Dutch scheme to maintain influence through 'puppet' states, this federation collapsed within months. It was formally dissolved into, and replaced by, the current unitary Republic on 17 August 1950, the fifth anniversary of the proclamation of Independence. The new constitution of the re-united Republic was not, however, the bare-bones document proclaimed in 1945. Instead, a version of the constitution of the United States of Indonesia, but without the federal component or the RIS' senate,[5] was used. Drafted in two months by a Committee for Preparation for the Unitary State, this new, third constitution included a version of the Universal

---

[4] Ricklefs, *A History Of Modern Indonesia* (n 1 above) 262–63, 269, 309. Sovereignty over Papua was transferred by the Dutch to the United Nations on 1 October 1962, who handed it to Indonesia on 1 May 1963 as required by the transfer agreement. The 'act of free choice' by Papuans themselves that was also required by that agreement took place in 1969, and has been much criticised as being anything but free (ibid, 337). For more on Papua, see Chapter 6 of this volume.

[5] G Kahin, *Nationalism and Revolution in Indonesia* (Ithaca, NY, Cornell University Press, 1952) 463.

Declaration of Human Rights and was provisional in nature, envisaging the election of an assembly to draft a permanent constitution.

Both the Federal and the 1950 Constitutions were much more detailed than the 1945 Constitution but neither was a product of national consultation. Both lacked political legitimacy. The task of creating a more detailed and final constitution was therefore revived in 1955, and given to a Constituent Assembly, the *Konstituante*. This was elected pursuant to Article 134 of the 1950 Constitution in December 1955 but did not sit until November the following year. A two-thirds majority was required for Konstitutante decisions, and it became deadlocked over the type of state that the Constitution should embody, including, in particular, whether the state should be based on Islamic law (*shari'ah*) – a proposition that had been the subject of debate well before Independence, as we show in Chapter 8.

In 1958, the army responded to continuing political instability by proposing a return to the 1945 Constitution, which had been briefly applied during the revolution, albeit only in Republican-controlled areas. The army – which considered itself to have the right of political intervention by virtue of its role in the struggle against the Dutch – organised popular demonstrations calling for the reinstatement of the 1945 Constitution. Playing into their hands, political parties reflecting fragmented communal allegiances jostled for dominance amid growing political turmoil. This was aggravated by rebellions in Aceh, Sumatra and Sulawesi involving disgruntled politicians, Islamist groups and army factions, sparking the fears of national disintegration that are a common theme of Indonesian politics. When the *Konstituante* failed to endorse a return to the 1945 Constitution, President Soekarno launched an autogolpe, backed by the military. He reinstated the 1945 Constitution by unilateral decree on 5 July 1959.[6]

The 'lightning constitution' suited Soekarno's needs. He had played a leading role in its creation in 1945, and its Spartan provisions lacked the checks and balances that might have thwarted the undemocratic 'Guided Democracy' dictatorship he now sought to create. Ruling directly, he presided over growing political rivalry between the army and the Indonesian Communist Party (*Partai Komunis Indonesia*, PKI), who competed for his favour.

---

[6] Under Interim Emergency Law 23 of 1959.

Soekarno's regime was marked by a capricious and personalised legal system he labelled *hukum revolusi* (revolutionary law), one of the many rhetorical and ideologically-loaded slogans he used to maintain political authority. Quoting Liebknecht, Soekarno stated that 'You cannot build a revolution with lawyers'[7] and political doctrine as enunciated by the 'Bearer of the Mandate of the People's Suffering' (as he called himself) soon came to overrule statutes and judicial decisions. The resulting regime established patterns that were later described as 'law without law'.[8] It collapsed in 1966 when a Leftist coup attempt and a rapid counter-coup by Major General Soeharto led to a bloody nation-wide purge of PKI members and those identified as fellow travellers by the military and Muslim groups working with it. The violence ran wild and lasted many months. It is believed to have led to the deaths of over half a million Indonesians.[9]

The military-backed Rightist dictatorship led by Soeharto that emerged from this violence to replace Soekarno kept the 1945 Constitution in place for the same reasons that Soekarno had reinstated it: it was 'top heavy' in that it gave broad and strong powers to the President, and was hence easily amenable to authoritarian rule. The new administration expanded Soekarno's Guided Democracy authoritarianism to create what was effectively an entrenched and coercive single-party system with power centralised in the presidency and enforced by the security and intelligence services. The regime inititially relied on emergency powers to administer what was essentially martial law but this eventually evolved into a sham democratic shell legitimised by reference to the 1945 Constitution, which left much of the detail of the operation of the organs of state to be determined by statutes (as we show in Chapters 2 and 3). For the three decades of the repressive New Order Soeharto established in 1966, the 1945 Constitution and the regime it enabled were presented as 'sacred', and their content immutable. Indeed, to propose

---

[7] This was an aphorism Soekarno often cited. Lev reports him using it, for example, at a national conference of Indonesian lawyers in 1961: DS Lev, 'Judicial Institutions and Legal Culture in Indonesia' in Claire Holt (ed), *Culture and Politics in Indonesia* (Ithaca, NY, Cornell University Press, 1972).

[8] JS Katz and RS Katz, 'The New Indonesian Marriage Law: A Mirror of Indonesia's Political, Cultural, and Legal Systems' (1975) 23(4) *American Journal of Comparative Law* 653, 653.

[9] R Cribb, *The Indonesian Killings of 1965–1966: Studies from Java and Bali* (Clayton Victoria, Centre of Southeast Asian Studies Monash University, 1991).

revision or replacement was seen as an act of subversion, punishable with imprisonment or worse.[10]

President Soeharto's corrupt and oppressive regime presided over a period of economic growth unrivalled since 1945 – consistently eight per cent overall in the 1990s, and 11 per cent in the industrial sector. Despite this, its 1998 collapse in the so-called 'Asian Economic Crisis' plunged Indonesia into financial and political disaster. By early 1998 Indonesia had slumped to seven per cent 'negative growth' (a fall of 13 per cent overall), unemployment had officially hit 12 per cent (in fact, it was certainly much higher), interest rates had climbed to over 75 per cent and the rupiah had plunged from 2,500 to the US$ to a catastrophic 17,000.[11] Around 80 per cent of banks and listed companies were insolvent, 'the savings of the middle class were wiped out and labourers were thrown out of work by the millions'.[12] Student and middleclass protest gave way to rioting and looting in urban centres across the archipelago that often targeted the ethnic Chinese, stereotyped as wealthy and exclusivist. Rival army factions manipulated the violence, seeking political advantage, and financial crisis quickly became 'kristal' or *krisis total*. Unable to form a cabinet, and with embryonic coups apparently afoot amid scenes of chaos in major cities, Soeharto resigned that month.

His resignation proved to be a watershed in Indonesian history. The freeing-up of politics that followed not only ended military-backed authoritarian rule but also rapidly ushered in a much more open and democratic society. It became clear soon after this process began that the 'minimalist' 1945 Constitution was not appropriate for the new polity that was emerging. As a result, it was substantially rewritten from 1999 to 2002 in intensely contested annual debates between legislators in the *Majelis Permusyawaratan Rakyat* (MPR, People's Consultative Assembly).

The revised constitution was much lengthier than the original brief document. It enshrined separation of powers and procedural democracy, as well as a set of human rights closely resembling those in the Universal Declaration of Human Rights. Ironically, in many respects it now resembles the provisional and liberal democratic constitution that

---

[10] AB Nasution, 'Towards Constitutional Democracy in Indonesia', *Adnan Buyung Nasution Papers on Southeast Asian Constitutionalism* (Asian Law Centre, University of Melbourne, 2011) 11.
[11] Ricklefs, *A History Of Modern Indonesia* (n 1 above) 379.
[12] ibid, 379.

had applied from 1950 to 1959, and which had been greatly reviled by both Soekarno and Soeharto. In any case, in substantially amended form, the 1945 Constitution has remained in force since 2002 and formed the framework for a largely successful transition to an open, liberal democratic system.

In the remainder of this chapter, we offer an account of the long-running battle between proponents of an authoritarian state and supporters of a liberal democratic model that has underpinned and informed the trajectory of Indonesian constitutional history just described. The implications of this for the constitutional status of the presidency, the legislature and the judiciary are explored in the next three chapters. The fifth chapter focuses on the most important source of constitutional interpretation in contemporary Indonesia – the Constitutional Court. The balance of the book then considers four other major areas of constitutional controversy in recent years, namely decentralisation, human rights, religion and the economy. We do this chiefly through an examination of the Constitutional Court decisions relevant to each theme, seeking to understand them both in their own terms and in their wider political contexts.

INTEGRALISM IN INDONESIAN CONSTITUTIONAL THOUGHT

The meetings of the Investigating Body for Preparatory Work for Indonesian Independence witnessed vigorous theoretical argument despite the sense of urgency and uncertainty that prevailed. The debate reflected three strains of opinion about the form the new Indonesian state should take: 'Integralistic' authoritarian, liberal-democratic or Islamic.[13] (There was a fourth opinion, favouring a Marxist state, but it was effectively wiped out by the purges of the mid-1960s. It has not since been revived, at least not in mainstream politics.)

Each of these three options have since proved persistent and resilient, and have influenced Indonesian constitutional thinking, albeit at different times and to different degrees. They re-emerged in the *Konstituante* debates from 1955 to 1959, and again from 1999 to 2002,

---

[13] HM Yamin, *Naskah Persiapan Undang-Undang Dasar 1945* (Jakarta, Yayasan Prapanca, 1959); AB Nasution, *The Aspiration for Constitutional Government in Indonesia: A Socio-Legal Study of the Indonesian Konstituante, 1956–1959* (Jakarta, Pustaka Sinar Harapan, 1992).

when constitutional amendments were finally made. For most of Indonesia's independent history, the Integralist model prevailed, but with liberal democracy applied in an interregnum in the 1950s and since 1999. The Islamist argument continues to be made with vigour (and occasionally violence) but has generally had little success at the national level. As discussed in Chapters 6 and 8, it has, however, had more impact on regional governments since post-Soeharto democratisation and decentralisation granted them greater political autonomy.

In 1945, those who supported the Integralist strain of opinion wanted Indonesia, so long dominated by foreign colonisers, to be a very strong state. The nation and the people would be one 'organic whole' led by a charismatic ruler who embodied his people's 'essence', drawn from their ancient traditions and historical experience. Although not explicitly labelled as such, Integralism was essentially a form of authoritarianism: it required that citizens unquestioningly obey state instruction. There was no room – indeed no need – for mechanisms to challenge state action, for example through judicial review by an independent judiciary.[14]

The *Integralistic Staatsidee*[15] argument was introduced by Professor Soepomo, then perhaps Indonesia's leading jurist. Addressing the Investigating Body for Preparatory Work for Indonesian Independence in May 1945,[16] he proposed that the state structure best suited to the character of indigenous Indonesian society reflected a combination of two foreign models, namely Nazi Germany and Imperial Japan (notwithstanding that both had just suffered comprehensive defeats in World War II). The German state, Soepomo argued, was based on the Integralistic or totalitarian theory of state, where the people and leaders were politically unified. The Japanese state, he contended, was founded on the idea of the family principle (*asas kekeluargaan*), with the Emperor as the spiritual centre of a unity between himself and the people.

Soepomo went on to propose that the 'organic' state and 'family principle' reflected the nature of Indonesian society, where unity of 'the outer and inner world, of the macrocosmos and the microcosmos, of

[14] TM Lubis, 'The *Rechsstaat* and Human Rights' in T Lindsey (ed), *Indonesia: Law and Society*, 1st edn (Annandale, NSW, Federation Press, 1999) 171–85.

[15] 'Integralist State Idea'.

[16] The following description is based on an extract of Soepomo's speech in H Feith and L Castles, *Indonesian Political Thinking, 1945–1965* (Ithaca, NY, Cornell University Press, 1970) 188–92.

the people and their leaders' is primary.[17] Each individual and group – and society as a whole – had obligations to achieve unity and harmony, and were thus inseparable. In this context, the state, which was at one with the people, must be sensitive to the community's sense of justice but must also transcend all groups in every field. According to Soepomo, this totalitarian or 'integralistic' ideal required a strong executive body, and there was no need to guarantee individual human rights against the state, because the individual was an organic part of the state.

> In the *Integralistic Staatsidee*, there is basically no dualism of state and individual, no conflict between the state organisation on the one hand, and the legal order of individuals on the other, no dualism of state and society-without state.[18]

On this model, Soepomo argued:

> There will be no need for any guarantee of *Grund- und Freiheitsrechte* [basic rights] of individuals against the state, for the individuals are nothing else than organic parts of the state, having specific positions and duties to realise the grandeur of the state.[19]

The 'family principle' was similar in nature, and was essentially a metaphor for the paternalistic and absolutist Integralistic state.

> The duties which father asks his wife and children to carry out are happily accepted, and there is no grumbling. What father says is right, because father is wise![20]

These comments were based on the notion that the ideal Integralist state – because it was 'integrated' – could never be at odds with individuals comprising it.[21] On this view, there was no need for a private legal sphere independent of the state and thus able to check the state, because the state *is* all citizens and their interests are therefore identical. As Nasution points out:[22]

> [e]vidently, there was no fear of abuse of power by the state nor any doubt that the state would always use its power appropriately. The state functionaries

---

[17] S Rahardjo, 'Between Two Worlds: Modern State and Traditional Society in Indonesia' (1994) 28(3) *Law and Society Review* 493, 495–96.

[18] Feith and Castles, *Indonesian Political Thinking*, n 16 above, 191.

[19] Yamin, *Naskah Persiapan Undang-Undang Dasar 1945*, n 13 above, 114.

[20] Feith and Castles, *Indonesian Political Thinking*, n 16 above, 185, citing Soeriokoesoemo.

[21] Yamin, *Naskah Persiapan Undang-Undang Dasar 1945*, n 13 above, 114.

[22] Nasution, *The Aspiration for Constitutional Government in Indonesia*, n 13 above, 93.

were assumed to be good and wise persons taking seriously the interests of the people as a whole, never thinking of their [own] interests. It was not astonishing that given these assumptions, Soepomo thought there was no need to put limits on state power or to guarantee individual rights.

Integralism's conception of the unity of people and state is quite different from the democratic metaphor of the state 'as the people', where the state is chosen by a majority of them and administered using constitutional processes of government. Rather, as Bourchier[23] and Burns[24] have shown, the Germanic Romantic notion of the state as the spiritual manifestation of the people, as a quasi-religious emanation of their racial and ethnic essence, is what is meant: the *Volksgeist*. Von Savigny and Puchta's ideas of the nation 'as an entity possessing an organic unity above and beyond the concerns of individuals'[25] had been filtered through the Leiden School of Law and disseminated in the East Indies, particularly by the influential Dutch colonial legal scholar, van Vollenhoven. Soepomo was a strong supporter of the School's notion of *Volksrecht*, the people's law, as opposed to *Juristenrecht*, lawyers' law. From this thinking sprang the so-called *adat* school of law, which saw Indonesian traditions as the only appropriate source of law because, Soepomo argued, it was the essence of 'Indonesian-ness', of the 'national identity'. This *Rechtsgeschichte* (legal genealogy) he interpreted as being based around notions of an imagined traditional village 'family' as the model of the state, with decisions made by consensus and the villagers' communal life rendering them identical with the village, represented by its leaders. He 'maintained that there was no place for divisive concepts of political rights in the constitution'.[26]

On Soepomo's reading, the state is *the* source of law because, in the Romantic tradition, the only valid law is that which expresses the *Volksgeist*, the spirit of the people. It follows that all state acts embody the *Volksgeist* and are, therefore, inherently legitimate and legally correct.

---

[23] D Bourchier, 'Positivism and Romanticism in Indonesian Legal Thought' in T Lindsey (ed), *Indonesia: Law and Society*, 2nd edn (Annandale, NSW, Federation Press, 2008) 94–104.

[24] P Burns, 'The Myth of Adat' (1989) 28 *Journal of Legal Pluralism and Unofficial Law* 1; and P Burns, *The Leiden Legacy: Concepts of Law in Indonesia* (Jakarta, PT Pradnya Paramita, 1999).

[25] This paragraph draws on Bourchier, n 23 above, and Burns, n 24 above.

[26] Bourchier, n 23 above, 99.

Both the Integralistic state and the 'family principle' and all they implied in theoretical terms were voted down by the Investigating Body for Preparatory Work for Indonesian Independence,[27] and neither concept appears in express form in the Constitution. Indeed, the General Elucidation[28] to the Constitution stated instead, that Indonesia is a 'law state' (*Rechtsstaat*), thereby implicitly rejecting Sopeomo's totalitarian ideas. The drafting of the Constitution itself was, however, left largely in Soepomo's hands.[29] The executive-heavy nature of state power in the document he produced reflected his thinking, as did the absence of significant checks and balances. In fact, Soepomo had consciously set out to create a Constitution which 'can give the greatest accent to the government', while being itself 'also accountable to the government and primarily the head of state'.[30] As a result, much of the Constitution simply establishes organs of state and leaves their powers and limits for later regulation, granting broad and undefined powers to the president (as we show in Chapter 3).

A second strain of opinion prominent among members of the Investigating Body for Preparatory Work for Indonesian Independence in July 1945 was that Indonesia should adopt Western-style liberal democracy, with state action being subject to judicial review, the judiciary independent, and human rights protected.[31] This position was represented, in particular, by Muhammad Yamin, a lawyer who was Soepomo's fiercest opponent in the Committee debates. Inspired by the US model, he argued for a bill of rights, a supreme court with powers of judicial review, and clear separation of powers. His ideas were based on values that were the polar opposite of Integralism, namely:

---

[27] TM Lubis, *In Search of Human Rights: Legal-Political Dilemmas of Indonesia's New Order, 1966–1990* (Jakarta, PT Gramedia Pustaka Utama in cooperation with SPES Foundation, 1993) 93.

[28] The elucidation is the explanatory memorandum that accompanies many types of Indonesian laws. During the post-Soeharto amendment process the elucidation to the Constitution was criticised for being overly influenced by Integralistic thinking, and was deleted. It was not replaced.

[29] DS Lev, 'Between State and Society: Professional Lawyers and Reform in Indonesia' in Tim Lindsey (ed), *Indonesia: Law and Society*, 2nd edn (Annandale, NSW, Federation Press, 2008) 53–54.

[30] RM Indra, *The President's Position under the 1945 Constitution* (Jakarta, Trisula, 1998).

[31] DS Lev, *The Transition to Guided Democracy: Indonesian Politics, 1957–1959* (Ithaca, NY, Cornell University, 1966); H Feith, *The Decline of Constitutional Democracy in Indonesia* (Ithaca NY, Cornell University Press, 1962).

a sharp distinction between state and society, recognition of individual interests and rights, limited government, and institutional controls over political authority.[32]

On 17 August 1945, Soekarno declared Indonesia's independence and became the nation's first president. The following day, he announced Indonesia's 1945 Constitution. The constitutional model it contained was ambiguous, at least about the theoretical battle between the proponents of Integralism and liberal democracy. On the one hand, the General Elucidation of the 1945 Constitution states, as mentioned, that 'Indonesia is a State based on law (*Rechsstaat*), not on power (*Machtsstaat*)', as Yamin and the liberal democrats sought. On the other hand, the Constitution did not clearly provide for the mechanisms often considered essential to the rule of law, such as an independent judiciary or separation of powers. It was, however, a document that could give significant authority and flexibility to the nationalist leadership as it fought to defend the new republic against its enemies, particularly the returning Dutch.[33] Most leaders of the embryonic state accepted that this took priority over other matters that were complex and disputed but less urgent. These included what forms the organs of government might take in a stable and secure state; how power should be divided between them; and what rights citizens should have. The absence from the Constitution of liberal democratic features thus seemed a relatively minor problem to many at the time.

The third main strain of opinion expressed during the debates of the Investigating Body in 1945 was that Indonesia should be an Islamic state, or at least that Indonesian Muslims should be constitutionally required to adhere to *shari'ah*, or Islamic law.[34] As discussed in more detail in Chapter 8, in the lead-up to the declaration of independence, Muslim groups had successfully lobbied for the inclusion of the so-called 'Jakarta Charter' (*Piagam Jakarta*) in the final draft of the 1945 Constitution. This was a version of the Preamble that included a phrase that would oblige Muslims to follow Islamic law (*shari'ah*). The phrase

[32] Lev, 'Between State and Society', n 29 above, 232.
[33] W Liddle, 'Indonesia's Democratic Transition: Playing by the Rules' in A Reynolds (ed), *The Architecture of Democracy: Constitutional Design, Conflict Management, and Democracy* (Oxford/New York, Oxford University Press, 2002).
[34] N Hosen, *Shari'a and Constitutional Reform in Indonesia* (Singapore, ISEAS, 2007); A Salim, *Challenging the Secular State: the Islamization of Law in Modern Indonesia* (Honolulu, University of Hawaii Press, 2008).

was, however, dropped from the Constitution of 1945 as promulgated, amid fears that it might lead to non-Muslims breaking away from the new-born republic.[35] While the struggle between liberal democracy and Integralism remained unresolved, the Islamists seemed roundly defeated.

THE PANCASILA

Indonesia did not, however, become an entirely secular state. The Pancasila – Indonesia's state philosophy; literally 'The Five Principles' – was included in the Preamble to the Constitution, where it remains today.[36] This was an attempt by Soekarno to articulate common ideological ground that could be accepted by the diverse nationalist leaders who were about to take control of the new state. It consists of the following principles.

1. *Ketuhanan Yang Maha Esa* (Belief in Almighty God);
2. *Kemanusiaan Yang Adil dan Beradab* (Just and Civilised Humanity);
3. *Persatuan Indonesia* (The Unity of Indonesia);
4. *Demokrasi* (Guided by Deliberations amongst Representatives) ; and
5. *Keadilan Sosial* (Social Justice).

Since 1945, the Pancasila has been seen by successive governments as, in principle, unassailable and, indeed, co-identical with the Indonesian

[35] The *Piagam Jakarta* and the circumstances of the deletion of the obligation to follow Islamic law are discussed in more detail in Chapter 8.

[36] The full text of the Preamble is as follows (with the Pancasila italicised): 'Whereas freedom is the inalienable right of all nations, colonialism must be abolished in this world as it is not in conformity with humanity and justice; And the moment of rejoicing has arrived in the struggle of the Indonesian freedom movement to guide the people safely and well to the threshold of the independence of the state of Indonesia which shall be free, united, sovereign, just and prosperous. By the grace of God Almighty and impelled by the noble desire to live a free national life, the people of Indonesia hereby declare their independence. Subsequent thereto, to form a government of the state of Indonesia which shall protect all the people of Indonesia and their entire native land, and in order to improve the public welfare, to advance the intellectual life of the people and to contribute to the establishment of a world order based on freedom, abiding peace and social justice, the national independence of Indonesia shall be formulated into a constitution of the sovereign Republic of Indonesia which is based on the *belief in Almighty God, just and civilized humanity, the unity of Indonesia, democracy guided by the inner wisdom of deliberations amongst representatives and the realisation of social justice for all people of Indonesia*'.

state. It is, for example, still formally said to be the 'source of all sources of law',[37] and was left untouched by the post-Soeharto amendments. Despite this, state implementation of the Pancasila has frequently been not much more than rhetoric – and has sometimes clearly breached the ideals the 'Five Principles' embody. Their interpretation has also shifted significantly over the years since 1945.

In any case, the Pancasila's first principle (which originally included the Jakarta Charter obligation on Muslims to observe *shari'ah*) requires government and citizens alike to give effect to belief in an 'almighty God'. The founding principles of the state, therefore, appear to establish adherence to one's religious beliefs as both a right and an obligation of Indonesian citizenship. They also appear to compel the government to not only safeguard religious freedom but also to use the machinery of the state to encourage and promote the exercise of faith, including Islam. Because the Pancasila mandates such a role for the state in matters of religion, the ideological door has remained ajar for some Muslim groups to continue seeking a more prominent place for Islamic principles in government and law. Further, as shown in Chapter 8, many Indonesian Muslims continue to regard Islamic doctrine as having independent legal potency, regardless of whether the state agrees.

THE PANCASILA AND INTEGRALISM

The liberal democratic system embodied in the 1950 Provisional Constitution effectively ended when Soekarno declared a 'state of war and siege' in 1957, as Indonesia grappled with regional conflict, ineffective and short-lived parliamentary governments, a deadlocked *Konstituante* and rising military assertiveness. The formal reintroduction of the 1945 Constitution in 1959 by unilateral presidential action merely confirmed the Realpolitik reversion to the Integralistic model Soepomo had inserted in his 'Trojan horse' constitution.

Soekarno's chaotic and authoritarian Guided Democracy was thus marked by an Integralistic personalisation of power and the president's self-identification with the state, symbolised most obviously by his appointment as 'President for Life' (a hubristic title lost after his fall in 1966). After Soekarno's removal, Soeharto's new regime – having secured

---

[37] Article 2, Law 10 of 2004 on Law-making.

the backing of the military from which it emerged, and annihilated political opposition in killings and detentions from 1965 to 1966 – continued to develop the Integralistic system, albeit without Soekarno's personality cult and flamboyant revolutionary rhetoric. Marsilam Simanjuntak[38] argues that the express public articulation of Integralistic state theory re-emerged in political and legal discourse from the early 1980s, about halfway through Soeharto's long rule. At this time, the New Order primarily used the Pancasila to promote the principle of national unity, rather than the other four principles,[39] thereby associating it with the Integralistic state's primary concern for 'oneness' and conformity.

The New Order also used this interpretation to justify its often repressive and sometimes violent approach to dissent. Laws 3 and 8 of 1985 on Social Organisations, for example, required all political parties and social organisations to adopt the Pancasila as their 'sole foundation', regardless of their actual ideological basis. Lubis[40] points out that, despite the Constitution's nominal deference to the *Rechtsstaat*, some government ideologues began to assert that the *Integralistic Staatsidee* was never actually rejected by the founding fathers in 1945, and that, constitutionally, the New Order was bound by it. Soon enough, some government officials began openly using the Integralistic interpretation of the Pancasila to justify government interference in judicial processes. In 1985, for example, the then Minister of Justice said in the DPR:

> [t]he Government actually is applying Integralistic principles in accordance with the spirit of the Pancasila and the 1945 Constitution in supervising the judges by emphasising a priority on togetherness and consultation between the government and the judiciary.[41]

This approach had also been given a statutory basis. The Elucidation to Article 14 of the 1970 Law on Judicial Power[42] provided that freedom to exercise judicial authority was not absolute, because the duty of a judge was to uphold law and justice based on the Pancasila. As Lubis says:[43]

---

[38] M Simanjuntak, *Pandangan Negara Integralistik: Sumber, Unsur, dan Riwayatnya dalam Persiapan UUD 1945* (Jakarta, Pustaka Utama Grafiti, 1994) 6–7.

[39] M Cammack, 'Islamic Law in Indonesia's New Order' (1989) 38(1) *International and Comparative Law Quarterly* 53, 53, fn 3.

[40] Lubis, *In Search of Human Rights*, n 27 above, 93.

[41] Lubis, *In Search of Human Rights*, n 27 above, 88, fn 5.

[42] Law 14 of 1970.

[43] Lubis, *In Search of Human Rights*, n 27 above, 98.

one would find it difficult to deny that the independence of the judiciary is not absolute because it is the power-holder who determines the meaning of upholding the law and justice based on the Pancasila.

Clearly, the formal re-emergence of the Integralistic state concept helped the government deflect calls for increased judicial independence and the introduction of judicial review. Being an organic whole, the Integralistic state does not anticipate a need to uphold individual rights at the expense of the interests of the state. Furthermore, *asas kekeluargaan* served to undermine the rationale for judicial review – namely, to check government power. Nasution[44] has summarised the effect of the principle succinctly:

> Opposition is interpreted as distrust of the good faith of the ruler; just as it would be inconceivable that children demand that their father account for his acts, it is inconceivable that the people demand that the ruler be accountable for his deeds.

THE PERSISTENCE OF LIBERAL DEMOCRATIC IDEAS:
LAW AS MEMORY

Nasution's words come from *The Aspiration for Constitutional Democracy in Indonesia*, a book he published in the early 1990s, when New Order Integralism had become overt state policy, articulated to saturation level in schools, government offices and the media, among others, through compulsory state indoctrination courses, known as 'P4'. In this book, Nasution argued cogently for revision of the 1945 Constitution. As he says:

> Of course, the New Order authorities were motivated to ban my discussion programmes because I always criticised their corruption, but what caused them the most consternation was my determination to pioneer a discourse of constitutional amendment in Indonesia.[45]

The regime, in fact, banned Nasution's book as soon as it was published but it circulated underground for years, and was later used as a reference for reformers involved in the post-Soeharto constitutional

---

[44] Nasution, *The Aspiration for Constitutional Government in Indonesia*, n 13 above, 423.

[45] Nasution, 'Towards Constitutional Democracy in Indonesia', n 10 above, 11.

amendment process.[46] The book thus stands as an important reminder that even at the height of Integralism's triumph under Soeharto, many of the alternative constitutional ideas debated in 1945 remained alive.

The key to this survival of liberal democratic values in New Order Indonesia was the bland statement in the General Elucidation of the 1945 Constitution that 'Indonesia is a State based on law (*Rechsstaat*), not on power (*Machtsstaat*)'. *Rechsstaat* is translated in Indonesian as *Negara Hukum*, a term that literally means 'law state', but is often understood to imply 'rule of law'. This phrase became the ideological hook from which its opponents hung their criticism of the New Order.

The Soekarno and Soeharto governments claimed to have implemented the *Negara Hukum* but while they were in power there was no real representative democracy and certainly no separation of powers. Final appeal sat formally in the hands of the Supreme Court but was consistently exercised in accordance with the dictates of the executive. International and Indonesian critics therefore frequently criticised Indonesian governments for failing to implement the 'rule of law'. Their use of Anglo-common law traditions of 'rule of law' to understand *Negara Hukum* was problematic,[47] however, because there was then no theoretical consensus in Indonesia as to precisely what *Negara Hukum* means. Dissident lawyers asserted, sometimes without recourse to much jurisprudence, that separation of powers is self-evidently implicit in the notion of *Negara Hukum*, equating it with the 'thick' Anglo-common law reading of rule of law.

For decades, leading orthodox Indonesian law professors and government lawyers countered with arguments drawing on European civil law constitutional traditions to support the 'thin' interpretation. On this view, *Rechsstaat* and *Negara Hukum* do not necessarily imply either representative democracy or separation of powers but simply a state based on laws, that is, a more formalistic and procedural version of 'rule by law'.[48] This was a system that both Soekarno and Soeharto had valorised as innately Indonesian.[49] They claimed that it reflected deep-seated, paternalistic and communitarian indigenous traditions of government that are the essence of an Indonesian *Volksgeist*. Under Soeharto, 'thin'

---

[46] Nasution, 'Towards Constitutional Democracy in Indonesia', n 10 above, 10.

[47] G Frankenburg, 'Critical Comparisons: Re-thinking Comparative Law' (1985) 26 *Harvard International Law Journal* 411–55.

[48] Bourchier, n 23 above.

[49] P Burns, 'The Myth of Adat'; P Burns, *The Leiden Legacy*, n 24 above.

rule of law Integralism acquired added legitimacy as the supposed protective shell for *pembangunan*, economic development. In other words, oppressive rule was seen as guaranteeing growth, trading rights for prosperity.

In this way, the New Order was able to marginalise the liberal democratic tradition of the 1950s through its ideological programme and, more particularly, by reinventing accounts of that period as a political failure that jeopardised the security and economic development of the republic.[50] The regime could never completely silence the liberal democratic discourse, however, which found shelter in political litigation. Subversion trials became the most dramatic legal forum for the expression of these ideas. In fact, in the hands of determined dissident lawyers they became elaborate performance pieces. In them, the New Order was repeatedly accused of failing to fulfil the promises it made after Soekarno fell to deliver the *Negara Hukum*. The trials of dissidents such as Muchtar Pakpahan,[51] Ratna Sarumpaet[52] and Sri Bintang Pamungkas,[53] among others, became 'Emperor's new clothes' set pieces, where arguments about democracy and the rule of law were regularly and provocatively aired,[54] in a tradition established, ironically enough, by Soekarno's own trial by the Dutch under similar provisions in the 1930s. The inevitable convictions in these cases were, in fact, political victories for the convicts and their lawyers because they focused attention on the illegitimacy of the process and its final result, rather than the subject matter of the dispute.

Resistance was led by the Indonesia Legal Aid Institute (LBH), a highly-influential NGO established by Nasution after he was dismissed as a state prosecutor for criticising the state.[55] LBH consciously set out

---

[50]   D Bourchier, 'The 1950s in New Order Ideology and Politics' in JD Legge and D Bourchier (eds), *Democracy in Indonesia, 1950s and 1990s*, Monash papers on Southeast Asia (Clayton, Victoria, Centre of Southeast Asian Studies, Monash University, 1994) 50–60.

[51]   The leader of the formerly-banned trade union, SBSI (*Serikat Buruh Sejahtera Indonesia*).

[52]   A well-known Indonesian dramatist and activist.

[53]   A former legislator and staunch critic of Soeharto, who has established his own opposition party.

[54]   For an engaging narrative of the gross injustice of political trials in the late New Order, see S Zifcak, 'But a Shadow of Justice: Political Trials in Indonesia' in T Lindsey (ed), *Indonesia: Law and Society*, 1st edn (Annandale, NSW, Federation Press, 1999).

[55]   Nasution, 'Towards Constitutional Democracy in Indonesia', n 10 above, 7, 11.

to resist the abuses of the regime and its blatant manipulation of the legal system. Its members did this by acting as paralegals and defence lawyers (and many are today leaders of the legal profession or senior government officials). They also maintained the liberal democratic constitutionalist discourse through what they called 'structural legal aid', that is, political activism. They did so defiantly and with considerable courage, despite abuse, loss of practicing licenses, imprisonment, violent attacks and, occasionally, death.[56] As Lev[57] has said:

> Private lawyers are a particularly important group in the history of constitutionalism . . . because they become the most articulate rationalizers of constitutionalist ideas . . . In Indonesia professional advocates, who suffered economically and ideologically under Guided Democracy, became the most fervent promoters of rule of law ideas in the New Order. And when it became clear that the New Order would not differ politically and institutionally all that much from the old, they prepared in effect for a longer struggle by creating the LBH . . . [which] represents a highly sophisticated constitutionalist movement. Not limiting itself to formal legal assistance, it . . . conceived its work more broadly as the cutting edge of political, social, and even cultural reform.

DISMANTLING INTEGRALISM

This persistent assertion of rule of law and universal legal values by lawyers at the margins of public life was one of the reasons why Indonesians were able to so rapidly dismantle the authoritarian state and its Integralistic dogma in Soeharto's wake, once they had won a voice in policy and law-making.

Even Soeharto's protégé and successor, Dr Bacharuddin Jusuf Habibie (May 1998–October 1999), was at pains to demonstrate that, unlike his patron, he was, in his own words, 'a democrat, a Western educated man'[58] and a supporter of the *Negara Hukum*, democratisation and human rights. Eager to win legitimacy by embracing the new *Reformasi* (Reformation) agenda, Habibie presided over a massive legislative

[56]   Nasution, 'Towards Constitutional Democracy in Indonesia', n 10 above, 9.

[57]   DS Lev, 'Social Movements, Constitutionalism and Human Rights: Comments from the Malaysian and Indonesian Experiences' in Douglas Greenberg et al (eds), *Constitutionalism and Democracy: Transitions in the Contemporary World* (Oxford, Oxford University Press, 1993) 145–46.

[58]   Personal communication to Lindsey, Jakarta, April 1999.

reform programme, including the amendment in 1999 of Law 14 of 1970 on Judicial Power to establish judicial independence. Habibie, in fact, sometimes took major decisions with little cabinet or government consultation in an effort to move Indonesia toward compliance with the standards advocated by multilateral global organisations. These included, among others, the United Nations (for example, ordering the referendum in East Timor against the army's wishes) and the International Labour Organization (making Indonesia the first Asian nation to sign all core ILO Conventions).

It was during Habibie's brief term in office that Indonesia began the major decentralisation, electoral, human rights and anti-corruption reforms that established the foundation of its transition to a functioning, stable and open democratic system. With these reforms, Integralism and its implicit claim to Indonesian authoritarian particularism, once so central to the Indonesian polity, seemed to vanish quickly from public discourse. Few in the legislature or the media sought to defend the New Order model in 1999, or to oppose liberal democratic notions of democracy, separation of powers and the universality of human rights that only a year or so earlier had been officially alien, Western and 'un-Indonesian'.

The initial chaos of the post-Soeharto Reformasi was consolidated and focused by the constitutional amendment process that began in 1999, again under Habibie's administration. The amendments effectively re-allocated the power of the state along liberal democratic lines to a number of sources, chief among them a democratically-elected legislature and newly-independent judiciary. In this way the key feature of the integralistic state, political power concentrated in the hands of the president and his inner circle, was dismantled.[59] To demonstrate this, we offer a brief summary of the main amendments.

The First Amendment

The First Amendment was passed on 19 October 1999 following the 1999 elections, which were widely considered democratic, free and fair,

---

[59] S Waddell, 'Shifting Visions of the Social and Legal Order in Indonesia: Implications for Legislative Style and Form' (2005) 7(1) *Australian Journal of Asian Law* 43, 52.

delivering an MPR with a clear mandate to introduce constitutional reforms.

Prior to the amendments, the 1945 Constitution did not clearly establish either a parliamentary or a presidential political system. Instead, it created a blended and uncertain hybrid that relied on the notion of 'distribution of powers' from the MPR (as the superior institution of state), through the president to the bureaucracy and to the DPR. The separation of powers and its system of checks and balances between the judiciary, legislature and executive, so fundamental for a democratic political system, were absent.

Under the old 1945 Constitution, the president was formally subservient to the MPR, which appointed him or her. In practice, however, Soeharto effectively controlled the MPR's membership (see Chapter 3). It met only every five years, and had not much else to do but appoint the president – and in the New Order this involved little more than rubber-stamping. The MPR had also proclaimed the general outlines of state policy, but only in very broad terms, and always at the behest of the government.

In reality, the president held sweeping power. He was both head of state and head of government, had an unlimited number of five-year terms, could make statutes and the regulations to implement them, could form a Cabinet and had broad emergency powers. The president and the ministers he appointed were not accountable to the DPR. They were accountable only to the MPR, which is to say they were hardly accountable at all.

This executive-heavy system was altered by the first round of amendments in 1999. Most significantly, the Constitution was altered to prevent the president from holding office for more than two five-year terms, a clear response to the dictatorships of Soekarno and Soeharto. Amendments also restricted the president's legislative powers in favour of the legislature (see Chapters 2 and 3).

The Second Amendment

On 18 August 2000, the Second Amendment was enacted, further curtailing the president's so-called 'legislative powers'. Now bills automatically come into force 30 days after being passed by the DPR, even if the president does not endorse them.

The MPR also agreed to abolish the appointment of members to the DPR over time, thus ending the long-standing practice of reserving seats for the military, a pillar of the New Order system.

The Second Amendment also involved the dramatic expansion of human rights provisions in the Constitution to embrace most of the Universal Declaration of Human Rights. Chapter XA of the Constitution, which contains these rights, is a lengthy and impressive passage, granting a full range of protections extending well beyond those guaranteed in most developed states. These rights are discussed in Chapter 7.

The Second Amendment also strengthened the post-Soeharto regional autonomy process through the grant of formal constitutional status to local governments. Elected regional legislative bodies were given new and broad law-making powers, restricted only by the reservation of several matters for the national government. The legal infrastructure for decentralisation is the focus of Chapter 6.

The Third Amendment

The Third Amendment, enacted a year after the Second Amendment, was also important. The MPR voted to strip itself of its power to appoint the president. Instead the president and vice-president are now directly elected by the people from pairs of candidates proposed by political parties. To win, candidates need to receive more than 50 per cent of the overall vote, plus at least 20 per cent of the votes in at least half of the provinces of Indonesia.

The Third Amendment also outlined procedures for the impeachment and dismissal of the president (see Chapter 2), and curtailed the MPR's powers to pass decrees and set state policy. It established the *Dewan Perwakilan Daerah* (DPD, Regional Representatives Assembly), or regional 'senate' (Chapter 3); and provided for the establishment of the Constitutional Court with power to review legislation (Chapter 6), Judicial Commission (Chapter 5) and an independent electoral commission (Chapter 3).

The Fourth Amendment

The Fourth Amendment was the final set of amendments. The MPR agreed that if none of the candidates for the presidency and vice-presidency received an absolute majority in the first round of a direct election, then a second direct election would be held between the two highest-scoring candidates. It was also agreed that the MPR would now comprise the members of the DPR and DPD, ending the system of appointments to national assemblies, entrenched since Soekarno (Chapter 3). The MPR also rejected an effort to reintroduce the 'Jakarta Charter', to require Muslims to observe *shari'ah* (Chapter 8).

The Reinvention of The Pancasila

Although the four amendments did not touch the Pancasila, which remains in the Preamble to the Constitution, the status of the state ideology has changed significantly. It is now widely accepted that the New Order 'betrayed' the values of the Pancasila, rendering it little more than political rhetoric used to promote conformity and to stifle dissent. Under Habibie the 1985 'sole foundation' statutes were rescinded, and in Decision XVIII/MPR/1998[60] the MPR decided to end Pancasila indoctrination in schools and universities because it was 'no longer consistent with developments'. As President Yudhoyono has said:

> Nowadays, if we discuss Pancasila, the 1945 Constitution, and unity of Indonesia, most people will quickly associate us with the New Order regime, which limited human rights and was an anti-reform movement.[61]

Despite this loss of credibility, the Pancasila is still recognised as having formal legal prominence, and government officials – including the president – have reaffirmed that the Pancasila remains the fundamental basis of national life. More recently, liberal democrats have argued for its revival and 'revitalisation' as a means to resist that third strain of constitutional opinion surviving from 1945: aspirations for an Islamic state. As discussed in Chapter 8, the liberals see 'Belief in Almighty God' as a guarantee of religious pluralism and a means of ideological resistance against those who push for the implementation of conservative understandings of Islamic law.

---

[60] This Decision revoked MPR Decree II/MPR/1978 on the Guide to Living and the Practice of the Pancasila.

[61] *Jakarta Post*, 'SBY urges end to debate on Pancasila's merits', 2 June 2006.

CONCLUSION

The theoretical arguments that accompanied the drafting of Indonesia's Constitution of 1945 were not resolved with its promulgation. Since Independence in August that year, at least three ideas about what the Indonesian republic should be like have competed for political pre-eminence: Integralism, liberal democracy and Islamism. These ideas are essentially incompatible, despite Soekarno's efforts to embrace them all in the Pancasila. They are, however, apparently inextinguishable as well.

Although the Committee for the Preparation of Indonesia Independence had explicitly rejected Soepomo's Integralistic state idea, the 1945 Constitution acted as a charter for this authoritarian ideology for four decades under two dictatorships, one of the Left and the other of the Right. Remarkably, the alternative liberal democratic account of the state, which seemed to have been defeated in 1959, survived in the form of a determined, if marginalised, opposition discourse focused on the constitutional promise of a *Negara Hukum*. It was revived in 1999.

The very success of Soeharto's Integralistic system, and the extreme and intrusive nature of the authoritarian state it legitimised, ensured its rejection when his New Order regime disintegrated. The slow but effective remaking of the 1945 Constitution over four years from 1999 by fractious law-makers was little short of extraordinary. More extraordinary still, this Constitution now resembles the 1950 Provisional Constitution it once displaced.

The process of amendment allowed an effective transition to a new and functioning liberal democratic system. The result is, admittedly, still a long way from being satisfactory. The amended Constitution remains an incomplete document and only a few of the changes it mandates have been fully implemented legislatively or institutionally, as this book shows. Most are yet to be tested and, it is hoped, refined; some already face great difficulties. There are other major problems to be surmounted too, the most obvious of which is institutionalised and widespread corruption inherited from the New Order, which continues to hinder reform. Another is the reassertion of the old calls for an Islamic state, sometimes accompanied by violence, and even occasional calls for a return to Integralism.

There are, however, grounds for some optimism. The flood of post-Soeharto reforms and the widespread examination and criticism they have received, together with the blossoming of civil society and the media, has generated a much broader public understanding of the importance of constitutional change and of legal and institutional reform than at any time since the 1950s. Indonesia now has a vigorous constitutionalist discourse, led by the active, energetic and professional Constitutional Court. The result is the emergence of a new and more civil Indonesian society that does not guarantee the pendulum will not swing back to Integralism but perhaps makes that less likely than at any time since 1945.

SELECTED READING

Lev, Daniel S, 'Between State and Society: Professional Lawyers and Reform in Indonesia' in Tim Lindsey (ed), *Indonesia: Law and Society*, 2nd edn (Annandale, NSW, Federation Press, 2008) 48–67.

Lubis, Todung Mulya, *In Search of Human Rights: Legal-Political Dilemmas of Indonesia's New Order, 1966–1990* (Jakarta, Published by PT Gramedia Pustaka Utama in cooperation with SPES Foundation, 1993).

Nasution, Adnan Buyung, *The Aspiration for Constitutional Government in Indonesia: A Socio-Legal Study of the Indonesian Konstituante, 1956– 1959* (Jakarta, Pustaka Sinar Harapan, 1992).

Nasution, Adnan Buyung, 'Towards Constitutional Democracy in Indonesia', *Adnan Buyung Nasution Papers on Southeast Asian Constitutionalism* (Asian Law Centre, University of Melbourne, 2011).

2

The Presidency

———◆———

Introduction – The Constitution and the Presidency Under the New Order – Amendment of Constitutional Provisions Relating to the President – Presidential Powers Under the Amended Constitution – The Vice-President – Election of the President and Vice-President – The Presidential Advisory Council – The Cabinet and Ministers – Replacement of the President – Impeachment and Dismissal – Conclusion

INTRODUCTION

WHEN SOEHARTO FELL in 1998, the *Reformasi* (Reformation) movement that toppled him demanded immediate change to create:

> an open society, symbolised and beginning with free elections . . . chastened and disciplined and regulated business and banking; a professionally focused armed forces . . . a decently paid civil service with one mission, public service; a thorough investigation of the recent pseudo-royal family's sources of wealth . . . and the stripping of neo-feudal values from Indonesian leadership style.[1]

The last of these demands was perhaps the most important, as it was, in many respects, the key to the others. This is because during his three decades of power Soeharto and his inner circle of family and friends created a parallel 'black' system backed by coercive state power to ensure

---

[1] T Friend, '*The Asian Miracle, The Asian Contagion, and the USA*' (Speech to the Foreign Policy Research Institute, 16 November 1998, copy in possession of the authors).

their access to rents. It was through this corrupt system that most business and administration was really carried out.

The system that emerged has been memorably described by McLeod[2] as an elaborate form of franchise. Put at its simplest, money derived from illegal rents flowed up from 'franchisors' (office holders or businesses) to the 'head franchisor' (Soeharto, and his inner circle) in return for political favour and patronage. Pervasive, powerful and sometimes violent, this franchise subverted 'official' formal systems, such as law and rational administration. Those who opposed it were politically marginalised or dealt with by the security forces and their associated criminal gangs and militias, sometimes with fatal consequences. One effect of the franchise was to institutionalise and entrench corruption and criminality throughout the bureaucracy.

THE CONSTITUTION AND THE PRESIDENCY UNDER
THE NEW ORDER

Creating a new constitutional system that would prevent a repeat of the Soeharto dictatorship and Soekarno's earlier, less brutal and corrupt but equally authoritarian, Guided Democracy regime, was not a simple matter. This was because the New Order's political 'franchise' had been accompanied by a legitimising constitutional theory that was supported by relentless political indoctrination, including through the regime's obligatory 'P4' Pancasila propaganda training programmes.[3] Adnan Buyung Nasution, a dissident legal aid lawyer during this period, argued in his seminal work *The Aspiration for Constitutional Democracy in Indonesia* (1992) that New Order constitutional thought was saturated by the *Integralistic Staatsidee*. As discussed in Chapter 1, this was the authoritarian theory of the state promoted by the Constitution's original principal drafter, Professor Soepomo, in 1945. For Soepomo:

[t]he head of state must be capable of leading the entire populace, the head of state must surpass all classes and have the quality of unifying the people

---

[2] RH McLeod, 'Soeharto's Indonesia: A Better Class of Corruption' (2000) 7(2) *Agenda.*

[3] See S Nishimura, 'The Development of Pancasila Moral Education' (1995) 33(3) *Southeast Asian Studies* 303–16 on P4 indoctrination and, for a more satirical approach, S Permana, 'Not your Local Member' in T Lindsey (ed), *Indonesia: Law and Society*, 1st edn (Sydney, Federation Press, 1999) 197–99.

and the state ... as a King or President, or as an Adipati like in Burma, or as a Fuhrer.[4]

This, Nasution says, meant that:

> the system of government proposed by Soepomo ultimately turned entirely on the ruler, and, in particular, the ruler's role as head of state. Soepomo believed, in fact, that there should be a 'concentration of responsibility and power in government.' Furthermore, he said that 'we desire a constitution which is accountable to the government, particularly to the head of state', and not the other way around ... [T]he Integralistic State idea ... places the state and the leader above all else, and strenuously rejects both the substance and procedure of democracy.[5]

Integralistic orthodoxy under Soeharto had it that Indonesia was a *Negara Hukum*, or law state, based on a *trias politika*, the 'political triad'. This term is now generally understood in Indonesia to mean 'separation of powers' but it was then interpreted as a reference to what was called the 'distribution' of executive, legislative and judicial powers *through* the president to subordinate state agencies.[6]

On this analysis, all state power stemmed from Indonesia's then-supreme sovereign body, the People's Consultative Assembly (*Majelis Permusyawaratan Rakyat* or MPR), and flowed directly to the president, as the sole bearer of its mandate. The president was thus answerable only to the MPR, and it was legitimate for him to influence and even control all the bodies to which he distributed that power, including the legislature (the DPR, *Dewan Perwakilan Rakyat*, People's Representative Assembly) and the judiciary. As discussed in Chapter 4, the judiciary was therefore not independent. Although the Elucidation to Article 1 of the Constitution required the judiciary to be free of external interference, this was qualified by the words 'except as provided by law'. The Constitution also granted no court power to review statutes. On the orthodox Integralistic reading of the Constitution, only the MPR as the repository of sovereignty had the right to do that. Accordingly, provided the president could control the MPR – as Soeharto did for most of his rule – his power was virtually unlimited.

[4]   AB Nasution, 'Towards Constitutional Democracy in Indonesia', *Adnan Buyung Nasution Papers on Indonesian Constitutionalism* (Asian Law Centre, University of Melbourne, 2011) 15–16.
[5]   ibid, 16.
[6]   TM Lubis, 'The *Rechsstaat* and Human Rights' in T Lindsey (ed), *Indonesia: Law and Society*, 1st edn (Annandale, NSW, Federation Press, 1999).

As shown in Chapter 1, Soepomo's expressly-stated points of reference for his Integralistic ideas were Nazi Germany and wartime imperial Japan.[7] He saw these as embodying the principle of *kekeluargaan*,[8] which for him was the proper basis of the new Indonesian Republic. The state was to function on paternalistic terms, with the children – the *rakyat* or people – following the will of the father – the president – and accepting punishment by him when their actions displeased him. In this way, Soepomo's Constitution gave Integralism what it required: the concentration of all power in the hands of the president at the expense of other branches of government. As Nasution puts it:

> Soeharto's leadership was based on . . . the principle of 'family'. He, in fact, appointed himself as 'Father of the Nation', presenting himself as father/leader of a nuclear family, where all the family members had to obey him, and criticism of the father was considered taboo. Soeharto thus perfectly put into practice Soepomo's integralistic concept . . . Branches of the state authorities were stripped of all independence and were rendered ineffective in performing their functions. Soeharto was truly like a king and everybody had to bow down and humble themselves before him. The legislative body and the executive body became mere ornaments of his absolute power.[9]

Decades of ideological indoctrination insisting on these ideas, and repression of critics of the New Order regime, led to a dearth of legal theory supporting alternative constitutional theories. Only a few marginalised, if outspoken, activists, such as Nasution, Todung Mulya Lubis and their circles, provided exceptions to this, although there was always a degree of popular cycnicism about government rhetoric. By the 1990s Integralistic theories about the supremacy of the presidency were largely unquestioned, in public at least. It was perhaps only the extreme and blatant nature of the abuses committed by Soeharto's regime under cover of these ideas that ensured they were rejected so comprehensively within just a few years of his resignation.

The post-Soeharto reformers were, in fact, remarkably successful in stripping power from the presidency during the constitutional amendment process conducted annually in the MPR from 1999 to 2002. The presidency inherited by Soeharto's successors was progressively diminished as authority was gradually transferred to other branches of the

---

[7] ibid, 92.
[8] Literally, 'familiness'.
[9] Nasution, 'Towards Constitutional Democracy in Indonesia', n 4 above, 16–17.

state, principally the DPR. Notorious as a 'rubber-stamp' under Soeharto, the legislature emerged in 2004 as the most powerful branch of government. This is true even though the decision to make the presidency a directly-elected office granted the executive a competing legitimacy it could never claim under the New Order, when, as we shall see, the MPR alone selected and appointed the president. In any case, the amendments set the scene for constant tussles between the DPR and the presidency for control of policy. These have marked Indonesian politics since then.

In this chapter, we offer a brief account of the constitutional amendments relating to the presidency, followed by a summary of the executive's constitutional powers as they now stand. We conclude by considering procedures for the impeachment and removal of the president, using the dismissal of former President Abdurrahman Wahid as a case study.

AMENDMENT OF CONSTITUTIONAL PROVISIONS RELATING TO THE PRESIDENT

As mentioned in Chapter 1, the First Amendment was passed on 19 October 1999, not long after the first truly democratic election in Indonesia for decades was held in June of that year.[10] The MPR that sat four months after that election was then, as now, the only body with authority to amend the Constitution, and voters expected it to exercise those powers to prevent another dictatorial presidency. Perhaps unsurprisingly, it began with amendments that handed elected legislators greater control of the legislative process.

Defining the separation of legislative power between the executive, the DPR and the MPR was a predominating concern as the constitutional amendments were deliberated. The position of these branches of government had long been ambiguous, largely because of the absence of the separation of powers in the Constitution. On the one hand, the MPR had been the supreme sovereign body, nominally at least. In the

---

[10] The only genuinely democratic election prior to New Order's establishment in 1966 was held in 1955. This election, with 91.5 per cent of registered voters participating, was more fair and open than the sham elections held every five years under Soeharto but it too has been criticised for being not truly democratic, due to religious and military pressures. See MC Ricklefs, *A History Of Modern Indonesia Since C. 1300*, 4th edn (Stanford CA, Stanford University Press, 2008) 286–87.

words of Article 1 of the Constitution as it then stood, 'sovereignty is in the hands of the MPR and is exercised in full by it'.[11] Chapter III of the Elucidation to the Constitution added that 'since the MPR is vested with the sovereignty of the state, its power is unlimited'. Section 6(III)(3) of the Elucidation spelled out the implications of this for the presidency:

> It is the MPR that holds the highest power of the state, whereas the President shall pursue the state policy outlined by the MPR. The President, who is appointed by the MPR, shall be subordinate and accountable to the MPR . . . The President is not in an equal position to, but is subordinate to, the MPR.

In theory, the MPR therefore enjoyed unfettered[12] discretion to select the president, and could also dismiss him or her on the basis of an 'interpolation' (*interpelasi*) reference for impeachment from the DPR, pursuant to a process discussed below. Read on their own, these provisions made the Indonesian system appear 'parliamentary'.

Yet the 1945 Constitution also provided for a very strong presidential system. It unambiguously stated that the 'President shall hold the power of government' (Article 4), and was thus at once both head of state and of government. The president could serve for an unlimited number of five-year terms (Article 7). The president also had power to make laws (Article 5(1)) and regulations to implement them (Article 5(2)); exclusive powers in respect of ambassadors, amnesties and pardons; exclusive authority over Ministers and the formation of cabinets (Articles 13, 14 and 17); and broad emergency powers (Article 12). The executive bias of these provisions was also supported by a clear statement in the Constitution that the president and ministers were not accountable to the legislature (the DPR) but solely to the MPR (Chapter 6, Parts V and VII of the Elucidation).[13] In reality, however, the MPR had only very occasionally asserted its authority against Soekarno and Soeharto – the two presidents who ruled independent Indonesia before 1998 – and then only when each had already lost political power.

---

[11] This sovereignty was removed in the course of the amendments. It is now 'in the hands of the people and is exercised in accordance with the Constitution' (Article 1(2)).

[12] The only mechanism to restrain the MPR was the requirement that it meet at least once every five years (Article 2(2)). For most of Soeharto's rule this meant it met only once every five years.

[13] Constitutionally, the President was on the same level as the legislature, the DPR, and as Chapter 6, Part V of the Elucidation to the Constitution stated, 'the President is not responsible to it'. It also provided, however, that the President 'must pay full attention to the voice of the DPR'.

The First Amendment did not completely clarify the distinction between presidential and parliamentary government, but it did significantly refine the formula to the benefit of the legislature. The notion that the system was, in principle, presidential was affirmed but the president's power to make statutes was greatly diminished. This shift was expressed in changes to Articles 5 and 20, which, in their original wording read: '[t]he President holds the power to make statutes (*undang-undang*) in conjunction with the DPR'. The new Article 20(1) states that the DPR 'holds the power to make statutes', while the President merely has the right 'to present bills to the DPR' (Article 5), a power he or she shares with all members of the DPR (Article 21(1)). Article 20(2) requires that bills be 'debated by the DPR and the President to reach joint agreement'.[14]

The First Amendment also gave the DPR a right to be heard in the appointment of ambassadors (Article 13) and the grant of amnesties (Article 14), and gave the Supreme Court (*Mahkamah Agung*) power to make recommendations to the president about clemency requests. Finally – and of great political resonance – the new Article 7 limits future presidents to two five-year terms. This was clearly a reaction to the 23-year reign of Soekarno and the 32 years enjoyed by Soeharto. Perhaps more than any other, this amendment was a strong indication of the intent to end authoritarianism in Indonesia.

On 18 August 2000, the MPR passed the Second Amendment, together with a complementary set of MPR Decrees. Only one amendment focused on the continuing tussle between the presidency and legislature but it was important. The president's ratification or assent, previously required for bills to become law, now became a mere courtesy. If the president refuses to sign into law a bill duly passed by the DPR, it automatically becomes law after 30 days in any case (Article 20(5)). This amendment makes the DPR Indonesia's principal national legislature. The MPR became a sort of supervisory assembly with special responsibility for the Constitution, as discussed in Chapter 3. The Second Amendment thus decisively shifted the locus of state power to the DPR, leaving Indonesia with a constitutionally-weaker presidency.

The Third Amendment, passed in August 2001, delivered another radical change to the original scheme of the Constitution. By unani-

---

[14] For further discussion of the relationship between the president and DPR in the making of laws, see Chapter 3 of this volume.

mous vote, the MPR finally stripped itself of the last remnants of the power it had enjoyed since 1945 to appoint the president (Article 6A). Instead, the president and vice-president are now directly elected in pairs proposed by political parties. The Constitution requires that, to win office, the pair must obtain more than 50 per cent of the vote, plus at least 20 per cent of the votes in at least half of Indonesia's provinces (Article 6A). After bitter argument, consensus was also reached on what would happen if no pair met this threshold. In the Fourth Amendment, the MPR decided that there would be a second-round direct election run-off between the two highest-scoring pairs (Article 6A(4)).

PRESIDENTIAL POWERS UNDER THE AMENDED CONSTITUTION

Section III of the Constitution as amended now sets out the powers of the president and vice-president. Article 4(1) states broadly that the 'President of the Republic of Indonesia is granted the power of government in accordance with the Constitution'. Professor Jimly Asshiddiqie, founding Chief Justice of the Constitutional Court, has questioned whether this wide grant of governmental authority allows the president to exercise other 'inherent' executive powers not expressly granted in the Constitution. Such powers might be vested in him or her by virtue of the wide ambit of the term 'government'. Asshiddiqie[15] concludes, however, that while this is certainly arguable, scholarly opinion in Indonesia remains 'unsettled' on the issue.

The specific executive powers that the Constitution does expressly grant to the president are as follows. He or she:

- formally ratifies bills upon which he or she, and the DPR, agree, but without a right to veto bills passed by the DPR (Article 20(4));
- is Supreme Commander of the Armed forces, Navy and Air Force (Article 10);
- declares war and peace, with DPR approval (Article 11(1));
- enters into treaties. The president must seek DPR approval where an international agreement has 'broad and fundamental consequences for the lives of the Indonesian people, creates burdens on the state's

---

[15] J Asshiddiqie, *The Constitutional Law of Indonesia: A Comprehensive Overview* (Selangor, Malaysia, Sweet and Maxwell Asia, 2009) 276.

finances, and/or requires amendments to laws or the enactment of new ones' (Article 11(2));

- declares states of emergency. This power is, however, circumscribed by statute (Article 12);
- appoints and dismisses ministers (Article 17(2));
- appoints ambassadors, after considering the views of the DPR, and consuls (Articles 13(1) and (2));
- accepts ambassadors from foreign countries, after considering the views of the DPR (Article 13(3));
- forms an advisory council to advise the president (Article 16);
- awards titles, decorations and other marks of honour as provided for by statute (Article 15);
- inaugurates members of the State Auditing Body (BPK), who are elected by the DPR, after considering the advice of the DPD (Article 23F(1));
- appoints Supreme Court judges proposed by the Judicial Commission and approved by the DPR (Article 24A(3));
- appoints and dismisses members of the Judicial Commission approved by the DPR (Article 24B(3)); and
- appoints Constitutional Court judges, after the Supreme Court, the DPR, and the president have proposed three judges each (Article 24C(3)).

The Constitution also gives the president quasi-judicial powers of clemency, including granting pardons (*grasi*) and rehabilitation (*rehabilitasi*), after considering advice from the Supreme Court (Article 14(1)); and granting amnesties and nullification (*abolisi*), after considering advice from the DPR (Article 14(2)). A person who has been prosecuted can seek a pardon from the president to alter, reduce or cancel a criminal sentence.[16] Rehabilitation is the process of restoring a person's honour and reputation following an acquittal.[17] Amnesty is a pardon initiated by the president. Abolition is similar to amnesty but it can be issued after a

---

[16] The procedure for granting pardons is governed by Law 22 of 2002 on Pardons.

[17] Procedures for rehabilitation are contained in Article 9 of Law 4 of 2004 on Judicial Power; Article 97 of the Criminal Procedure Code (*Kitab Undang-Undang Hukum Acara Pidana*, KUHAP); Article 35 of Law 26 of 2000 on Human Rights; and Government Regulation 3 of 2002 on Compensation, Restitution and Rehabilitation of Victims of Gross Human Rights Violations.

prosecution has commenced.[18] Although Article 14 of the Constitution requires the president to consider advice of the Supreme Court before deciding to grant a pardon or rehabilitation, and of the DPR before granting amnesty or abolition, their opinions do not bind the president. He or she has exclusive and unreviewable authority in the exercise of these powers.[19]

The Constitution reserves some powers for the president in the legislative process, although, as mentioned, these are now limited. Specifically, the president can propose bills to the DPR (Article 5(1)); propose a bill on the state budget to be discussed by the DPR, after considering the views of the DPD (Article 23(2)); and issue government regulations to implement laws (Article 5(2)).

During times of crisis, the president can also issue interim emergency laws (*peraturan pengganti undang-undang*, 'Perpu', regulations in lieu of statute). These have constitutional status equivalent to statutes but, to remain in force, the DPR must approve them at its next sitting (Articles 22(1) and (2)). Several legal issues relating to interim emergency laws have been controversial in recent years, two of which we briefly mention here. First, whether a 'pressing situation' exists is something the president can subjectively determine. It is not for a court to second-guess the president's judgement. The Constitutional Court has therefore refused to review the propriety of the president's determination of a situation as 'pressing'.[20] Instead, only the DPR is given authority to objectively determine, at its next sitting and with the benefit of hindsight, whether there really was an emergency, and whether it remains.

Secondly, confusion has arisen because of the vague terminology used in Article 22 of the Constitution. Article 22(2) states that the interim law 'must' obtain the approval of the DPR at its next sitting but Article 22(3) states that 'if the interim law does not obtain the approval of the DPR, then it must be revoked'. Although the Constitution itself

---

[18] Asshiddiqie, *The Constitutional Law of Indonesia*, n 15 above, 288, 290, 297. Both amnesty and abolition are regulated by Interim Emergency Law 11 of 1954 on Amnesty and Abolition.

[19] Article 2(3) of Law 22 of 2002 on Pardons says that pardons may generally only be applied for once. However, where a first appeal for clemency is denied, another application can be made after two years. Additionally, a convict on death row who applies for, and obtains, a pardon to commute his or her sentence to life may apply for another pardon after two years.

[20] See Constitutional Court Decision 3/PUU-III/2005.

does not mention how revocations should take place, Article 25(4) of Law 10 of 2004 on Law-making declares that if the DPR rejects the Perpu, it must be revoked by a bill that the president introduces into the DPR and that the DPR endorses. It seems, therefore, that repeal is not automatic if the DPR simply votes against the interim law. It is also unclear whether an interim law will remain in force if the DPR does not explicitly reject it, or if the president declines to introduce a bill to revoke it.[21]

The Vice-President

Article 4(2) of the Constitution states that 'in exercising his or her duties, the President shall be assisted by a vice-president'. Under Article 8, the vice-president acts as president in the latter's absence.

Perhaps because the vice-president is viewed merely as an assistant to the president, the powers of the vice-president are not detailed in the Constitution, or indeed in any other law. Instead, they are dictated by convention. Asshiddiqie[22] argues, presumably on the basis of democratic principles, that because the vice-president is directly elected on a joint ticket with the president (Article 8), he or she outranks all Ministers, who are directly appointed and dismissed by the president (Article 17).

Election of the President and Vice-President

Articles 6 and 6A of the Constitution require the president and vice-president to be directly elected. These elections are regulated by Law 42 of 2008 on the General Election of the President and Vice-President,[23] a statute that has survived several Constitutional Court challenges,[24] discussed in Chapter 5.

---

[21] For further discussion of some of these issues, see Harsono, Yuli 'Polemik Penolakan Perpu JPSK', *Hukumonline*, 19 January 2010.

[22] Asshiddiqie, *The Constitutional Law of Indonesia*, n 15 above, 273.

[23] Law 42 of 2008 replaced Law 23 of 2003 on the General Elections of the President and Vice-President (see Article 261 of Law 42 of 2008).

[24] See, for example, Constitutional Court Decisions 51-52-59/PUU-VI/2008; 56/PUU-VI/2008; and 104/PUU-VII/2009.

Article 6A(1) of the Constitution requires that the president and vice-president be directly elected as a pair. Presidential and vice-presidential candidates must be Indonesian citizens from birth; have never been of another nationality of their own volition; have never betrayed their country; and be mentally and physically capable of carrying out duties as president or vice-president (Article 6(1)).[25] Constitutional Court Decision 008/PUU-II/2004 dealt with an application by former President Abdurrahman Wahid and former Foreign Minister Alwi Shihab. Partially blind and having suffered several strokes, Wahid had failed to pass the medical check-up the Electoral Commission required for all would-be presidential candidates. He therefore asked the Constitutional Court to consider the constitutionality of provisions of Law 23 of 2003 on the General Election of the President and Vice-President, which purported to prohibit candidates from standing for president on the basis that they were physically and mentally incapable of performing the role. The Court pointed out that Article 6(1) of the Constitution itself requires presidential candidates to be physically and mentally capable of performing the tasks and responsibilities of the president and vice-president. The Law was, therefore, constitutional.

Political parties and coalitions must propose their presidential and vice-presidential candidates prior to a general election (Article 6A(2)). These requirements are reiterated in Article 8 of Law 42 of 2008, which was the subject of a Constitutional Court challenge by a number of activists in the year it was passed. They argued that it allowed the 'monopolising' of presidential candidacy by political parties and should therefore be invalidated. The Court, however, upheld the legislation, pointing out that the reference to political parties in this context is expressly made in the Constitution.[26]

Article 9 of Law 42 of 2008 also requires that to propose a pair of presidential and vice-presidential candidates a party or coalition must hold at least 20 per cent of the total number of seats in the DPR or 25 per cent of the total number of valid votes in the previous general

---

[25] Article 5 of Law 42 of 2008 adds a number of other conditions of candidacy.

[26] Constitutional Court Decision 56/PUU-VI/2008, pp 120–21. It should be noted, however, that similar provisions in Law 32 of 2004 on Regional Government sought to require that local regional head election candidates be proposed by political parties – thereby preventing independent candidates from standing. These provisions were declared unconstitutional in Constitutional Court Decision 5/PUU-V/2007. This case is discussed in Chapters 3 and 5 of this volume.

election for the DPR.[27] As mentioned above, Article 6A(3) also requires that candidates must also win more than 50 per cent of the vote across more than half of Indonesia's provinces; and, if that threshold is not met, then the two pairs receiving the most votes compete in a run-off (Article 6A(4)).

THE PRESIDENTIAL ADVISORY COUNCIL

Article 16 of the Constitution states that 'the President is to set up an advisory council, which has the task of advising the President and which is to be further regulated by law'. Under Soeharto, a Supreme Advisory Council (*Dewan Pertimbangan Agung*) operated pursuant to an earlier version of Article 16 but was ineffectual and was wound up after his fall.[28] It has now been replaced by the Presidential Advisory Council (*Dewan Pertimbangan Presiden* or *Wantimpres*). While an entirely separate body to the cabinet (which is discussed below), the Wantimpres has had some influence on policy formation under President Yudhoyono.

The Presidential Advisory Council was established through Law 19 of 2006 on the Presidential Advisory Council, which cites Article 16 of the Constitution in its Preamble. Like Article 16, the Law states that the Presidential Advisory Council is a 'government institution tasked with advising the president' in the course of his or her duties (Article 1). It is responsible solely to the president (Article 2). Its members must give advice as necessary to the president, and may do so regardless of whether he asks for it (Article 4(2)). At the request of the president, they may attend Cabinet meetings or accompany the president on state or working visits (Article 6(2)). Advice can be given to the president by individual members or by the Council as a whole but must always be kept confidential (Articles 4(3) and 6(1)). This rule seems to be honoured more in the breach than in the observance, however, as various members of the Presidential Advisory Council have often publicly discussed advice they have given to President Yudhoyono.

The Constitution is silent on the membership of the Presidential Advisory Council but Chapter III of Law 19 of 2006 details the Team's

---

[27] This provision was upheld by Constitutional Court Decision 51-52-59/PUU-VI/2008.

[28] Asshiddiqie, *The Constitutional Law of Indonesia*, n 15 above, 300.

composition and selection process. It comprises nine members, appointed by the president, and one chair (Articles 7(1) and 9). The chair rotates amongst the members at the president's discretion (Article 7(2)). Article 8 requires a potential candidate to be devoted to almighty God; an Indonesian citizen; and loyal to Pancasila, the Constitution and the 1945 Proclamation of Independence. They must also possess statesperson-like qualities; have mental and physical health; and be honest, fair, and of good character. They must have never been sentenced by a court for an offence carrying a jail term of five years or more; and must have particular expertise in government.

Presidential Advisory Council members are prohibited from serving in other positions while on the Council. For example, they must not lead political parties, NGOs, foundations, private or public companies, professional organisations, or private or public educational institutions (Article 12). They serve for the duration of the president's term (Article 10) but the president may dismiss council members at his or her discretion, including for breach of Article 8 (Article 11(1)(d)–(e)).

THE CABINET AND MINISTERS

The Constitution makes no mention of the Cabinet but Article 17 refers to the Ministers who are part of it and provides that their role is to assist the president. Appointed and dismissed by the president, they are responsible to him or her for a specific portfolio. All 34 current ministers – of whom 20 are Departmental Ministers, 10 are Ministers of State, four are Coordinating Ministers and one is Secretary of State – are members of President Yudhoyono's 'Second United Indonesia' Cabinet, although Deputy Ministers are not.[29] Ministers need not be elected members of the national legislature, although some are. Also appointed to the Cabinet are so-called 'Ministerial-Level Officials' (*Pejabat Setingkat Menteri*), such as Indonesian Armed Forces, National Police and State Intelligence Agency heads and the Attorney General/Chief Public Prosecutor (*Jaksa Agung*), although there is no clear regulatory basis for

---

[29] The profiles of Cabinet Ministers can be found at www.presidenri.go.id/index. php/statik/kabinet.html. The functions of the 34 Ministers and the Ministries they lead are further regulated by Law 39 of 2008 on Ministers of State; and Government Regulation 47 of 2009 on the Establishment and Organisation of State Ministries.

their inclusion.[30] The president typically installs the Cabinet by decree and a new decree listing its members is required every time a new Cabinet is formed.[31]

Most Cabinets since Soeharto have been made up of a mixture of technocrats appointed from the bureaucracy and civil society, and politicians representing a range of different parties. This reflects the fact that no government since Soeharto has enjoyed a majority in the DPR and all have therefore been forced to broker unreliable coalitions to rule. Seats in Cabinet are much sought-after by competing parties and there is an expectation that they will be distributed as incentives to support the government. While this often results in the appointment of Ministers who lack competence in the areas allocated to them, it is a reflection of political reality and is probably necessary for stability. It is nonetheless the source of much criticism.

REPLACEMENT OF THE PRESIDENT

If the president dies, resigns, is impeached, or is unable to perform his or her duties, Article 8(1) of the Constitution provides that the vice-president replaces the president until the end of his or her term. If the position of vice-president becomes vacant, the MPR must convene within 60 days to select a vice-president from two candidates nominated by the president (Article 8(2)).

If the positions of both president and vice-president become vacant simultaneously, or if both are unable to carry out their duties, then a troika of the Minister of Foreign Affairs, the Minister of Home Affairs and the Minister of Defence is to perform the presidential functions (Article 8(3)). Within 30 days of the vacancy or incapacity, the MPR must convene to elect a president and vice-president to serve the remainder of the term. In doing so, the MPR must choose from:

> two pairs of Presidential and Vice Presidential candidates proposed by the political parties or coalitions whose . . . pairs received the first and second highest votes in the previous general election (Article 8(3)).

[30] PNH Simanjuntak, *Kabinet-kabinet Republik Indonesia: dari awal kemerdekaan sampai reformasi* (Jakarta, Djambatan, 2003). For a current list of Ministerial-Level Officials in Cabinet, see www.indonesia.go.id/in/kabinet-indonesia-bersatu-ii/setingkat-menteri.html.

[31] See, for example, Presidential Decision 84/P of 2009.

IMPEACHMENT AND DISMISSAL

The Constitutional provisions on presidential impeachment and dismissal, and in particular, their absence prior to 2001, have had great political significance in the years since Soeharto's resignation. As mentioned, in no post-Soeharto election has the political party from which the president is drawn won a majority of seats in the DPR. This, combined with the diminished powers of the president and continued tensions between legislature and executive, has led to repeated threats by the DPR to impeach the president or vice-president.

On one occasion, the DPR acted upon this threat, dismissing President Abdurrahman Wahid in July 2001. The result was political crisis. These events led to the amendment of the impeachment and dismissal process, and the grant of a decisive role in it to the Constitutional Court. These amendments now make it more difficult for legislators to remove the president. Although various attempts have been made to impeach Wahid's successors, Megawati Soekarnoputri (2001–04) and Susilo Bambang Yudhoyono (2004–), none have succeeded. We now offer a short account of Wahid's dismissal and the ensuing constitutional amendments.

The Dismissal of Abdurrahman Wahid

Abdurrahman Wahid was appointed president by MPR majority vote on 20 October 1999, just one day after the First Amendment was passed.[32] The winner of the democratic legislative elections held earlier that year was, however, not Wahid's party, PKB,[33] but Megawati Soekarnoputri's PDI-P.[34] Its plurality of 36 per cent put it well ahead of its nearest rival, *Golkar*[35] (the former political vehicle of Soeharto), which won only 21 per cent. PKB scored a distant 11 per cent but Wahid became president nonetheless, with Megawati as his vice-president.

---

[32] D Indrayana, *Indonesian Constitutional Reform, 1999–2002: An Evaluation of Constitution-Making in Transition* (Jakarta, Kompas Book Publishing Indrayana, 2008) 159.

[33] *Partai Kebangkitan Bangsa*, National Awakening Party.

[34] *Partai Demokrasi Indonesia – Perjuangan*, Indonesian Democracy Party – Struggle.

[35] *Golongan Karya* – Functional Groups.

This was possible because at the time the MPR held absolute discretion to appoint the president, under Article 6 of the Constitution. It was obliged only to choose a president who was a 'native Indonesian citizen'. Wahid won the presidency by garnering the support of a 'central axis' (*poros tengah*) of Muslim political parties in the MPR. He also secured the support of members of *Golkar*, probably because they feared that Megawati, Soekarno's daughter and the leading opposition politician under Soeharto, would seek vengeance against them. In any case, Wahid was able to secure the numbers necessary to defeat Megawati in the MPR, despite his party's poor performance in the elections.

The instability and administrative paralysis that marked Wahid's rule was not surprising, as he never long controlled a significant minority in the newly-strengthened legislature, let alone a majority. Moreover, the 'winner' of the popular election was his vice-president – and she was ready and willing to replace him. Wahid was therefore forced to go to extraordinary lengths to piece together temporary coalitions to implement even routine decisions or pass laws. The result was very weak government. By late 2000, ethnic and religious conflict was growing across the archipelago, Wahid appeared to be losing control of the military, and serious allegations of corruption were being made against him.[36]

In August 2000, the DPR formed a Special Committee (*Panitia Khusus, Pansus*) to investigate two corruption scandals linked to Wahid. The first was the withdrawal of Rp 35 billion by Wahid's masseur and former business partner from Bulog, the state-owned logistics agency. The second related to the handling of a US$ 2 million donation by Sultan Hassanal Bolkiah of Brunei.[37] These events seemed to implicate Wahid and even members of the central axis turned against him, with 151 of the DPR's 550 members presenting a petition in November calling for his impeachment.[38]

The Existing Procedure for Impeachment and Dismissal in 2000

The unamended 1945 Constitution did not include a procedure for impeachment of the president. Given Soepomo's aim of empowering the president at the cost of other state institutions, this is not surprising.

---

[36] G Barton, *Abdurrahman Wahid: Muslim Democrat, Indonesian President; a View from Inside* (Honolulu, University of Hawaii Press, 2002) 306.

[37] D Indrayana, *Indonesian Constitutional Reform, 1999–2002*, n 32 above, 229.

[38] Barton, *Abdurrahman Wahid*, n 36 above, 345.

Rather, impeachment was covered in MPR Decree III of 1978 on the Position and Relations of the Highest State Institutions, and MPR Decree II of 1999 on the Standing Orders of the MPR. Article 4 of the 1978 MPR Decree gave power to the MPR to dismiss the president if he or she requests to be dismissed, is continually absent or commits a serious violation of state policy. Article 4(e) of the 1999 MPR Decree added that the president could be dismissed for 'committing a serious violation of the broad national policy platform and/or the Constitution'. What constituted a 'serious violation' was left to the MPR to decide.[39]

Article 7 of the 1978 MPR Decree outlined the dismissal process for serious violations of state policy. The DPR was required to first issue memoranda to notify the president of the violation (Article 7(2)). If the president did not respond to the memorandum within three months, the DPR could issue a second memorandum (Article 7(3)). If the president ignored the memorandum for a further month, then the DPR could then request the formation of a Special Session (*Sidang Istimewa*) for the president to answer the complaints. If it was dissatisfied with the president's answer, it could then vote for dismissal.

The Dismissal

In late January 2001, the Special Committee established by the DPR to investigate the Bulog and Brunei corruption allegations issued a report finding that it was 'reasonable to suspect' that the President was involved in corruption.[40] On 27 January 2001, Wahid told a gathering of university rectors that if Indonesia 'descended into anarchy' he would dissolve the DPR.[41] This led to a significant shift of opinion against the President, who now appeared increasingly draconian and authoritarian.

On 1 February 2001, the DPR voted 393 to 4 to issue the first memorandum against President Wahid.[42] This alleged that Wahid had committed a serious violation of the Constitution and national policy in two, somewhat vaguely described, ways. First, he had violated the oath of office he took under Article 9 of the Constitution, by which he stated he would 'hold firmly to the Constitution and fully implement all Laws and

---

[39] International Crisis Group, 'Indonesia's Presidential Crisis', *Indonesia Briefing* (Jakarta/Brussels, 2001) 6.

[40] Indrayana, *Indonesian Constitutional Reform*, n 32 above, 233.

[41] Barton, *Abdurrahman Wahid*, n 36 above, 347–48.

[42] Indrayana, *Indonesian Constitutional Reform*, n 32 above, 233.

Regulations'. Secondly, he had failed to implement MPR Decree XI of 1998 on Clean Governance Free from Corruption, Collusion and Nepotism.[43]

In March 2001, Wahid sacked Cabinet Ministers who had publicly criticised him and responded to the first memorandum, rejecting the constitutional validity of the Pansus and denying that failure to implement the 1998 MPR Decree amounted to a serious breach of state policy.[44] Events then degenerated rapidly into a political stand-off between President Wahid and legislators, and government became paralysed. On 30 April, the DPR voted by 365 to 52 (with 42 abstentions) to send a second memorandum to the President. Wahid formally responded to the second memorandum on 29 May 2001, arguing that the memorandum was invalid for failing to specify the pledge of office he was alleged to have breached.[45]

Dissatisfied with this response, the DPR decided by majority vote (365 to 4, with 39 abstentions) on 30 May 2001 that the MPR would call a Special Session.[46] The MPR fixed the date for 1 August 2001 but it was brought forward when Wahid attempted to move against the national police chief, General Surojo Bimantoro.[47] On 2 June 2001, Wahid breached MPR Decree VII of 2000 by suspending Bimantoro, as the Decree required DPR approval for appointment and dismissal of the heads of the army and the police.[48] In response to what was perceived as the President's increasingly erratic behaviour, a 'Plenary Session' of the MPR was called to consider voting to create a 'Special Session'. The standing rules of the MPR, re-drafted in 2000, did not then provide for 'Plenary Sessions' but the MPR met regardless, and duly voted on 21 July to convert the session to a 'Special Session'.[49] The Special Session

---

[43]   International Crisis Group, 'Indonesia's Presidential Crisis', n 39 above, 7.

[44]   E Bjornlund, 'Indonesia's Change of President and Prospects for Constitutional Reform: A Report on the July 2001 Special Session of the People's Consultative Assembly and the Presidential Impeachment Process' (Jakarta/Washington, National Democratic Institute for International Affairs, 2001) 12.

[45]   ibid, 13.

[46]   Indrayana, *Indonesian Constitutional Reform*, n 32 above, 234.

[47]   This decision to bring forward the date of the Special Session has been criticised for contravening MPR Decree III of 1978 (A Ellis, 'The Indonesian Constitutional Transition: Conservatism or Fundamental Change?' (2002) 6(1) *Singapore Journal of International and Comparative Law* 116).

[48]   Bjornlund, 'Indonesia's Change of President and Prospects for Constitutional Reform', n 44 above, 13.

[49]   ibid, 14.

decided that it would meet to hear from the President on 23 July. The MPR Speaker, Amien Rais, wrote to Wahid requesting that he appear at the session to present his report. Wahid replied that he would not attend because the session was unconstitutional.[50]

Around 1 am on 23 July 2001, the President issued a *maklumat* or decree requiring the army to 'take necessary special actions and steps, by coordinating with all elements of the security forces, to overcome the crisis and uphold order, security and the law as quickly as possible'. The crisis he referred to was described as 'the emergency political situation that we are facing because of controversies over the possibility of the Special Session of the MPR and the possibility of a Presidential Decree'. He then purported to order the dissolution of the DPR and MPR and the arrest of their members but the armed forces ignored his orders. At 7 am, the Supreme Court, responding to a request from the DPR, issued an opinion declaring that the *maklumat* was legally invalid. This was undoubtedly correct, for several reasons.

In issuing the *maklumat*, Wahid appeared to rely on Article 12 of the Constitution, which provides that '[t]he President may declare a state of emergency. The conditions for such a declaration and the measures to deal with the emergency shall be governed by law'. The Law then governing states of emergency was Interim Emergency Law 23 of 1959, confirmed as a statute by the DPR in 1961. Politically, this instrument was highly controversial, as it was the instrument used by Soekarno to end democracy and initiate his authoritarian 'Guided Democracy' regime in 1959. In any case, Article 1 requires that there be a declaration by the president of a state of civil emergency, a state of military emergency or a state of war before the president can exercise emergency powers in Article 10. In Wahid's case, however, it appears such a formal declaration never occurred, so the authority he needed to order the army to act was never invoked.

Furthermore, the order expressed itself to be a *maklumat* – an order or decree. The *maklumat* was an instrument commonly used by President Soekarno but was removed from the formal hierarchy of laws after his fall, as later confirmed by MPR Decree III of 2000. Wahid's *maklumat* could thus be overruled by DPR statutes or MPR Decrees, such as those issued by the MPR on 23 July. In any case, it seemed clear that what he was trying to do was constitutionally impossible. Chapter 6, Part VII of

---

[50] ibid, 14.

the Elucidation to the Constitution states that the 'position of the DPR is strong. The DPR cannot be dissolved by the President.' As for the MPR, which included all members of the DPR, its position vis-à-vis the president was not expressly stated but is arguably the same. As mentioned above, the Constitution was then clear that the MPR was absolutely superior to its mandatory, the president, even if the political reality was more often the opposite.

The second sitting of the Special Session continued at 8 am on 23 July. As was by then inevitable, the MPR voted to dismiss Wahid, replacing him with his vice-president, Megawati, pursuant to Article 8 of the Constitution. Specifically, it issued four decrees. The first rejected Wahid's *maklumat* as invalid (MPR Decree I of 2001); the second dismissed Wahid immediately (MPR Decree II of 2001); the third appointed the vice-president to serve as acting president (MPR Decree III of 2001); and the fourth declared that the MPR would install a new vice-president following an election (MPR Decree IV of 2001).

The New Process for Impeachment and Dismissal

The events just described proved to be a watershed in the constitutional amendment process. The legislature had survived the crisis and asserted its constitutional authority over a president who had sought military support to act in an authoritarian and undemocratic fashion. However, in the process, weaknesses in the formal relationship between the executive and legislators surviving from the First Amendment had been exposed. These included an interpolation process that many now saw as vulnerable to political exploitation, as well as the root cause of the crisis – the MPR's ability to select a president whose party had, in fact, lost the election and lacked workable numbers in the legislature. In addition, the chaotic process had publicly discredited all actors to some extent – including the MPR.

Accordingly, the Third Amendment was designed to avert future similar crises. As mentioned, it introduced direct presidential elections. Articles 3, 7A, 7B and 8 were amended and added to establish a clearer impeachment process that excluded removal from office on policy grounds but specifically included corruption. The old procedure requiring a reference from the DPR to the MPR was retained but the final decision was now subject to review by the Constitutional Court. As also mentioned, the amendments confirmed that the vice-president would succeed the president if dismissed (Article 8(1)). Finally, the new Article 7C expressly restated the basic constitutional principle, previously mentioned only in the Constitution's Elucidation, that the President could not suspend or dismiss the DPR.

In summary, these provisions of the Constitution, together with Law 27 of 2009 on the MPR, DPR, DPD and DPRD, now prescribe the following process for presidential and vice-presidential impeachment.

- A special plenary session of the DPR is called to decide whether to ask the Constitutional Court to investigate the conduct of the president or vice-president. This is referred to as interpolation (*interpelasi*). A two-thirds majority of at least two-thirds of DPR members is required.[51]
- The DPR's request for investigation is then submitted to the Constitutional Court. Pursuant to Articles 7B(1) and (4), the Court must investigate and decide whether any of the conditions for dismissal outlined in Article 7A have been satisfied.[52] These are treason, corruption or any other felony; misconduct; and no longer fulfilling the requirements of office. The Court must issue its decision within 90 days of receiving the request (Article 7B(4)).
- If the Constitutional Court decides that the Article 7A conditions have been met, the DPR must next convene a further plenary session to decide whether to submit a proposal to the MPR to impeach the president or vice-president (Article 7B(5)). If the DPR decides to submit such a proposal, then the MPR must convene a plenary session to consider it within 30 days of receipt (Article 7B(6)). A quorum of three-quarters of the MPR's membership is required (Article 7B(7)).

---

[51] Article 7B(3) of the Constitution. Law 27 of 2009 sought to increase both these requirements to three-quarters (Article 184(3)) but the Constitutional Court struck this down in Decision 23-26/PUU-VIII/2010. Specifically, the Court held that increasing the quorum requirement to three-quarters would constitute an excessive burden upon DPR members. The Court held that, as it would be difficult to reach this consensus, a constitutional check and balance on the power of the executive would be eroded.

[52] The Constitutional Court has power to perform this investigation under Article 24C. See Regulation of the Constitutional Court 17 of 2009 on Procedural Guidelines for Disputes about the Result of the Election of the President and Vice-President, available at www.mahkamahkonstitusi.go.id/pdf/PMK_PMK_17.pdf.

- At the MPR plenary session, the president or vice-president is given an opportunity to explain his or her conduct (Article 7B(7)). The president or vice-president can be dismissed if at least two-thirds of MPR members present support the DPR proposal (Articles 7A and 7B(7)).

This process has been invoked several times, although, as mentioned, it has not led to the dismissal of a president. President Yudhoyono, for example, was called for interpolation in June 2007 over his signing of United Nations Security Council Resolution 1747 on the Iranian nuclear crisis,[53] and again in June 2008 over a rise in fuel prices.[54] Political parties also threatened to impeach him in October 2008 in relation to the appointment of Governors and Vice Governors in North Maluku;[55] and in 2010 for alleged involvement in the Bank Century corruption scandal.[56] Two failed attempts were also made to impeach Vice-President Boediono in April 2010, again over the Bank Century crisis.[57]

CONCLUSION

With the passage of the Fourth Amendment on 10 August 2002, the MPR diminished both its own authority and that of the presidency in favour of a directly-elected DPR. It also completed a gradual constitutional transition, from an authoritarian 'top-heavy' system that had twice allowed dictators to emerge, to a liberal representative democracy with a new institutional framework intended to enforce a working separation of powers between the executive and the other branches of government. Generally speaking, post-Soeharto governments have usually complied with the new constitutional arrangements.

This new system has, however, encountered problems, most of which have arisen from the inability of post-Soeharto presidents to command

[53] I Fadil, 'Cegah Konflik Baru, SBY Diminta Jawab Langsung Interpelasi', *Detik News*, 5 June 2007.

[54] MH Faiq, 'Hak Angket Masih Jauh dari Pemakzulan', *Kompas*, 26 June 2008.

[55] Sutarmi, 'Pemakzulan SBY-JK, Golkar Belum Tentukan Sikap', *Okezone*, 6 October 2008.

[56] *Antara News*, 2 March 2010.

[57] HD Tampubolon, 'Impeachment initiative starts rolling', *Jakarta Post*, 13 March 2010; BBT Saragih and D Christanto, 'Boediono Brushes Off Threat of Impeachment', *Jakarta Post*, 15 January 2011; MJ Sihaloho, 'Court Ruling Fails to Kill Impeachment Petition', *Jakarta Globe*, 3 May 2010.

a loyal majority in the DPR – even when they have constructed a coalition supposedly bound by written agreements, as did President Yudhoyono. The consequences of this proved catastrophic for Wahid and hampered the ability of both Presidents Megawati and Yudhoyono to implement their programmes. It has led to backlogs in law-making and intense political contests over most policy issues. It has also encouraged corruption in the DPR, as members haggle over the terms by which legislation may progress in the house. Nasution[58] suggests that the constitutional relationship between the executive and legislature therefore needs further major reform:

> Tensions in the relations between the [DPR] and the government that might lead to deadlock are always a possibility in Indonesia today. This is because the current system grants dual legitimacy to the President and the [DPR], because both are directly elected. These difficulties increase when the party that backs the president does not control the majority vote in [the DPR], as is now the case . . . These problems are not new, and have been viewed for a long time as a weakness typical of the juxtaposition of the juxtaposition of a presidential system with a multiparty system . . . I therefore believe we should consider another alternative, that is, the semi-presidential system applied in France, and in various other countries, including South Korea . . . [T]he superiority of the semi-presidential system derives from the fact that it has a mechanism for cohabitation (mixture of power) between the prime minister and the president if the elected president obviously does not control the majority support in parliament.

This proposal has often been discussed in post-Soeharto Indonesia but has met with only limited support. Implementing it would involve a major remaking of the current political model. It would, for example, require yet another significant cession of power from the presidency, this time to a prime minister who would, presumably, lead the largest party or coalition in the DPR. Nasution's proposal does not, however, lack for precedent. The 1945 Constitution operated with both a president and a prime minister during the revolution, as did the provisional constitutions that replaced it in the 1950s. Even under President Soekarno's Guided Democracy from 1959 to 1966 multiple prime ministers were appointed (although real power remained with the president). It is doubtful, however, that political support exists at present for the creation of prime minister who would share power with the DPR and

---

[58] Nasution, 'Towards Constitutional Democracy in Indonesia', n 4 above, 31.

the president, and thus dilute the power of both. There also appears to be deep reluctance to allow a new round of amendments to the Constitution for fear of re-opening controversial political issues, such as Islam or regional autonomy.

SELECTED READING

Asshiddiqie, Jimly, 'Creating a Constitutional Court for a New Democracy', *Centre for Comparative Constituional Studies and Asian Law Centre Public Lecture* (Melbourne, Melbourne Law School, 2009).

Bjornlund, Eric, 'Indonesia's Change of President and Prospects for Constitutional Reform: A Report on the July 2001 Special Session of the People's Consultative Assembly and the Presidential Impeachment Process' (Jakarta/Washington, National Democratic Institute for International Affairs, 2001).

International Crisis Group, 'Indonesia's Presidential Crisis', *Indonesia Briefing* (Jakarta/Brussels, 2001).

Nasution, Adnan Buyung, 'Towards Constitutional Democracy in Southeast Asia', *Adnan Buyung Nasution Papers on Indonesian Constitutionalism* (Asian Law Centre, University of Melbourne, 2011).

3

National Legislatures, Representative Assemblies and Elections

————◆◆◆————

Introduction – The Reconstruction of Indonesia's Legislative System – The Indonesian Legislative System Today – General Elections – The Constitutional Court's Candidacy and Electoral Jurisprudence – General Electoral Commission – Conclusion

INTRODUCTION

IN ITS ORIGINAL form, the Constitution vested significant executive, judicial and legislative powers in the presidency, as discussed in the previous two chapters. As for legislative powers, Articles 5 and 20 allowed the president to make statutes (*undang-undang*), with 'the approval of the *Dewan Perwakilan Rakyat*' (DPR, People's Representative Assembly, the national legislature). For most of the history of the Republic the power of the presidency made this approval a given. Article 5 also gave the president power to issue government regulations to implement or enforce legislation. This broad grant of legislative power to the president was strengthened by the Constitution's 'completely insufficient' regulation of the powers of the DPR, or even of its basic structure.[1]

Under Soekarno's Guided Democracy (1959 to 1966), this did not matter much. After Soekarno reinstated the 1945 Constitution in 1959 the president ruled directly under the emergency powers in Article 12 of the Constitution, without elections. He dissolved the DPR in June 1960 and

---

[1] P Ziegenhain, *The Indonesian Parliament and Democratization* (Singapore, ISEAS, 2008) 45.

replaced it with a new 'DPR-GR',[2] the members of which were appointed at his discretion, and the legislature became largely moribund. Soekarno also began what was to become a long-running practice of appointing members of so-called 'functional groups' (*golongan karya*) to the legislature, including representatives of the military (who were by this stage a significant political component of the idiosyncratic and personalised political system he was developing). By 1962, the DPR had 281 members, all appointed: 130 from 10 political parties, 150 from 20 'functional groups' and one representative of West Irian (Papua), then not yet incorporated into Indonesia. The other national representative assembly, the MPR (*Majelis Permusyawaratan Rakyat* or People's Consultative Assembly), was also appointed directly by Soekarno on a temporary basis. It was made up of the DPR members, together with additional 'functional group' and regional representatives, numbering around 616. It was generally just as subservient to Soekarno as the DPR.

When Soeharto came to power in 1966, his regime sought to present itself as complying with the 1945 Constitution – in form at least – seeking legitimacy in nominal legalism. In reality, however, the DPR and MPR remained as firmly under the control of the presidency as it had been when Soekarno was in power, perhaps even more so. The New Order promulgated Law 15 of 1969 on Elections, and amended it in 1975, 1980 and 1985. Each successive amendment made victory for Soeharto's electoral vehicle, Golkar (*Golongan Karya*, Functional Groups), at the token elections held every five years[3] ever more certain.[4] From 1975, for example, the only entities allowed to contest elections were Golkar (officially said to be not a political party) and the two official political parties, PPP[5] and PDI,[6] both amalgams of other parties forcibly merged by the government in 1973. The activities and leadership of these two parties were constantly subject to government interference, overt and covert, and elections were marked by 'a lot of dirty tricks, with

---

[2]   'GR', *Gotong Royong*, 'mutual self-help' or co-operation.

[3]   Under Soeharto general elections were held in 1971, 1977, 1982, 1987, 1992 and 1997.

[4]   A Schwarz, *A Nation in Waiting: Indonesia's Search for Stability* (Boulder CO, Westview Press, 2004) 271–72; P Ziegenhain, *The Indonesian Parliament and Democratization* (n 1 above) 46.

[5]   *Partai Persatuan Pembangunan*, United Development Party, an amalgamation of Islamic parties.

[6]   *Partai Demokrasi Indonesia*, Indonesian Democracy Party, an amalgam of nationalist, Christian and other non-Muslim parties.

the military, the bureaucracy, and Golkar colluding in all kinds of illegal and improper methods to preserve Soeharto's power'.[7] Indonesia's five-yearly 'festivals of democracy' (*pesta demokrasi*) eventually became such a sham that Soeharto was routinely able to accurately predict the results to within a few percentage points. The DPR elected through these contrivances was thus dominated by Soeharto loyalists, and had little more independence than its equivalent under Soekarno.

The president's de facto, but virtually absolute, control of legislative power enabled Soeharto's sustained authoritarian rule until 1998.[8] For most of this period, the DPR was famously a kind of 'rubber-stamp' for the regime's legislative programme.[9] As Sherlock says:[10]

> Legislation was created either to legitimise the arbitrary enforcement of state power or to facilitate it through deliberately obscure, declamatory and ambiguous wording and through inconsistency between different laws. Rare instances of behind the scenes debate in the DPR only occurred when competing interests within the ruling elite clashed. But usually the only role for the DPR was formally to pass instruments of executive power into law.

The DPR thus virtually never produced a law on its own initiative, and the common Indonesian joke was that it was famous for the five 'Ds' – '*datang, duduk, diam, dengar, duit*' (loosely, 'arrive, sit down, shut up, listen, take money') – because its members did little else. By the end of the New Order the DPR had become an object of popular contempt, and reform of Indonesia's legislative system was high on the agenda after Soeharto's resignation in May 1998. As we shall see, this agenda for the reform of the legislature was closely entwined with reform of the executive: strengthening the DPR was understood to necessarily involve

---

[7] AB Nasution, 'Towards Constitutional Democracy in Indonesia', *Adnan Buyung Nasution Papers on Southeast Asian Constitutionalism* (Asian Law Centre, University of Melbourne, 2011) 18.

[8] D Indrayana, *Indonesian Constitutional Reform, 1999–2002: An Evaluation of Constitution-Making in Transition* (Jakarta, Kompas Book Publishing, 2008) 176.

[9] Schwarz, *A Nation in Waiting* (n 4 above) 272. This only began to shift to towards the end of Soeharto's rule. Ziegenhain, *The Indonesian Parliament and Democratization* (n 1 above) 45, for example, argues that during the latter period of the New Order, the DPR did on a few occasions use some of its legislative powers in efforts to rein in President Soeharto.

[10] S Sherlock, 'The Indonesian Parliament after Two Elections: What has Really Changed?', *CDI Policy Papers on Political Governance* (Canberra, Centre for Democratic Institutions (CDI), 2007) 37.

a corresponding weakening of the presidency.

How this was to be done was a matter for the MPR – then, as now, the only body with power to amend the Constitution. At the time, Articles 3 and 37 of the Constitution allowed the MPR to amend it by a two-thirds majority vote, provided that two-thirds of MPR members were present.[11] Article 2 provided that all members of the DPR were also automatically members of the MPR, 'augmented by delegates from the regions and groups as further regulated by law'.[12] Membership varied over time, reaching 920 under Soeharto after the 1971 elections and 1000 in the period 1997 to 1999. By the time of the amendments in 1999, however, the 500 DPR members were a majority of the MPR's 700 members. This meant they could largely determine the future constitutional position of their own chamber. More significantly still, when the MPR passed the First Amendment to the Constitution in October 1999, 462 of the DPR members sitting in it had been elected a few months earlier in Indonesia's first genuinely democratic elections in decades, perhaps ever. They had a democratic mandate to introduce reforms that would prevent the emergence of another dictatorship, and they did so by paring back the powers of both the presidency (as described in the previous chapter) and the MPR, appropriating them for the DPR.

This rest of this chapter is divided into two parts. First, we briefly describe how Indonesia's legislative system was reconstructed through the four constitutional amendments that began in 1999. The amendments made the DPR the single most powerful political institution in Indonesia. Secondly, we provide an overview of the current structure and operation of the legislative system. This section also includes summaries of the rules governing elections and the operation of the General Electoral Commission (*Komisi Pemilihan Umum*, or KPU).

---

[11] In its final form after the Fourth Amendment, Article 37 still requires attendance of two-thirds of members (Article 37(3)) but amendments may be effected by a simple majority: 'fifty per cent plus one member' (Article 37(4)). In addition, a proposal for amendment requires the support of one-third of members to be placed on the MPR agenda for consideration (Article 37(1)).

[12] The balance of the 500 members was then made up of 38 seats reserved for the armed forces. As discussed below, all members of the DPR and MPR are now elected. Since 2004, the MPR's membership has been limited to 700 and is currently constituted by the 560 members of the DPR sitting with the 132 members of the DPD (*Dewan Perwakilan Daerah* or Regional Representatives Council) (Article 2(1)).

THE RECONSTRUCTION OF INDONESIA'S LEGISLATIVE SYSTEM

The First Amendment

As mentioned, Article 5 of the Constitution originally read, 'the president holds the power to make statutes with the approval of the DPR'. The First Amendment, passed on 19 October 1999, changed Article 20(1) to provide that it was now the DPR that had the right to make statutes. Article 5 was also altered so that the president's rights were restricted simply to submitting bills to the DPR, a power he or she shared with all DPR members (Article 21). Article 20(2) originally provided that a bill refused by the DPR could not be resubmitted in the same session. This prohibition was retained in Article 20(3) and Article 20(2) now requires that bills be 'debated by the DPR and the President to reach joint agreement'.

As explained in the previous chapter, the First Amendment also gave the DPR an advisory role in the appointment of ambassadors by the president (Article 13) and, with the Supreme Court, in the grant by the president of clemency, such as amnesties and abolitions (Article 14(2)). These changes reflect the Reformasi legislature's determination to monitor the executive closely but they were minor reforms compared to the new authority the DPR had acquired over law-making.

The Second Amendment

The DPR's dominance of the legislative process was confirmed by the Second Amendment of 18 August 2000, which removed the president's power to veto statutes. Article 20(5)) now provides that statutes passed by the DPR automatically come into force after 30 days, even if the president withholds consent.

The DPR did not, however, acquire an absolute monopoly on law-making in Indonesia. The Second Amendment also spawned a new category of independent lawmakers. As discussed in Chapter 6, the 'big bang' decentralisation process that had begun in 1999 under President Habibie granted wide-ranging law-making powers to hundreds of regional legislatures and executive governments. To confirm this devolution of power, Article 18 of the Constitution was rewritten and

Articles 18A and 18B were added. The new Article 18(6) provides that 'Regional Governments have the right to enact regional regulations (*peraturan daerah*) and other regulations in order to implement autonomy and the duty to assist [the central government]'. This legislative power is broad, with Article 18(5) allowing the Regional Governments to 'implement autonomy to the fullest extent except in matters of government that are determined by statute to be matters for the Central Government'.[13] The definition of 'Regional Government' is also very broad, with Article 18(1) stating that 'The Unitary State of the Republic of Indonesia shall be divided into Provinces and these Provinces divided into Counties (*kabupaten*) and Cities, and each of these Provinces, Counties and Cities shall have Regional Governments, regulated by statute'. Under Article 18(3), these regional governments are all to be elected, and Article 18(4) provides that the governors, regents and mayors, who are the respective heads of the regional governments of the provinces, counties and cities, are likewise to be 'democratically elected'.

Law-making is now more dispersed than at any other time in the history of the Republic. As we show in Chapter 6, decentralisation has triggered an avalanche of local legislation. In many cases, regional regulations are poorly drafted or unenforceable, overlap, or are in direct conflict with national laws. Despite this, little has been done in a systematic, consistent or reliable fashion to resolve the many legal and political problems this creates.[14] The DPR has, instead, generally chosen to ignore its regional regulatory competitors.

The Third Amendment

The Third Amendment was passed in the aftermath of a national political and constitutional crisis. The newly strengthened authority of legislators was tested in a direct confrontation with the president who replaced Habibie, Abdurrahman 'Gus Dur' Wahid, the charismatic,

---

[13] The areas reserved were foreign affairs, defence and security, justice-sector matters, religious affairs and certain economic policy areas (Article 10(4) of Law 32 of 2004 on Regional Government). For more details, see Chapter 6 of this volume.

[14] For this paragraph, see T Lindsey and S Butt, 'Unfinished Business: Law Reform, Governance and the Courts in Post-Soeharto Indonesia' in M Künkler and A Stepan (eds), *Indonesia, Islam and Democratic Consolidation* (New York, Columbia University Press, 2012).

eccentric and blind former leader of the world's largest Islamic organisation, Nahdlatul Ulama. As described in the previous chapter, the MPR ultimately dismissed Wahid following allegations of misconduct made by the DPR, replacing him with Megawati Sukarnoputri, pursuant to Article 8 of the Constitution. The process for impeachment and dismissal that the MPR applied was, however, hotly disputed, and there was little clear authority for it in the Constitution. Ultimately, public perceptions of the crisis discredited all involved, including the MPR and DPR, as well as Wahid.

Accordingly, the Third Amendment sought to democratise and clarify the limits of power exercised by each branch. In particular, it aimed to prevent any future impeachment crisis by offering a clear constitutional answer to the question of exactly how a president should be removed. In the event, although the MPR was victorious in its struggle with President Wahid, the reforms eroded three of its constitutional powers. First, the MPR lost its power to appoint the president and vice-president, who would now be directly elected (Article 6A). Secondly, the MPR's role in any future attempt to remove the president and vice-president was now restricted by Article 3(3) to a new process established in Articles 7A and 7B that gave a decisive role to the new Constitutional Court, as described in the previous chapter.

Thirdly, the MPR's previous authority to set the Broad Guidelines of State Policy (GBHN, *Garis-Garis Besar Haluan Negara*) was removed entirely from Article 3. This power was significant, because it was the source of the MPR's right to hold the president accountable for his or her implementation of the GBHN. This had, in turn, given rise to an implicit power to remove a president whose account was deemed lacking. This authority was first demonstrated in mid-1966, in the aftermath of the bloody annihilation of Soekarno's Leftist supporters by the army and Muslim militias. President Soekarno gave his *Naksawara* (Nine Points) speech to the MPR(S),[15] intended to explain the bloody coup and counter coup of the previous year. The MPR(S) found the speech 'fell short of fulfilling the expectations of the people'. It revoked the Presidency for Life it had previously conferred on Soekarno and in 1967 stripped him of power, appointing Soeharto Acting President.[16] The MPR's power to hold

---

[15] The 'S' stood for *sementara* (temporary) and reflected the fact that this body was an interim one appointed by Soekarno, not an elected body.

[16] Soeharto was confirmed as full President by the MPR in March 1968.

the president to account was, however, a theoretical one for most of Soeharto's oppressive reign, when his accountability speeches routinely met with standing ovations. It was revived when President Habibie responded to the MPR's rejection of his accountability speech in October 1999 by withdrawing his candidature for reappointment.

In any case, the MPR's power to appoint the president was now lost, and so was the need for it to set the GBHN and thus approve the presidential accountability speech. Perhaps reflecting this, the MPR's previously unlimited power to exercise the sovereignty of the people 'in full', granted by Article 1, was also removed. Instead, sovereignty is now nominally 'in the hands of the people'. It seems to float with no specific locus, presumably above all three branches of government. The new Article 1(1) simply states that the sovereignty of the people is to be 'exercised in accordance with the Constitution'.

The Third Amendment also established the Regional Representatives Council (the *Dewan Perwakilan Daerah* or DPD). Reflecting the political importance of the decentralisation process that had been constitutionally recognised by the Second Amendment, the DPD's role was to represent the regions at the highest levels of national government. It could do little else, however. Its creation did not diminish the centrality of the DPR, as the DPD was not given law-making powers. Instead, Article 22D(1) only granted it power to submit laws to the DPR. Under Article 22C its members are to be elected from each province at the general elections and must sit once a year, as must the DPR, the members of which are also chosen by general election (Article 19).

The increasing authority of the DPR as the constitutionally dominant branch of government was confirmed by the addition of Article 7C, which provides that the president cannot dissolve or 'freeze' (*membeku-kan*) the DPR. This was obviously a reaction to Wahid's failed attempt to repeat Soekarno's dissolution of the legislature of 1960 and order the army to arrest its members, as discussed in Chapter 2.

Reflecting the newly expanded importance of general elections for the DPR, the DPD and hundreds of local governments, their administration was no longer left to the Minister for Home Affairs, as under Soeharto, when elections became little more than a tool of the regime. Instead a new General Electoral Commission (*Komisi Pemilihan Umum*, or KPU) was established as a constitutional body independent of government (Article 22E(5)). Given the torrid history of electoral manipulation under the New Order, this was a vital reform.

The Fourth Amendment

The Fourth Amendment completed the marginalisation of the MPR and the rise of the DPR. By unanimous vote, the MPR removed the last remnants of the power it had enjoyed since 1945 to appoint the president (Article 6A). It was agreed that if none of the pairs running for the presidency and vice-presidency received an absolute majority in the first round of a direct election, then, rather than the matter being left to the MPR to decide, a second direct election would be held between the two highest-scoring pairs (Article 6A(4)). The MPR retained only the ceremonial role of inaugurating the duly-elected president and vice-president and taking their oaths of office (Articles 3(3) and (9)) – a power that, could, in any case, be alternatively exercised by the DPR (Article 9).

The MPR also reconfigured its own composition. As mentioned, this had changed over the course of the New Order. By the end of Soeharto's rule the DPR comprised 425 elected members from PPP, PDI and Golkar, together with 75 army members appointed by the government. 500 additional members were added to the DPR's total of 500 to form the MPR's 1000 members. These were made up of 213 regional party representatives (allocated to PPP, PDI and Golkar according to their percentages in the DPR, with Golkar thus taking more than 60 per cent); a further 38 representatives of the armed forces (who were loyal to Soeharto); 100 'functional group' representatives (ultimately approved by Soeharto); and 149 non-party regional representatives nominated by regional legislatures (controlled by the regime, which appointed provincial governors).[17] Soeharto's dictatorship was thereby entrenched; loyalists always occupied at least 57 per cent of the MPR, the only body that could remove him.[18]

The new Article 2 of the Constitution provided that DPD members would replace the appointed members. The MPR thus became a joint sitting of the DPR and DPD. It was of great significance that the new Article 22C also provided that DPD members could not exceed one-third of the numbers of the DPR. As mentioned, since 2004, the MPR's membership has been limited to 700, constituted by the 560 elected members

---

[17] S Permana, 'Not your Local Member' in T Lindsey (ed), *Indonesia: Law and Society*, 1st edn (Sydney, Federation Press, 1999) 197, 198.

[18] ibid, 198.

of the DPR sitting with the 132 elected members of the DPD. This ensures the DPR – and not the DPD or the president – controls the MPR.

These changes also meant that the armed forces would lose their appointed seats in the MPR and DPR. In return, it was agreed that members of the military would now have the right to vote in elections as individuals. Under Soeharto, members of the armed forces had forgone voting rights in return for guaranteed seats that were hugely dispropor-tionate to their numbers.[19] This represented the formal end to another pillar of the New Order system – the *dwifungsi* (dual function) of the military: the notion that serving members of the armed forces should play an institutionalised political role as well as a military one. Since the military's departure from the MPR and DPR, some former senior offic-ers have remained active in politics. President Yudhoyono, for example, is a former army general, and his first cabinet in 2004 included five for-mer members of the armed forces. His second, in 2009, had two former senior officers. The military have so far not, however, sought to inter-vene in politics as an institution, for example by forming a party, launch-ing a coup or destabilising government. The formal demilitarising of the legislature achieved by the Fourth Amendment of 2002 appears, therefore, to have been a success – so far, at least.

THE INDONESIAN LEGISLATIVE SYSTEM TODAY

Asshiddiqie[20] has argued that the Indonesian legislative system produced by the four constitutional amendments described above is unique in that it is neither unicameral nor bicameral. It is certainly true that at the national level the Indonesian legislative system involves three institu-tions of importance – the MPR, the DPR and the DPD – and they are complemented at the local level by hundreds of DPRDs, or Regional People's Representative Councils (*Dewan Perwakilan Rakyat Daerah*), in provinces, cities (*kota*) and counties (*kabupaten*). Asshiddiqie's account is,

---

[19]   In theory, each member of the DPR was said to represent 400,000 people. Given that the population of Indonesia under Soeharto reached over 200 million and the armed forces never numbered more than 500,000, the DPR's 75 military representatives were clearly disproportionate (ibid, 197–98). If anything, however, their numbers in the DPR understated the military's real level of political influence in the New Order.

[20]   J Asshiddiqie, *The Constitutional Law of Indonesia: A Comprehensive Overview* (Selangor, Malaysia, Sweet and Maxwell Asia, 2009) 130.

however, somewhat misleading, for three reasons. First, the DPD lacks any legislative power of its own: it can only *propose* bills to the DPR. Secondly, the stripped-down MPR, now controlled by the DPR, plays a largely symbolic role and has not exercised its key residual power to amend the constitution since 2002. Thirdly, DPR legislation formally trumps laws produced by any local government.

In the next section, we outline the current structure, powers and responsibilities of the MPR, DPR and DPD, and the mechanisms for the election of their members. DPRDs are dealt with in Chapter 6. This next section demonstrates that despite having a diversity of elected bodies, Indonesia now operates essentially as a unicameral legislative system, with the DPR constitutionally at the centre of Indonesian politics.

The MPR

Section II of the 1945 Constitution outlines the composition, powers, and procedural rules of the MPR. It is supplemented by the provisions of Law 27 of 2009 on the MPR, DPR, DPD and DPRD.

Article 2(1) of the 1945 Constitution and Article 2 of Law 27 of 2009 state that the MPR, as mentioned, comprises the members of the DPR and DPD, chosen in general elections. The term of MPR members is five years and ends when a new MPR member takes the oath or is sworn into office. MPR members are accorded certain rights – for example, to propose amendments to the Constitution, to vote, and to claim immunity from prosecution for acts performed while exercising their duties as members. They are also formally subject to obligations, including to 'uphold the Pancasila' and 'put the interests of the state ahead of private or group interests'.[21] Article 2(2) of the Constitution obliges the MPR to meet in the capital at least once every five years,[22] and Article 2(3) of the Constitution requires that all MPR decisions be taken by majority vote.

As mentioned, the MPR can amend the constitution. The scope of subject matter for amendment is unlimited, except that Article 37(5) prohibits the unitary state of the Republic of Indonesia from being altered, a provision intended to prevent the creation of another federation like the

---

[21] Articles 9 and 10(d) of Law 27 of 2009.
[22] See also Article 3 of Law 27 of 2009.

failed United States of Indonesia (RIS, *Republic Indonesia Serikat*) of 1949–50.[23] Article 37 also sets out the procedure for amendment. It allows a proposed amendment supported by one-third of the MPR members to be put on the agenda for an MPR session. Two-thirds of all MPR members must attend that session (Article 37(3)). To be passed, 50 per cent of all the members of the MPR (not just those present for voting), plus one member, must support the proposal (Article 37(3)).

Under Articles 3(2) and (3) of the Constitution, the MPR can inaugurate and dismiss the president and vice-president pursuant to provisions discussed in the section on impeachment in Chapter 2. The Constitutional Court now plays a role in this process but under Article 7B(7) the MPR has the final vote on whether the president should be dismissed. The MPR also plays a role in replacing a president or a vice-president, for example, in the case of their death, as was also discussed in the previous chapter.

The DPR

Section VII of the Constitution deals with the DPR. As mentioned, Article 19(3) requires that the DPR meet at least annually. Article 19(2) provides that the DPR's organisation is to be regulated by statute, that is, by the DPR itself. Article 19(1) of the Constitution and Article 67 of Law 27 of 2009 stipulate that DPR members are to be elected at general elections, discussed later in this chapter. As also mentioned, pursuant to Article 21 of Law 10 of 2008 and Article 74(1) of Law 27 of 2009 there are now 560 seats contested in DPR elections.

Rights and obligations of DPR members

Once elected, DPR members enjoy constitutional rights 'to ask questions, to make proposals and to give other opinions, with a right to immunity' (Article 20A(3)). They also have rights of 'interpellation, of enquiry, and of expressing opinions' (Article 20A(2)). DPR members are, however, also subject to various obligations set out in Article 79 of Law 27 of 2009. These are similar to those imposed upon MPR members and include a duty to 'uphold and practise Pancasila values'.

---

[23] The RIS and the historical reasons for Indonesia's strong political aversion to federalism are discussed in Chapter 1 of this volume.

These obligations are significant, because Article 22B of the 1945 Constitution provides that members can be dismissed under statutory procedures for breach of their duties. Law 27 of 2009 sets out procedures for suspension, interim removal, dismissal and replacement of DPR members.[24] Their political parties can replace them for several reasons, including if they die, resign, or are dismissed (Article 213(1)). There are a number of grounds for dismissal, including violation of the DPR Code of Ethics, continuous and unexplained absence for three months or more, or conviction by a court for an offence carrying a jail term of five years or more. For some types of dismissals, such as for violating the DPR Code of Ethics, the DPR Honour Board (*Badan Kehormatan DPR*) must first investigate (Article 215(1)). DPR members may be suspended on two grounds only: if indicted and convicted of an offence carrying a jail term of five years or more; or if indicted for 'special crimes' (*tindak pidana khusus*) (Articles 219(1)–(3)).

Functions of the DPR

The Constitution grants the DPR extensive authority to perform 'legislative, budgetary and oversight functions' (Article 20A(1)).

Individual DPR members can introduce a bill (Article 21) but for it to be passed the DPR and president must first discuss and 'jointly approve' it (Article 20(2)).[25] If a bill gains their joint approval, the president is to ratify it to become law (Article 20(4)). If they cannot reach joint approval, then the bill cannot be re-introduced to the house within the same session, although it may be introduced at a later date (Article 20(3)). If the president does not ratify a bill within 30 days of it achieving joint approval, it becomes law in any case (Article 20(5)).

As mentioned in Chapter 2, the president can unilaterally exercise legislative power, that is, the power to create an Interim Emergency Law (*peraturan pengganti undang-undang* or Perpu)[26] without DPR approval, in emergency situations (Article 22(1)). However, the DPR must approve such regulations at its next session, failing which they are revoked (Articles 22 (2) and (3)).[27]

---

[24]   Articles 213–216 and 219.
[25]   See also Article 20(1) of the Constitution and Articles 69–71 of Law 27 of 2009.
[26]   Literally 'regulation in lieu of a statute'.
[27]   See also Chapter 2 of this volume for a discussion of controversies surrounding the revocation of Interim Emergency Laws.

Article 20A of the Constitution and Article 69 of Law 27 of 2009 deal with the DPR's budgetary and supervisory functions. For instance, the DPR has power to 'supervise the implementation of legislation and the state budget' (Article 69(i)). Its members can use their powers of 'interpellation, of enquiry, and of expressing opinions' to these ends by requiring state or government officials, members of the judiciary or members of the community to provide information about an issue of importance to the state.[28]

The DPD

Section VIIA of the Constitution covers the DPD's composition and powers. Article 22C(1) of the Constitution requires members to be elected from each province.[29] General elections for the DPD are to be held every five years and voters choose from individuals rather than political parties, by contrast to DPR and DPRD elections (Articles 22E(1) and (4)). Candidates must be domiciled in the province in which they are seeking election, and have an office in that province's capital.[30]

As mentioned, the Constitution restricts the size of the DPD to ensure that the DPR controls the MPR. Each province is to have the same number of representatives in the DPD (Article 22C(2)) and no more than four DPD representatives can be elected from any one province.[31]

Article 22D(4) declares that DPD members can be removed from office under statutory conditions and procedures that mirror those applicable to DPR members, discussed above.[32]

Article 22D grants three powers to the DPD but, as mentioned, stops short of permitting it to enact laws. First, Article 22D(1) allows it to submit bills to the DPR about the following regional issues:

- regional autonomy;
- relations between the central government and the regions;
- establishing, developing and merging regions;

---

[28] Article 20A(2) of the Constitution; Article 72 of Law 27 of 2009.

[29] See also Article 221 of Law 27 of 2009.

[30] Article 227(4) of Law 27 of 2009. See Chapter 5 of this volume for discussion of the *DPD Domicile case*, in which the Constitutional Court decided that DPD candidates must be 'from' the provinces in which they seek election.

[31] Article 227(1) of Law 27 of 2009.

[32] These conditions are set out in Articles 283–288 of Law 27 of 2009.

- the management of natural and other economic resources; and
- the financial balance between the central government and the regions.

Secondly, Article 22D(2) gives the DPRD power to participate in DPR debates about these regional issues, and to provide recommendations to the DPR about bills concerning the national budget, taxation, education and religion. Thirdly, the DPD can 'supervise the implementation' of laws relating to most of these issues[33] and report its findings to the DPR 'as material for consideration and further action' (Article 22D(3)). In practice, these limited powers have so far proved to have little political significance and the DPD has often seemed irrelevant to policy formation and implementation.

GENERAL ELECTIONS

Article 22E covers elections. It states that they are to be used to elect members of the DPR, DPD and DPRD and the president and vice-president. 'Participants' in DPR and DPRD elections are political parties, whereas in DPD elections 'participants' are individuals (Article 22E(4)).[34]

Article 22E(1) of the Constitution requires that general elections take place every five years and be organised in a 'direct, public, free, secret, honest, and fair way'. As mentioned, Article 22E(5) adds that elections are to be run by a national, permanent and independent Commission, discussed below.

Article 22E(6) provides that general elections are to be regulated in more detail by statute. At the time of writing, these included Law 2 of 2008 on Political Parties (as amended by Law 2 of 2011); Law 10 of 2008 on General Elections for Members of the DPR, DPD, and DPRD;

---

[33] 'Matters related to the financial balance between the central government and the regions' are included among the areas covered by the powers to submit bills and debate in Articles 22D(1) and (2) but not those covered by the supervisory and reporting power in 22D(3). The other powers in 22D(3) are probably wide enough to prevent this being a material restriction.

[34] As mentioned, pursuant to Article 21 of Law 10 of 2008 and Article 74(1) of Law 27 of 2009 there are now 560 seats contested in a DPR election. The number of seats contested in the DPD is calculated according to the rules described above, based on the number of DPR seats. Pursuant to Article 23(1) of Law 10 of 2008 there are between 35 and 100 seats contested in each DPRD.

Law 27 of 2009 on the MPR, DPR, DPD and DPRD; and Law 42 of
2008 on the Election of the President and Vice-President. Other
national legislation touches on elections in particular regions.[35] Regional
regulations[36] and a range of other subordinate regulations – including
various decisions of the Electoral Commission on technical issues –
also govern the conduct of elections.

THE CONSTITUTIONAL COURT'S CANDIDACY AND
ELECTORAL JURISPRUDENCE

As mentioned in Chapter 1 and discussed in more detail in Chapter 5, the
Indonesian Constitutional Court has jurisdiction to review the constitutionality of statutes. Indonesia's electoral laws have been among those
most regularly challenged before the Court, because they now determine
the configuration of political power across Indonesia, at every level. In
this section we discuss cases in which the Court has assessed statutes that
regulated vote-counting and candidacy requirements, as these have direct
impact on the form of Indonesia's new democratic system.

Candidacy Cases

In the *PKI case*, the Constitutional Court struck down provisions in the
2003 General Elections Law[37] that banned former members of the
Indonesian Communist Party, other prohibited organisations, and people involved in the 30 September 1965 coup attempt,[38] from being nominated for candidature in local, regional and national elections.[39]
According to the Court, this legislation breached citizens' constitutional
rights to participate in government and to be free from discrimination.

[35] See, for example, Law 30 of 2003 on the Formation of the County of West
Sumbawa in the Province of West Nusa Tenggara.

[36] See, for example, Regulation of the Province of Nanggroe Aceh Darussalam 4
of 2006 on Financial Assistance for Political Party Participants in the 2004 Elections
that Obtain a Seat in the Provincial DPRD.

[37] Law 12 of 2003 on General Elections for Members of the DPR, DPD and
DPRD.

[38] On the Indonesian Communist Party and the 1965 coup attempt, see R Cribb,
The Indonesian Killings of 1965–1966: Studies from Java and Bali (Clayton, Centre of
Southeast Asian Studies Monash University, 1991).

[39] Constitutional Court Decision 011-017/PUU-I/2003.

In the *Political Crimes cases*, the Constitutional Court upheld Electoral Law provisions prohibiting candidates from running if they had previously been convicted of a crime that attracts a maximum of five years' imprisonment.[40] According to the Court, candidates who run for public office must be trustworthy, and so the legislature can legitimately require that candidates have high levels of moral integrity. However, the Court held that the prohibition could not apply to those convicted of political crimes and minor offences (although it did not define the types of minor crimes it meant).[41] If the prohibitions applied to political crimes – which the Court defined as crimes arising from the 'expression of a political view' – they would be discriminatory, it held, and hence unconstitutional, because they would be susceptible to subjective determination according to the political views of those in power.[42]

In a similar 2009 case, a would-be politician who had completed a prison term of nine years and eight months in 1981 challenged Articles 12(g) and 50(1) of the 2008 Election Law and Article 58(f) of Law 32 of 2004 on Regional Government, all of which disqualified him from running as a candidate in legislative elections because he was a former convict.[43] He argued these provisions infringed his constitutional rights to equal treatment (Articles 27(1), 28D(1) and 28D(3)). The Constitutional Court agreed, holding that the provisions could be applied only to appointed officials and not elected public officials and even then only for a period of five years after punishment has been completed. It added that the restrictions should never be applied to convicted persons who honestly and openly admit to the public that they were formerly subject to criminal punishment but should always apply to repeat felony offenders.

Also in 2007, the Court struck out several words from provisions of the 2004 Regional Government Law[44] that purported to allow only candidates put forward by political parties or coalitions to run in local elections for governor or deputy governor, regent or deputy regent, or mayor

---

[40] Constitutional Court Decisions 14-17/PUU-V/2007 and 15/PUU-VI/2008.

[41] In Constitutional Court Decision 14-17/PUU-V/2007, one of the applicants had been involved in an attempted murder and, in Constitutional Court Decision 15/PUU-VI/2008, the applicant had been convicted for aggravated assault.

[42] Constitutional Court Decision 14-17/PUU-V/2007, p 132.

[43] Constitutional Court Decision 4/PUU-VII/2009.

[44] Law 32 of 2004 on Regional Government.

or deputy mayor.[45] The effect of this decision was to allow independent candidates to stand in these elections.[46]

In the *DPD Domicile case*,[47] a 5:4 majority of the Court found that Articles 22C(1) and (2) of the Constitution require that DPD candidates be 'from' the provinces in which they seek election.[48] The Court made the constitutionality of Articles 12 and 67 of the 2008 Electoral Law – which set out candidacy requirements and did not impose this domicile obligation – conditional on their being interpreted to include domicile in the province as a requirement.

Voting Cases

Indonesia has used different types of electoral systems for its national elections. At the 2009 general election for the DPR, a semi-open proportional representation system was used.[49] This system gave voters three options. They could select a party, a candidate or both. To be

[45] Constitutional Court Decision 5/PUU-V/2007. For further discussion see Chapter 5 of this volume.

[46] The Court's reasoning was as follows: Article 18(4) of the Constitution provides that 'Governors, County Heads and Mayors, as heads of provincial, county and city governments respectively, are to be democratically elected'. Articles 56 and 59 of Law 32 of 2004 on Regional Government sought to apply Article 18(4) by requiring general elections to fill those positions but by allowing only candidates put forward by parties or party coalitions. The Court found that, in isolation, Articles 56 and 59 did not contradict Article 18(4). However, in 2006 the national government enacted the Aceh Government Law, which provided that, in Aceh, these positions could be filled by parties and coalitions as well as individuals – that is, independent candidates (Article 67). This, too, the Court held, was within the confines of Article 18(4). The result was, however, that the provisions of both the 2006 Aceh Government Law and 2004 Regional Government Law had Article 18(4) of the Constitution as their legal basis but one allowed independent candidates and the other did not. This, according to the Court, led to 'dualism' in the implementation of Article 18(4): individuals outside Aceh did not receive equal treatment because they could not nominate themselves as independent candidates. The Court held that this breached Article 28D(1) of the Constitution, which guarantee a right to equal treatment before the law and government. The Court's solution was to give independent candidates the right to be nominated under the Regional Government Law, rather than to declare that the Aceh Government Law was unconstitutional.

[47] Constitutional Court Decision 10/PUU-VI/2008.

[48] With Natabaya, I Dewa Gede Palguna, Moh Mahfud MD and H Harjono dissenting.

[49] Article 5(1) of Law 10 of 2008.

elected, candidates were required to achieve at least 30 per cent of the Vote Division Number (*Bilangan Pembagi Pemilu*, or BPP). The BPP is calculated by dividing the total valid votes in one district by the number of seats available in that district. Where no candidate achieved 30 per cent of the BPP, the first candidate listed on the ballot of the political party that gained the most votes was elected. Accordingly, being in a 'winnable position' on the candidate list was initially important.

In the *Female Candidates case*, the Constitutional Court annulled this part of Law 10 of 2008, making positioning on the candidate list less decisive.[50] The Court was asked to review Article 55(2) of Law 10 of 2008, which requires that at least one in every three candidates on the list be female.[51] It was also asked to review Articles 214(a)–(e), which set out the system of semi-open proportional representation just described. The applicants argued that the combined effect of the two Articles was to make it easier for women to win seats, because one would always be included in the top three candidates on any political party's list. This, the applicants argued, was discriminatory.

A majority of the Court held that the state could legislate to positively discriminate in favour of women and that Article 55 of the 2008 General Election Law was therefore not unconstitutional.[52] The majority reasoned that through Article 55 Indonesia sought to fulfil its international legal obligations to provide gender equality, and emphasised Article 28H(2) of the Constitution, which allows the state to use 'special measures' (*perlakuan khusus*) to ensure that every person in Indonesia is accorded equality, equal opportunity and justice. However, the majority also found that Article 214 created inequality before the law, because candidates, whatever their gender, were more likely to win seats because of their position in the list. The electoral system, it held, should favour the candidate who wins the most votes from the people. It should not give power to political parties to interfere with the will of the people by giving candidates a greater chance of winning because of their position

[50] Constitutional Court Decision 22-24/PUU-VI/2008.

[51] The minimum quota for women members of the DPR was introduced by Article 65 of Law 12 of 2003 on General Elections, which 'recommended' that political parties consider a 30 per cent gender quota when fixing their candidate lists. Article 55(2) of the 2008 Law expanded affirmative action, making a minimum quota of 30 per cent compulsory for all political parties participating in elections. Article 8(1)(d) imposed a similar 30 per cent female membership requirement for the boards of political parties.

[52] This was an 8:1 majority with Judge Maria Farida Indrati dissenting.

on the candidate list. Accordingly, Article 214 was inconsistent with Article 28D(1) of the Constitution.

In the *Sisa Suara case*, the Constitutional Court determined how 'surplus votes' (*sisa suara*) in national elections would be used to allocate seats in the legislature.[53] As mentioned, under Law 10 of 2008,[54] the number of votes required for each seat in the national or regional legislatures is determined by dividing the number of registered voters in a particular electoral area by the number of seats allocated to that electoral area. Once a party's votes meet the threshold, it obtains a seat. Of course, not all seats can be filled in this 'first phase'. Some parties will not receive enough votes to obtain a seat; others obtain seats, but their 'left over' votes are insufficient to obtain a further seat. There are, therefore, surplus seats and surplus votes (*sisa suara*). The Constitutional Court held that votes that had been used to obtain a seat in the first phase were, in effect, exhausted and could not be used again. Any surplus seats would be allocated proportionally by reference to the surplus votes alone in a so-called 'second phase'.

In the *Electoral Roll case*, the Court heard objections to parts of the Presidential and Vice-Presidential Elections Law[55] requiring citizens to register with the Electoral Commission (*Komisi Pemilihan Umum*, KPU) in order to vote in elections.[56] Finding that citizens had a constitutional right to vote that could not be hampered by administrative requirements, the Court decided that unregistered citizens could vote provided they produced a valid identity card (KTP, *Kartu Tanda Penduduk*), family card (KK, *Kartu Keluarga*) or passport on election day.

GENERAL ELECTORAL COMMISSION

As mentioned, the constitutional authority for the General Electoral Commission is Article 22E(5), which states that 'general elections shall be organised by a general electoral commission that shall be national, permanent and independent'. Article 22E(6) simply notes that 'further provisions regarding general elections are to be regulated by statute'. There is no other mention of the Electoral Commission in the Constitution.

---

[53] Constitutional Court Decision 110-111-112-113/PUU-VII/2009.
[54] Law 10 of 2008.
[55] Law 42 of 2008 on Presidential and Vice-Presidential Elections.
[56] Constitutional Court Decision 102/PUU-VII/2009.

Law 22 of 2007 on the Organisation of General Elections covers the Electoral Commission.[57] It details its membership (Part 2); tasks, authority and obligations (Part 3); appointment and dismissal of members (Part 5); mechanisms for decision-making (Part 6); responsibilities (Part 7); membership selection committee (Part 8); and secretariat (Part 9). Article 8(1) deals with DPR, DPD, and DPRD elections, Article 8(2) with presidential and vice-presidential elections, and Article 8(3) with elections for regional heads and their deputies.

Composition of the Electoral Commission

Article 2(6) of Law 22 of 2007 provides that the Electoral Commission has seven members, of whom at least 30 per cent must be women. The members serve a five-year term and choose the head of the Electoral Commission from among themselves.

Article 11 lists the criteria for membership of the Electoral Commission,[58] and Article 13 sets out the selection process. The president forms a Selection Committee Team of five to help develop a list of candidates, who then undergo 'fit and proper' assessment by the DPR. To give an example of how this process works, in 2007, 545 applicants applied to the Team for appointment to the Electoral Commission. Of these, 270 passed initial administrative screening but only 45 passed the next written test. Their track records were then publicised; comments were sought from the public and extensive submissions received. The president then recommended 21 of these candidates to the DPR for 'fit and proper' testing. The DPR then chose the seven applicants whom it ranked highest, and announced their appointment at a DPR

---

[57] This statute was intended to be a consolidation of provisions relating to the Commission that previously appeared in Law 12 of 2003 on DPR, DPD and DPRD General Elections and Law 23 of 2003 on Presidential and Vice-Presidential General Elections.

[58] Members must be Indonesian citizens; at least 35 years old; loyal to the Pancasila, Constitution and the ideals of the Proclamation of Independence; have integrity, a strong personality, and be honest and fair; possess knowledge and expertise in a field connected with the running of elections or have experience as an election organiser; have a Bachelor's degree; live in Indonesia; be healthy; have never been a member of a political party; have never served time in jail; not currently occupy a political, structural, or functional state position; be available to work full time; and not occupy a state position for the duration of office.

plenary session.[59] This process gave rise to significant controversy over the exclusion of experienced candidates and allegations of political favouritism.[60]

Election Supervisory Board

Law 22 of 2007 also establishes the Election Supervisory Board (Bawaslu, *Badan Pengawas Pemilihan Umum*). This is an ad hoc institution formed when preparations for each general election commence and disbanded when winners are inaugurated after the election. It is responsible for supervising the Electoral Commission and the electoral process.[61]

Although the Election Supervisory Board has been criticised for being a 'paper tiger' because it lacks a clear power to resolve conflicts between electoral participants (matters usually handled by the Electoral Commission or the Constitutional Court), there has been a history of animosity between the Electoral Commission and the Election Supervisory Board. This has chiefly related to disputes about demarcation between the two bodies, for example over who should choose the members of *Panwas* (regional Election Supervisory Councils), a power held by the Electoral Commission under Law 22 of 2007 but which the Election Supervisory Board argues it should exercise. These disputes have been exacerbated by widespread allegations of Electoral Commission corruption and incompetence. Some of these claims have been justified[62] and many senior members of the former Electoral Commission, including a former Chair, Nazaruddin Sjamsuddin, have been jailed for corrupt procurement practices.[63]

---

[59] KPU, 'Profil Komisi Pemilihan Umum', 2011: www.kpu.go.id/index.php?option=com_content&task=view&id=32&Itemid=50>, accessed 20 July 2011.

[60] R Sukma, 'Indonesian Politics in 2009: Defective Elections, Resilient Democracy' (2009) 45(3) *Bulletin of Indonesian Economic Studies* 317.

[61] A Schmidt, 'Indonesia's 2009 elections: Performance Challenges and Negative Precedents' in Edward Aspinall and Marcus Mietzner (eds), *Problems of Democratisation in Indonesia: Elections, Institutions and Society* (Singapore, ISEAS, 2010) 105.

[62] Although compare S Butt, '"Unlawfulness" and Corruption under Indonesian Law' (2009) 45(2) *Bulletin of Indonesian Economic Studies* 179–98.

[63] Schmidt (above n 61) 104.

Criticism of the Electoral Commission

The Electoral Commission's integrity and competence is of fundamental importance for the successful implementation of the model of democracy established by the four amendments made to the 1945 Constitution.

Adnan Buyung Nasution served as Deputy Chair of Indonesia's first independent Electoral Commission, established in 1999. He observes that 'the three legislative general elections and two direct presidential elections of the Reformation Era must be counted a happy improvement on what went on under Soeharto' but admits that '[t]he 2009 General Elections unfortunately attracted much criticism, including allegations of fraud in the vote counting'.[64] Others claim that the electoral roll was marred by the omission of millions of eligible voters and the inclusion of fictitious or dead voters[65] and that over 14 percent of votes cast were invalid.[66]

Schmidt[67] argues that in 2009 the Electoral Commission struggled to direct resources to meet rigid election timelines because of very stringent financial rules introduced in response to the corruption of previous Electoral Commission members. He accuses the Electoral Commission of incompetence, however, claiming that it failed to adequately educate voters and train electoral staff, or maintain a transparent vote-counting process, auditable publication of results and an accurate electoral roll. Sukma[68] agrees, and concludes that 'electoral management problems will continue to undermine the quality of Indonesia's democracy.'

These problems are particularly acute at the local level,[69] where 'direct regional-head elections . . . have been very problematic, dirtied by money politics. They have triggered horizontal conflict in some regions, leading even to riots'.[70] It is a measure of the increasing severity of these

---

[64] AB Nasution, 'Towards Constitutional Democracy in Indonesia' (n 7 above) 18–19.

[65] R Sukma, 'Indonesian Politics in 2009' (n 60 above) 56.

[66] A Schmidt, 'Indonesia's 2009 elections' (n 61 above) 114–15.

[67] A Schmidt, 'Indonesia's 2009 elections' (n 61 above) 103, 109.

[68] R Sukma, 'Indonesian Politics in 2009' (n 60 above) 56.

[69] HS Nordholt and GA van Klinken (eds), *Renegotiating Boundaries: Local Politics in Post-Suharto Indonesia* (Verhandelingen van het Koninklijk Instituut voor Taal-, Land- en Volkenkunde, Leiden, KITLV Press, 2007).

[70] AB Nasution, 'Towards Constitutional Democracy in Indonesia' (n 7 above) 20.

problems that even a prominent advocate of democratisation such as Nasution can now suggest that it may be necessary to reconsider whether local heads should be elected at all,[71] supporting recent government proposals to abolish these elections in favour of direct appointment by the national government.

CONCLUSION

Under Soekarno and Soeharto, Indonesia's legislatures were rendered powerless and politically corrupted. This was possible because the Constitution that established the MPR and DPR gave them few powers, rights or protections. Post-Soeharto, Indonesia's representative assemblies have asserted their independence from the executive. The DPR has, in fact, become constitutionally the most powerful institution in Indonesia. Its theoretical dominance of the law-making process is now enshrined in a range of constitutional provisions that it was largely responsible for drafting and adopting, by virtue of its members' control of the MPR during the amendment process from 1999 to 2002.

It is therefore ironic that the DPR has now become notorious not for political corruption, in the sense of compliance with the will of a dictatorial ruler as in the past, but for 'money politics' and incompetence. Today its members are often seen as among the most corrupt holders of public office in Indonesia. Its initials are said to stand for *Datang, Paraf, Rupiah* (Come, Sign, Money), and members are criticised for being cynical, greedy and lazy. These perceptions have only been strengthened by a regular flow of sex and ethics scandals, and the successful prosecution by Indonesia's Corruption Eradication Commission (*Komisi Pemberantasan Korupsi*, KPK) of DPR members from all political parties.

Likewise, the DPR has been unimpressive in performing its core task – passing statutes – persistently failing to even come close to meeting its own legislative targets, with bills routinely facing long delays. These targets are set out in the Prolegnas (*Program Legislasi Nasional*, National Legislation Programme), agreed with the government at the start of every five-year term. This document is, however, usually a fairly crude and arbitrary 'wishlist' that obviously cannot anticipate political developments half a decade after its creation. Likewise, despite the DPR's

---

[71] ibid, 20.

dominance of legislative power, it is still the government that generates most bills and it is certainly able to influence the speed of the legislative process if it chooses. Nonetheless, the DPR's failure to either meet Prolegnas targets or develop more realistic planning mechanisms is testimony to wider institutional managerial and administrative problems in the legislature.[72] As Sherlock says:

> The DPR has ended the monopoly on decision-making once exercised by the President and government ministries and has become a conduit for new players in the political process. But despite the DPR's entry into political and policy debate through its powers to summon ministers and to give opinions on the issues of the day, it has not yet been able to use its legislative and policy review functions effectively. The difficulty of having policy transformed into legislation is emerging as a major obstacle to governance in Indonesia.[73]

It is equally concerning that the Electoral Commission, the other key constitutional organ relevant to the formation of legislatures and representative assemblies in Indonesia, has faced constant scandals relating to the corrupt behaviour or incompetence of its members. If voters do not generally accept the integrity of the electoral process, then the legitimacy of legislatures and executives chosen through them is weakened too. The danger, then, is that the legitimacy of the broader democratic transition achieved in Indonesia over the past decade through a complex process of constitutional reform may also come into question.

SELECTED READING

Indrayana, Denny, *Indonesian Constitutional Reform, 1999–2002: An Evaluation of Constitution-Making in Transition* (Jakarta, Kompas Book Publishing, 2008).

Lindsey, Tim, 'Constitutional Reform in Indonesia: Muddling towards Democracy' in Tim Lindsey (ed), *Indonesia: Law and Society* (Sydney, Federation Press, 2008) 23–47.

Mietzner, Marcus, 'Political Conflict Resolution and Democratic Consolidation in Indonesia: The Role of the Constitutional Court' (2010) 10(3) *Journal of East Asian Studies* 397–424.

---

[72] S Sherlock, 'The Indonesian Parliament after Two Elections' (n 10 above) 36.
[73] ibid, 55.

Nasution, Adnan Buyung, 'Towards Constitutional Democracy in Indonesia', *Adnan Buyung Nasution Papers on Southeast Asian Constitutionalism* (Asian Law Centre, University of Melbourne, 2011).

Schmidt, Adam, 'Indonesia's 2009 elections: Performance Challenges and Negative Precedents' in Edward Aspinall and Marcus Mietzner (eds), *Problems of Democratisation in Indonesia: Elections, Institutions and Society* (Singapore, ISEAS, 2010).

Sherlock, Stephen, 'The Indonesian Parliament after Two Elections: What has Really Changed?', *CDI Policy Papers on Political Governance* (Canberra, Centre for Democratic Institutions, CDI, 2007).

Ziegenhain, Patrick, *The Indonesian Parliament and Democratization* (Singapore, ISEAS, 2008).

4

Judicial Power

———≫•◦•≪———

Introduction – The Lower Courts – Special Courts within the General Courts – The Supreme Court – Judicial Appointments and Tenure – Judicial Reform – The Judicial Commission – The Ombudsman – Conclusion

INTRODUCTION

DURING SOEHARTO'S THREE decades in power (1966–98) the 1945 Constitution formally bound the government and declared Indonesia to be a 'law state' (*Rechtsstaat*), but no judicial institution had power to hold the government to account for breaching it.[1] By most accounts, the majority of judges were corrupt and lacked independence from government.[2] The result was a dysfunctional legal system that consistently failed citizens but served the New Order regime well, providing almost complete legal impunity for many

[1] DS Lev, 'Judicial Authority and The Struggle for An Indonesian Rechsstaat' (1978) 13 *Law and Society Review* 37.

[2] See on this Lev, above n 1; S Pompe, *The Indonesian Supreme Court: A Study of Institutional Collapse* (Ithaca, NY, Cornell University, 2005); RS Assegaf, 'Judicial Reform in Indonesia, 1998–2006' in N Sakumoto and H Juwana (eds), *Reforming Laws and Institutions in Indonesia: An Assessment* (Ciba, Japan: Institute of Developing Economies (IDE)/Japan External Trade Organization (JETRO), 2007), to name just a few among the many who have contributed to the large literature on judicial desuetude in Indonesia. In this chapter, we also draw on our own previous work in S Butt and T Lindsey, 'Unfinished Business: Law Reform, Governance and the Courts in Post-Soeharto Indonesia' in Mirjam Künkler and Alfred Stepan (eds), *Indonesia, Islam and Democratic Consolidation* (New York, Columbia University Press, 2012); S Butt and T Lindsey, 'Judicial Mafia: Corruption and the Courts in Indonesia' in E Aspinall and G Van Klinken (eds), *The State and Illegality in Indonesia* (The Netherlands, KITLV Press, 2011) 189–216.

state actors, including, in particular, military perpetrators of human rights abuses.[3] Lev has described the state as 'reduced to institutional shambles' by 1998, with the judicial system marked by 'corruption, incompetence, mis-orientation, and organisational breakdown . . . [the] legal process had little integrity left'.[4]

In these circumstances, it was only natural that a key demand of the popular Reformasi movement that emerged in 1998 was an overhaul of the Indonesian judicial system. This movement was originally driven by civil society but the idea that the courts required urgent and radical reform soon became mainstream. The reform process began with the constitutional position of the judiciary, set out in Chapter IX of the 1945 Constitution, entitled 'Judicial Power'. This was revised to reflect the basic scheme of the Constitution – a liberal democratic system based on the separation of executive, legislative and judicial powers (*trias politika*). Chapter IX now reads as follows.

Article 24

(1) Judicial power is an independent power used to run a system of courts that uphold law and justice.

(2) Judicial power is exercised by a Supreme Court and the general, religious, military and administrative courts below it, and by a Constitutional Court.

(3) Other bodies whose functions relate to judicial power are to be regulated by statute.

Article 24A

(1) The Supreme Court has jurisdiction to adjudicate at the cassation level, to review laws of a level lower than statutes as against statutes, and has other jurisdiction provided for by statute.

(2) Supreme Court judges must have integrity and irreproachable character, be just and professional, and have legal experience.

(3) Supreme Court candidate judges are to be proposed to the DPR by the Judicial Commission for approval and are then to be appointed by the President.

---

[3] J Herbert, 'The legal framework of human rights in Indonesia' in T Lindsey (ed) *Law and Society in Indonesia* (NSW, Federation Press, 2008).

[4] DS Lev, 'Comments on the judicial reform program in Indonesia' (paper presented at Seminar on Current Developments in Monetary and Financial Law, International Monetary Fund, Washington, DC, 3 June 2004): http:// www.imf. org/external/np/leg/sem/2004/cdmfl/eng/lev.pdf. p 2.

(4) The Chief Justice and Deputy Chief Justice of the Supreme Court are to be appointed from and by Supreme Court judges.

(5) The organisation, position, membership and procedural law of the Supreme Court and the courts below it are to be regulated by statute.

Article 24B

(1) The Judicial Commission is independent and has the power to propose Supreme Court judicial appointments. It has other powers that relate to ensuring and upholding the honour, dignity, and [good] behaviour of judges.

(2) Members of the Judicial Commission must have legal knowledge and experience, and have integrity and irreproachable character.

(3) Members of the Judicial Commission are appointed and dismissed by the President with the approval of the DPR.

(4) The composition, position and membership of the Judicial Commission are to be regulated by statute.

This chapter describes the current functions and powers of Indonesia's Supreme Court, the courts 'below it', and the Judicial Commission. We begin by outlining the relative jurisdictions of the general, religious, administrative and military courts, before turning to the specialised courts established in the post-Soeharto era. We consider the Supreme Court's cassation, judicial review and *peninjauan kembali* '(Reconsideration') functions and then describe procedures for the appointment and dismissal of Supreme Court judges. Important post-Soeharto developments are also assessed, including the *Satu Atap* (One Roof) reforms, by which the Supreme Court was granted administrative control over most other courts. We conclude by outlining the functions of the Judicial Commission and describing some of the resistance, much of it successful, that the Commission has faced from the Supreme Court and the Constitutional Court (which we cover separately in Chapter 5). Throughout this chapter, we also consider the slow progress of broader efforts to reform the court system and some of the many challenges remaining.

THE LOWER COURTS

Four branches of the judicature exist under the Supreme Court: the general courts (*pengadilan umum*), the military courts (*pengadilan militer*), the religious courts (*pengadilan agama*), and the administrative courts (*pengadilan tata usaha negara*).

General courts. Most civil litigation and criminal proceedings are heard in one of Indonesia's 330 first instance general courts.[5] These courts operate at the county (*kabupaten* or Regency) and city (*kota*) level. They have jurisdiction over any matter not falling within the jurisdiction of other courts, including general criminal and civil cases, as well as many commercial matters.[6]

Religious courts. Although their name might suggest broad jurisdiction over legal issues concerning a variety of religions, Indonesia's 343 first instance religious courts in fact only adjudicate on disputes between Muslims. These courts have jurisdiction over specified areas of Islamic law, such as marriage, inheritance, trusts and Islamic finance. Approximately 90 per cent of the cases they hear are divorce applications.[7]

Administrative courts. Indonesia's 26 first instance administrative courts have jurisdiction to hear disputes between Indonesian citizens and the government over alleged infringements of the law or misuse of power by a state organ or official but only after other administrative avenues have been exhausted.[8]

The administrative courts initially emerged as an important, albeit largely unexpected, departure from the Integralist policies[9] and oppressive dominance by the executive that characterised the New Order. They

---

[5] The data on the number of courts in each branch is from Mahkamah Agung, *Laporan Tahun 2010* (Jakarta, Mahkamah Agung, 2011) 373–74.

[6] Law 2 of 1986 on the General Courts, amended by Law 8 of 2004 and Law 49 of 2009. In 2010, 3,037,036 cases were lodged with the general courts, of which around 98 per cent were decided. The vast majority of these were criminal cases, 95 per cent of which involved traffic infringements and misdemeanours. By contrast, the general courts heard only 56,337 civil cases in 2010 (Mahkamah Agung, *Laporan Tahun 2010* (Jakarta, Mahkamah Agung, 2011) 58, 61).

[7] See generally C Sumner and T Lindsey, *Courting Reform: Indonesia's courts and justice for the poor*, Lowy Paper no 31 (Double Bay, Lowy Institute for International Policy, 2010). The primary statute covering the religious courts is Law 7 of 1989 on the Religious Courts (amended by Law 50 of 2009). Indonesia's religious courts heard 377,230 cases in 2010 (Mahkamah Agung, *Laporan Tahun 2010* (above n 5) 58, 64).

[8] The administrative courts are governed by Law 5 of 1986 on the Administrative Courts (amended by Law 51 of 2009). The administrative courts heard only 1,768 cases in 2010, with a clearance rate of around 75 per cent per year (Mahkamah Agung, *Laporan Tahun 2010* (above n 5) 67).

[9] On Integralism, see Chapter 1 of this volume.

had early victories, including the widely-celebrated *Tempo case*.[10] In that case, a panel of the Jakarta Administrative Court chaired by Judge Benjamin Mangkoedilaga invalidated a government decision to revoke the publishing licence of *Tempo* magazine, one of few publications of the time brave enough to criticise the Soeharto regime.[11] This decision was, however, later overturned by the Supreme Court and proved to be of only symbolic value.

More than a decade later, however, the administrative courts face atrophy and even a crisis of relevance. They now hear very few cases compared to the general and religious courts, largely because their previous jurisdiction over taxation and labour issues has been transferred to the specialised taxation and labour courts described below. Most of the cases they hear involve land law disputes and should probably be heard in the general courts rather than the administrative courts in any case.[12] The government's refusal to comply with many of their decisions, combined with their small caseload, undermines the efficacy of the administrative courts and raises questions about their future viability.

Military courts. The military judicature comprises general military courts (*pengadilan militer*); high military courts (*pengadilan tinggi militer*); and supreme military courts (*pengadilan utama militer*).[13] These courts hear matters involving military officers and alleged breaches of military law.[14]

---

[10] B Quinn, *The Administrative Review Act of 1986: Implications for Legal and Bureaucratic Culture* (Honours thesis, Faculty of Asian Studies, Australian National University, 1994).

[11] J Millie, 'The *Tempo* Case: Indonesia's Press Law, the *Pengadilan Tata Usaha Negara* and the Indonesian *Negara Hukum*' in T Lindsey (ed), *Indonesia: Law and Society* 1st edn (Sydney, Federation Press, 1999).

[12] A Bedner, '"Shopping forums": Indonesia's administrative courts' in A Harding and P Nicholson (eds), *New courts in Asia* (London/New York, Routledge, 2010) 214.

[13] Law 31 of 1997 remains the primary legislation regulating the military courts. In 2010, Indonesia's 19 military courts of first instance heard 3641 cases and decided 87 per cent of them (Mahkamah Agung, *Laporan Tahun 2010* (above n 5) 57).

[14] Article 65(2) of Law 34 of 2004 on the Indonesian Armed Forces. Under Soeharto, and for several years into the post-Soeharto era, military personnel tended to be tried in the military courts, even if the alleged crime was not committed in the course of duty and appeared to be non-military in nature. The use of the military courts to try soldiers for crimes clearly committed in their capacity as civilians caused great controversy – largely because military court processes tended to produce acquittals or lighter sentences for military officers than would probably have been imposed by a civil court – and has now been restricted by law.

The jurisdiction of these courts depends on the rank of the officer being tried and the type of breach alleged.[15]

Appeals courts. Appeals from all these first instance courts are heard by high courts (*pengadilan tinggi*) located in Indonesia's provincial capitals.[16] These are divided into four branches: the high general court (*pengadilan tinggi umum*); the high religious court (*pengadilan tinggi agama*); the high administrative court (*pengadilan tinggi tata usaha negara*); and the high military courts (*pengadilan tinggi militer* and *pengadilan utama militer*).[17] Appeals from these courts can be heard on cassation (*kasasi*) by the Supreme Court, as discussed below.

Most of these courts are filled with so-called 'career judges'. As is customary in many European-tradition civil law countries, these are recruited soon after completing law school and, after training and internships, begin work as judges. They generally begin in a first instance court and, through promotions, make their way up the judicial hierarchy.

SPECIAL COURTS WITHIN THE GENERAL COURTS

The general courts house what are referred to as 'special courts' (*pengadilan khusus*). These include the Anti-corruption Court (*Pengadilan Tindak Pidana Korupsi*, or *Pengadilan Tipikor*), the Commercial Court (*Pengadilan Niaga*), the Human Rights Court (*Pengadilan Hak Asasi Manusia*), the Industrial Relations Court (*Pengadilan Hubungan Industrial*), the Fishery Court (*Pengadilan Perikanan*), and the Taxation Court (*Pengadilan Pajak*).

Many of these special courts were established so that particular types of cases that fell within the general court's jurisdiction could be handled by specially-trained judges. This was deemed necessary because of the perceived lack of expertise, competence or impartiality of general court judges. Unlike Indonesia's other courts, some of these special courts therefore employ ad hoc judges. The term 'ad hoc' is a misnomer in this

---

[15]   See Law 31 of 1997.

[16]   In 2010, appeals courts accepted 17,324 cases and decided 81 per cent of them (Mahkamah Agung, *Laporan Tahun 2010* (above n 5) 57).

[17]   The high general courts, of which there are 30, decided 10795 cases, the 29 high religious courts decided 2252, the four high military courts (including the sole supreme military court) decided 374, and the four high administrative courts decided 751 (Mahkamah Agung, *Laporan Tahun 2010* (above n 5) 373–74).

context, however. In Indonesia, the term refers to non-career judges employed to sit on a court for a particular period, rather than being 'called in' to sit in specific cases relating to their particular areas of expertise.

From most specialised courts, such as the Human Rights and Anti-corruption Courts, parties can appeal to similarly-constituted panels at the provincial high court and then to the Supreme Court. For others, such as the Commercial and Industrial Relations Courts, there is no right of appeal to the high courts; instead, parties must appeal directly to the Supreme Court. For the Taxation Court, there is no right of appeal, though *peninjauan kembali* (reconsideration) by the Supreme Court, discussed below, may still be available.[18]

Commercial Courts. Indonesia's five Commercial Courts are located in Jakarta, Medan, Semarang, Surabaya and Makassar. These courts were established in the wake of Indonesia's economic collapse that began in 1997.[19] The establishment of the Commercial Courts was, in fact, a specific condition imposed in government Letters of Intent that were the basis of IMF-led bail-out packages. The jurisdiction of these courts is primarily over insolvency and civil intellectual property matters. Case lodgement rates are relatively low,[20] apparently because of a widespread lack of faith in the court's proceedings and decisions, perhaps a result of its early highly-controversial decisions.

Anti-corruption Courts. In 2004, a single Anti-corruption Court was established in Central Jakarta to hear the corruption cases that the Anti-corruption Commission (*Komisi Pemberantasan Korupsi*, KPK) investigated and prosecuted.[21] It was established to circumvent the general courts, which were commonly regarded as complicit in protecting

[18] The lack of a right of appeal to both the high and Supreme Courts was the basis of a constitutional challenge to Law 14 of 2002 on the Taxation Court (Constitutional Court Decision 4/PUU-II/2004). The Court declared that it lacked jurisdiction to hear the case, but also explained that, because the Supreme Court oversaw the legal and judicial aspects of the Taxation Court, including by hearing *peninjauan kembali* applications against its decisions, the Taxation Court was 'under' the Supreme Court as required by the Constitution.

[19] The courts were established by Law 4 of 1998, which has been subsequently amended by Law 37 of 2004 on Bankruptcy and Repayment of Debt Obligations.

[20] Only 254 cases were lodged with the court in 2010, up from 164 in 2009 (Mahkamah Agung, *Laporan Tahun 2010* (above n 5) 62).

[21] Law 30 of 2002 on the Anti-corruption Commission.

corruptors, and – at the very least – capable of being unresponsive or incompetent in the administration of justice.[22]

Three ad hoc judges and two specially-trained general court judges sat on each Anti-corruption Court panel and it maintained a 100 per cent conviction rate in over 200 cases.[23] This conviction rate was largely attributed to the Court and the Anti-corruption Commission having higher levels of professionalism than ordinary judges and prosecutors. In 2009, however, the DPR enacted a new Anti-corruption Court Law that required the establishment, by late 2011, of Anti-corruption Courts within the general courts of Indonesia's 33 provincial capitals.[24] These new courts have exclusive jurisdiction over all corruption cases, which can now be brought before them by ordinary public prosecutors (*Jaksa*) as well as the Anti-corruption Commission. Further, the new Law still requires that ad hoc judges sit on each Anti-corruption Court case but allows chairperson of the district court in which the Anti-corruption Court is housed to appoint a majority of career judges to sit on corruption case panels, if he or she so chooses. It is assumed in Indonesia that benches dominated by career judges would be susceptible to influence from defendants in corruption cases.

This new Law does not bode well for the future of Indonesia's anti-corruption drive: it makes the participation of ordinary law enforcers in the investigation and adjudication of corruption cases more likely, thus exposing the Anti-corruption Courts to the same problems that have so long bedevilled the general courts. Indeed, within only a few months of the passage of the Law, Jakarta's Anti-corruption Court issued its first acquittal, in a case brought by an ordinary public prosecutor.[25] Many other acquittals followed soon after in provincial Anti-corruption courts.[26]

Human Rights Court. The Human Rights Court can adjudicate cases of 'genocide' and 'crimes against humanity', which the 2000 Human Rights Court Law defines in line with the Rome Statute of the

---

[22] S Fenwick, 'Measuring Up? Indonesia's Anti-Corruption Commission and the New Corruption Agenda' in T Lindsey (ed), *Indonesia: Law and Society*, 2nd edn (Annandale, NSW, Federation Press, 2008).

[23] S Butt, *Corruption and Law in Indonesia* (London, Routledge, 2011) 45–47, 121.

[24] Law 46 of 2009 on the Anti-corruption Court.

[25] S Butt, 'Anti-corruption Reform in Indonesia: an Obituary?' (2011) 47(3) *Bulletin of Indonesian Economic Studies* 381–94.

[26] ibid.

International Criminal Court.[27] The two other crimes punishable under the Rome Statute – war crimes and crimes of aggression – are not specifically prohibited under the Law and thus fall outside the jurisdiction of these courts. Three ad hoc non-career judges are to preside over each five-judge panel of the Court. There are rights of appeal to identically-weighted panels in the high court and the Supreme Court.

Article 43(1) of the Human Rights Court Law authorises the national legislature to form ad hoc human rights tribunals to hear and adjudicate alleged human rights violations committed before the 2000 Law was enacted. This provision was the subject of an unsuccessful constitutional challenge by former East Timor Governor Abilio Soares, discussed in Chapter 5. These tribunals have been established to hear allegations of abuses in Abepura in 2000, East Timor in 1999 and Tanjung Priok in 1984.[28]

Industrial Relations Court. Industrial Relations Courts have been established in Indonesia's provincial capitals.[29] They have jurisdiction over specified employment-related disputes.[30] General and ad hoc judges preside over each case. The Court also formally registers and enforces settlements of employment disputes arrived at by conciliation, arbitration and mediation.[31]

Fishery Court. Indonesia has fisheries courts in the Medan, Pontianak, North Jakarta, Bitung and Tual District Courts.[32] The main jurisdiction of these courts is fishery-related crime.[33]

---

[27] Law 26 of 2000 on the Human Rights Court. Article 8 of the Human Rights Court Law is almost a direct translation of the definition of genocide contained in Article 2 of the Convention on the Prevention and Punishment of the Crime of Genocide, as adopted by Article 6 of the Rome Statute. Similarly, Article 9 of the Law adopts the definition of 'crimes against humanity' contained in Article 7 of the Rome Statute.

[28] D Cohen, *Intended to Fail: the Trials before the Ad Hoc Human Rights Court in Jakarta* (New York, International Center for Transitional Justice, 2003).

[29] Law 13 of 2003 on Labour and Law 2 of 2004 on Settlement of Industrial Relation Disputes.

[30] Their jurisdiction is enlivened, however, only if alternative dispute resolution fails.

[31] The Industrial Relations Courts accepted 1,417 cases in 2010 and decided around 70 per cent of them (Mahkamah Agung, *Laporan Tahuna 2011* (above n 5) 63).

[32] These courts were established by Law 31 of 2004 on Fishery.

[33] These Courts heard 123 cases in 2010 and decided almost all of them (Mahkamah Agung, *Laporan Tahuna 2011* (above n 5) 59).

Taxation Court. Indonesia has only one Taxation Court, located in Jakarta.[34] It decides taxation disputes between taxpayers and government tax authorities.[35] This Court is unique in Indonesia because the Supreme Court does not administer it, as it does all other courts (except the Constitutional Court). Instead, the Taxation Court is under the authority of the Finance Ministry. The Supreme Court does, however, supervise 'technical-legal' aspects of the Taxation Court's work. Although many of its judges are career judges, appointed by the president from a list of names proposed by the Minister after obtaining the agreement of the Supreme Court Chief Justice, ad hoc judges can also be appointed to the Court.[36]

THE SUPREME COURT

As mentioned, Article 24A of the Constitution grants the Supreme Court jurisdiction to decide cassation applications and to exercise limited 'judicial review' powers.[37]

Cassation. The Supreme Court can overturn lower court decisions on a number of grounds, including if the lower court lacked or exceeded its jurisdiction; or wrongly applied or broke the law.[38] There are few restrictions on the types of cassation applications the Supreme Court will hear. Provided the application is not an appeal against a pre-trial hearing (*praperadilan*) or against a decision in a criminal case involving a crime for which the maximum punishment is one year of imprisonment or less, or a fine,[39] the Supreme Court will consider it – so long as the administrative requirements for lodgement are met and there is a question of law to be answered. Clearly, these grounds are extremely broad; they

---

[34] These courts were established by Law 14 of 2002 on the Taxation Court.

[35] In 2010, the Tax Court handled 16,617 cases and decided 42 per cent of them. 1272 *peninjauan kembali* applications were lodged (Mahkamah Agung, *Laporan Tahuna 2011* (above n 5) 68).

[36] See Articles 8–9 of Law 14 of 2002 on the Taxation Court.

[37] See also Article 11(2)(b) of Law 4 of 2004 on Judicial Power; Article 31(2) of Law 14 of 1985 on the Supreme Court (as amended in 2004 and 2009).

[38] Article 30 of Law 14 of 1985 on the Supreme Court.

[39] Article 45A(1) and (2) of Law 14 of 1985 on the Supreme Court. Cassation is also not available for administrative law cases concerning a decision of a regional official if the decision is regional in scope.

give most litigants the right to have the Supreme Court consider their cases. This lack of limitation contributes significantly to the Supreme Court's massive caseload, discussed below.

Cassation hearings, a feature of many civil law countries, are similar to appeals within the common law system but have traditionally been concerned only to ensure that the lower courts have applied the law correctly.[40] Essentially, the main function of cassation is to ensure the uniform application of the law. However, although the Supreme Court is theoretically not required to reconsider the facts of the case or the evidence produced by the parties, it often does so,[41] usually by defining the issue in question as a legal one.

Cassation is generally conducted 'on the papers'. A panel of at least three Supreme Court judges reviews the case file (which should include the decisions at first instance or on appeal, if applicable) and written arguments submitted by the parties. Cassation generally does not involve the presentation of oral arguments or the questioning of witnesses, although exceptions are sometimes made. When this happens, the Supreme Court usually does not conduct the examination. Instead, it orders the first instance court to hear new witness testimony or other evidence, and provide it with a report. The Supreme Court's cassation decision is, in theory at least, immediately executable, although enforcement problems are very common.[42]

Judicial review.[43] The Supreme Court can review laws below the level of statutes in the so-called hierarchy of laws to ensure that they comply with statutes. The hierarchy is contained in Article 7(1) of Law 10 of 2004 on Law-making (as amended in 2011), which reads:

---

[40] Article 30(b) of Law 14 of 1985 on the Supreme Court. R Subekti, *Law in Indonesia* (Jakarta, Center for Strategic and International Studies, 1982); J Merryman, *The Civil Law Tradition: an Introduction to the Legal Systems of Western Europe and Latin America* (Stanford, CA, Stanford University Press, 1984).

[41] S Pompe, *The Indonesian Supreme Court: A Study of Institutional Collapse* (Ithaca, NY, Cornell University, 2005).

[42] S Butt, 'Surat sakti: The Decline of the Authority of Judicial Decisions in Indonesia' in T Lindsey (ed), *Indonesia: Law and Society*, 2nd edn (Annandale, NSW, Federation Press, 2008).

[43] We use the term 'judicial review' here to describe the mechanisms under which courts review laws for their compliance with other laws. The term is often misused to refer to the *peninjauan kembali* (PK or reconsideration) process, by which the Supreme Court can re-open cases – discussed below.

The types and hierarchy of laws are:

a. The 1945 Constitution (*Undang-undang Dasar 1945*);
b. MPR Decrees (*Ketetapan MPR*);
c. Statutes/Interim Emergency Laws (*Undang-Undang/Peraturan Pemerintah Pengganti Undang-Undang*);
d. Government Regulations (*Peraturan Pemerintah*);
e. Presidential Regulations (*Peraturan Presiden*);
f. Provincial Regulations (*Peraturan Daerah Propinsi*); and
g. County/City Regulations (*Peraturan Daerah Kabupaten/Kota*).

The Court also has the power to review the formal validity of lower-level laws – that is, it can review whether the procedures under which such a law was drafted and enacted were complied with.[44] If the Court decides that a lower-level law is inconsistent with a statute, it is to declare that lower law invalid and without binding force.[45] As we explain in more detail in Chapter 6, this judicial review jurisdiction is quite limited and therefore problematic: the Court lacks power to assess the constitutionality of any type of law or the consistency of lower-level laws as against each other. Further, although the Constititional Court has the power to review the constitutionality of statutes, as we show in Chapter 5, it cannot review lower-level laws. There is in fact no court in Indonesia that can review such laws against the Constitution, and it is becoming clear that this is a serious lacuna in the contemporary Indonesian legal system.

Other powers. Article 28A of the Constitution authorises the Supreme Court to exercise other powers provided to it by statute. For example, the Supreme Court is to provide 'its legal opinion to the President on requests for pardons and rehabilitation'. It also supervises the lower courts, a power it actively exercises.[46]

---

[44] In 2010, for example, the Court decided 61 judicial review cases. It was asked to review nine government regulations, three presidential decisions, 12 local laws, 14 ministerial regulations, six ministerial decisions, two electoral commission decisions, nine electoral commission regulations, one mayoral decision, one governor's decision, and one 'circular letter' (*surat edaran*) (Mahkamah Agung, *Laporan Tahuna 2011* (above n 5) 65).

[45] Article 31(4) of Law 14 of 1985 on the Supreme Court. Before the 2004 amendment, if the Supreme Court found a lower-level law to be inconsistent with a statute, it was to 'firmly state that the law is invalid and not generally applicable'. However, the Court could not itself strike down the law.

[46] Articles 32, 32A and 35 of Law 14 of 1985 on the Supreme Court.

Peninjauan Kembali (**PK or Reconsideration**). This is often regarded as the final stage of appeal – and, indeed, litigants often treat it as such – but PK is more correctly understood as the Supreme Court re-opening a case. Using this power, the Supreme Court can review 'permanently binding' decisions from all courts below it and can even review its own decisions. If reviewing one of its own decisions, the panel of judges presiding over the PK will be different to the one that heard the original cassation application.

To bring a PK application, the applicant must establish at least one of a number of grounds, such as that the decision appealed against was tainted by a clear mistake or judicial error, or that new evidence or circumstances have since come to light which, if known at the time the case was heard, would have likely changed the outcome of the case.[47] The PK is the final formal avenue of judicial recourse for litigants. The Supreme Court cannot 'conduct a PK of a PK'.[48]

JUDICIAL APPOINTMENTS AND TENURE

The Supreme Court has 51 judicial positions, although in 2010 only 39 of these were filled.[49] Of these, there is one Chief Justice, one Deputy Chief Justice, and six Junior Chief Justices.[50] The Court is divided into eight 'chambers', each led by a senior judge.

To be appointed as a Supreme Court judge, candidates who have worked as career judges must meet various requirements, including being an Indonesian citizen, over 45 years old, physically healthy and 'devoted to Almighty God'. They must also have a law degree; at least 20 years' experience (including at least three years in a high court); and

---

[47] For a list of grounds, see Article 67 of Law 14 of 1985 on the Supreme Court; Article 263(2) of the Criminal Procedure Code.

[48] Article 23(2) of the Judicial Power Law. This provision was subject to unsuccessful constitutional challenge in two cases – Constitutional Court Decisions 16/PUU-VIII/2010 and 10/PUU-IX/2011 – discussed in Chapter 4 of this volume.

[49] Mahkamah Agung, *Laporan Tahuna 2011* (above n 5) 8.

[50] The Supreme Court's Chief and Deputy Chief Justices are 'elected by Supreme Court judges and appointed by the President' (Article 8(7) of Law 14 of 1985 on the Supreme Court). Junior Chairpersons are appointed by the president from among Supreme Court judges put forward by the Supreme Court Chief Justice (Article 8(8) of Law 14 of 1985 on the Supreme Court).

integrity, irreproachable character and professionalism.[51] Candidates can also apply for a position on the Supreme Court as a so-called 'non-career' judge if they have not had a previous judicial career. The age, religious, health and character requirements are the same. In addition, they must have at least 20 years' experience in the legal profession or as a legal academic; hold a master's degree in law or another degree that provides legal expertise; and not have been convicted of a crime for which the applicable prison sentence is five years or more.[52] The Judicial Commission proposes candidates to the national legislature. The latter then conducts 'fit and proper' screening tests that often attract public controversy and media speculation before it passes names on to the president for formal appointment.[53]

The Supreme Court Law regulates honourable discharge and dismissal from judicial office. Supreme Court judges can be honourably discharged upon their own request or death; or if they cannot adequately perform their duties due to illness or other reasons. Supreme Court Judges will also be honourably discharged if they reach the mandatory retirement age of 70.[54] In addition, Supreme Court judges can be dishonourably dismissed by the president on the recommendation of the Chief Justice for improper conduct; continual neglect of their work; breaching their oath or pledge of office; holding a prohibited concurrent position; or committing a felony.[55] While there has been much public criticism of Supreme Court judges, these dismissal provisions have rarely been invoked, for reasons we explain below when we discuss the Judicial Commission.

JUDICIAL REFORM

One of the most significant post-Soeharto reforms to Indonesia's judicial system was the transfer, in 2004, of the organisational, administrative and financial affairs of the lower courts to the Supreme Court – the so called 'One Roof' (*Satu Atap*) reforms.[56]

---

[51] Articles 6A and 7 of Law 14 of 1985 on the Supreme Court.
[52] Article 7 of Law 14 of 1985 on the Supreme Court.
[53] Article 8 of Law 14 of 1985 on the Supreme Court.
[54] Article 11 of Law 14 of 1985 on the Supreme Court.
[55] Articles 11A and 12 of Law 14 of 1985 on the Supreme Court.
[56] See Law 35 of 1999, amending Law 14 of 1970 on Judicial Power, which

Before the reforms, the Supreme Court could exercise control over lower courts' 'technical-judicial' functions by hearing cases on appeal from them, supervising them and helping to train their judges but the Ministry of Justice had organisational, administrative and financial control over the general and administrative courts, the Religious Affairs Ministry over the religious courts and the Defence and Security Department over the military courts. This departmental control was often cited as the main cause for very low levels of judicial independence from government, particularly from the early to mid-1970s.[57] Judges were reliant on the government for employment, pay and promotion, and were said to be reluctant to 'bite the hand that fed them'.[58] The result was that the government could – and often did – dictate the decisions it wanted.

With the *Satu Atap* reforms, the Supreme Court assumed ultimate responsibility for the appointment, education, transfer, promotion and dismissal of judges. It also embarked on an unprecedented program of internal reform. In partnership with a leading legal reform NGO, LeIP,[59] the Court developed ambitious Judicial Reform Blueprints, which, although imperfectly and incompletely implemented, have now become a central part of the court's routine administration. It is generally accepted that these reforms have achieved their primary goal – Indonesia's courts are now far more independent of government.[60] It is now rare to hear allegations of political case-fixing by the government, allegations that were common during the Soeharto period.[61] In fact, the government now finds the courts quite willing to find against it in ways that were unheard of under the New Order.

provided a five-year deadline for the transfer; Law 4 of 2004 on Judicial Power; and Law 14 of 1985 on the Supreme Court. Presidential Decision 21 of 2004 transferred authority over the organisation, administrative and financial affairs of the general, administrative and religious courts to the Supreme Court on 31 March 2004.

[57] S Pompe, *The Indonesian Supreme Court: A Study of Institutional Collapse* (above n 41) 125–29.

[58] DS Lev, 'Judicial Authority and The Struggle for An Indonesian Rechsstaat' (1978) 13 *Law and Society Review* 37, 55–57.

[59] Institute of Advocacy and Study for an Independent Judiciary (*Lembaga Kajian dan Advokasi untuk Independensi Peradilan*). For more information on the Blueprint, see RS Assegaf, 'Judicial Reform in Indonesia, 1998–2006' (n 2 above).

[60] S Butt and T Lindsey, 'Unfinished Business: Law Reform, Governance and the Courts in Post-Soeharto Indonesia' in M Kunkler and A Stepan (eds), *Indonesia, Islam and Democratic Consolidation* (New York, Columbia University Press, 2010).

[61] ibid.

While *Satu Atap* appears to have reduced judicial dependence on government, it has not solved other problems facing the Indonesian courts. The problems of judicial incompetence and bribery – in both the Supreme Court and the courts below it – remain acute, but have been well-documented elsewhere so we will not discuss them in detail here.[62] In the words of the Supreme Court itself:

> The struggle is not over. The Supreme Court must actually work even harder to prepare for the future by cleaning itself, improving quality, increasing integrity, becoming more efficient and productive so that the Court can be authoritative and respected as quickly as possible.[63]

Indeed, some problems appear to have worsened under *Satu Atap*. As we have noted elsewhere, there is a perception that judicial corruption, in the sense of litigants being able to 'buy' decisions, is now more prevalent than ever before.[64] Some also argue that *Satu Atap* has reduced the quality of the Court's decision-making because of the burdensome administrative responsibilities it has imposed upon the Court.[65] The Court must now administer Indonesia's 806 courts and almost 36,000 personnel, including around 7,500 judges and 11,000 clerks and bailiffs.[66] It must do all this while hearing and deciding more than 10,000 cases per year.[67] It is hardly surprising, then, that one of the Court's

---

[62] See A Aspandi, *Menggugat Sistem Hukum Peradilan Indonesia Yang Penuh Ketidakpastian* (Surabaya, LeKSHI and Lutfansah, 2002); Pompe, *The Indonesian Supreme Court* (n 57 above); Lev, 'Judicial Authority and The Struggle for An Indonesian Rechsstaat' (n 58 above); Assegaf, 'Judicial Reform in Indonesia, 1998–2006' (n 2 above); S Butt and T Lindsey, 'Who Owns the Economy? Privatisation, Property Rights and the Indonesian Constitution' in Aileen McHarg, et al (eds), *Property and the Law in Energy and Natural Resources* (Oxford, Oxford University Press, 2010); S Butt and T Lindsey, 'Unfinished Business: Law Reform, Governance and the Courts in Post-Soeharto Indonesia' (n 60 above); and S Butt, *Corruption and Law in Indonesia* (London, Routledge, 2011).

[63] Mahkamah Agung, *Laporan Tahuna 2011* (above n 5) 20.

[64] S Butt and T Lindsey, 'Unfinished Business: Law Reform, Governance and the Courts in Post-Soeharto Indonesia' (n 60 above).

[65] ibid.

[66] Mahkamah Agung, *Laporan Tahunan 2007* (Jakarta, Mahkamah Agung, 2008) i; Mahkamah Agung, (above n 5) 374.

[67] In 2010 alone 13,480 cases were lodged with the Supreme Court and 8,835 were carried over from 2009. The Court decided 13,891 of these 22,315 cases – the most decided in any one year in Supreme Court history (Mahkamah Agung, *Laporan Tahuna 2011* above n 5) 71).

future priorities, set out in its Blueprint for 2010–35, is to reduce the number of cases that come before it.[68]

THE JUDICIAL COMMISSION

Article 24B of the Constitution provides:

(1) The Judicial Commission is independent and has power to propose Supreme Court judicial appointments. It has other powers related to ensuring and upholding the honour, dignity, and [good] behaviour of judges.

(2) Members of the Judicial Commission must have legal knowledge and experience, and integrity and irreproachable character.

(3) Members of the Judicial Commission are appointed and dismissed by the President with the approval of the DPR.

(4) The composition, position and membership of the Judicial Commission are to be regulated by statute.

The Judicial Commission began operating in 2005. It is the main accountability mechanism put in place to counterbalance the greatly increased autonomy the *Satu Atap* reforms brought to the Supreme Court and the courts it supervises.

Law 22 of 2004 on the Judicial Commission is the primary statute governing the Commission,[69] although amendments made in 2009 to Indonesia's various judiciary laws are also relevant.[70] The 2004 Law restates and expands Article 24B. It declares that the Judicial Commission is to be independent when exercising its powers – that is, it must be free from interference or influence from other sources (Article 2). It requires that the Commission comprise seven members, drawn from the ranks of former judges, legal practitioners, legal academics and community members (Articles 6(1) and 6(3)). Its chair and single deputy chair are elected by the other members (Articles 5 and 7(1)).

---

[68] *Cetak Biru Pembaruan Peradilan 2010–2035* (Jakarta, Mahkamah Agung, 2010). Another priority is to increase efficiency by establishing a chamber system, so that judges with particular expertise handle cases falling within that area of expertise.

[69] At time of writing, significant amendments to this Law had just been enacted, which cannot be covered in this volume.

[70] Law 48 of 2009 on Judicial Power; Law 49 of 2009, amending Law 2 of 1986 on the General Courts; Law 50 of 2009, amending Law 7 of 1989 on the Religious Courts; Law 51 of 2009, amending Law 5 of 1986 on the Administrative Courts.

The 2004 Judicial Commission Law also affirms the Judicial Commission's two primary functions, as mentioned in Article 24B(1) of the Constitution. The first is helping propose Supreme Court judicial appointments.[71] To this end, the 2004 Law requires the Commission to register and select candidates to submit to the DPR for consideration (Article 14(1)). Amendments to Indonesia's various judiciary laws in 2009 added the task of helping the Supreme Court select general, religious and administrative court judges.[72]

The Commission's second function – helping to ensure and uphold the honour, dignity, and good behaviour of judges – has been far more controversial. When first enacted, the 2004 Law required the Judicial Commission to supervise the performance and behaviour of judges from all Indonesian courts, including the Supreme and Constitutional Courts, as part of this function (Articles 13(b) and 20). This it does largely by reference to an Ethics Code and Judicial Behaviour Guidelines developed with the Supreme Court.[73] To this end, Article 22(1) of the 2004 Judicial Commission Law requires the Commission to:

a. receive reports from the community about the behaviour of judges;
b. seek periodic reports from courts about the behaviour of their judges;
c. investigate suspected breaches of proper judicial behaviour;
d. call and seek explanations from judges suspected of breaching the code of ethics for judicial behaviour; and
e. report the findings of investigations, make recommendations and convey them to the Supreme Court and/or the Constitutional Court, and send a copy to the President and the DPR.[74]

---

[71] See also Article 20(2) of the 2009 Judicial Power Law.

[72] Article 14A(2) of Law 2 of 1986 on the General Courts; Article 14A(2) of Law 5 of 1986 on the Administrative Courts; Article 13A(2) of Law 7 of 1989 on the Religious Courts.

[73] Article 41(3) of the 2009 Judiciary Law; Article 13E(2) of Law 2 of 1986 on the General Courts; Article 13EA(2) of Law 5 of 1986 on the Administrative Courts; Article 12E(2) of Law 7 of 1989 on the Religious Courts.

[74] Similarly, the 2009 judiciary law amendments specifically allow the Commission to receive complaints about potential breaches of the Code from the community and the Supreme Court and investigate the allegations, including by sitting in on trials or calling the judge in question to account. It can then 'issue a decision' based on the results of the investigation (Article 13D(2) of Law 2 of 1986 on the General Courts; Article 12D(2) of Law 7 of 1989 on the Religious Courts; Article 13D(2) of Law 5 of 1986 on the Administrative Courts).

If the Judicial Commission finds that a judge has committed a violation of the ethics code, it can, depending on the gravity of the alleged breach, propose that the judge be punished by written reprimand, suspension or dismissal.[75] However, the Commission's sanctioning powers are strictly circumscribed – presumably so that its work does not interfere with judicial independence. Only the Commission's recommendations to issue a written reprimand against a judge are binding. If the Commission recommends suspension or dismissal, it can take no further direct action. It can only send the proposed sanction and reasons for suggesting it to the Supreme or Constitutional Court leadership for further action.[76] In other words, the statute allows the Commission to review the performance of judges but the final decision on whether 'real' action is taken lies with other judges.

It is clear, then, that the 2004 Law presupposes an effective working relationship between the Commission, the Supreme Court and the Constitutional Court. This is true also of the 2009 Judiciary Law amendments, which require the Commission and the Supreme Court to 'coordinate' when supervising judges,[77] and specify circumstances in which joint investigations are necessary.[78] The Judicial Commission is almost entirely dependent on the willingness and ability of those Courts to act on its proposals and recommendations. Unfortunately, the Commission's relationship with these institutions – particularly the Supreme Court – has been frosty at best and, more often, openly hostile.

The Supreme Court maintains that Judicial Commission investigations into it and other courts do, or might, compromise judicial independence.[79] In reply, the Judicial Commission cites Supreme Court

---

[75] Article 23(1) of the 2004 Judicial Commission Law.

[76] Article 23(2) and 23(3) of the 2004 Judicial Commission Law. The Commission can also propose to the Supreme or Constitutional Court that a judge be recognised for his or her achievements or service in upholding the honour and dignity, or ensuring the good behaviour, of judges (Article 24(1)).

[77] Article 13C(1) of Law 2 of 1986 on the General Courts; Article 12C(1) of Law 7 of 1989 on the Religious Courts; Article 13C(1) of Law 5 of 1986 on the Administrative Courts.

[78] Article 13C(2) of Law 2 of 1986 on the General Courts; Article 12C(2) of Law 7 of 1989 on the Religious Courts; Article 13C(2) of Law 5 of 1986 on the Administrative Courts.

[79] Komisi Yubisial, *Laporan Tahunan* 2010 (Jakarta, Komisi Yudisial, 2011) 277.

resistance as the main impediment to the performance of its duties,[80] claiming that the Supreme Court has persistently failed to respond to many Commission proposals and investigations. For example, the Judicial Commission investigated 376 judges in 2005–10 and recommended to the Supreme Court that 97 of them be sanctioned by written reprimand, suspension or dismissal.[81] The Supreme Court simply ignored the Judicial Commission's proposals in 31 of these cases, and in 41 others declared that the alleged breach was 'technical-judicial', and should, for reasons of judicial independence, be taken out of the Commission's hands.[82] The Supreme Court followed-up only 12 cases and just four of the judges the Commission named were brought before the Judges' Honour Council.[83]

Animosity between the Supreme Court and the Judicial Commission was on-going at time of writing[84] but the peak of discontent was in 2006. In December 2005, Professor Bagir Manan, the then Supreme Court Chief Justice, refused to allow the Judicial Commission to investigate several Supreme Court judges, including himself, for alleged corruption. After a list of so-called 'problematic' or corrupt judges was leaked to the media, several Supreme Court judges reported the then Judicial Commission Chairperson, Busyro Muqoddas, to the police for defamation. In early 2006, the judges increased the pressure, asking the Constitutional Court to strike out provisions of the 2004 Judicial Commission Law that purported to permit the Commission to supervise Supreme Court judges. The Supreme Court judges argued that these provisions contradicted guarantees of judicial independence in Chapter IX of the Constitution.

[80] ibid, 100–01. The Commission has, in fact, lodged a written complaint about the Supreme Court's attitude with the DPR (Judicial Commission Letter 893/P. KY/XI/2010 of 4 November 2010): ibid, 101.

[81] ibid, 60. The Commission proposed that 45 be given a written warning, 36 be suspended for between six months and two years, and 16 be dismissed (ibid, 61).

[82] ibid, 2.

[83] ibid, 62. The remaining five judicial misconduct cases brought before the Council in 2005–10 were initiated by the Supreme Court itself (ibid, 65).

[84] For example, in May 2010, the Judicial Commission sought to interview Supreme Court judges over alleged breaches of the judicial code of ethics and behaviour. The Supreme Court Chief Justice refused to cooperate, claiming that the Commission had been reviewing the substance of its decisions when, in fact, it only had jurisdiction to investigate and monitor judges' compliance with the judicial code of ethics and behaviour (*Hukumonline*, 'Hakim Agung Mangkir, KY Akan "Vonis" secara in absentia', 24 May 2010).

The Constitutional Court began its decision in the *Judicial Commission case*[85] by excluding itself from Judicial Commission supervision, on the basis that one of the Court's functions was to settle disputes between state institutions. Given that the Commission was one such institution, the Court held that if the Commission could supervise the Court, this might affect the Court's independence in cases heard before it to which the Commission was a party. Next, the Court found that judicial independence also precluded the Commission from supervising the Supreme Court's exercise of judicial powers. The nub of the Court's decision was as follows.

> [E]ven though assessing the technical-judicial skills of judges by reading judicial decisions might assist the Judicial Commission to identify a breach of a code of conduct or ethics, reviewing judicial decisions might place unjustifiable pressure on judges, thereby breaching judicial independence. Only the courts can review judicial decisions, and then only through the appeals process – not by evaluating and directly interfering with decisions or by influencing judges.[86]

The result of this decision was to create great uncertainty about what the Judicial Commission was, constitutionally, permitted to do in exercising its duty to supervise judges.[87] The Constitutional Court decision gave the Supreme Court a shield to deflect many Commission proposals to examine particular judges for impropriety. The Supreme Court can, as it did many times in 2010 (discussed above), declare that any alleged impropriety was 'technical-judicial' in nature and was therefore a matter for the Supreme Court alone. Judges also point to provisions in the 2009 Judiciary Law amendments that declare that supervision, whether internal or external, 'must not reduce the independence of judges when examining and deciding cases'.[88]

---

[85] Constitutional Court Decision 005/PUU-IV/2006, a unanimous decision.

[86] S Butt, 'The Constitutional Court's Decision in the Dispute Between the Supreme Court and the Judicial Commission: Banishing Judicial Accountability?' in RH McLeod and AJ MacIntyre (eds), *Indonesia: Democracy and the Promise of Good Governance* (Singapore, ISEAS, 2007) 192 (references omitted).

[87] Despite this, the Judicial Commission, with a number of universities, has published two volumes analysing judicial decisions of the lower courts: Komisi Yudisial *Menemukan Substansi Dalam Keadilan Prosedural: Laporan Penelitian Putusan Kasus Pidana Pengadilan Negeri* (Jakarta, Komisi Yudisial, 2009); and Komisi Yudisial *Potret Profesionalisme Hakim Dalam Putusan: Laporan Putusan Pengadilan Negeri* (Jakarta, Komisi Yudisial, 2008).

[88] Article 41(2) of the 2009 Judiciary Law; Article 13E(3) of Law 2 of 1986 on the General Courts; Article 13E(3) of Law 5 of 1986 on the Administrative Courts; and Article 12E(3) of Law 7 of 1989 on the Religious Courts.

Amendments made to the Supreme Court Law in 2009 were intended to clarify the types of supervisory activities the Judicial Commission can perform. They divide responsibility for supervising judges between the Supreme Court and the Judicial Commission. On the one hand, the Supreme Court is responsible for 'internal' supervision of judicial behaviour, including judicial tasks, administration and finance. On the other, the Judicial Commission performs 'external' supervision of judicial conduct based on the Ethics Code and Judicial Behaviour Guidelines.[89]

Whether the Judicial Commission can analyse the decisions of a particular judge in order to assess his or her integrity or conduct remains a highly vexed question. The Supreme Court Law does not specifically permit the Judicial Commission to examine Supreme Court judgments for any purpose. The 2009 amendments to several other judiciary-related laws, however, purport to specifically permit the Commission to analyse the decisions of lower courts in order to maintain judicial integrity and good conduct – but only to determine whether a judge should be transferred to another judicial post.[90]

Although these amendments were enacted in response to the Constitutional Court decision discussed above,[91] in our view, they are susceptible to challenge in the Constitutional Court along the same lines as the 2004 Judicial Commission Law. It is conceivable that the Judiciary Law amendments purporting to permit the Commission to examine specific decisions of particular judges could be invalidated on the grounds that they do, or could, affect judicial independence.

Detecting and punishing judicial impropriety is now, in a formal sense, almost exclusively a matter for the Supreme Court but it has little incentive to actively pursue misconduct, particularly allegations of judicial corruption, in its own ranks. Quite apart from the embarrassment

---

[89] Articles 40(1) and (2) of the 2009 Judiciary Law; Articles 13A(2) and 13D(1) of Law 2 of 1986 on the General Courts; Articles 13A(2) and 13D(1) of Law 5 of 1986 on the Administrative Courts; Article 12A(2) of Law 7 of 1989 on the Religious Courts.

[90] Article 42 of the 2009 Judiciary Law; Article 13F of Law 2 of 1986 on the General Courts; Article 13F of Law 5 of 1986 on the Administrative Courts; Article 12F of Law 7 of 1989 on the Religious Courts.

[91] As declared in the Elucidations (explanatory memoranda) to all the Judiciary Law amendments: Law 3 of 2009 on the Supreme Court; Law 48 of 2009 on Judicial Power; Law 49 of 2009 on the General Courts; Law 50 of 2009 on the Religious Courts; and Law 51 of 2009 on the Religious Courts.

this might cause, corruption brings significant financial benefits to judges personally and provides funds that help with the running of the Supreme Court and the courts for which it is responsible.

Even if the Supreme Court were inclined or pressured to pursue particular allegations, corruption is, by its very nature, a difficult crime to detect, and the Court has few investigatory powers and little experience in this area. Accordingly, responsibility for dealing with judicial misconduct in Indonesia has largely shifted from the formal sector to the informal. Most revelations of judicial misbehaviour in recent years have come not from the courts or the Judicial Commission, or the police or public prosecution service, or even from the two agencies that have reported large numbers of public complaints about judicial corruption: the Anti-corruption Commission and the Ombudsman.[92] Rather, the most active judicial 'watchdog' is still civil society and, in particular, the media and the NGOs that were in the vanguard of the legal and governance *Reformasi* movement a decade or so ago.[93] The result is that there are still few apparent disincentives for corruption in the Supreme Court, other than the risk of being 'shamed' by the media and NGOs.

THE OMBUDSMAN

The Ombudsman was established by Presidential Decree in 2000[94] and as a statutory authority in 2008.[95] It has authority to investigate complaints about public services and allegations of maladministration, including judicial impropriety, the most common matter complained of.[96] To these ends,

---

[92] The majority of complaints lodged with Indonesia's National Ombudsman Commission relate solely to the judiciary. It has, however, had very little success in resolving such complaints to the satisfaction of the public (M Crouch, 'Indonesia's National and Local Ombudsman Reforms: Salvaging a Failed Experiment?' in T Lindsey (ed), *Indonesia: Law and Society* (Annandale, NSW, Federation Press, 2008) 386).

[93] These include, among others, the Institute of Advocacy and Study for an Independent Judiciary (*Lembaga Kajian dan Advokasi untuk Independensi Peradilan* – LeIP); the Indonesian Centre for the Study of Law and Policy (*Pusat Studi Hukum dan Kebijakan Indonesia* – PSHKI); the Legal Aid Institute of Indonesia (*Lembaga Hukum Indonesia* – LBHI); and, in particular, Indonesia Corruption Watch (ICW).

[94] Presidential Decree 44 of 2000.

[95] Law 37 of 2008.

[96] Article 7 of Law 37 of 2008; and see M Crouch, 'Indonesia's National and Local Ombudsman Reforms' (n 92 above) 386.

the Ombudsman can formally request reports from impugned government institutions; examine documents held by a complainant or respondent to verify the truth of allegations and complaints; call complainants or respondents for interview; resolve complaints through mediation and conciliation; make recommendations, including that compensation be paid; and publicise findings and recommendations, if in the public interest.[97] To improve public services, the Ombudsman can make recommendations to the president, regional heads of government and other government leaders. It can also suggest regulatory reform to prevent maladministration.[98]

Though initially flooded with complaints,[99] the Ombudsman is now considered 'toothless' as a check on government action and has become largely irrelevant to public life in Indonesia. A variety of reasons – such as insufficient budget and political support – are commonly cited as causes of its impotence.[100] The Ombudsman's main weakness, however, is its inability to compel government officials and departments to respond to its inquiries and recommendations. The 2008 legislation did not give it coercive powers and many officials simply ignore the Ombudsman's requests and findings.[101] For the most part, the Ombudsman can only attempt to 'shame' impugned officials and government departments through the media and hope that they remedy the problem. This strategy has not proved particularly successful.

CONCLUSION

Indonesia's courts are now in position of greater power and autonomy than at any time in the last four decades at least. In theory, the judiciary

[97] Article 8 of Law 37 of 2008.

[98] Article 8 of Law 37 of 2008.

[99] The Ombudsman received 1723 complaints in its first year, mostly about court and police corruption and maladministration (M Crouch, 'Indonesia's National and Local Ombudsman Reforms' (n 92 above) 386). After a sharp drop in complaints, it received 1237 official complaints in 2009 (up 17.23% from 2008) and 1154 in 2010 (Ombudsman Republik Indonesia (2010) *Laporan Tahunan 2009: Ombudsman Republik Indonesia* (Jakarta: Ombudsman Republik Indonesia)).

[100] World Bank, *Combating corruption in Indonesia: enhancing accountability for development* (Jakarta, World Bank Office Jakarta, 2004) 13.

[101] S Sherlock, 'Combating Corruption in Indonesia? The Ombudsman and the Assets Auditing Commission' (2002) 38(3) *Bulletin of Indonesian Economic Studies* 367, 369–70.

is now a key arbiter of the post-Soeharto *Reformasi* process that has sought to roll back the overwhelming power of the authoritarian state built by the New Order and replace it with a more open, transparent system of governance in which individual rights have greater currency and the powers of the executive and the legislature are hemmed in by institutionalised democratic checks and balances.[102]

Many judicial reforms have failed, however, despite the best efforts of reformers within civil society, the courts and government. Others have had only very limited impact, and some have themselves spawned new problems. Nevertheless, the post-Soeharto judicial reform process has produced positive, albeit very slow, change to Indonesia's legal system, although this is often overlooked and discounted in assessments of Indonesia's post-Soeharto *Reformasi*. In part, this is because legal system reform is an inherently complex and slow process in any country, regardless of the type of system involved. In part, it is because the changes that have taken place within the Indonesian judiciary are often not immediately apparent to the public, who observe the day-to-day activity of the courts through the (very critical) lens of the media and local politics. Controversial political cases and corruption scandals are rarely an accurate measure of the complex business of court reform.

Nevertheless, the fact remains that the Supreme Court's own continuing dysfunction and corruption still prevent it, and many of the courts below it, from effectively performing key judicial tasks. The result is that unless a matter falls within the jurisdiction of the Constitutional Court (discussed in the next chapter),[103] citizens cannot rely on the courts to decide disputes impartially in civil and commercial matters, to convict defendants by reference to applicable law and relevant evidence in criminal cases or acquit in the absence of such evidence, or to ensure that government abides by the law in its dealings with citizens. The last half-decade has shown that the institutional independence granted to

---

[102] T Lindsey, 'History Always Repeats? Corruption, Culture and "Asian Values"' in T Lindsey and H Dick (eds), *Corruption in Asia: rethinking the governance paradigm*, 2nd edn (Sydney, Federation Press, 2002) 1–23; T Lindsey, 'Indonesia: Devaluing Asian Values, Rewriting Rule of Law' in R Peerenboom (ed), *Asian Discourses of Rule of Law* (London and New York, Routledge, 2004) 286–323.

[103] The religious courts (*Pengadilan Agama*) are also often considered an exception to the general corruption and dysfunction of the other courts. See C Sumner and T Lindsey, *Courting Reform: Indonesia's Islamic courts and justice for the poor*, Lowy Paper no 31 (Double Bay, Lowy Institute for International Policy, 2010).

the courts by the amendment of Chapter IX of the Constitution is, unfortunately, not enough to deliver a just and open judicial system.

SELECTED READING

Assegaf, Rifqi S, 'Judicial Reform in Indonesia, 1998–2006' in N Sakumoto and H Juwana (eds), *Reforming Laws and Institutions in Indonesia: An Assessment* (Ciba, Japan, Institute of Developing Economies (IDE)/Japan External Trade Organization (JETRO), 2007).

Butt, Simon and Lindsey, Tim, 'Judicial Mafia: Corruption and the Courts in Indonesia' in E Aspinall and G Van Klinken (eds), *The State and Illegality in Indonesia* (The Netherlands, KITLV Press, 2011) 189–216.

Colbran, Nicola, 'Courage under fire: the first five years of the Indonesian Judicial Commission' (2009) 11 *Australian Journal of Asian Law* 273– 301.

Lev, Daniel S, 'Judicial Institutions and Legal Culture in Indonesia' in Claire Holt (ed), *Culture and Politics in Indonesia* (Ithaca, NY, Cornell University Press, 1972).

Lev, Daniel S, 'Judicial Authority and The Struggle for An Indonesian Rechsstaat' (1978) 13 *Law and Society Review* 37.

5

The Constitutional Court and its Jurisdiction

Introduction – Powers of the Constitutional Court – The Constitutional Court's Composition – Judicial Review – Disputed Returns and Election-Related Jurisdiction – Expanding its own Jurisdiction – 2011 Amendments to the Constitutional Court Law – The Court Strikes Back – Conclusion

INTRODUCTION

ESTABLISHMENT OF INDONESIA'S first Constitutional Court was mandated by the Fourth Amendment of the Constitution in 2002 and it began operating in late 2003. Of all the state institutions created by the amendments, it has had the most impact on constitutional law in Indonesia. In fact, litigation in this court quickly began to create the body of sophisticated constitutional jurisprudence that independent Indonesia had always lacked.

As explained in Chapter 1, there was no room under the authoritarian rule of Soekarno (after 1957) and Soeharto (1966–98) for mechanisms to challenge state action, such as judicial review conducted by an independent judiciary.[1] In fact, the very notion of constitutional checks and balances on the overwhelming power of the executive was seen as inherently subversive. The state system was presented as 'sacred' (*sakti*) and fixed, and any proposal for change was potentially treasonable. Despite this, judicial review was always a central component of the liberal democratic system persistently called for since 1945 by opponents of the authoritarian Integralistic state (described in Chapter 1) that prevailed

---

[1] TM Lubis, 'The *Rechsstaat* and Human Rights' in T Lindsey (ed), *Indonesia: Law and Society*, 1st edn (Annandale, NSW, Federation Press, 1999) 171–85.

for four decades.[2] When the New Order finally collapsed amid economic chaos in 1998, the creation of an independent judicial body that could ensure that laws passed by the national legislature did not threaten the new democratic political agreement embodied in the amended constitution was seen as a vital. The notion of judicial review had survived decades of repression to become a key part of the post-Soeharto *Reformasi* (Reformation) agenda.

In this chapter, we show that over the last decade the Constitutional Court has provided both Indonesia's first public forum for serious debate on the interpretation and application of the Constitution, and its first significant and easily accessible body of detailed, reasoned decisions. While it is certainly possible to criticise individual judgments of this court, it must be acknowledged that its judges, and, in particular, its first and second Chief Justices, have made great efforts both to create a new model of judicial decision-making and explain the workings of Indonesia's new liberal democratic system. This is essential if that system is to survive and develop. After briefly discussing the Constitutional Court's powers and composition, we consider how the Court has defined and exercised its jurisdiction in judicial review and electoral dispute cases.

In this chapter we also show that the very success of the Court in establishing itself as clean and fiercely independent, willing to assert its authority and even expand its powers to influence the making and application of laws, has brought it into direct conflict with the most powerful political entity in democratic Indonesia, the national legislature (*Dewan Perwakilan Raykat*, DPR). Tensions between legislatures and courts with the power of judicial review are common in democracies but they have escalated significantly in Indonesia in recent years. We therefore consider ways in which the Court has resisted attempts by the DPR to limit its jurisdiction, as well as cases where the Court appears to have, in fact, expanded its jurisdiction. We then discuss the DPR's legislative response to this judicial 'activism' – the 2011 Amendments to the 2003

---

[2] AB Nasution, *The Aspiration for Constitutional Government in Indonesia: A Socio-Legal Study of the Indonesian Konstituante, 1956–1959* (Jakarta, Pustaka Sinar Harapan, 1992); AB Nasution, 'Towards Constitutional Democracy in Indonesia', *Adnan Buyung Nasution Papers on Southeast Asia Constitutionalism* (Asian Law Centre, The University of Melbourne, 2011); TM Lubis, *In Search of Human Rights: Legal-Political Dilemmas of Indonesia's New Order, 1966–1990* (Jakarta, PT Gramedia Pustaka Utama in cooperation with SPES Foundation, 1993); Lubis, 'The *Rechsstaat* and Human Rights' (n 1 above).

Constitutional Court Law – before considering the Court's controversial invalidation of parts of that legislation in October 2011. The outcome of this battle for the final say in policy formation and implementation remains uncertain but it will be of central importance for the future of democracy in Indonesia.

POWERS OF THE CONSTITUTIONAL COURT

According to Article 24C(1) and 24C(2) of the 1945 Constitution as amended and Article 10 of Law 24 of 2003 on the Constitutional Court, the Court's main functions are to resolve disputes about the relative jurisdiction of state institutions, the dissolution of political parties and general election results. As discussed in Chapter 2, it must also 'provide a decision' if the DPR suspects that the president or vice-president has committed treason or corruption, another serious crime or form of misconduct, or otherwise no longer fulfils the constitutional requirements to hold office. And, of course, the Court can also engage in judicial review, as mentioned, that is, it can assess statutes to ensure that they are consistent with, and do not breach, the Constitution.

This constitutional review function is particularly important given the breadth and depth of Indonesia's recent constitutional reforms, which include the insertion of a Bill of Rights in Chapter XA of the Constitution, as discussed in Chapter 7 of this volume. The Constitutional Court is, in fact, the only Indonesian court since independence to have been granted jurisdiction to review the constitutionality of national statutes.[3] As discussed below and in Chapter 6, the Constitutional Court was quick to exhibit its independence and a strong willingness to actively exercise its judicial review powers with some rigour and transparency. It has, in fact, become a model for reform within a judicial system that, for around half a century, has generally been corrupt and incompetent.[4]

---

[3] Articles 130(2) and 156(1) of the federal Constitution of the United States of Indonesia (Republik Indonesia Serikat, RIS), which was in force for less than a year from 1949 to 1950, permitted judicial review of state, but not federal, statutes (P Lotulung, 'Judicial Review in Indonesia' in Y Zhang (ed), *Comparative Studies on the Judicial Review System in East and Southeast Asia* (The Hague, Kluwer Law International, 1997) 77).

[4] In 2010–11, several corruption allegations were made against Constitutional Court judges and officials. The Court responded to these swiftly and, as discussed below, they appear not to have seriously damaged the court's reputation of integrity.

THE CONSTITUTIONAL COURT'S COMPOSITION

The Constitutional Court consists of nine judges. The DPR, president and Supreme Court select and appoint three judges each,[5] presumably to ensure diversity on the bench and encourage judicial independence.[6] Constitutional Court judges can serve a maximum of two five-year terms.[7] They elect their own Chief and Deputy Chief Justices, who hold their positions for two years and six months.[8]

By law, Constitutional Court judges must have high levels of integrity; be of impeccable character; be fair and just; have a complete understanding of constitutional and administrative law; and refrain from holding government office.[9] Other prerequisites include Indonesian citizenship; having an undergraduate law degree, as well as a Masters and a doctoral degree; being between 47 and 65 years of age at the time of appointment; not having been convicted of a crime that carries a prison sentence of five years or more; never having been declared bankrupt; and having at least 15 years' experience working in the law or as a state official.[10] In addition, Article 27B(a) of the Constitutional Court Law requires that judges obey the law; attend court sessions; adhere to procedural law; comply with the Code of Ethics and Behaviour Guidelines for Constitutional Court Judges; treat parties justly, impartially and without discrimination; and hand down objective decisions based on the facts and the law. Article 27B(b) prohibits Constitutional Court judges from breaching their oaths, directly or indirectly receiving a thing or a promise from parties involved in a case before the Court, or issuing an opinion or statement outside court about a case the Court is handling before that case has been decided.

Under Article 23 of the Constitutional Court Law, Constitutional Court judges can be honourably discharged if they die, step down or turn 70; if their term of office expires; or if they are physically or men-

---

[5] Article 24C(3) of the Constitution; Articles 4(1) and 18(1) of the Constitutional Court Law.

[6] M Mietzner, 'Political Conflict Resolution and Democratic Consolidation in Indonesia: The Role of the Constitutional Court' (2010) 10(3) *Journal of East Asian Studies* 397, 404.

[7] Article 22 of the Constitutional Court Law.

[8] Article 4(3) of the Constitutional Court Law.

[9] Article 24C(5) of the Constitution; Article 15 of the Constitutional Court Law.

[10] Article 15 of the Constitutional Court Law.

tally ill for three consecutive months so they cannot continue to perform their functions.

Constitutional Court judges can be dismissed if they are convicted of a crime for which imprisonment is a punishment, act reprehensibly, fail to attend five consecutive Court sessions that they are required to attend, or breach their oath of office. They can also be dismissed if they deliberately impede the Court providing a decision within 90 days of a request by the national legislature to investigate whether the president or vice-president has committed treason, corruption, another serious crime or reprehensible act, or whether the president or vice-president no longer fulfils the requirements of office.[11] Dismissal can also take place if a Constitutional Court judge breaches prohibitions on holding other positions while also serving on the bench, no longer fulfils the requirements to be a Constitutional Court judge, or breaches the Constitutional Court's Code of Ethics and Behaviour Guidelines.[12]

Before being dismissed, judges must be given the opportunity to defend themselves before the Constitutional Court Honour Council (*Majelis Kehormatan Mahkamah Konstitusi*) (Article 23(3)). Dismissal is by a Presidential Decision issued at the request of the Chief Justice of the Constitutional Court (Article 23(4)). At the date of writing no Constitutional Court judges had been dismissed under these provisions, although in the face of unproven corruption allegations, one retired early to maintain the reputation of the Court, as discussed below.

JUDICIAL REVIEW

As mentioned, Article 24C(1) of the Constitution empowers the Constitutional Court to review statutes against the Constitution. Article 57(1) of the Constitutional Court Law states that if the Court declares that provisions of statutes breach the Constitution then those provisions 'have no binding legal force' (*tidak mempunyai kekuatan hukum mengikat*).

In this section we discuss the scope of the Court's judicial review jurisdiction, which both the Constitution and the legislature have sought

---

[11] Article 7A of the Constitution requires the Constitutional Court to provide such a decision if requested.

[12] Article 23(2) of the Constitutional Court Law.

to limit. In fact, the Constitution prohibits the Court from reviewing the constitutionality of most of Indonesia's laws and regulations, though as we will explain below when we discuss the Court's 'conditional constitutionality' cases, the Court has sometimes circumvented this restriction. The legislature also attempted to restrict the Constitutional Court to reviewing only statutes enacted after October 1999 but the Court has eliminated this limitation.

Despite the Court's resistance to external attempts to limit its jurisdiction, it has itself, on occasion, sought to limit the exercise and effect of its judicial review powers. It has, for example, refused to strike down statutes it has declared invalid where doing so would, in its view, be particularly undesirable, despite Article 57(1) apparently requiring it to do so. The Court has also generally sought to prevent itself from reviewing the implementation or effect of statutes, declared that it will not interfere with government policy, and given its decisions prospective effect only. Yet, as we shall see, in several cases the Court also appears to have avoided even these self-imposed limits. The result is significant uncertainty about exactly how far its powers extend and a good deal of tension between the Court, the government and the national legislature.

Judicial Review of Constitutionality of Statutes Only

Under Article 24C(1) of the Constitution, the Constitutional Court can only assess whether national statutes (*undang-undang*) – that is, laws enacted by the DPR – are consistent with the Constitution. It cannot review the constitutionality of other types of laws or actions of government.

This is a significant restriction because most Indonesian laws are in fact, so-called 'lower-level' laws, that is, laws below the level of statute. These include, for example, government regulations (*peraturan pemerintah*); presidential decisions (*keputusan presiden*), instructions (*instruksi presiden*) and regulations (*peraturan presiden*); ministerial regulations (*peraturan menteri*) and decisions (*keputusan menteri*); and laws enacted by local government legislatures and executives called *Perda* (*peraturan daerah*).[13] Only the Supreme Court has jurisdiction to review these laws, but it cannot do so against the Constitution. Rather, as discussed in Chapter 4, the

---

[13] For the formal hierarchy of these laws, see Article 7(1) of Law 10 of 2004 on Law-making, which is reproduced at p 88 of this volume.

Supreme Court has jurisdiction only to review lower-level laws to ensure their compliance with national statutes.[14] There is, therefore, no mechanism to judicially review the constitutionality of lower-level laws. This is highly problematic: the need for effective review of lower-level laws is arguably more acute than for statutes, because most of these regulations are issued without the transparent debates that often accompany a statute's passage in the national legislature.

Reviewing Statutes Enacted Before 19 October 1999

Article 50 of the Constitutional Court Law states that 'Statutes for which a review can be sought are statutes enacted after the amendment of the Constitution'. The Elucidation to Article 50 adds that 'After the amendment of the Constitution' means the First Amendment to the Constitution on 19 October 1999. The DPR clearly intended Article 50 and its Elucidation to prevent the Constitutional Court from reviewing statutes passed before 19 October 1999.

Soon after its establishment, however, the Court was asked to review legislation enacted well before 19 October 1999. In only its fourth case, the *Supreme Court Law case*,[15] the Court was asked to review Law 14 of 1985; in its sixth, the *Regional Land Affairs case*,[16] it was asked to review Law 22 of 1999; and in the *Kadin Law case*,[17] Law 1 of 1987. In all three cases, a 6:3 majority held that Article 50's attempts to limit the Court's review powers did not bind the Constitutional Court. Simply put, the majority's reasoning was as follows. The Constitution grants jurisdiction to the Constitutional Court to review statutes and does not prohibit the Court from reviewing statutes passed before the first amendment. Because the Constitution trumps statutes, Article 50 of the Constitutional Court Law cannot restrict the Court's jurisdiction provided under the Constitution.[18]

---

[14] Article 24A(1) of the Constitution; Article 11(2)(b) of the Judicial Power Law; Article 31(2) of the Law No 1 of 1985 on the Supreme Court.

[15] Constitutional Court Decision 004/PUU-I/2003, discussed further below.

[16] Constitutional Court Decision 009/PUU-I/2003.

[17] Constitutional Court Decision 066/PUU-II/2004.

[18] The Court invalidated Article 50 in the *Kadin Law case* (n 17 above) because the applicants asked it to. In the earlier *Supreme Court Law* (n 15 above) and *Regional Land Affairs cases* (n 16 above), the applicants did not seek review of Article 50, so the majority decided not to invalidate it, preferring to 'set it aside' (*mengesampingkan*) in order to hear the review.

The Court stated:

> It must be understood that the Constitutional Court is a state institution, the powers and jurisdiction of which are determined by the Constitution. The Court is not an organ of legislation, but rather is an organ of the Constitution. Therefore, the basis upon which the Constitutional Court carries out its constitutional tasks and exercises its constitutional jurisdiction is the Constitution. Every person and every institution must adhere to legislation and other laws, but only laws that do not conflict with the Constitution.[19]

Strictly speaking, the Court's invalidation of Article 50 of the Constitutional Court Law did not expand its jurisdiction; it simply thwarted legislative efforts to limit its constitutionally-delineated jurisdiction. Yet, for the Court to 'stand up' to the legislature so soon after its establishment by invalidating Article 50 indicated that the Court intended to actively exercise its judicial review powers.[20]

Invalidating Article 50 was also important to the broader development of a legal culture of human rights in Indonesia, something markedly absent under the New Order. Article 50 was an obstacle to Indonesia's Constitution – including its Bill of Rights – having any real meaning. If Article 50 had been allowed to stand, the new Bill of Rights would have been irrelevant to all but the statutes enacted after 19 October 1999. Article 50 would therefore have allowed the mass of pre-*Reformasi* statutes to remain in force, many of which had been passed during Soeharto's authoritarian rule. Yet it is often these older laws – rather than the laws enacted after the First Amendment, which were

---

[19] Constitutional Court Decision 066/PUU-II/2004, p 55.

[20] The Court's intent was also clear from the invalidation of the Electricity Law in its first case, discussed in Chapter 9 of this volume. The Article 50 cases drew the ire of members of the DPR. The then DPR Speaker, Agung Laksono, stated, for example, that the Court's Article 50 decisions had 'got the attention of the DPR', claiming that the decisions contradicted the Constitutional Court Law, and warning that they would 'have implications for relationships between state institutions' (*Hukumonline*, 'DPR Tanggapi Serius Implikasi Perluasan Kewenangan MK', 3 May 2005). Likewise, the then Justice and Human Rights Minister, Yusril Ihza Mahendra, criticised the Article 50 decisions, arguing, predictably, that the Court should simply have followed Article 50 of the Constitutional Court Law (*Hukumonline*, 'Mengupas "Itjihad" Kontroversial Mahkamah Konstitusi', 6 January 2004). Similar criticisms were made by prominent constitutional law scholar Dr Maria Farida Indrati (see BK Harman, 'Peranan Mahkamah Konstitusi dalam Mewujudkan Reformasi Hukum' in R Harun, ZAM Husein and Bisariyadi (eds), *Menjaga Denyut Konstitusi: Refleksi satu tahun Mahkamah Konstitusi* (Jakarta, Konstitusi Press, 2004) 231), who later became a judge of the Court.

passed by a democratically-elected DPR and President – that are most likely to encroach upon the new human rights of citizens. They are, therefore, more likely to be in need of review. Article 50 would have allowed statutes passed before Indonesia's Constitution was amended that breach human rights to continue breaching them until amended or revoked – a process that may have taken a long time, if indeed it took place at all.

Invalidation 'Too Undesirable'

In several early cases, the Court has declared a statute unconstitutional but, because the consequences of invalidating the statute would be too great, has refused to strike it down. It has preferred instead to ask the government to make further attempts at compliance or has imposed a deadline for legislative reform.

The series of cases in which the Court was asked to review the national state budget demonstrates this. Article 31(4) of the Constitution requires that the DPR allocate at least 20 per cent of the state budget to education. This provision reflects a general deterioration of the Indonesian education system in recent years and deep concern about the social damage this is causing, with claims of a 'lost generation' being created as result of falling educational standards. Article 31(4) has proved to be a controversial provision and successive governments have struggled to fulfil it. In cases filed annually from 2004, the Indonesian Teachers' Association, among others, asked the Court to invalidate state budgets that have failed to meet this target.[21] Because the budget is a statute passed by the DPR, the Court can assess it under its judicial review jurisdiction. Each year, the Court found that the budgets did not meet the 20 per cent target for education and were, therefore, unconstitutional. In each case, however, the Court declined to invalidate them, explaining that budgets are highly political and usually delicately balanced, and citing the likelihood of ensuing financial chaos.

In the *2005 Budget Law case*,[22] for example, a majority of Constitutional

[21] Constitutional Court Decision 011/PUU-III/2005; Constitutional Court Decision 026/PUU-III/2005; Constitutional Court Decision 026/PUU-IV/2006; Constitutional Court Decision 013/PUU-VI/2008.

[22] Constitutional Court Decision 012/PUU-III/2005, reviewing Law 36 of 2004 on the 2005 National Budget.

Court judges acknowledged that the government and the DPR had, in good faith, attempted to meet the allocation required by Article 31(4) by deciding to increase the budget allocation for education each year until the 20 per cent allocation was reached. The government had, also in good faith, decided to remove teachers' salaries and funds for in-house government training from inclusion in the allocation, because if included, the 20 per cent allocation would be close to being met already, leaving Article 31(4) with very little effect.[23] This good faith was not enough for the majority of the Court, however, which interpreted Article 31(4) strictly and declared the Budget Law unconstitutional.[24] Despite this, they declined to strike down the 2005 Budget. The judges explained that doing so would require the government to redraft the Budget and withdraw funds from other sectors, causing legal uncertainty and placing great strain on government time and finances. According to the majority, removing the statute would cause a *'governmental disaster* in state financial administration'.[25] Further, the Constitutional Court noted that if it were to declare the budget invalid, then Article 23(3) of the Constitution would force the government to revert to the previous year's Budget. This would, in fact, disadvantage the applicants, because the 2004 budget had allocated even less to education than the 2005 budget.[26]

Despite not invalidating budgets for failure to meet the Article 34(1) requirements, the Court appears, nevertheless, to have helped push the

---

[23] Constitutional Court Decision 012/PUU-III/2005, p 60.

[24] The *Education Law case* (Constitutional Court Decision 011/PUU-III/2005) was handed down on the same day as the *2005 Budget Law case* and raised very similar issues. In it, the applicants questioned the constitutionality of the Elucidation to Article 49(1) of the Education Law (Law 20 of 2003 on the National Education System). The text of Article 49(1) largely mirrored Article 31(4) of the Constitution. The Elucidation to Article 49(1) stated, however, that the 20 per cent allocation would be 'achieved in stages'. The applicants argued that the Constitution required the allocation to be made immediately and that the Elucidation to Article 49(1) could not, therefore, allow the allocation to be achieved incrementally. A majority of the Court agreed with this argument and struck down the Elucidation. After referring to several constitutional provisions on education and declaring that one of the government's prime responsibilities was to provide basic education, the majority decided that 'the implementation of constitutional provisions cannot be delayed. The Constitution has expressly stated that a minimum of 20 per cent of the budget must be prioritised . . . [and this] cannot be reduced by laws below it in the hierarchy' (p 101).

[25] Constitutional Court Decision 011/PUU-III/2005, p 62. (emphasis in the original)

[26] Constitutional Court Decision 011/PUU-III/2005, p 62.

government to reach this requirement, increasing the budget for education from year to year. In the *2006 Budget Law case*, the Court even began prohibiting the DPR from capping the maximum to be allocated to the education sector.[27] According to the Court, this allowed the government to divert any surplus funds from other sectors to education.[28] The DPR eventually allocated 20 per cent of the state budget to education from 2009, but only because teachers' salaries were included in it.[29]

In the *Anti-corruption Court case*,[30] the Court again decided that striking down an unconstitutional statute would lead to undesirable outcomes. In that case, the Court was asked to review the constitutionality of the Anti-corruption Court's establishment, under Article 53 of the Anti-Corruption Commission Law. The Court decided that Article 53 was unconstitutional because it established the Anti-corruption Court to hear the cases that the Anti-corruption Commission investigated and prosecuted, but left Indonesia's general courts to hear the cases the Commission chose not to pursue. There were, therefore, parallel judicial processes for corruption cases, and this had, in fact, led to very different decisions in similar cases depending on the court before which the cases were heard. For example, at the time, the Anti-corruption Court had a 100 per cent conviction rate in corruption cases, whereas the ordinary courts' rate was closer to 50 per cent.[31] According to the Constitutional Court, this created legal 'dualism' that breached the constitutional right to equality before the law.[32]

Despite this, the Constitutional Court did not invalidate the provisions establishing the Anti-corruption Court, admitting that it was making significant dents in corruption levels in Indonesia. Anticipating that the Anti-corruption Court would likely be shut down if the statute was invalidated with immediate effect, the Constitutional Court gave the DPR three years to enact a new, constitutionally-valid statute to provide a proper legal basis for the Anti-corruption Court.[33] The Constitutional

---

[27] Constitutional Court Decision 026/PUU-III/2005.

[28] Constitutional Court Decision 026/PUU-III/2005, p 86.

[29] AD Hapsari, 'Court Ruling Won't Affect Education Budget', *Jakarta Post*, 4 March 2010; Soedijarto, 'Some Notes on the Ideals and Goals of Indonesia's National Education System and the Inconsistency of its Implementation: A Comparative Analysis' (2009) 2 *Journal of Indonesian Social Sciences and Humanities* 1–11.

[30] Constitutional Court Decision 012-016-019/PUU-IV/2006.

[31] S Butt, *Corruption and Law in Indonesia* (London, Routledge, 2011).

[32] ibid.

[33] The DPR met this deadline, enacting Law 46 of 2009 on the Anti-corruption

Court explained that it was concerned to restrict the legal consequences arising from a declaration of unconstitutionality of a statute in the 'greater public interest', fearing that striking down Article 53 immediately would disrupt Anti-corruption Court trials and cause legal chaos.[34] It emphasised the disastrous effects corruption had brought upon the nation and wanted to allay concerns that it was weakening efforts to eradicate corruption:

> The Court views corruption, which has damaged the social and economic rights of the Indonesian community, as an 'extraordinary crime' and a 'common enemy of the community and nation as a whole'. Therefore, the human rights sought to be upheld through this review of the Anti-corruption Commission Law were small-scale in comparison to the protection of the economic and social rights of the majority of the community damaged by corruption. Corruption has weakened the ability of the state to provide adequate public services and has impeded the effective functioning of the state. This has become a heavy economic burden because it has created high macroeconomic risk that has endangered financial stability, public security, law and order. Moreover, it can undermine the legitimacy and credibility of the state in the eyes of the people.[35]

The Court's decisions in the *Anti-corruption Court case* and the *Budget Law cases* may well be pragmatic and directed towards protecting important and desirable ends. Both decisions are problematic, however, because in them the Court has not delineated the circumstances in which the effects of striking down a statute will be so dire as to justify its endorsement of an unconstitutional law, even for a limited time. Many of the other Constitutional Court cases discussed in this chapter and Chapter 7 have involved statutes that appeared geared towards protecting similarly critical interests, such as freedom of speech, yet the Court was willing to invalidate them.

We speculate that in recent decisions the Court has dealt with these types of cases by holding the impugned provisions 'conditionally constitutional' rather than leaving them in force. As discussed below, a finding of conditional constitutionality allows the Court to avoid striking

Court on 29 October 2009. See S Butt, 'Indonesia's anti-corruption drive and the Constitutional Court' (2009) 4(2) *The Journal of Comparative Law* 186–204; S Butt, 'Anti-corruption reform in Indonesia: an obituary?' (2011) 47(3) *Bulletin of Indonesian Economic Studies* 381–94.

[34] Constitutional Court Decision 012-016-019/PUU-IV/2006, p 288.
[35] Constitutional Court Decision 012-016-019/PUU-IV/2006, p 287.

down the statutory provision in question, thereby creating legal lacunae. Instead it attempts to remedy the constitutional defect 'on the spot', often by issuing what are effectively instructions to the government and the legislature.

Cannot Review Implementation or Effect of Statutes

In many decisions, the Court has declared that it is concerned only with the substance of a statute, not the way the statute is interpreted or applied in practice. For example, for a statute to be reviewable for breach of the freedom from retrospective prosecution under Article 28I(1), the statute would need to seek to permit itself to apply retrospectively, as did the Law in question in the *Bali Bombing case*, discussed in Chapter 7. In that case, the applicant challenged Law 16 of 2003. This was a very short statute that merely declared that Indonesia's Terrorism Law (Interim Emergency Law 2 of 2002) could be applied to investigate, prosecute and try the Bali Bombers. This Interim Emergency Law was enacted after the bombings took place. Law 16 was reviewable because its substance sought to allow the retrospective operation of a law that would allow a prosecution for terrorism to take place.

If, however, a law enforcement institution charged an individual with an offence under a statute that did not exist at the time the alleged criminal act was committed, the Court would likely refuse to review the constitutionality of the application of that statute. The statute would not be reviewable for breach of the retrospectivity freedom unless a provision in the statute – part of the 'substance' of the statute – purported to authorise the statute to operate retrospectively.

The *Manoppo case* provides an illustrative example of the distinction between 'substance' and 'application'.[36] In this case, Bram Manoppo challenged Article 68 of the Anti-corruption Commission Law,[37] claiming that it had retrospective application. This provision allowed the Anti-corruption Commission to take over corruption investigations and prosecutions in particular circumstances. Manoppo complained that the Anti-corruption Commission had used the provision to investigate him for a crime allegedly committed before Article 68 itself was enacted,

---

[36] Constitutional Court Decision 069/PUU-II/2004.
[37] Law 30 of 2002.

thereby breaching the Constitution's retrospectivity prohibition. The Court held that, as a matter of fact, Article 68 had not been applied against the applicant but noted that even if the Anti-corruption Commission's investigation

> could be construed as a retroactive act, this would not have been a matter relating to the constitutionality of the Law, but rather a matter relating to the application of the statute, which does not fall within the jurisdiction of the Constitutional Court.[38]

Similarly, in the *Wijaya and Lubis case*,[39] the Constitutional Court was asked to consider whether certain Criminal Code (*Kitab Undang-Undang Hukum Pidana*) defamation provisions breached constitutional rights, including freedom of speech. As discussed in Chapter 7, the Court ultimately turned down the application. In response to applicants' submissions that the defamation provisions were misused in practice to stifle legitimate criticism and debate, the Court declared that it lacked power to assess the constitutionality of the application of statutes. Indeed, the Court noted that if it had jurisdiction to invalidate Criminal Code provisions for misapplication, then it might have already invalidated much of the Code, because law enforcers regularly misused it in ways that prevented citizens pursuing their democratic rights.[40]

The *KPK Commissioners case*,[41] however, directly contradicts the Court's previous jurisprudence prohibiting itself from reviewing the implementation or effect of statutes. In that case, several anti-corruption reformists and Indonesia Corruption Watch (one of Indonesia's leading anti-corruption NGOs) sought a review of Article 34 of the 2002 Anti-corruption Commission Law. Article 34 states that Anti-corruption Commission commissioners hold office for four years and can serve for a maximum of two terms. Busyro Muqoddas, former academic and Chairperson of the Judicial Commission, had been selected to replace Anti-corruption Commission Chairperson, Antasari Azhar (who was dismissed following his conviction for ordering the assassination of businessman Nasruddin Zulkarnaen).[42] The DPR and President had

---

[38] Constitutional Court Decision 069/PUU-II/2004, pp 73–74.
[39] Constitutional Court Decision 14/PUU-VI/2008.
[40] Constitutional Court Decision 14/PUU-VI/2008, pp 279–80.
[41] Constitutional Court Decision 5/PUU-IX/2011.
[42] See Butt, *Corruption and Law in Indonesia'*, n 31, above, for a detailed discussion of this case.

sought to limit Muqoddas to serving out Azhar's term.[43] The applicants argued that, under Article 34, Muqoddas should serve a full four-year term. According to the Court, the DPR and President's interpretation of Article 34 caused legal uncertainty, principally because it contradicted the apparently clear words of Article 34. The Court also found that Article 34 was discriminatory because, despite undergoing similarly rigorous, time-consuming and costly selection processes, replacement commissioners received shorter terms than other commissioners.

For present purposes, the primary significance of the *KPK Commissioners* decision is that the Court decided to evaluate the constitutionality of the way the DPR and President had interpreted Article 34, rather than the substance of Article 34 itself.

> [T]he DPR and the President can interpret a statute to implement that statute. However, the Court has jurisdiction to review the constitutionality of the interpretation of a statutory norm implemented by the DPR or the President, if that interpretation threatens the respect, protection and fulfilment of the constitutional rights of citizens, in the context of guaranteeing the implementation of the mandate and norms of the Constitution. By so doing the Court does not exceed its jurisdiction to review statutory norms as against the Constitution ... Article 1(2) of the Constitution – which declares that 'Sovereignty is in the hands of the people and is implemented in accordance with the Constitution' – requires that the administration of the state by the organs of the state must be based on the Constitution. It is on this basis that Indonesia is a state adhering to constitutional government ... If the Court discovers the implementation of a statutory norm that breaches, diverges from or is inconsistent with the norms and spirit of the Constitution, then by virtue of its function, tasks and jurisdiction to uphold the constitution, the Court has jurisdiction to review the constitutionality of the interpretation of a statutory norm.[44]

Although the *KPK Commissioners case* seems to make it clear that the Court can now consider the constitutionality of the implementation of statutes in addition to the substance of statutes, the Court did not declare explicitly whether its decision overturned its own jurisprudence,

[43] DPR Decision 01/DPR RI/II/2010-2011 on the Agreement of the DPR upon the Candidate to Replace the KPK Commissioner with Dr Muhammad Busyro Muqoddas to Continue the Term as KPK Commissioner for 2007–2011, Ending on December 2011; Presidential Decision 129/P of 2010 on the Appointment of Muhammad Busyro Muqoddas as Replacement KPK Commissioner and Chairperson.
[44] Constitutional Court Decision 5/PUU-IX/2011, pp 70–71.

or whether this was merely an exceptional case. The circumstances in which it will, in future cases, choose to evaluate the interpretation of statutes thus remain very unclear.

Government Policy Unreviewable

The Constitutional Court has repeatedly declared that it lacks jurisdiction to assess government policy. In the Court's view, its task is to determine the 'corridor of constitutionality' within which government can legitimately operate. This issue is discussed only briefly here, and is canvassed in more detail in Chapter 9, which deals with the Court's interpretation of Article 33 of the Constitution in cases involving socio-economic rights.

In the *KPK Law case*, the Court gave perhaps its most detailed discussion of the limits of its judicial review function vis-à-vis government policy. In this case, the Law under review established the Anti-corruption Commission.[45] One of the Law's purposes was to subsume a pre-existing Commission – the Public Official Asset Investigation Commission (the *Komisi Pemeriksa Kekayaan Penyelenggara Negara*, or KPKPN) – into the Anti-corruption Commission's structure. Some of the applicants were KPKPN employees who objected to this on a number of grounds. These included that the KPKPN had been effective and that merging it with the Anti-corruption Commission might undermine corruption eradication efforts.

A majority of the Court refused to strike down the Law, deciding that, although the Constitution intended that corruption be eradicated,[46] the government had discretion to choose the means to achieve this end. According to the majority, the Constitutional Court should, therefore, not evaluate the means the legislature chooses to achieve that end, nor the effectiveness of those means.

---

[45]   Law 30 of 2002 on the KPK.

[46]   From our reading, the majority did not attempt to substantiate its declarations that the Constitution sought to eradicate corruption. It emphasised anti-corruption legislative reform in the post-Soeharto era but did not point to constitutional provisions. On this point, minority judges were perhaps more convincing, attempting to connect anti-corruption efforts to the Constitution through the Preamble. According to Justice Siahaan: 'The people's aspirations . . . for protection for the nation and for social justice for all Indonesians, as is promised in the Preamble to the Constitution, demand the eradication of corruption and a state administration free of corruption, collusion and nepotism': Constitutional Court Decision 006/PUU-I/2003, p 117.

[I]f the Constitution has underlined that the statute must contain the means to achieve a purpose, that is, it chooses an instrumental policy, lawmakers (the DPR and the President) can choose between a number of alternatives. Whichever alternative the lawmakers choose will be valid, provided that it remains within the *corridor* stipulated by the Constitution. The Constitutional Court does not have jurisdiction to review the instrumental policy chosen by lawmakers.

... In a democratic country in which the people are represented through elections, it is presumed that the people's will is represented by people's representative institutions. Upon this premise, one can syllogistically ... conclude that the people's aspirations are represented by elected people's representative institutions.

Instrumental policy also relates to the *effectiveness* of a statute; that is, the extent to which the means chosen by lawmakers has successfully achieved the purposes mandated by the Constitution. The Constitutional Court's jurisdiction does not extend to evaluating a statute's effectiveness. This does not mean that a statute's effectiveness cannot be reviewed [at all]. It can be reviewed at any time by lawmakers through *legislative review*.[47]

The majority proceeded to apply these principles. The applicants had argued that the Law was inadequate because it regulated only the prevention of corruption, not its eradication. The Court rejected this argument as a matter of fact, accepting that the Law contained 'both preventative and repressive measures to eradicate corruption'.[48] The majority also indicated, however, that, even if the Law was inadequate, the Court did not have jurisdiction to declare it invalid.[49]

As for subsuming the Public Official Asset Investigation Commission within the Anti-corruption Commission, the Constitutional Court stated that this

indicates that lawmakers had made a policy decision ... to establish the Anti-corruption Commission and make the Public Official Asset Investigation

[47] Constitutional Court Decision 006/PUU-I/2003, p 95. Emphasis in the original.
[48] Constitutional Court Decision 006/PUU-I/2003, p 100.
[49] 'The original intent of the Constitution was ... to eradicate corruption, and the means to achieve that intent was an *instrumental policy* about which lawmakers have power to choose from a number of available alternatives. The contrast between the Anti-corruption Commission's repressive and preventative functions as contained in the Law represents a choice of *instrumental policy*, chosen by the DPR and President from a variety of alternatives, as the best way to eradicate corruption ... The Constitutional Court cannot declare a statute to conflict with the Constitution merely because the statute does not effectively fulfil its Constitutional mandate': Constitutional Court Decision 006/PUU-I/2003, pp 100–01. Emphasis in the original.

Commission a part of the Anti-corruption Commission. [Legislators have the power to] . . . choose this alternative. The Constitutional Court decides that [this] choice . . . does not conflict with the provisions and spirit of the Constitution.[50]

On the other hand, the majority noted that the Court could review and invalidate statutes that did not comply with detailed and specific constitutional provisions but instead take 'a different or contrary direction . . . against the Constitution's provisions and spirit'.[51]

Invalidations Operate Prospectively

Article 58 of the Constitutional Court Law states:

> Statutes reviewed by the Constitutional Court remain in force until there is a decision declaring that the statute conflicts with the Constitution.

The Constitutional Court's preferred interpretation of Article 58 is that unconstitutional statutes are invalid only from the moment the Court reads out its decision invalidating them in open court. Anything done under the statute before the Constitutional Court invalidated the statute remains legal and does not need be to 'undone'. In other words, Constitutional Court decisions operate only into the future.[52]

The Court has applied Article 58 to this effect in several cases. In the *Electricity Law case*,[53] discussed in detail in Chapter 9, the Court invalidated the entire Electricity Law[54] on the basis that it breached Article 33

---

[50] Constitutional Court Decision 006/PUU-I/2003, p 102.

[51] 'When performing material review, the Constitutional Court must differentiate between [types of] legislation . . . If the Constitution's provisions and spirit [require] a statute to contain detail to achieve a particular aim, but the statute takes a different or contrary direction, then the statute will go against the Constitution's provisions and spirit. The Constitutional Court then has jurisdiction to declare that statute to conflict with the Constitution and to declare that the statute has no binding legal force': Constitutional Court Decision 006/PUU-I/2003, pp 94–95.

[52] On our reading, however, Article 58 could, alternatively, be interpreted to mean merely that while the Constitutional Court is reviewing a statute, that statute is presumed legal and remains in force. Once the Court decides that the statute is unconstitutional it is considered invalid from the moment it was enacted (S Butt and T Lindsey, 'Indonesian Judiciary in Crisis (parts 1 and 2)', *Jakarta Post*, 6–7 August 2004).

[53] Constitutional Court Decision 001-021-022/ PUU-I/2003.

[54] Law 20 of 2002 on Electricity.

of the Constitution. However, the Court held that contracts made under the statute remained valid because they were made under the statute when it was still in force:

> It must be stressed that, in accordance with Article 58 of the Constitutional Court Law, Constitutional Court decisions have legal effect after they are read out and are prospective in operation – they do not have retrospective operation. Therefore, all contracts or permits relating to the electricity industry that were signed and issued under the Electricity Law remain in force until the contract or permit becomes invalid or expires.[55]

In the *Bali Bombing case*, the applicant, Masykur Abdul Kadir, had been sentenced to 15 years' imprisonment for assisting the Bali bombers in their murderous attack on Kuta nightclubs on 12 October 2002. The Court found that the applicant, who lived in Bali, helped some of the bombers from Java to find rental accommodation and drove them around Bali to survey possible targets ahead of the attack. It was alleged also that he met up with some of the bombers after the blasts.[56] As discussed above and in Chapter 7, the Constitutional Court decided by a bare majority that one of the statutes under which the Bali bombers were investigated and ultimately convicted was unconstitutional because it was enacted after the bombings took place. The decision could not, however, be used to undo actions taken under a Law that the Constitutional Court held was unconstitutional. In other words, the Bali bombers did not need to be set free or retried, as their conviction under the Law took place before the Constitutional Court had invalidated it.

The *Death Penalty case*,[57] discussed in Chapter 7, was brought by several inmates of Indonesia's 'death row', including three Australian members of the so-called 'Bali Nine' gang who had been convicted and sentenced to death for attempting to smuggle heroin out of Indonesia. They asked the Court to consider whether imposing the death penalty in narcotics cases contradicted the right to life granted by Articles 28A and 28I(1) of the Constitution. In the *Firing Squad case*,[58] three of the Bali bombers asked the Court to assess whether the way the death penalty is

[55] Constitutional Court Decision 001-021-022/PUU-I/2003, p 350.

[56] S Butt and D Hansell, 'The Masykur Abdul Kadir Case: Indonesian Constitutional Court Decision No 013/PUU-I/2003' (2004) 6(2) *Australian Journal of Asian Law* 176, 198.

[57] Constitutional Court Decision 2-3/PUU-V/2007.

[58] Constitutional Court Decision 21/PUU-VI/2008, reviewing law 2/PNPS/1964 on the Method of Carrying Out the Death Penalty.

carried out in Indonesia – by firing squad – was a cruel and inhumane punishment, prohibited by the Constitution in Articles 28G(2) and 28I(1). The Court turned down both applications but even if the Court had declared the death penalty unconstitutional, the executions would probably have proceeded because the death penalties in each case had been imposed under the Law before the Court could invalidate it. If the Bali bombers had succeeded in the *Firing Squad* case, however, they may have been able to avoid death by firing squad because the Law under which they were to be executed had not yet been applied to them, that is, they had not yet been executed. They could, presumably, have still been executed by other means, as the firing squad case dealt only with the means of execution and not the validity of the death penalty itself.

Finally, in the *Mahendra case*,[59] the Constitutional Court decided that the Attorney General had held office unconstitutionally for several months for reasons discussed later in this chapter. The Court made it clear, however, that its decision would operate only into the future. That is, although the Court required the Attorney General to vacate his position, it declared that acts that he had performed while holding office unconstitutionally, but before the Court's decision, were not thereby rendered invalid or otherwise legally flawed. Instead, the Constitutional Court simply ordered him to step down, effective from the moment the Constitutional Court finished reading its decision in open court.[60]

The Court's insistence that its decisions operate prospectively is not unique. A number of the world's constitutional courts issue only pro- spective decisions (*ex nunc*) or can decide whether their decisions should apply *ex nunc* or *ex tunc* (retroactively), depending on the circumstances.[61] This stance is by no means unjustifiable, given that avoiding the need to 'undo' acts performed under laws later declared unconstitutional pro-

---

[59]   Constitutional Court Decision 49/PUU-VIII/2010.

[60]   *Hukumonline*, 'Hendarman Supandji Harus Berhenti', 22 September 2010; *Hukumonline*, 'MK: Masa Jabatan Jaksa Agung Konstitusional Bersyarat', 22 September 2010; 'Old Hand at the Helm', *Tempo*, 7 December 2010.

[61]   M Patrono, 'The Protection of Fundamental Rights by Constitutional Courts – A Comparative Perspective' (2000) 2 *Victoria University of Wellington Law Review* 24; M Hartwig, 'The Institutionalization of the Rule of Law: The Establishment of Constitutional Courts in the Eastern European Countries' (1991–92) 7 *American University Journal of International Law and Policy* 449, 467; G Harutyunyan and A Mavcic, *Constitutional Review and its Development in the Modern World (a Comparative Constitutional Analysis)* (1999) [online text], Armenian Constitutional Court, www. concourt.am/Books/harutunyan/monogr3/book.htm.

motes legal certainty.[62] It also tends to soften the political impact of constitutional court decisions, making them more politically palatable to government, particularly the legislature. This is an important consideration given that the Indonesian Constitutional Court has, as discussed below, virtually no enforcement powers at its disposal.

Yet by taking this position the Constitutional Court has significantly undermined its own authority and credibility as 'guardian of the Constitution', because it has allowed unconstitutional statutes to be applied. What would prevent the DPR from enacting a blatantly unconstitutional law to achieve a particular purpose in the short-term, for example, a statute that allowed the state to torture particular dissidents, contradicting the Constitution's right to be free from 'inhumane torture' under Article 28G(2)? The statute would apply – and the dissidents could legally be tortured – until the Court declared it invalid.

Furthermore, by taking this approach, the Constitutional Court appears to be creating strong disincentives for applicants to lodge applications with the Court. Applicants get no benefit from judicial decisions that operate only prospectively.[63] As we have argued elsewhere:

> If Constitutional Court decisions in constitutional review cases . . . only apply prospectively, then the absurd situation is created whereby no litigant – no matter how deserving and badly treated – could ever receive the benefit of a win in the Court. What would be the point of a litigant aggrieved by an apparently unconstitutional law going to the effort and expense of challenging the legality of that law knowing that the decision will not actually benefit him or her in any way? This is a particularly tragic outcome if the litigant is wrongfully facing long imprisonment or, worse still, the death penalty . . . the unconstitutional law would apply until the Court could hear the case, during which time the law could do significant damage.[64]

There is perhaps no clearer example of this problem than the *Lèse Majesté case*,[65] discussed in Chapter 7. In that case, the Constitutional Court considered the constitutionality of Criminal Code provisions that

[62] O Pollicino, 'Legal Reasoning of the Court of Justice in the Context of Principle of Equality between Judicial Activism and Self-Restraint' (2004) 5(3) *German Law Journal* 283, 304.

[63] T Koopmans, 'Retrospectivity Reconsidered' (1980) 39(2) *Cambridge Law Journal* 287, 299.

[64] S Butt and T Lindsey, 'Indonesian Judiciary in Crisis (parts 1 and 2)', *Jakarta Post*, 6–7 August 2004.

[65] Constitutional Court Decision 013-022/PUU-IV/2006.

prohibited insulting the president or vice-president. When the Court began hearing the case, the trial of one of the applicants, Sudjana, had already commenced in the Central Jakarta District Court.[66] It was adjourned pending the outcome of the Constitutional Court case. The challenge was successful and the Court invalidated the Criminal Code provisions under which Sudjana was being prosecuted. When his trial resumed after the Constitutional Court's decision was handed down, however, the Central Jakarta District Court held that the defendant had insulted the president and vice-president before the provisions were invalidated. It therefore convicted him and imposed a suspended three-month sentence.[67]

Exceptions?

In the *Sisa Suara case*,[68] the Court noted that Article 58 required it to give prospective operation to its decisions. It decided, however, that an exception was justified in this case. In the words of the Court:

> [T]he Constitutional Court Law does not provide an exception to the general principle of the non-retroactivity doctrine, and does not provide for judicial discretion to determine [whether a decision must apply retrospectively]. However [exceptions and discretion] are required in particular circumstances, [such as] to achieve the purposes of the statute under review.

Noting that the decisions of other courts – including the administrative, criminal and civil courts – generally have retrospective application,[69] the Court declared that: 'A decision that is not applied retrospectively can, in some circumstances, lead to the non-fulfillment of protections provided by legal mechanisms'.[70] In particular:

> [t]he Court's decisions in election cases, including disputes over counting and the allocation of parliamentary seats, must be able to be applied to the very voting and allocations disputes [complained of]. If not, then the pur-

---

[66]   Constitutional Court Decision 012-022/PUU-IV/2006, p 52.

[67]   N Royan, 'Increasing Press Freedom in Indonesia: The Abolition of the Lese Majeste and "Hate-sowing" Provisions' (2008) 10(2) *Australian Journal of Asian Law* 90.

[68]   Constitutional Court Decision 110-111-112-113/PUU-VII/2009.

[69]   As the Court put it: 'The decisions of these courts apply from the moment of the "illegal" act, not from the time the decision is announced in open court' (Constitutional Court Decision 110-111-112-113/PUU-VII/2009, p 106).

[70]   Constitutional Court Decision 110-111-112-113/PUU-VII/2009, pp 106–07.

pose of the constitutional protections provided by electoral disputes and judicial review . . . will not be fulfilled as the constitution intends.[71]

The Court explained that it had exercised discretion in past cases to issue types of decisions for which the Constitutional Court Law did not explicitly provide. For example, the Court noted, it had declared statutes 'conditionally constitutional', 'conditionally unconstitutional', or applicable for a stipulated time. It reasoned that it could therefore give its decisions retrospective effect despite Article 58's apparent prohibition against doing so. After all, the Court noted, constitutional courts of other countries could give their decisions retrospective effect. The Court continued:

> For decisions that provide an interpretation on the constitutionality of a norm (interpretative decisions), it would be natural for them to be retrospective from the time the law under interpretation was enacted . . . therefore, even though the Constitutional Court Law stipulates that the Constitutional Court's decisions operate prospectively, for this case, because of its special characteristics, it must be given retrospective operation for the allocation of DPR, provincial DPRD and city DPRD seats from the 2009 elections, without compensation for the consequences of previous laws.[72]

The Court's justification was unconvincing, however. It did not seek to explain why this decision and not others that also involved particularly important issues – such as the execution of an applicant – could apply retrospectively. This gives an air of arbitrariness to the *Sisa Suara case*.

Despite this, the Court followed the *Sisa Suara case* in the *KPK Commissioners case*.[73] In this case the Constitutional Court, as mentioned, considered the constitutionality of the way the DPR and President had interpreted Article 34 of the Anti-corruption Commission Law. At stake was the term of office as Anti-corruption Commission Chairperson of Busyro Muqoddas, a well-regarded reformer. The President had appointed him to replace Antasari Azhar for one year – the remainder of what would have been Azhar's term. Pointing to Article 34, which provides that commissioners serve four-year terms, the applicants sought a declaration from the Court that Muqoddas should serve a four-year term rather than a one-year term.

---

[71] Constitutional Court Decision 110-111-112-113/PUU-VII/2009, p 107.

[72] Constitutional Court Decision 110-111-112-113/PUU-VII/2009, p 108. See S Butt 'Indonesia's Constitutional Court – the conservative activist or pragmatic strategist?' in Dressel, B (ed) *Judicialisation of Politics in Asia* (Routledge, 2012).

[73] Constitutional Court Decision 5/PUU-IX/2011.

The Court accepted the application, for reasons outlined above, and held that Article 34 was conditionally unconstitutional unless interpreted to apply to both commissioners appointed during general selection rounds and commissioners appointed to replace a commissioner mid-term. The problem was, however, that the Court's decision would not apply to allow Muqoddas to serve a full term unless given retrospective effect – Article 34 had already been applied to him (albeit erroneously, in the eyes of the Court). The Court therefore decided that its decision could operate prospectively:

> Even though according to Article 47 of the Constitutional Court Law, Constitutional Court decisions operate prospectively, in the interests of utility (a universal legal norm and objective) the Court can give its decisions retrospective effect in certain cases. This became jurisprudence in [the *Sisa Suara* decision] . . . The reasons for declaring that a particular decision operates retrospectively include that the law had been, and is continuing to be, erroneously interpreted, leading to legal uncertainty and constitutional damage that must cease. To [do this, the decision] must operate retrospectively from the time the erroneous interpretation was stipulated – the moment when the legal uncertainty and constitutional damage began . . . Therefore, to avoid legal uncertainty in the transition period as a result of this decision, this decision applies to commissioner replacements who have already been chosen.[74]

The circumstances in which the Court will give its decisions retrospective effect therefore remain unclear. As mentioned in the above extract, the Court cited as reasons for doing so the 'interests of utility' and, in particular, the danger of erroneous interpretation of the law leading to constitutional damage. However, the Court did not specify what type of erroneous interpretation leading to constitutional damage would allow the Court to apply its decision retrospectively. How much constitutional damage was required? Would enough damage to give an applicant standing be sufficient? And in what form must the erroneous interpretation be? Need it be a law, or could it be government action? It is hard to understand how preventing the unconstitutional prosecution and killing of a prisoner cannot be seen to satisfy the 'interests of utility' test, while extension of an official's term of appointment can.

---

[74] Constitutional Court Decision 5/PUU-IX/2011, p 76.

Enforcement of Constitutional Court Decisions in Judicial Review Cases

The Constitution, the Constitutional Court Law and Constitutional Court Regulations provide no mechanisms by which the Court can enforce its decisions or impose sanctions for breaches of Constitutional Court decisions. Yet, for the most part, its decisions have been respected,[75] albeit sometimes reluctantly, by DPR members and politicians. There have, however, been exceptions.

Of course, enforcement difficulties are not limited to the Constitutional Court. The problem of enforcement of judicial decisions is acute in all Indonesian courts.[76] It is also commonly experienced by constitutional courts in other countries.[77] The Constitutional Court of Indonesia is, however, particularly vulnerable in this regard. A prime example was the government's response to the *Electricity Law case*,[78] the Constitutional Court's first case. In it, a unanimous bench invalidated the entire Electricity Law that the DPR had enacted in the previous year.[79] As discussed in Chapter 9, the Court found that the Law's attempts to allow private sector control over various aspects of electricity production and distribution breached the state's obligation under Article 33 of the Constitution to control 'important branches of production'.

The Constitutional Court's decision in the *Electricity Law case* put the Indonesian government in a difficult position. The decision significantly impeded Indonesia's compliance with the conditions of International Monetary Fund (IMF) bailouts in the aftermath of the 1997 Economic

---

[75] For example, Preamble section (c) of Law 12 of 2008 – the second amendment to Law 32 of 2004 on Regional Government – refers to the need to respond to the Constitutional Court's decision on independent candidates (Constitutional Court Decision 5/PUU-V/2007). See Chapter 3 of this volume for further discussion.

[76] S Butt, 'Surat sakti: The Decline of the Authority of Judicial Decisions in Indonesia' in T Lindsey (ed), *Indonesia: Law and Society*, 2nd edn (Annandale, NSW, Federation Press, 2008).

[77] V Autheman, 'Global Lessons Learned: Constitutional Courts, Judicial Independence and the Rule of Law', *IFES Rule of Law White Paper Series* (International Foundation of Electoral Systems (IFES), 2004) 1.

[78] Constitutional Court Decision 001-021-022/ PUU-I/2003. See generally, S Butt and T Lindsey, 'Economic Reform when the Constitution Matters: Indonesia's Constitutional Court and Article 33' (2008) 44(2) *Bulletin of Indonesia Economic Studies* 239–62.

[79] Law 20 of 2002 on Electricity.

Crisis. It also thwarted government efforts to make electricity supply more reliable and to extend it to more parts of Indonesia by inviting private sector involvement and competition with the State Electricity Company (PLN). To this end, the government was about to host a major summit promoting private investment in infrastructure projects, including power projects valued at US $6 billion, or 25 per cent of Indonesia's power infrastructure needs.[80]

Within two months of the Constitutional Court's decision, the central government had issued Government Regulation 3 of 2005 on the Provision and Exploitation of Electricity.[81] The Regulation appeared intended to reinstate the main thrust of the Electricity Law and, indeed, has been described as the re-enactment of the Electricity Law 'in new clothes'.[82] Yet although this regulation probably also breaches Article 33, the Constitutional Court has no jurisdiction to review government regulations and other types of lower-level laws, as discussed earlier in this chapter. The government, therefore, successfully circumvented the Constitutional Court's decision – in fact, it subverted it.[83]

The government appeared to adopt a similar strategy to pre-empt an unfavourable decision in the *Water Law case*.[84] Like the Electricity Law, the Water Resources Law[85] sought to allow private sector involvement in the provision of drinking water (though it arguably relinquished less government control over the sector than had the Electricity Law). While the Constitutional Court was hearing this case (but before it had handed down its decision), Government Regulation 16 of 2005 on the Development of a Drinking Water Availability System was issued.[86] This

---

[80] Price Waterhouse Coopers, 'Summary of Electricity Law no 15/1985 and Government Regulation no 3 /2005' (Available at: www.pwcglobal.com/Extweb/ pwcpublications.nsf).

[81] Amending Government Regulation 10 of 1989.

[82] *Hukumonline*, 'PP Listrik Swasta Diajukan Uji Materiil', 17 July 2005.

[83] We note, however, that a new Electricity Law was enacted in 2009 (Law 30 of 2009). Again, it was subject to constitutional challenge but the Court held that the 2009 Law complied with Article 33 (Constitutional Court Decision 149/PUU-VII/2009). It did allow for private sector involvement and competition but did not relinquish enough state control to breach Article 33 of the Constitution. See further, Butt and Lindsey, 'Economic Reform when the Constitution Matters . . .' n 78, above.

[84] Constitutional Court Decisions 058-059-060-063/PUU-II/2004 and 008/ PUU-III/2005.

[85] Law 7 of 2004 on Water Resources.

[86] *Walhi*, 'Pemerintah harus ubah PP Air Minum yang Mendorong Privatisasi' (updated 20 October 2005) www.walhi.or.id/kampanye/air/privatisasi/kamp_

Regulation appears to achieve part of what the Water Law aims to do –
to allow for private sector involvement in the provision of drinking
water. As discussed in Chapter 9, the Constitutional Court ultimately did
not invalidate provisions of the Water Law but we think it reasonable to
speculate that, given the timing of the Regulation, it was intended as
'insurance' against the invalidation of some or all of the Water Law.

DISPUTED RETURNS AND ELECTION-RELATED JURISDICTION

Participants in DPR, presidential, regional head and Regional
Representative Council elections can bring challenges before the
Constitutional Court in respect of official vote counts announced by
the National Electoral Commission.[87] To claim, applicants must be able
to clearly describe the mistake the Commission has made, and establish
what they believe should be the correct result.[88]

The Court heard over 900 objections to the 2004 and 2009 national
general election results, upholding around 100 of them and reallocating
seats where required.[89] The Court has also heard challenges to presidential election results brought by a number of candidates, including former Commander-in-Chief of the Indonesian Army Wiranto (who ran
for President in 2004 and Vice-President in 2009) and former President
Megawati Soekarnoputri and her Vice-Presidential candidate, former
Commander of Army Special Forces Prabowo Subianto (who ran in
2009). The Court rejected both applications.[90]

tolak_priv_air_info/; *Walhi*, 'PP Air Minum Muluskan Privatisasi' (updated 15 July
2005) www.walhi.or.id/kampanye/air/privatisasi/kamp_tolak_priv_air_info/.

[87] Article 74 of the Constitutional Court Law.
[88] Article 75 of the Constitutional Court Law.
[89] See S Harijanti and T Lindsey, 'Indonesia: General elections test the amended
Constitution and the new Constitutional Court' (2006) 4(1) *International Journal of
Constitutional Law* 138, 148; M Mahfud, 'The Role of the Constitutional Court in the
Development of Democracy in Indonesia' (Cape Town, South Africa, 2009) 27–29;
J Asshiddiqie, *The Constitutional Law of Indonesia: A Comprehensive Overview* (Selangor,
Malaysia, Sweet and Maxwell Asia, 2009) 11; R Sukma, 'Indonesian Politics in 2009:
Defective Elections, Resilient Democracy' (2009) 45(3) *Bulletin of Indonesian Economic
Studies* 317, 322; M Mietzner, 'Political Conflict Resolution and Democratic
Consolidation in Indonesia: The Role of the Constitutional Court' (2010) 10(3)
Journal of East Asian Studies 397, 407.
[90] Mietzner, ibid, 407; Harijanti and Lindsey, ibid, 140.

The Court's election-related judicial review cases have also been important. In these the Court has been asked to determine the constitutionality of Indonesia's electoral system and its candidacy restrictions. These are discussed in Chapter 3.[91]

EXPANDING ITS OWN JURISDICTION

This section focuses on two categories of Constitutional Court decisions in which the Court seems to be expanding its jurisdiction beyond even the boundaries it has set for itself. The first category covers cases in which the Court has been asked to determine whether statutes comply with the constitutional right to 'legal certainty'. The Court has, in these cases, acted beyond its power. It has exercised jurisdiction that should, we argue, be exercised by the Supreme Court and the courts below it. The second category includes cases in which the Court has declared statutory provisions to be 'conditionally constitutional' – that is, constitutional provided that they are *interpreted* in a particular way.

In subsequent chapters of this book, we discuss other categories of cases that are also examples of the Court operating beyond its jurisdiction. These include the cases in which the Court has appeared to 'discover' or 'imply' rights that are not explicitly mentioned in the Constitution (see Chapter 7). They also include cases in which the Court appears to have reviewed government policy, despite its clear declarations, described above, that it cannot do so (see Chapter 9).

Right to Legal Certainty

Article 28D(1) of the Constitution states that:

> Every person has the right to legal recognition, guarantees, protection and certainty that is just, and to equal treatment before the law.

Article 28D(1) is a vague and open-ended provision, yet legal certainty is one of the rights most often relied on in Indonesian judicial review cases. It is, however, often invoked along with other rights, rather than as the sole constitutional basis for invalidation.

---

[91] For further discussion of other election-related cases, see Mietzner, ibid.

In legal certainty cases, the Court has struck down statutes that it declares uncertain in two sets of circumstances. The first is that they are inconsistent with other statutes. The second is that they are internally unclear or contradictory. We now turn to some of the more prominent of these two categories of cases before critiquing the Court's use of the right to legal certainty in its decision-making.

Inconsistent statutes

One of the first cases in which the Court invalidated a provision of a statute because it contradicted another statute was the *Supreme Court Law case*.[92] In this case, the Court accepted that the 1985 Supreme Court Law (amended in 2004) and the Advocates Law (Law 18 of 2003) contradicted each other because they nominated different institutions to supervise advocates.[93] Article 36 of the Supreme Court Law required the government and the judiciary to supervise advocates but Article 12 of the Advocates Law authorised the professional advocates' organisation to supervise advocates to ensure that they abided by the advocates' code of ethics and the law. When the Supreme Court Law was amended in 2004, the legislature left Article 36 untouched.

The Constitutional Court decided that when the Advocates Law was enacted, it indirectly amended Article 36 of the Supreme Court Law. Nevertheless, it concluded that the legislature's failure to amend Article 36 in 2004 had caused legal uncertainty. To remove this uncertainty, the Court invalidated Article 36 of the Supreme Court Law.

> [I]t is clear to the Constitutional Court that lawmakers did not carefully exercise their powers and that this has resulted in an inconsistency between one statute and another. This inconsistency has caused doubt over the implementation of the relevant statute, which has caused legal uncertainty. This has the potential to breach the constitutional right contained in Article 28D(1), [that is,] '*Every person has the right to legal recognition, guarantees, protection and certainty which is just, and to equal treatment before the law*'. Legal uncertainty is also inconsistent with the spirit of . . . the principles of the *Negara Hukum* as mandated by Article 1(3) of the Constitution, which states clearly that Indonesia is a *Negara Hukum*, of which legal certainty is a prerequisite.[94]

[92] Constitutional Court Decision 067/PUU-II/2004.
[93] Constitutional Court Decision 067/PUU-II/2004, p 21.
[94] Constitutional Court Decision 067/PUU-II/2004, p 31. Emphasis in the original. The Court did not, in its published reasons, consider the argument that the

Another example is the *Book Banning Law case*.[95] In it, the Court was asked to rule on the constitutionality of the Attorney General's power under a 1963 Law to ban and seize books, in this case history books dealing with the still hugely-controversial events of the mid-1960s that led to the killing of hundreds of thousands of Indonesians and the rise of Soeharto.[96] The Court found that the 1963 Law caused legal uncertainty because it contradicted Article 38(1) of the Criminal Procedure Code (*Kitab Undang-undang Hukum Acara Pidana*, KUHAP), which requires prior written judicial consent before investigators can seize property. It decided that this inconsistency caused legal uncertainty that breached Article 28D(1) and therefore struck down the disputed provision of the 1963 Law.[97]

In the *General Election Campaign Advertising case* and *Presidential Campaign Advertising case*,[98] the Court was asked to review provisions of Law 10 of 2008 on the General Election of Members of the People's Legislative Assembly and Law 42 of 2008 on the General Election of the President and Vice-President. These gave the Press Council and the Indonesian Broadcasting Commission power to issue sanctions against press organisations and broadcasters respectively if they breached regulations relating to campaign advertisements.[99] These sanctions included revoking print media and broadcasting licences. Although the Constitutional Court found some parts of the Presidential and General Election Laws invalid for breach of the constitutional rights to information and free expression, the Court's main concern was the right to legal certainty.

DPR did not amend Article 36 because it wanted it to continue in force. On this view, the retention of Article 36 two years after the Advocates' Law was enacted rendered the Advocates' Law invalid to the extent of any inconsistency. If the Court had followed this reasoning, it should have declared Article 12 of the Advocates' Law invalid, rather than Article 36 of the Supreme Court Law.

[95] Constitutional Court Decision 6-13-20/PUU-VIII/2010.

[96] Article 6 of Law 4/PNPS/1963 on Securing Printed Materials that Impede Public Order. See generally, R Cribb, *The Indonesian Killings of 1965–1966: Studies from Java and Bali* (Clayton, Centre of Southeast Asian Studies Monash University, 1991).

[97] As shown in in Chapter 7 of this volume, the Court's main concern was that the Attorney General's power to determine whether a book threatened 'public order' and then to seize it was unfettered because no prior judicial authorisation was required. This, the Court held, breached constitutional due process protections and the right to not have property taken arbitrarily.

[98] Constitutional Court Decisions 32/PUU-VI/2008 and 99/PUU-VII/2009.

[99] Articles 56(2) and (3), 57(1) and (2) of the President and Vice-President Election Law; Articles 98–99 of the General Election Law.

The Presidential and General Election Law provisions under review purported to regulate together two separate arms of the press – print media and broadcasting institutions. These entities were, however, already regulated by their own separate statutes: Law 40 of 1999 on the Press and Law 32 of 2002 on Broadcasting.

According to the applicants, uncertainty arose as to whether these entities should follow their separate specific-purpose statutes or the Presidential and General Election Laws. The Court agreed and held that the Presidential and General Election Laws created ambiguity that breached Article 28D(1).[100] The main sources of the uncertainty were the provisions in the Laws that allowed the Council and Commission to revoke press and broadcasting licences respectively. The Court emphasised that the Press Council could not revoke a publishing licence, because the Press Law stipulates that the print media no longer requires a publishing licence.[101] The Broadcasting Law permitted only the Communication and Information Minister to revoke a broadcasting licence. To resolve the conflict and, hence, the uncertainty, the Court limited the application of the Presidential and General Election Laws to the extent that they were consistent with the earlier Press and Broadcasting Laws.

Uncertainty within a single statute

As mentioned, the Constitutional Court has also invalidated statutory provisions that are vague or open to multiple interpretations. In these cases, the Court's approach seems to be that

> the right to obtain legal certainty is . . . first and foremost that statutes . . . must not lead to multiple interpretations that can be disputed.[102]

In the *Sisa suara case*, discussed above, the Court found that in provisions of the 2008 Election Law the word 'vote' was susceptible to at least three interpretations. This, the Court found, rendered the provisions legally uncertain and had caused significant concern and controversy within the community.[103] As discussed below, instead of invalidating the provisions, however, the Court held them to be 'conditionally constitutional' – that is, valid, provided that they were applied in line with the

---

[100] Constitutional Court Decision 99/PUU-VII/2009, p 33.
[101] Constitutional Court Decision 99/PUU-VII/2009, pp 33–34.
[102] Constitutional Court Decision 110-111-112-113/PUU-VII/2009, pp 100–01.
[103] Constitutional Court Decision 110-111-112-113/PUU-VII/2009, p 101.

Constitutional Court's own interpretation of them. Pointing to recent scholarship on the rights of minorities in democracies, the Court held that 'sisa suara' referred to votes that had not yet been 'converted' into a seat. To do otherwise, the Court noted, would allow a vote that had *already* been converted into a seat to be used twice. This, it held, had no place in the proportional electoral system based on democratic principles employed in Indonesia.

As mentioned, in the *Mahendra case*,[104] former Justice Minister Yusril Ihza Mahendra challenged the constitutional validity of the Law under which the Attorney General held office. His challenge centred upon Article 22(1)(d) of the Public Prosecution Law, which sets out the grounds upon which the Attorney General can be honourably discharged, including 'the expiry of his or her term of office'. Yet beyond this bare statement, the Law does not explain how the term might come to an end. The Constitutional Court held that Article 22(1)(d) caused unconstitutional legal uncertainty about the way the Attorney General's office expired that required legislative redress. It presented four alternative ways the term could end, from which the legislature could choose. In the interim, however, the Court decided that Article 22(1)(d) would remain constitutional, conditional upon its interpretation being that the Attorney General's term ended upon the expiry of the term of the president or Cabinet.[105]

The Court also appears to have decided that provisions that allow an individual or institution to subjectively determine whether they are breached might fall foul of the legal certainty right. The *Lèse Majesté case*, discussed in more detail in Chapter 7, seems to provide an example of this. In it, the Constitutional Court held that that Criminal Code provisions that prohibited insulting the president breached legal certainty, among other constitutional rights, although it provided scant reasoning for this. According to the Court, these provisions were 'extremely susceptible' to (subjective) interpretation (presumably by the president or vice-president) as to whether a protest, declaration or thought constituted a criticism of or insult to the president or vice-president.[106]

---

[104] Constitutional Court Decision 49/PUU-VIII/2010.

[105] The other three options were upon expiry of a fixed period; on the Attorney General's retirement; or at the discretion of the President or the official who appointed the Attorney General.

[106] Constitutional Court Decision 013-022/PUU-IV/2006, p 60.

Observations

In our view, the Court has used the legal certainty right in these cases to expand its judicial review jurisdiction. As mentioned, this jurisdiction allows the Court to decide whether statutes conflict with the Constitution.[107] In the legal certainty cases, however, the Court tests whether statutes conflict with other statutes or tries to resolve internal ambiguity within statutes (and therefore does not assess the statute's compliance with another legal instrument). These cases do not really involve 'constitutional' issues; they are matters of ordinary statutory interpretation that fall within the jurisdiction of other Indonesian courts – particularly the Supreme Court and the courts below it, discussed in Chapter 4 of this volume.[108]

In some cases, the Constitutional Court has found a breach of legal certainty after attempting to apply two of the maxims of statutory interpretation that general Indonesian courts commonly use to resolve inconsistencies between statutes and finding that the maxims fail to resolve the uncertainty. The first is *lex specialis derogat lex generalis*. According to this principle, if two inconsistent laws are applicable to the case at hand, the more specific of the two overrules the law of more general application.[109] The second is *lex posteriori derogat lex priori*. Under this rule, if two laws conflict with each other, then the more recently-enacted law prevails.[110]

Again, we think this approach is problematic. The maxims' failure to resolve the uncertainty should not automatically make the uncertainty a constitutional issue. It remains a matter of ordinary statutory interpretation, and one more properly decided by other Indonesian courts. Yet even if one accepts that this type of statutory interpretation is acceptable in constitutional cases, the Constitutional Court's application of these maxims has been highly questionable. In particular, the Constitutional Court seems to have ignored the *lex posteriori derogat lex priori* principle, when applying that principle might have resolved the

---

[107] Article 24C(1) of the Constitution and Article 10 of the Constitutional Court Law.

[108] Indeed, the government and the DPR have made this point when defending the constitutionality of their statutes. See, for example, Constitutional Court Decision 067/PUU-II/2004, pp 13–16.

[109] A Hamzah, *Kamus Hukum* (Jakarta, Ghalia, 1986) 352.

[110] ibid.

uncertainty. For example, in the *Supreme Court Law case*,[111] the Court decided that *lex specialis derogat lex generalis* could not be applied to the Supreme Court Law and the Advocates Law 'because both laws actually regulated two different issues, so that one was not the *lex specialis* of the other'.[112] Although the Constitutional Court did not clearly explain what it intended by this statement, it seems reasonable to speculate that it meant that the principle was inapplicable because both statutes were equally specific – that is, the Supreme Court Law regulated the issue from the specific perspective of the Supreme Court, and the Advocates Law from the viewpoint of the advocates' association. Yet the Constitutional Court appeared to jump to the conclusion that the Advocates Law prevailed over the Supreme Court Law without considering the *lex posteriori derogat lex priori* principle at all. Applying this rule, the Supreme Court Law, amended in 2004, would clearly overrule the Advocates Law of 2003.

Another example of this can be found in the *General Election Campaign Advertising* and *Presidential Campaign Advertising cases*.[113] As mentioned, in these cases the Court decided that the Presidential and General Election Laws created ambiguity that breached Article 28D(1) of the Constitution. The Court's reasoning was that the Press Law and Broadcast Law already regulated the Press Council and the Broadcasting Commission, and did not provide them with power to revoke licences.[114] The Press Law and the Broadcasting Law were therefore inconsistent with the Presidential and General Election Laws. In both cases the Court considered the *lex generalis lex specialis* maxim, deciding that the impugned laws were *lex generalis* and did not, therefore, displace the rules contained in the prior statutes, which were more specific. It was on this basis that the Constitutional Court decided that provisions of the Presidential and General Election Laws should cede to the Press and Broadcasting Laws and not vice-versa. Yet, once again, the Court did not attempt to apply *lex posteriori*. Surely the legislature can enact a new statute to implicitly override provisions of a previous one? It is hard to see what else it could do in circumstances such as this, where the legislature merely sought to temporarily allow the Press Council and the Broadcasting Commission

---

[111] Constitutional Court Decision 067/PUU-II/2004.
[112] Constitutional Court Decision 067/PUU-II/2004, p 32.
[113] Constitutional Court Decisions 32/PUU-VI/2008 and 99/PUU-VII/2009.
[114] Law 32 of 2002 on Broadcasting; Law 40 of 1999 on the Press.

to issue specific sanctions for actions performed during the three days leading up to the election and on election day itself.

The Court's decision in the *Book Banning Law case*, mentioned above, deserves special note in this context. From our reading, the Court did not apply either statutory interpretation maxim in this case. Yet if it had done so, it might have been able to resolve the uncertainty it identified. Applying *lex posteriori*, the Court might have argued, for example, that the Code of Criminal Procedure of 1981 was more recently enacted and should, therefore, override the 1963 Law. More significant, however, is the fact that there were key differences between the relevant provisions of the Code and the 1963 Law that, we argue, made the application of each quite clear. In particular, Article 38(1) of the Code applies only to *penyidik* – that is, police (see Articles 1(1) and 6(1) of the Code) – so it cannot be applied to prevent prosecutors seizing property. On this reading, it seemed open to the Court to decide that the Code and the 1963 Law were not inconsistent at all.

Further, the Court has inconsistently applied the right to legal certainty. In some cases, the Constitutional Court has refused to strike down statutes for breach of legal certainty in circumstances similar to cases in which it has struck down other statutes. For example, in the *Taxation Law case*,[115] the applicant objected to Articles 33(1) and 77(1) of the Taxation Court Law.[116] Article 33(1) states that the Tax Court is the court of first and final instance in tax disputes; and Article 77(1) states that Tax Court decisions are final and have permanent binding force. These provisions, the applicant claimed, breached provisions of judiciary statutes that provided the right to an appeal to a high court and to lodge a cassation request with the Supreme Court. The majority refused to adjudicate, claiming that it lacked jurisdiction to decide upon the validity of statutes as against each other. Rather, the Constitutional Court declared, it had jurisdiction only to review statutes as against the Constitution.[117]

The Court's decisions in which it has found internally unclear or contradictory statutes to breach the right to legal certainty are equally problematic. Again, resolving uncertainties within statutes is a matter of ordinary statutory interpretation. The Constitutional Court arguably has jurisdiction to undertake statutory interpretation only to determine

---

[115] Constitutional Court Decision 004/PUU-II/2004.
[116] Law 14 of 2002 on the Taxation Court.
[117] Constitutional Court Decision 004/PUU-II/2004, p 46.

whether a statute conflicts with the Constitution. If *Sisa suara* and *Mahendra* in particular are taken as guides, then legal uncertainty could be used as a ground to invalidate almost any Indonesian statute. Inevitably, the vast majority of Indonesian laws – like most laws elsewhere – contain some degree of legal uncertainty. The Court has, thus far, failed to specify the degree of legal uncertainty necessary to make a provision or statute unconstitutional, thereby putting it at risk of being swamped with applications based on Article 28D(1). Ironically, the Constitutional Court's failure to distinguish between what is and what is not unconstitutional uncertainty has created uncertainty over how the Court will apply the right to legal certainty in future cases.

Conditional Constitutionality

Several years after its establishment, the Court began adopting the practice of declaring laws to be 'conditionally constitutional' – that is constitutional and kept 'on the books' provided they were implemented or applied in a way the Court thought was constitutional. In many of these cases, the Court has claimed that striking down the statute under review would result in a legal vacuum and thus uncertainty – itself prohibited under Article 28D(1) of the Constitution. In other cases, the Court has provided no (or only vague) justification for not simply invalidating and striking down the provision or statute under review.

In the 2007 *Political Crimes case*, the Constitutional Court attempted to justify its finding of conditional constitutionality in the following way:

> The Court is bound by Article 56 of the Constitutional Court Law, which sets out three types of decisions the Court can make: 'the application cannot be accepted' (that is, the applicant or the application do not meet the requirements), the 'application is upheld' (that is, the application has foundation), or the 'application is rejected' (that is, the application is without foundation). The fact is that, in the present case, the decision cannot be fitted within one of these three possibilities. Therefore, the only answer is to declare that [the impugned] provisions are 'conditionally constitutional', [that is, constitutional] upon the conditions set out [above].[118]

In more recent years, the Court has begun declaring some statutes conditionally unconstitutional – that is, unconstitutional and therefore

---

[118]   Constitutional Court Decision 14-17/PUU-V/2007, p 134.

invalid, unless implemented or applied in a way the Court thinks is constitutional. In the *Tobacco Excise case*, the Court offered the following explanation of this approach.

> In several decisions, the Constitutional Court has declared the statute under review to be conditionally constitutional. Experience has shown that [these decisions] have not been immediately adhered to and that, therefore, the decisions have not been effective. To uphold the Constitution, both by those who implement and those who make statutes, the Court will . . . declare that the provision under review conditionally breaches the Constitution. This means that the provision is unconstitutional if the requirements the Constitutional Court stipulates are not met . . . The provision under review has, therefore, no binding force if, when implemented, the requirements stipulated by the Court are not fulfilled.[119]

Most of these conditional constitutionality/unconstitutionality cases share one common factor – the Court adds norms to, or removes norms from, statutes. By so doing, the Constitutional Court seems to breach its self-proclaimed limitation of acting only as a 'negative' rather than a 'positive' legislator; that is, it is authorised only to invalidate unconstitutional statutes or parts thereof, not amend or add to them.

In the following section, we discuss possible motivations for, and the implications of, the Court's approach in conditional constitutionality cases, after discussing some prominent examples.

Case examples

The Court has issued a significant number of conditional constitutionality decisions in a range of cases described in detail elsewhere in this book. In summary, the conditional constitutionality/unconstitutionality aspects of these decisions were as follows.

In the 2007 and 2008 *Political Crimes cases*, the Court held that provisions preventing candidates from seeking a particular office if convicted of a crime with a maximum penalty of five years' imprisonment or more were conditionally constitutional – that is, constitutional provided they did not include political offences and minor offences.

In the *Mahendra case*, the Court decided that Article 22(1)(d) of the Public Prosecution Law, which provides that the Attorney General can be honourably discharged after 'the expiry of his or her term of office',

---

[119] Constitutional Court Decision 54/PUU-VI/2008, para 3.22.

was legally uncertain. The Court allowed Article 22(1)(d) to continue in force, provided it was interpreted to mean that the Attorney General held office until the expiry of the term of the president or cabinet.

In the *Tobacco excise case*, discussed in Chapter 9, the provincial government of West Nusa Tenggara challenged Article 66A(1) of the 1995 Excise Tax Law, which required the central government to allocate two per cent of the tobacco excise it levied on the sale of cigarettes to regions that 'produced tobacco excise revenue'. The central government had interpreted Article 66A(1) to require it to allocate this revenue only to provinces that housed cigarette factories, and not to those that merely produced tobacco. The Court held Article 66A(1) conditionally unconstitutional – that is, unconstitutional unless interpreted to require distribution to tobacco-growing provinces as well as provinces with cigarette factories.[120]

In the *Electoral Roll case*, the Court held that provisions of the Presidential and Vice-Presidential Elections Law that required that citizens be registered in order to vote in elections were conditionally constitutional. The conditions included that citizens must be permitted to vote if they provided a valid identity card or passport.

On the one hand, this conditional constitutionality technique appears to show deference to the DPR. With it, the Court airs the constitutional problems it finds in a Law but does not require the DPR to take action, thereby avoiding the time and effort associated with the legislative process. The Court requires only the party or institution that implements the Law to take any action in response to its decision. For example, in the *Censorship case*, discussed below, the Court asked the Censorship Board to change the way it interpreted the Film Law. In the *Sisa Suara case*, the Court purported to require the Electoral Commission to issue a regulation implementing the Constitutional Court's decision. The reality, however, is that the conditional constitutionality method effectively allows the Court to amend statutes. Although, as mentioned, the Court regularly claims that it is not a 'positive legislator', it assumes precisely that function when it declares a statute to be conditionally constitutional. By imposing an interpretation of the statute that is not clearly expressed in that statute, it is, in effect, making de facto change to that statute.

---

[120] Constitutional Court Decision 54/PUU-VI/2008, p 60.

The Court also appears to be exceeding its jurisdiction when it makes the constitutionality of a statute conditional upon the 'implementation' of the statute being consistent with the Court's interpretation of that statute. As mentioned above, the Court has declared that it lacks power to review the constitutionality of the implementation of statutes but in the conditional constitutionality cases the Court purports to dictate how statutes are implemented. In fact, the Court has begun imposing very specific conditions in recent years, compared with earlier cases such as the *Censorship case*.[121] In that case, actors, producers and others involved in the film industry asked the Constitutional Court to consider provisions of the Film Law,[122] particularly those that authorised the Censorship Board to censor films. A majority of the Court declared that the statute's provisions on censorship were behind the 'spirit of the times', that is, the 'spirit of democracy' and 'respect for human rights'.[123] Nevertheless, fearing that striking down the statute would create a vacuum and legal uncertainty, the Court allowed the provisions to remain in force 'provided that, in their implementation [by the Censorship Board], they are given a new spirit to uphold democracy and human rights'.[124] The Court left the constitutionality of the provisions dependent on the Censorship Board's meeting these conditions but provided no specific guidance for the Censorship Board to follow so that it could be certain it was complying with them.[125]

By contrast, in later decisions – and, in particular, the *Unions* and *Sisa Suara cases*– the Court's conditions were detailed and cast almost as legislative amendments. In the *Unions case*,[126] employees and union representatives from Bank Central Asia (BCA) asked the Constitutional Court to review the constitutionality of Article 120 of the Labour Law,[127] which deals with negotiations between unions and employers. Article 120(1) provides that if more than one union represents employees in a company, the union entitled to negotiate with the employer company is the union representing more than 50 per cent of the total number of

---

[121] Constitutional Court Decision 29/PUU-V/2007.

[122] Law 8 of 1992.

[123] Constitutional Court Decision 29/PUU-V/2007, p 230. Marzuki was the sole dissenting judge.

[124] Constitutional Court Decision 29/PUU-V/2007, pp 230–31.

[125] Constitutional Court Decision 29/PUU-V/2007, p 231.

[126] Constitutional Court Decision 115/PUU-VII/2009.

[127] Law 13 of 2003 on Labour.

workers in that company. Article 120(2) allows unions to form coalitions to make up the 50 per cent. Article 120(3) states:

> if the requirements of Article 120(1) and (2) are not fulfilled, then the unions are to form a negotiating team, the membership of which is to be determined proportionally, based on the respective number of employees belonging to each union.

As discussed in more detail in Chapter 7, the Court found that Article 120(1) and (2) denied the constitutional rights of unions and workers to 'proportional representation', so it struck down both provisions. Article 120(3), on the other hand, embodied the very type of representation that the Court endorsed. It therefore decided to retain Article 120(3) on two conditions. The first was that Article 120(3)'s reference to Article 120(1) and (2) be excised, given that they were no longer relevant.[128] The second reflected the Court's concerns that Article 120(3) would allow too many unions to participate in negotiations and this could impede agreements being reached between unions and the company. The Court required Article 120(3) to be read in the following way:

1. If in one company there is more than one union, a maximum of three unions or coalitions of unions, each representing at least ten per cent of the company's workers can participate in the negotiations with the company;
2. If (1) is not fulfilled, then the unions are to establish a negotiating team, the membership of which is to be determined proportionally based on the respective membership [of employees in the union].[129]

The *Sisa Suara case*[130] again deserves emphasis as an example of how the Court seems to be expanding its jurisdiction by purporting to dictate how a statute should be applied. To explain, we need to discuss events leading up to the case being lodged with the Constitutional Court. The Electoral Commission had, by internal regulation (15 of 2009), decided that seats left over after the first phase would be allocated more or less

---

[128]   Constitutional Court Decision 115/PUU-VII/2009, p 51. The Court declared that leaving Article 120(3) with its references to Article 120(1) and (2) intact would breach legal certainty – itself a constitutional norm.

[129]   Constitutional Court Decision 115/PUU-VII/2009, p 55.

[130]   Constitutional Court Decision 110-111-112-113/PUU-VII/2009. This description of the case draws from S Butt, 'Two at the top: the Constitutional Court and the Supreme Court' (2009) XI(8) *Van Zorge Report on Indonesia* 12–20.

proportionally by reference to the surplus votes alone.[131] Electoral Commission regulations are among the 'lower-level laws', mentioned above, that the Supreme Court can assess for compliance with statutes. Several Democratic Party (*Partai Demokrat*) members who missed out on seats because of this allocation method had asked the Supreme Court to assess whether the Electoral Commission's regulation complied with the Election Law. The Supreme Court decided that it did not, interpreting the Law to require that seats left over from the first phase be allocated towards seats in the second round by reference to the proportion of overall votes that parties received, including those votes that had already gone towards obtaining a seat. The Supreme Court invalidated and struck down the Electoral Commission regulation. This result clearly favoured the major parties because their votes would, in effect, be counted twice: once to determine whether they had met the quota for a seat; and again, when the proportion of overall votes they had obtained would be used to determine how many of the 'surplus' seats they would acquire.[132]

Some of the parties who anticipated that they would lose seats as result of this then asked the Constitutional Court to intervene.[133] As mentioned, the Constitutional Court upheld their arguments, holding that, in order to be constitutional, the Electoral Law's provisions on 'surplus votes' needed to be interpreted to refer to 'left over' votes, not all votes. A preliminary matter was whether the Constitutional Court could, in fact, hear the case at all. It lacks power to review Supreme Court decisions, let alone overturn them, and, unlike the Supreme Court, the Constitutional Court cannot assess whether an Electoral Commission regulation is consistent with a national statute, as its review jurisdiction is restricted to the constitutionality of statutes. The Court's response was as follows:

> In this decision, the Constitutional Court is not assessing or reviewing a Supreme Court Decision, or a General Electoral Commission regulation. By reviewing General Electoral Commission Regulation 15 of 2009, the

---

[131] The effect of this regulation was very similar to the Constitutional Court's decision in the *Sisa Suara case*, discussed above.

[132] The Supreme Court's decision required 66 seats to be reallocated in the DPR, and around 1,300 in regional legislatures. President Yudhoyono's Democratic Party would have benefitted most, gaining an additional 31 seats, with PDI-P and Golkar gaining somewhere between 16 to 19 seats each.

[133] Including Prabowo Subianto's Gerindra Party, Wiranto's Hanura Party, the United Development Party (PPP) and the Prosperous Justice Party (PKS).

Supreme Court has acted within its jurisdiction; likewise, the Commission has regulated within the confines of its jurisdiction. Even so, because the Constitutional Court has determined that Articles 205(4), 211(3) and 212(3) of Law 10 of 2008 are constitutionally [conditional], then all regulations and judicial decisions that are not in accordance with this decision become invalid because the legal basis for them no longer exists.[134]

By approaching the dispute in this way, the Constitutional Court deprived a Supreme Court decision of legal effect by 'altering' the statute upon which the Supreme Court had based its decision. On another view, the Constitutional Court has overturned a Supreme Court decision and given itself power to require the Electoral Commission to issue a type of law over which the Constitutional Court lacks jurisdiction, and then to dictate the contents of that law. As mentioned above, even the Court's justification for bringing this matter within its own jurisdiction in the first place – that the Legislative Election Law's use of the term 'sisa suara' had at least three potential interpretations and caused uncertainty, as evidenced by the diverging interpretations of the Electoral Commission and Supreme Court – was highly questionable.

2011 AMENDMENTS TO THE CONSTITUTIONAL COURT LAW

In June 2011, the DPR enacted amendments to the 2003 Constitutional Court Law designed to address two concerns.[135] The first was that the Constitutional Court had been exceeding its jurisdiction in its decision-making in some of the ways described earlier in this chapter. The second was that the mechanisms under which Constitutional Court judges could be pursued for impropriety and dereliction of duty were insufficient or unclear. We discuss these two issues in turn.

Reining in the Court?

Three provisions in the amendments seek to curb the Court's decision-making. First, Article 50A is directed towards preventing the Court from

---

[134] Constitutional Court Decision 110-111-112-113/PUU-VII/2009, para 3.37.

[135] The amendments also made a number of minor changes to requirements to hold office as a Constitutional Court judge and to the term of office of Chief and Deputy Chief Justices.

using the constitutional right to legal certainty to strike down statutes that are either inconsistent with other statutes or internally unclear. It reads:

> When reviewing statutes against the Constitution, the Constitutional Court is not to use another statute as the basis for its legal considerations (*pertimbangan hukum*).

As mentioned, in most legal certainty cases the Court has done precisely this. It has used inconsistencies between statutes and statutory provisions susceptible to multiple interpretations as grounds to make declarations of unconstitutionality. In our view, Article 50A, if applied, would render much of the Court's jurisprudence on legal certainty redundant.

The second provision designed to rein in the Court is Article 57(2a). This seems to preclude the Court from making future declarations of conditional constitutionality or unconstitutionality. Indeed, former Law and Human Rights Minister, Patrialis Akbar, who introduced the bill amending the Constitutional Court Law, announced that the amendments would prevent the Court from acting as a 'positive legislator'.[136] Under the original 2003 Law, Articles 57(1) and (2) stated:

(1) If the Constitutional Court declares that the contents of a subsection, provision and/or part of a statute conflict with the Constitution, then the contents of that subsection, provision and/or part of the statute no longer have binding force.
(2) If the Constitutional Court declares that requirements, based on the Constitution, for the enactment of the statute were not fulfilled, then that statute no longer has binding force.

Articles 57(1) and (2) were retained in the amendments, but a new Article 57(2a) was inserted, which reads:

Constitutional Court decisions are not to contain:

(a) declarations other than those referred to in Article 57(1) and (2).
(b) orders to law-makers.
(c) formulations or norms to replace the norms of legislation that are declared to conflict with the Constitution.

The Court's conditional constitutionality decisions appear to be caught by Article 57(2a)(a) because they purport to do more than simply declare a statute unconstitutional and, therefore, invalid. By making

---

[136] *Hukumonline*, 'MK Legowo Sambut UU Baru', 22 June 2011.

constitutionality subject to the addition or removal of words in statutes – as the Court has regularly done in conditional constitutionality cases – the Court seems to be providing the 'formulations or norms to replace the norms of the legislation' that are prohibited by Article 57(2a)(c).

Further, Article 57(2a)(b)'s prohibition on the Court issuing 'orders to law-makers' seems to preclude future decisions such as those in the *Anti-corruption Court case* and the *Budget Law cases*, though much would turn on how the word 'orders' is interpreted. As mentioned, in the *Anti-corruption Court case*, the Court gave the legislature a three-year deadline to enact a new statute. In the *Budget Law cases*, the Court decided that the national budget was invalid, but declined to invalidate it, instead urging the government to increase the allocation for education from year to year. Both types of decision could be interpreted as 'orders'. Article 57(2a)(b) appears to require the Court to strike down, with immediate effect, any laws it finds to be unconstitutional.

Finally, Article 45A states that:

> Constitutional Court decisions cannot contain a holding that was not sought by applicants, or which exceeds what the application sought, except in respect of particular matters related to the basis of the application.

Although the meaning of 'except in respect of particular matters related to the basis of the application' is unclear, the provision seems directed towards cases in which the Court has reviewed and invalidated a statutory provision for breach of a constitutional provision that the applicants did not, themselves, put forward as a basis for invalidity. For example, in the *General Election Campaign case*,[137] discussed in Chapter 3, the Court found that provisions of the 2008 General Elections Law[138] breached the constitutional right to freedom of information in Article 28F, even though the applicants did not mention Article 28F in their submissions as they appear in the case transcript. Article 45A also appears to prevent the Court in future cases adopting the approach it relied on in the *Electricity Law case*. In that case, the applicants only sought the invalidation of several provisions of the statute but the Constitutional Court instead invalidated the entire statute.

---

[137] Constitutional Court Decision 32/PUU-VI/2008.
[138] Law 10 of 2008 on the General Election of Members of the People's Legislative Assembly.

Disciplinary Procedures

The 2011 amendments to the Constitutional Court Law also require the Constitutional Court to develop a Code of Ethics and Guidelines for Judicial Behaviour with which judges must comply so as to guard their integrity and 'irreproachable, just and stately characters' (Article 27A). It is unclear why the amendments sought to require the Constitutional Court to develop a Code of Ethics; it had, in fact, developed one in its first year of operation and has since revised it.[139] The Code is based on the Bangalore Principles, which require judges to display independence, impartiality, integrity, propriety, equality, competence, diligence and wisdom, and sets out how each concept is to be applied in practice.

The 2011 Law provides more detail about the so-called Constitutional Court Honour Council (*Majelis Kehormatan Mahkamah Konstitusi*), charged with upholding the Code and Guidelines (Article 27A(2)). The Council comprises a Constitutional Court judge, a Judicial Commission member, a DPR member with responsibility over legislative affairs, a government official who deals with legal issues and a Supreme Court judge (Article 27A(2)). The Council can impose punishments on Constitutional Court judges who breach the Code and Guidelines, including written reprimand, suspension or dismissal (Article 27A(5)).

These provisions appear to be responses to recent allegations of impropriety against two Constitutional Court judges. First, in October 2010, a former Constitutional Court judges' assistant and lawyer, Refly Harun, published an opinion piece in *Kompas* newspaper, alleging that the Court was no longer free from corruption. He claimed to have seen Rp one billion that was to be used to bribe Constitutional Court judge Akil Mochtar. Constitutional Court Chief Justice Mahfud established an independent fact-finding team, led by Harun himself, but it was unable to find conclusive evidence against Mochtar.[140] The second 'scandal' involved Constitutional Court judge Arsyad Sanusi, who resigned in February 2011 over allegations that his daughter and brother-in-law had, in 2008, accepted bribes from an applicant in a 2009 Constitutional

---

[139] Constitutional Court Regulation 2/PMK/2003 on the Ethics Code and Behaviour Guidelines for Constitutional Court Judges; Constitutional Court Regulation 7/PMK/2005 on Applying the Ethics Code and Behaviour Guidelines for Constitutional Court Judges; Constitutional Court Regulation 2/PMK/2006 on Applying the Ethics Code and Behaviour Guidelines for Constitutional Court Judges.

[140] *Jakarta Post* 22 December 2010; Pasandaran 2010; Savitri 2010.

Court case. Though the Constitutional Court Honour Council found no evidence that Arsyad knew about the bribes, he resigned after the Council decided that he must take responsibility in the interests of upholding the reputation of the Court.[141]

THE COURT STRIKES BACK

Some of the 2011 amendments were challenged in the *Constitutional Court Law Amendment case No 1*[142] and the *Constitutional Court Law Amendment case No 2*,[143] both decided on 18 October 2011. The applicant in *No 1* had been convicted for drug possession under Article 112 of the 2009 Narcotics Law.[144] He claimed that Article 112 should not have been applied against him because he was a mere drug user and that a provision imposing a lesser penalty should have been employed. In effect, he asked the Constitutional Court to make it clear that Article 112 applied to dealers, not users, by adding to the provision the requirement that drug possession must be with intent to 'distribute or for use by another person'.[145] He also argued that he had a constitutional right to rehabilitation and asked the Court to compel the state to provide it, again by adding such a requirement to the Narcotics Law.[146] Both requests required the Court to make 'conditional constitutionality' rulings, so the applicant also asked the Court to invalidate Articles 57(2a) and 45A of the 2011 Amendment. A unanimous Constitutional Court invalidated Articles 45A and 57(2a) but rejected the applicant's challenge to the 2009 Narcotics Law.

[141] *Hukumonline*, 'Putusan Majelis Kehormatan MK Bakal Digugat', 14 February 2011; D Sagita, 'Constitutional Court Justice Steps Down Over Kin's Alleged Bribery', *Jakarta Globe*, 12 February 2011.

[142] Constitutional Court Decision 48/PUU-IX/2011.

[143] Constitutional Court Decision 49/PUU-IX/2011.

[144] Law 35 of 2009 on Narcotics.

[145] Article 112 of Law 35 of 2009 on Narcotics imposes between four and 12 years' imprisonment for 'possessing, storing, controlling or providing' Category I non-plant narcotics. As for rehabilitation, the applicant argued that Article 127(1)(a), which states that drug users are subject to a maximum of four years' imprisonment, should specifically require judges to order rehabilitation.

[146] The applicant pointed to Articles 28G(1) ('the right to protection of one's person), 28G(2) ('the right to be free from treatment that undermines human dignity') and 28H(1) ('the right to health services'): Constitutional Court Decision 48/PUU-IX/2011, pp 8–9.

No 2 was brought by eight constitutional law academics. They claimed that 10 provisions of the 2011 Amendment were unconstitutional, including those concerning the composition of the Constitutional Court Honour Council and pre-requisites for appointment to the Court. An 8:1 majority of the Court agreed to strike down most of these provisions.[147]

In the following analysis, we show that, on the whole, the Court's reasoning in both cases was highly questionable. In our view, only the Court's justification for invalidating Articles 27A(2) and 50A was legally defensible, albeit not without flaws. Our reading of the decision suggests that the Court may have been more concerned with repelling DPR attempts to rein it in, and projecting itself as strong and defiant, than with sound argument.

For reasons of space, we limit ourselves to discussing the Court's reasons for invalidating Articles 45A, 57(2a), 50A and 27A(2) – provisions, mentioned above, that appeared geared towards restricting the Court's decision-making and taking the investigation of its judges for impropriety out of its hands. We also briefly consider the Court's reasons for invalidating Articles 4(f)–(g), 59(2) and 15(2h), which, in our view, were particularly weak.

Article 27A(2)

Article 27A(2) requires that representatives from the DPR, the government, the Supreme Court and the Judicial Commission sit alongside a Constitutional Court judge on Honour Councils established to determine whether Constitutional Court judges have engaged in misconduct.

In *No 2*, the Court decided that Article 27A(2) of the 2011 Amendment was contrary to Article 24(1) of the Constitution, which provides for judicial independence.[148] In the Court's view, including the DPR,

---

[147] The Court refused the applicants' request to invalidate Article 15(2)(d), which required Constitutional Court judges to be between 47 and 65 years old, and found Article 15(2)(h), discussed below, to be conditionally constitutional. The applicants in *No 2* also asked the Court to consider the constitutionality of Articles 45A and 57(2a) but the Court refused on the basis that they had already been invalidated in *No 1*. Justice Harjono issued a dissenting opinion in *No 2*, which we do not consider for reasons of space.

[148] The Court also found Article 27A(3), (4), (5) and (6) – which deal with the powers, procedures and sanctions of the Council – invalid because they were closely interrelated with Article 27A(2).

government and Supreme Court on the Council 'directly and indirectly' threatened the independence of Constitutional Court judges in performing their functions, largely because these institutions could appear before the Constitutional Court as parties to disputes.[149] This view is consistent with the Court's decision in the *Judicial Commission case*, discussed above in Chapter 4, to which it pointed as justification for rejecting the judicial commission representative. In the *Judicial Commission case*, the Court had held that the Judicial Commission could not supervise the Constitutional Court, again for reasons of judicial independence.

Article 45A

As mentioned, Article 45A seeks to prevent the Court from striking down statutory provisions about which the applicant did not complain. The Court's primary reasons for invalidating Article 45A in *No 1* were as follows. In civil cases, judges cannot grant something that the plaintiff did not seek in its application because civil matters involve protecting individual interests and only bind the parties to the case. By contrast, judicial review cases are 'public' cases because they involve assessing laws that apply generally to citizens and government.[150] The public interest requires that, if necessary, judges can enforce the constitution beyond the confines of the individual interests represented in the application.

In our view, the Court's reasoning on this point was sound. Of course, the Court should not be overly distracted by constitutional arguments incidental to the case at hand and should not waste time actively seeking them out. However, its function is to ensure that statutes are consistent with the Constitution. The narrow interests of applicants should therefore not confine the Court's decision-making. Nevertheless, we observe that the Court was not required to consider, let alone invalidate, Article 45A in order to resolve *No 1*. As mentioned, Article 45A purported to prohibit the Court from invalidating provisions that applicants do not ask it to review. In *No 1*, the Court did not need to avoid this prohibition; the applicant's requests were precise and the Court did not 'exceed' them.

---

[149] Constitutional Court Decision 49/PUU-IX/2011, p 72.
[150] Constitutional Court Decision 48/PUU-IX/2011, p 92.

Article 50A

As mentioned, Article 50A purports to prohibit the Constitutional Court from using one statute as the basis to declare another statute unconstitutional. As mentioned, this provision seemed to be directed at preventing the Court from declaring statutes or statutory provisions invalid for legal uncertainty because they contradicted another statute or provision.

In *No* 2, the Court claimed that it had never employed this approach in judicial review cases, declaring that 'in practice, constitutional court decisions have never used [other] statutes as a basis for their reasoning'. Rather, the Court explained its approach in material judicial review cases as follows:

> [I]n particular applications, the Constitutional Court is required to see statutes as a part of a system that cannot contradict itself so that if the Court finds that one statute conflicts with another other statute, this will contravene legal certainty as guaranteed in the Constitution.[151]

This approach is justifiable as a matter of principle and could properly be used as a basis for future legal uncertainty cases. In our view, however, it significantly misrepresents the Court's past approach to the legal certainty cases discussed above. It clearly does not account for decisions in which the Court has invalidated statutes for being internally inconsistent. As we have shown in our discussion of these cases, the Court has – quite regularly and with great specificity – compared statutes under review with other statutes to determine whether they are consistent.

Even putting aside this objection, it is unclear why the Court considered it necessary to invalidate Article 50A. If, as the Court suggests, it in fact assesses the consistency of a statute with the entire body of

---

[151] Constitutional Court Decision 49/PUU-IX/2011, p 75. The Court did, however, distinguish between formal and material review. The Constitution, it said, did in fact authorise it to use statutes as bases for declarations of unconstitutionality when performing 'formal judicial review'. The purpose of formal review is to ensure that the law-making process complies with formal procedures but the Constitution does not specify these formal procedures. Article 22A of the Constitution merely stipulates that law-making procedures will be regulated by statute. At time of writing, the relevant statute was Law No 10 of 2004 on Law-making as amended in 2011 and supplemented by the DPR's standing orders. According to the Court, assessing the 'formal validity' of laws by reference to this statute and the standing orders is permissible because they are mandated by, or are implementations of, Article 22A.

Indonesian legislation rather than with other individual statutes in legal uncertainty cases, then it is not using 'another statute as the basis for its legal considerations' and so its endeavours do not fall within Article 50A. On this interpretation, Article 50A does not affect the Court's approach to legal certainty cases and, therefore, the Court could have simply allowed Article 50A to stand.

Article 57(2a)

As mentioned, Article 57(2a) seems to preclude declarations of conditional constitutionality. The Court's justification for invalidating it was scant. What follows is the entirety of its reasoning in *No 1*:

> According to the Court, Article 57(2a) of [the 2011 Amendments] conflicts with the purpose of establishing the Constitutional Court: to uphold law and justice, particularly in the framework of upholding the constitutionality of the norms of statutes in accordance with the Constitution. Article 57(2a) impedes the Court in (i) reviewing the constitutionality of norms; (ii) filling in legal gaps as a result of a Constitutional Court decision declaring a norm to conflict with the Constitution and no longer having binding force. Creating new statutes takes so long that it is not possible to fill the legal vacuum quickly; (iii) fulfilling the obligations of Constitutional Court judges to uncover, follow and understand the legal values and sense of justice alive within the community.[152]

This explanation for the invalidity of Article 57(2a) is problematic beyond its brevity and vagueness. It is difficult to see how Article 57(2a) impedes the Court in reviewing the constitutionality of norms and following community legal values; Article 57(2a) relates solely to what the Court can 'do' or order once it has already reviewed the law and decided that it is constitutionally flawed. The Court also failed to explain by reference to the Constitution why it, rather than the legislature, should remedy constitutional defects in statutes or fill legal vacuums left by declarations of invalidity.

---

[152] Constitutional Court Decision 48/PUU-IX/2011, p 94.

Articles 4(f)–(g)

These provisions deal with the election of Constitutional Court chief and deputy chief justices. Article 4(f) requires that they be elected at a single meeting. The candidate obtaining the most votes becomes Chief Justice (Article 4(g)) and the second-most becomes Deputy Chief Justice (Article 4(h)).

In *No 2*, the Court invalidated these provisions because while law-makers have scope to determine how state leaders, including judges, are elected, rules that cause 'legal deadlocks and impede the performance of state institutions' can 'cause constitutional damage to citizens'.[153] Articles 4(f), 4(g) and 4(h) contained such rules. If all nine judges voted, one candidate would always obtain more votes that all others (thereby qualifying for chief justice) but more than one candidate might obtain the second-highest number of votes. The vote would need to be annulled and retaken, even though the prospective Chief Justice had already obtained a majority, thereby affecting the legitimacy of the elected chief and deputy.[154] The provisions therefore had potential to impede the performance of the Court and that, in turn, could damage the constitutional rights of citizens guaranteed by Article 28D(1).

In our view, the Court's invalidation of these provisions was unnecessary. Any impasse could quite easily be resolved by a run-off between prospective deputies. As the DPR had pointed out during argument in *No 2*, Article 24(5) of the Constitution gives the Constitutional Court power to issue regulations to govern procedures for the election of chief and deputy chief justices. In response, the Court held that it was precluded from issuing such a regulation because the words of Article 4(f) were clear and the Court therefore had no scope to supplement it. Again, we find it difficult to accept this position – Article 4(f) requires only that Chief and Deputy Chief Justices be appointed at a single meeting. The provision does not preclude a run-off election between potential deputies being performed at that one meeting, if required.

---

[153] Constitutional Court Decision 49/PUU-IX/2011, p 66.
[154] Constitutional Court Decision 49/PUU-IX/2011, p 67.

Article 59(2)

Article 59(2) states that:

> If it is necessary to make changes to statutes that have been reviewed, the DPR or the president is to immediately follow up the Constitutional Court decision . . . in accordance with the law.

On the Court's reading, the phrase 'If it is necessary' gave the DPR and the president discretion to respond to Constitutional Court decisions. This, the Court held in *No 2*, breached Article 24C(1) of the Constitution, which stipulates that Constitutional Court decisions are final, thereby rendering them generally applicable (*erga omnes*) and self-executing, and making compliance with them mandatory for citizens and the state.[155]

There is little to commend the Court's interpretation of Article 59(2). On our reading, 'If it is necessary to make changes' (*Jika diperlukan perubahan*) does not necessarily imply that the DPR and president have discretion to ignore a Constitutional Court decision. It simply means that if the DPR and president need to respond to the decision – such as if the decision invalidates a statutory provision and, legislation is, therefore, required to replace the provision – then the DPR and President should respond without delay. The reality is, however, that most Constitutional Court decisions uphold the constitutionality of the statute for which review is sought and, therefore, require no legislative or government response.[156]

---

[155] Constitutional Court Decision 49/PUU-IX/2011, p 76.

[156] The Court also found that Article 59(2) contained an error. Article 20(2) of the Constitution requires that all draft laws be discussed together by the DPR and the president to obtain agreement before passage. For the Court, the phrase 'DPR or the president' was inconsistent with Article 20(2). The correct formulation was the 'DPR and the president'. Again, the Court's reasoning appears to be misdirected. Surely either the DPR or the president must initiate the law-making process. They are separate institutions and cannot be expected to propose legislative amendments at precisely the same moment. Rather, current practice is for one of them to initiate a bill for discussion between them with the aim of achieving the requisite mutual agreement. Ultimately both the DPR and the president should agree to the amendments as required by Article 20(2) but, in our view, they do not need to act together to initiate legislative change.

Manufacturing Legal Uncertainty?

For reasons of space, we do not detail the Court's reasons for invalidating Articles 10, 15(2h) and 26(5) in *No 2* – all on the grounds of legal uncertainty – but we note that the Court's reasoning was, again, unconvincing. We limit ourselves to outlining the Court's treatment of Article 15(2h). This provision requires that Constitutional Court judges 'have at least 15 years' work experience in the field of law and/or have been a state official'. The Court found that this provision caused legal uncertainty because it could be interpreted 'cumulatively' – that is, to require 15 years' experience and having served as a state official – or could be interpreted in the alternative, whereby experience or work as a state official would suffice. For the Court, this was problematic because not all people who have worked as state officials fulfil the requirements to become a Constitutional Court judge and, conversely, many people who have not been a state official will fulfil the requirements for being a Constitutional Court judge.

In our view, there is no logical basis for the Court's declaration that Article 15(2h) has led to legal uncertainty. The provision is clear: in addition to the many other prerequisites imposed by the 2003 Constitutional Court Law as amended, candidates must have 15 years' legal experience or have worked as a public official, or both. The 'and' may be redundant but it has not created uncertainty.

Comments

On the whole, the Court's reasoning in these two cases is highly problematic. As argued above, the Court provided scant reasons, misinterpreted provisions, manufactured legal uncertainty and even reviewed provisions that had no bearing on the case before it. In our view, only the Court's discussion of Article 27A(2) is legally defensible (although of all the Court's invalidations, this one drew the most negative press, chiefly because of widespread public concern regarding judicial accountability).

We speculate that the weaknesses in the Court's reasoning reflect the Court's overwhelming desire to defeat the DPR's efforts to rein it in. It seemed determined to push back at the DPR for attempting to 'interfere' with it – and to do so at the earliest opportunity. (The applications were lodged soon after the 2011 Amendment was enacted, and the Court issued its decisions only several months later.) Judge Harjono seemed to recognise this in the following statement from his impassioned sole dissent in *No 2*:

> It appears the Constitutional Court has been too eager to decide this case. Where are you going (*Quo Vadis*), Mahkamah Konstitusi?[157]

Given the Court's previous 'activism' and the jurisdictional expansion described above, one might have expected the majority to have gone further and invalidated the 2011 Amendments in their entirety – after all, in *No 2*, the Court was at pains to emphasise that it could revoke whole statutes. In our view, the fact that it did not indicates that these decisions should not be seen as a mere 'grab for power' by a majority of the Court. Rather, these judges appear to consider the future of Indonesian constitutionalism as being at stake, with the Court battling to protect its achievements from a reactionary DPR that regards it as excessively interventionist.

As the Constitutional Court is determined not to give ground, the DPR may need to seek amendment of the Constitution to restrict the Court's powers if it wants to 'win' this fight.[158] The DPR, however, will be reluctant to do this, both because its own legitimacy has been increasingly tarnished by corruption scandals and because the political elite are wary of the consequences of re-opening debate about other, politically contentious provisions of the Constitution discussed elsewhere in this book (including, in particular, those touching upon decentralisation and freedom of religion).

CONCLUSION

The Constitutional Court has, on the whole, proved to be the most professional judicial institution in post-Soeharto Indonesia, if not even Indonesian legal history. Under the very capable leadership of Chief Justices Jimly Asshiddiqie (2003–08) and Mohammad Mahfud

---

[157]   Constitutional Court Decision 49/PUU-IX/2011, p 87.
[158]   As explained in Chapters 1 and 3, the power to amend the Constitution is held by the MPR (*Majelis Permusyawaratan Rakyat*, People's Deliberative Council), which is effectively controlled by the DPR.

Mahmodin (known as Mahfud MD) (2008–), it has embraced its self-proclaimed role of 'guardian of the Constitution' and energetically defended itself from attack, including from legislators. Its exercise of the power to review statutes has put it at the forefront of Indonesia's transition from authoritarianism to become the most democratic and free country in Southeast Asia.[159] As a result, the Constitutional Court has made itself a critical part of the maintenance of the separation of powers, constitutional order, democracy and human rights in Indonesia.

The first judicial institution to enjoy its functions in independent Indonesia, the Court has generally performed them competently, reliably and impartially. It has, however, sometimes been inconsistent in its application of the principles of interpretation it has articulated. It has also sometimes used those principles to expand its own authority, seeking to determine how the government should make laws or apply them. This has brought it into conflict with the DPR, which, as mentioned in Chapter 3, is now the principal locus of power in democratic Indonesia. This is a significant potential danger for the Court. The 2011 Amendments to the 2003 Constitutional Court Law described in this chapter are the product of a frustrated DPR, resentful of the Court's increasing power and its willingness to interfere with legislation. Although the Court has deflected the DPR's most recent attacks, the battle between them is far from over.

SELECTED READING

Butt, Simon, *Corruption and Law in Indonesia* (London, Routledge, 2011).

Butt, Simon and Lindsey, Tim, 'Economic Reform when the Constitution Matters: Indonesia's Constitutional Court and Article 33' (2008) 44(2) *Bulletin of Indonesia Economic Studies* 239–62.

Harijanti, Susi and Lindsey, Tim, 'Indonesia: General elections test the amended Constitution and the new Constitutional Court' (2006) 4(1) *International Journal of Constitutional Law* 138–50.

Mietzner, Marcus, 'Political Conflict Resolution and Democratic Consolidation in Indonesia: The Role of the Constitutional Court' (2010) 10(3) *Journal of East Asian Studies* 397–424.

---

[159] According to Freedom House (www.freedomhouse.org).

6

Decentralisation

—————◆◆◆—————

Introduction – Background – Regional Government Institutions – Regional Government Jurisdictions – Avenues for Central Government Control – Jurisdictional Dispute Resolution – Creating new Regions – Special Autonomy – Conclusion

INTRODUCTION

BEFORE THE POST-SOEHARTO constitutional amendment process began in 1999, Article 18 constituted the entirety of Chapter VI of the 1945 Constitution. It was a bare-bones provision:

> The division of the territory of Indonesia into large and small regions shall be regulated by statute in consideration of, and with due regard to, the principles of deliberation in the government system and the inherited rights of the Special Regions.

During the second round of amendments in 2000, Article 18 was rewritten, and a new expanded Chapter VI on 'Regional Government' was inserted. It now contains the following three provisions.

Article 18

1. Indonesia is divided into provinces (*propinsi*); provinces are divided into counties (*kabupaten* or Regency) and cities (*kota*). Each province, county and city has its own regional government, regulated by statute.
2. Provincial, county and city governments are to regulate and administer matters of government themselves under the principles of autonomy and assistance [to other tiers of government] (*pembantuan*).
3. Provincial, county and city governments are to have Regional People's Representative Councils (*Dewan Perwakilan Rakyat Daerah*, DPRD) whose members are voted in by general election.

4. Governors, Regents and Mayors are the heads of provinces, counties and cities respectively and are to be democratically elected.
5. Regional governments are to exercise wide-ranging autonomy, except in matters that national legislation reserves for the Central Government.
6. Regional governments have power to enact regional regulations (*Perda*) and other regulations in the exercise of their autonomy and assistance.
7. The structures and procedures for the administration of regional government are to be regulated by statute.

Article 18A

1. The relative authority of the central government and provincial, county and city governments, and between provincial, county and city governments, is to be regulated by statute, having regard to regional uniqueness and diversity.
2. The relationship between the central and regional governments in matters of finance, public services, and the utilisation of natural and other resources, shall be regulated and implemented justly and harmoniously in accordance with legislation.

Article 18B

1. The State recognises and respects special (*khusus/istimewa*) regional governments, as regulated by statute.
2. The State recognises and respects *adat* law communities and their traditional rights, provided that they remain in existence and accord with community developments and the principle of the Unitary State of the Republic of Indonesia, as regulated by statute.

In this chapter, we discuss how Indonesia's decentralisation, or 'regional autonomy' (*otonomi daerah*) as it is usually described in Indonesia, has been implemented. Our focus is on how Articles 18, 18A and 18B of the Constitution have been fleshed out by statute – particularly Law 32 of 2004 on Regional Government[1] – and by the Constitutional Court. After providing a background to regional autonomy post-Soeharto, we consider the structure, jurisdictions and law-making powers of regional government institutions; avenues for central government control over them; and the legal means available to resolve jurisdictional disputes between tiers of government. We also consider the processes for establishing new regions. We conclude with a brief account of the so-called 'special' (*khusus* or *istimewa*) autonomy awarded to a few provinces.

---

[1] As amended by Interim Emergency Law 3 of 2005 (confirmed by Law 8 of 2005) and Law 12 of 2008.

BACKGROUND

Indonesia's history since Independence in 1945 has been marked by constant objections to centralised government. Regional rebellions dogged the early years of the new Republic. The *Darul Islam* movement sought the establishment of an Islamic state and in the 1950s attracted a large following, particularly in West Java, South Sulawesi and Aceh. The *PRRI-Permesta* rebellion, based in West Sumatra and South Sulawesi, rose against the central government in the late 1950s. Military operations that in some cases lasted years were required to crush these uprisings. Later, insurgent groups – particularly in Aceh, Papua and East Timor – sought the removal of their provinces from the Indonesian state on various grounds including ideological and religious differences, and local separatist traditions. Complaints about heavy-handed military intrusion and central bureaucratic interference were also common, particularly under Soeharto. Many regions, particularly those with abundant natural resources, protested that most of the spoils of natural and other resources located in their regions were channelled to the centre – particularly to the Soeharto family.

The New Order government was, for the most part, able to resist these objections. Regional separatist movements such as the Free Papua Organisation (*Organisasi Papua Merdeka,* or OPM) and the Free Aceh Movement (*Gerakan Aceh Merdeka,* or GAM) were met with military force. Although local governments existed at the provincial, municipal, city and village level, the central government's bureaucratic presence was so pervasive and controlling that regional governments were effectively the central government's representatives in the regions.[2]

Law 5 of 1974 on Regional Government was the principal legal instrument by which the New Order controlled sub-national governments.[3] The 1974 Law created a division between so-called 'autonomous regional government' and 'regional administration', which were given different areas of authority. The former was supposed to allow

---

[2] H Crouch, *Political Reform in Indonesia after Soeharto* (Singapore, ISEAS, 2010) 88.
[3] Law 5 of 1974 on Regional Government. Crouch, *Political Reform in Indonesia after Soeharto* (above n 2) 88; P Holland, 'Regional Government and Central Authority in Indonesia' in T Lindsey (ed), *Indonesia: Law and Society*, 1st edn (Annandale, NSW, Federation Press, 1999) 200, 207.

regions to legislate for their constituents, whereas the latter was intended as a top-down channel, allowing the central government to control regional governments by implementing its policies in the regions.[4] Despite creating this division, the 1974 Law also required that one individual – the 'regional executive' – serve as the head of both the 'regional government' and 'regional administration'. The regional executive was appointed by and was directly accountable to the central government[5] and largely dictated the issues which regional governments would regulate. Regional governments also relied on the central government for fiscal resources. Together, this financial dependence and control over the regional executive enabled the central government to largely determine the way regions exercised their so-called 'real and responsible local autonomy'[6] in a way that made this phrase little more than rhetoric.

With Soeharto's fall, public expressions of resentment at the parasitic, controlling and often-brutal centralised polity over which he had presided became overwhelming. Many feared that Indonesia would 'Balkanise' unless it quickly introduced meaningful decentralisation reform. The response of Soeharto's successor, his former Vice-President, Bacharuddin Jusuf Habibie, was therefore to hastily create a new legal apparatus for regional autonomy – a process the World Bank describes as a 'Big Bang'.[7] Within a year of Soeharto's resignation the national legislature, the DPR, had enacted two key regional autonomy statutes: Law 22 of 1999 on Regional Government and Law 25 of 1999 on Fiscal Balance between the Central and Regional Governments. These required the transfer of central government power and resources by early 2001.

Law 22 of 1999 radically reconfigured the Indonesian polity, transforming it from one of the world's most authoritarian and centralised states to one of its most democratic and decentralised. The Law gave broad and wide-ranging autonomy to counties (*kabupaten*) and municipalities (*kota*) to manage their own affairs, reserving only a few matters for central government control. Even villages were granted their own, albeit limited, powers. As part of the process, the central government

---

[4] DK Emmerson, *Indonesia beyond Suharto: Polity, Economy, Society, Transition* (Armonk, NY, ME Sharpe Inc, 1999) 78.

[5] ibid, 79.

[6] Holland, 'Regional Government and Central Authority in Indonesia' (above n 3) 215.

[7] World Bank, *Decentralizing Indonesia: a Regional Public Expenditure Review Overview Report* (Washington, DC, World Bank, 2003) 1.

transferred to regional governments control and responsibility over 2.8 million civil servants, 16,000 service facilities (including schools and hospitals) and several thousand government offices.[8]

In 2000, Article 18 of the Constitution was amended, and Articles 18A and 18B were added to the Constitution, as set out above. In 2004, Law 32 on Regional Government and Law 33 on Fiscal Balance between the Central and Regional Governments were enacted, replacing the 1999 statutes. At time of writing, the 2004 Regional Government Law remained the primary statute implementing Articles 18, 18A and 18B.[9] In this chapter, all references to legislative provisions are to this Law unless otherwise specified.

In 1998, Indonesia had approximately 292 local governments outside Jakarta, including 27 provinces.[10] Since Soeharto's fall, this number has grown as various provinces, municipalities and cities split into two or more, using processes described below. By 2003, there were around 440 cities and counties.[11] At time of writing, Indonesia had 33 provinces and almost 500 counties and cities.[12]

REGIONAL GOVERNMENT INSTITUTIONS

Provincial, county and city administrations each have their own executive and legislature. The 2004 Law defines the 'regional administration' (*pemerintahaan daerah*) as having two arms. The first is the 'regional government' (*pemerintah daerah*). This is the local executive, and com-

---

[8]   ibid, 1.

[9]   Although other statutes – notably, Law 27 of 2009 on the Organisation and Composition of the MPR, DPR, DPD, and DPRD – are also relevant and discussed in this chapter.

[10]   F Fitrani, B Hofman and K Kaiser, 'Unity in Diversity? The Creation of New Local Governments in a Decentralising Indonesia' (2005) 41(1) *Bulletin of Indonesian Economic Studies* 57, 58.

[11]   ibid, 57; P Smoke, 'The Rules of the Intergovernmental Game in East Asia: Decentralisation Frameworks and Processes' in World Bank (ed), *East Asia Decentralizes: Making Local Government Work* (Washington DC, World Bank, 2005).

[12]   See www.depdagri.go.id. As Booth points out, 'this process has in fact been going on since the 1950s, but has taken on new momentum in the last decade, especially at the sub-provincial levels of government' (A Booth, 'Splitting, Splitting and Splitting Again: A Brief History of the Development of Regional Government in Indonesia Since Independence' (2011) 167(1) *Bijdragen tot de Taal-, Land- en Volkenkunde* 31, 32).

prises the 'regional head' (*kepala daerah*) and the government apparatus. The second is the regional legislature: the DPRD (Article 3).

Regional Heads

The 2004 Regional Government Law provides that regional heads in provinces are governors (*gubernur*). In counties (*kabupaten*) they are regents (*bupati*), and in cities (*kota*) they are mayors (*walikota*). Each regional head also has a deputy (Article 24(4)). The primary functions of regional heads are to lead the administration of regional government using policies they have set with the DPRD, to enact laws with the DPRD and to issue regulations to implement those laws.

Many of the provisions of the 2004 Regional Government Law and its 2008 amendment deal with processes and rules for the election of regional heads. Heads and deputy heads of regions are, like the national president and vice-president, elected in teams. Once elected, the Home Affairs Minister, in the name of the president, appoints governors at a provincial DPRD session. The governor, in the name of the president, inaugurates regents and deputy regents, and mayors and deputy mayors, during sessions of the relevant county or city DPRD.

DPRDs (Regional Legislatures)

The primary statute governing DPRDs is Law 27 of 2009 on the Organisation and Composition of the MPR, DPR, DPD, and DPRD. Although many provisions of Law 27 of 2009 restate, or are very similar to, provisions in the 2004 Regional Government Law, Law 27 of 2009 is more detailed.

Each DPRD has commissions, a consultative body, a regional legislative body, a budget body and an Honour Council.[13] DPRDs have legislative, budgetary and supervisory functions.[14] In particular, they can enact

---

[13] Article 46(1) of the 2004 Regional Government Law; Articles 302 and 353 of Law 27 of 2009.

[14] Article 41 of the 2004 Regional Government Law; Article 292 of Law 27 of 2009 (for provincial DPRDs); Article 343 of Law 27 of 2009 (for county/city DPRDs).

Perda (*Peraturan Daevah*, Regional Regulations), including annual local government budgets. They can also supervise the implementation of those Perda and other laws, including regulations issued by regional heads, and even government policies. DPRDs can also advise regional government about international agreements; question their regional head about the administration of government; propose the appointment and dismissal of regional heads and deputy heads; and supervise the Regional Electoral Commission's performance in regional head elections.[15] DPRDs are required to issue standing orders and procedures for the exercise of their tasks and functions, and to issue Perda outlining codes of ethics.[16]

DPRD members are democratically elected for five-year terms. Each provincial DPRD is to have between 35 and 100 members,[17] and each county or city DPRD between 20 and 50.[18] Each member must belong to a DPRD 'faction' (*fraksi*).[19] DPRD decisions are to be taken by 'deliberation to reach consensus' (*musyawarah untuk mufakat*) and, if consensus cannot be reached, by majority vote (*suara terbanyak*).[20]

Like members of the national legislature, DPRD members have rights to interpellation (*interpelasi*), inquire (*angket*), express opinions (*menyatakan pendapat*), and immunity (*imunitas*). Using the right to interpellation, DPRD members can 'request an explanation' (*meminta keterangan*) from their regional head about regional government policies that are 'important and of broad strategic significance to the community and the state'.[21] The right to 'inquire' allows members to investigate regional government policies that are 'important and of broad strategic significance to the community and the state' but which they suspect are contrary to law.[22] DPRD members can 'express opinions' about the policy of a regional head or about 'extraordinary events (*kejadian luar biasa*) that occur in the region', and then recommend how to resolve the problem.

---

[15]   Article 42 of the 2004 Regional Government Law; Article 293 of Law 27 of 2009 (for provincial DPRDs); Article 344 of Law 27 of 2009 (for county/city DPRDs).

[16]   Articles 293(2), 325–326, 343(2), 376–377 of Law 27 of 2009.

[17]   Article 294 of Law 27 of 2009.

[18]   Article 345 of Law 27 of 2009.

[19]   Articles 301 and 352 of Law 27 of 2009.

[20]   Articles 321 and 372 of Law 27 of 2009.

[21]   Articles 298(2) and 349(2) of Law 27 of 2009. The 2009 Law sets the minimum number of DPRD members needed to support such a motion: Articles 306–307 and 357–358.

[22]   Articles 298(3) and 349(3) of Law 27 of 2009. The 2009 Law sets out further requirements and procedures in Articles 308 and 359–363.

This right is often exercised as a follow-up to the rights of interpellation and inquiry.[23] The right to immunity means that DPRD members cannot be prosecuted or removed for statements, questions or opinions they put forward during DPRD sessions.[24]

Villages

Village administrations have jurisdiction over matters relating to their pre-existing 'customary' or 'original' rights (*hak asal-usul desa*), and government matters that are delegated to them by levels of government above it (Article 206). Village administrations comprise the village head (*kepala desa*) and the village deliberation board (*badan permusyawaratan desa*) (Article 200(1)). Village heads are directly elected, can hold office for a maximum of two six-year terms (Articles 203–204)[25] and run the village administration (Article 208).[26]

The village deliberation board enacts village regulations (*peraturan desa*) together with the village head (Article 209). Although the 2004 Regional Government Law states that board members are 'representatives' (*wakil*) of villages, they are not democratically elected. Rather, they are appointed by deliberation and consensus (*musyawarah dan mufakat*), for six-year terms (Article 210). The board's leaders are chosen by, and from among, the board members.

REGIONAL GOVERNMENT JURISDICTIONS

The 2004 Regional Government Law purports to grant local governments – provincial, county and city – the broadest autonomy (*otonomi*

[23] Articles 298(4) and 349(4) of Law 27 of 2009. The 2009 Law sets the minimum number of DPRD members needed to support the motion (Articles 313–314, 364–365).

[24] Articles 315 and 366 of Law 27 of 2009. Legislators may, of course, leave office for other reasons covered in the 2009 Law, including as a result of removal for misconduct and retirement: Articles 332–340, 383–391 of the 2009 Law.

[25] The Elucidation to Article 204 adds that local customary law can dictate the term of office of village heads, provided that the law 'lives' in the community and is then confirmed in a Perda.

[26] The 2004 Regional Government Law provides no details of what this entails, leaving it to later government regulation (Article 208).

seluas-luasnya) in order to 'improve the prosperity of the community, public services and regional competitiveness' (Article 2). The Law gives them specific rights to regulate and manage the affairs of their administrations; to choose their regional head; to manage regional institutions and assets; to impose regional taxes and user charges; to share in the yields of the exploitation of natural and other resources in their regions; and to obtain other legal sources of income (Article 21). The Law does not give regional governments *carte blanche*, however. It imposes several restrictions upon them. First, some matters are reserved exclusively for the central government: foreign affairs; defence; security; judicial affairs; national monetary and fiscal matters; and religion (Article 10(3)). The central government can, however, delegate its jurisdiction to regulate these matters to local governments (Article 10(4)).

Second, the Law imposes 'obligations' (*urusan wajib*) upon regional governments. In particular, it specifies fundamental public services that regional governments must provide and functions that they must perform. These include development and spatial planning; public order and security; public facilities and infrastructure; health care; education; environmental controls; small-medium enterprises support; land and general government administration; and assistance for investment and civil registration (Articles 13(1) and 14(1)). The Law also requires regional governments to protect the community; ensure that national unity and harmony is maintained; improve the quality of life of the community; develop democratic life; ensure justice and equality; improve basic education services; provide acceptable social and public facilities; develop a social security system and productive regional resources; protect the environment and socio-cultural values; and manage population administration (Article 22).[27] The Law does not make clear how these responsibilities are to be fulfilled. Presumably, local governments have broad discretion to decide how to meet them.

Third, the 2004 Regional Government Law sets out 'Principles of Government Administration' (*Asas Penyelenggaraan Pemerintahan*) with which regional governments must comply. These principles are legal certainty, order, public interest, openness, proportionality, professionalism, accountability, efficiency and effectiveness (Article 20). Although

---

[27] The Law also allows regional governments to engage in 'optional responsibilities' (*urusan pilihan*), which are vaguely described as being 'closely related to the unique and particular potential of the region' (Elucidation to Article 22).

cast as requirements, these principles are so vague as to be virtually meaningless; and the Law provides no mechanisms for impartial review of compliance or redress for breach.

The fourth limitation is that local governments are legally required to assist higher-tier governments to perform functions within their regions, if requested. Governments can require assistance from any of the tiers of government below them under the so-called 'duty to assist' (*tugas pembantuan*) (Article 1(9)). The duty is defined as the 'participation of regions, or villages, including the community, in a task from the central government or a regional government, to perform a particular government function' (General Elucidation, part 3). Central government requests must be accompanied by funding and necessary equipment (Article 12).

Law-making

The 2004 Regional Government Law gives both the executive and legislative arms of provincial, county and city governments power to draft and enact laws about matters over which they have jurisdiction (Article 22).[28] Regional laws are commonly referred to as 'Perda', regardless of the institution and level of government from which they originate. The term has a narrower legal meaning, however, which we adopt in this chapter. Technically, it refers only to the laws enacted by provincial, county or city *legislatures*. The laws passed solely by regional heads – governors, regents and mayors – are properly termed either regulations (*peraturan*) or decisions (*keputusan*) of heads of regions, or, more specifically, governor regulations or decisions, regent regulations or decisions, and mayoral regulations or decisions.

Draft Perda can originate from the local legislature or regional head and should be directed towards 'implementing regional autonomy' (Article 136(2)) – that is, regulating the matters over which the 2004 Regional Government Law grants local governments jurisdiction. Perda can also seek to assist the central government to implement central government policy (Article 136(2)). Perda should accommodate the special

---

[28] Villages also have regulatory powers, exercised by the village deliberation board together with the *kepala desa* (Article 209). The 2004 Regional Government Law does not regulate them in detail, however, and we mention them here only for completeness.

characteristics of the region in which they are enacted (Article 136(3)), and must not contravene the public interest or higher-level laws (Article 136(4)).[29] Community members have the right to provide written or oral input when Perda are being formulated (Article 139(1)). The central government can review and veto Perda using processes discussed below. Once deliberated, enacted and approved (if necessary), they are brought into law (*ditetapkan*), or assented to, by the regional head (Article 136(1)). The regional head can then implement Perda by issuing regulations or decisions (Article 146(1)). A civil police unit (*pamong praja*) can be established to help the regional head enforce these laws (Article 148(1)).[30]

Many regional laws have been well-received, meeting regional government obligations to provide adequate services such as health care or education, or setting meaningful environmental standards. Many others, however, have been criticised for being unclear, unnecessary, misdirected, exploitative of citizens and investors, or even unconstitutional. Of particular concern has been the propensity of local governments to issue Perda imposing taxes and user charges to raise revenue, rather than to provide or improve public services for their constituents.

AVENUES FOR CENTRAL GOVERNMENT CONTROL?

Central Government Review and Veto Powers

The 2004 Regional Government Law gives the central government power to review, and the president power to veto by regulation, any Perda for being against public order or inconsistent with a higher-level law (Article 145(2)). The Law also requires central government preapproval for some types of Perda – for example, those that seek to impose taxes or user charges or constitute regional budgets or spatial plans.[31] Most types of Perda, however, must be sent to the central government within seven days after enactment. These laws automatically come into

---

[29] Perda are not permitted to impose more than six months' imprisonment and a Rp 50 million fine (Article 143(2)).
[30] Formal criminal investigations and prosecutions, however, must be conducted by national police and prosecutors (Article 149(1)).
[31] Articles 185–189 of the 2004 Law; Law 28 of 2009 on Regional Tax and User Charges. This constitutes a departure from the 1999 Autonomy Law, which proscribed post-enactment review for all Perda (Article 113 of Law 22 of 1999).

force after 60 days unless the central government objects to them (Article 145(3) and (7)). In practice, the president appears to have delegated invaliding Perda and local executive regulations to the Home Affairs Minister, who generally invalidates them by issuing a Ministerial Decision (*Keputusan Menteri*).[32] Although the Ministry of Home Affairs (MOHA) reviews provincial laws, it has purported to delegate power to review county and city Perda and regent/mayor regulations to the provincial governments in which they are located.[33]

Criticism of these review processes is widespread in Indonesian legal circles and the literature.[34] While many thousands of Perda are said to have been submitted to the central government for review, reports indicate that some regional governments have not done so.[35] Observers suspect that of those Perda that are submitted, many, if not most, are not reviewed within statutory timeframes because MOHA and provincial governments lack capacity and resources to deal with the mass of laws they receive. The central government appears mainly – perhaps almost exclusively – concerned about reviewing and invalidating regional laws

[32] Home Affairs Ministerial Regulation 53 of 2007 purports to make this and the other delegations described in this paragraph. The Finance Ministry is usually involved in reviews of finance-related Perda, such as those imposing taxes or setting out regional budgets.

[33] For discussion of the legality of these delegations and the legal instruments used to invalidate regional laws, see S Butt, 'Regional Autonomy and the Proliferation of Perda in Indonesia: An Assessment of Bureaucratic and Judicial Review Mechanisms' (2010) 32(2) *Sydney Law Review* 177.

[34] D Ray, *Decentralization, Regulatory Reform, and the Business Climate* (Jakarta Indonesia, Partnership for Economic Growth, 2003); S Butt, 'Regional Autonomy and the Proliferation of Perda in Indonesia' (n 33 above); S Butt and T Lindsey, 'Unfinished Business: Law Reform, Governance and the Courts in Post-Soeharto Indonesia' in M Kunkler and A Stepan (eds), *Indonesia, Islam and Democratic Consolidation* (New York, Columbia University Press, 2012). We draw on the last two publications throughout this chapter.

[35] Estimates vary, but, in the earlier days of decentralisation it seems that local governments were sending somewhere between only 30 and 40 per cent of their Perda to the central government (BD Lewis, 'Tax and Charge Creation by Regional Governments under Fiscal Decentralization: Estimates and Explanations' (2003) 39(2) *Bulletin Of Indonesian Economic Studies* 178). According to T Ismail, 'Kebijakan Pengawasan atas Perda Pajak Daerah dan Retribusi Daerah' in *Decentralization, regulatory reform, and the Business Climate* (Jakarta Indonesia, Partnership for Economic Growth, 2003) 89, between August 2001 and January 2003, for example, only nine of Indonesia's then-30 provinces, and 83 of Indonesia's 370 counties and cities, had sent any Perda to the central government.

imposing taxes or user charges.[36] Many Perda therefore seem to survive the 'review' process unchecked, and automatically come into force, despite questionable compliance with national laws and apparent flouting of constitutionally-guaranteed rights.[37]

National Laws Trump Regional Laws

Despite regional governments being granted powers to regulate a wide variety of issues, their law-making powers are not exclusive. Article 10(5) of the 2004 Regional Government Law gives the central government power to enact laws about matters that fall beyond those reserved exclusively for it in Article 10(3), discussed above. Legally speaking, the central government can continue to regulate any matter over which regional governments also have jurisdiction. This is important because in the event of inconsistency between most types of national laws and a regional government law, the national law prevails.[38] In practice, however, we suspect that many Perda that contradict national statutes and regulations remain on the books because, first, inconsistencies are not detected at the time that the central government reviews them; and, second, the mechanisms for resolving jurisdictional conflicts, discussed below, have been largely ineffectual.

---

[36] Many of the 1691 laws invalidated by the Ministry of Home Affairs in 2004–2009 were such laws (S Butt, 'Regional Autonomy and the Proliferation of Perda in Indonesia' (n 33 above); *Hukumonline*, 'PERMA Hak Uji Materiil Perlu Direvisi', 25 March 2011; B D Lewis, 'Tax and Charge Creation by Regional Governmenst under Fiscal Decentralization' (n 36 above) 178; E Susi Rosdianasari, N Anggriani and B Mulyani, *Dinamika Penyusunan, Substansi dan Implementasi Perda Pelayanan Publik* (Jakarta, World Bank Justice for the Poor Project, 2009) ix).

[37] A Swamurti, 'Komnas Perempuan Desak 154 Perda Diskriminatif Dibatalkan', *Tempo*, 29 January 2010.

[38] The so-called hierarchy of laws (contained in Article 7(1) of Law 10 of 2004 on Law-making) is discussed in Chapter 4 of this volume. This hierarchy ranks the Constitution, MPR Decrees, statutes, government regulations and presidential regulations above provincial and county/city Perda, in the sense that Perda may be overruled by any of these instruments.

Empowering Provinces, Potential Roll-back?

The 1999 Regional Government Law had granted only limited jurisdiction to provincial governments.[39] Provinces were confined largely to mediating disputes between districts, cross-county development, and representing the central government within the province. Provincial governments were not 'naturally' superior to counties and cities in the new scheme of governance created by the legislation.[40] They therefore could not trump the decisions or laws of local governments in the counties and cities within the province. By most accounts, this was a strategy to guard against Indonesia's disintegration. Provinces are more feasible as states than the smaller counties and cities[41] and politicians at the national level were chary of granting them quasi-federal status.

The 2004 Regional Government Law dramatically changed this balance. As mentioned, it gave provinces powers to regulate their own affairs like those enjoyed by counties and cities. It also positioned provincial governments as central government representatives in the regions. Articles 37 and 38, for example, make governors responsible to the President. Article 382(1) gives power to governors to 'guide and supervise governance in counties and municipalities' and to 'coordinate the implementation of central government affairs in provinces, counties and municipalities'.[42]

In this way, the central Indonesian government can, at least theoretically, retain some control through governors and provincial governments over the way sub-provincial governments exercise their powers. Indeed, as mentioned, provincial administrations have been charged with reviewing laws enacted by these governments. Even without these controls, however, the 2004 Regional Government Law gives the central government quite direct power to 'influence' local governments. It

---

[39] Elucidation, point h.

[40] G Ferrazzi, 'Using the "F" Word: Federalism in Indonesia's Decentralization Discourse' (2000) 30(2) *Publius: The journal of federalism* 73; F Fitrani, B Hofman and K Kaiser, 'Unity in Diversity? The Creation of New Local Governments in a Decentralising Indonesia' (2005) 4(1) *Bulletin of Indonesian Economic Studies* 58, 60.

[41] E Aspinall and G Fealy, 'Introduction' in E Aspinall and G Fealy (eds), *Local Power and Politics in Indonesia: Decentralisation and Democratisation* (Singapore, ISEAS, 2003) 4.

[42] The 2011 amendments to Article 7(1) of Law 10 of 2004 on Law-making place provincial laws above county and city laws in the hierarchy of laws.

authorises the central government to help develop the administration of regional governments. This it can do by co-ordinating the different levels of government; providing guidelines for the performance of government functions; supervising and consulting with regional governments about government matters; and educating and training, planning, researching, developing, monitoring and evaluating (Article 217).

JURISDICTIONAL DISPUTE RESOLUTION

Local legislatures and executives can challenge the central government's revocation of their laws in the Supreme Court.[43] The Supreme Court hears very few of these cases each year. In 2010, for example, it reviewed just six ministerial decisions,[44] only some of which may have sought to invalidate Perda.

Commentators have criticised the Supreme Court's appeal decisions in these cases. Butt[45] has argued, for example, that many of them lack persuasive reasoning, with the Court merely declaring that the subject matter of the law, being a local political matter, falls within the jurisdiction of the local government. Another problem was that the Court imposed a 180-day deadline for lodgement of review applications that ran from the date the impugned law was enacted.[46] Once this deadline had expired, the Perda would become unreviewable. The Court would, with few exceptions, throw out cases that did not strictly comply with the deadline, regardless of the egregiousness of the Perda in question.[47] Fortunately, however, the Supreme Court removed this limitation in 2011.[48]

The Supreme Court can, it seems, also review regional legislation and executive regulations as part of its general judicial review jurisdiction. As mentioned in Chapter 4, the Constitution authorises the Supreme Court

---

[43] Article 145(5) of the 2004 Autonomy Law.

[44] Mahkamah Agung, *Laporan Tahun 2010* (Jakarta, Mahkamah Agung, 2011) 75.

[45] S Butt, 'Regional Autonomy and the Proliferation of Perda in Indonesia' (n 33 above) 192.

[46] Article 2(4) of Supreme Court Regulation 1 of 2004; Article 5(4) of Supreme Court Regulation 1 of 1999.

[47] S Butt, 'Regional Autonomy and the Proliferation of Perda in Indonesia' (n 33 above).

[48] *Hukumonline*, 'Telah Terbit PERMA Hak Uji Materiil 2011', 20 June 2011.

to review against statutes any laws of a level below statutes.[49] These lower-order laws include national government and presidential regulations, and local laws. Citizens have asked the Supreme Court to exercise this jurisdiction to review Perda that they believe do not comply with national legislation. Until 2011, this type of case was also subject to the 180-day lodgement deadline, which allowed local governments to avoid review proceedings simply by holding back the publication of their enacted laws until the deadline had passed. Perhaps in part because of that deadline, the Supreme Court has heard only a handful of these cases in recent years. In 2010, for example, the Supreme Court reviewed nine Perda, one governor decision and one mayor regulation.[50] With the deadline lifted, the Court might be expected to hear more of these applications in the future.

In any case, the Supreme Court's general judicial review jurisdiction is of limited utility in the review of Perda. The Court does not have power to resolve all types of conflicting laws issued by the various tiers of government. Take, for example, the situation in which a regional law is thought to contradict either a central-government lower-order law, or a local law from another tier of regional government. Both events are very likely to happen. Provincial governments on the one hand, and county and city governments on the other, have virtually the same obligations under Articles 13 and 14 of the 2004 Regional Government Law. They are, therefore, likely to pass laws purporting to regulate the same or similar subject matter and, as mentioned, the central government has power to regulate any matter over which regional governments also have jurisdiction. These scenarios do not appear to fall within the Supreme Court's review jurisdiction, however, because the Court can review lower-order laws only against national statutes and not against national lower-order laws. There are, to our knowledge, no mechanisms available to help resolve these conflicts.[51]

---

[49] See also Article 31 of Law 14 of 1985 on the Supreme Court.

[50] Mahkamah Agung, *Laporan Tahun 2010* (above n 44) 75.

[51] One legal solution might be for the Supreme Court to grant itself jurisdiction to review Perda as against lower-order laws by reasoning that the 2004 Regional Government Law – a statute – prohibits the enactment of Perda that contradict higher-level laws and that this includes national government, presidential and ministerial regulations and decisions. The Perda would, therefore, be inconsistent with the 2004 Law if it breached a 'higher' law, even if that law was below the level of a statute. Presumably this reasoning could be applied to allow the review of a city or county Perda as against a provincial Perda. To our knowledge, this argument has not yet been put to the Supreme Court.

CREATING NEW REGIONS

The 2004 Regional Government Law provides that new regions can be established by merging (*penggabungan*) two pre-existing regions, or splitting (*pemekaran*) a region into two or more (Article 5(3)). The Law provides little guidance about the processes for merging or removing regions, however. It merely permits it if a region is 'unable' to engage in regional autonomy (Article 6(1)) and if a government regulation is issued to support the merger (Article 6(3)). Likewise, the 2004 Autonomy Law provides a regulatory outline of various administrative, technical and physical requirements that must be fulfilled to establish new regions but leaves the detail to government regulations (Articles 5(1) and 8).[52] The administrative requirements include obtaining the permission of other DPRDs and heads of governments who would be affected by the new region, as well as of the Home Affairs Minister. New provinces must secure the agreement of the DPRD of the counties and cities that are to fall within the new province and of the provincial DPRD and government from which it will split, and the Home Affairs Minister's recommendation (Article 5(2)). New counties and cities need approval from the relevant DPRD and the regent/mayor in question and the provincial DPRD and governor, as well as endorsement by the Home Affairs Minister (Article 5(3)).

The 2004 Regional Government Law vaguely casts the technical requirements as: economic capacity; 'regional potential' (*potensi daerah*); sufficient population and size; adequate defence and security; socio-cultural and socio-political capability; and 'other features' that make it possible for the region to engage in regional autonomy (Article 5(4)). Those proposing a new province must be able to bring at least five counties and cities under them; new counties must bring at least five sub-districts (*kecamatan*) and cities four sub-districts; and all new regions must nominate a capital city, in addition to providing equipment and infrastructure for government (Article 5(5)). Before being split, provinces must have been in existence for at least 10 years, and counties and cities seven years (Article 4(4)). Villages can be established, removed and merged on the initiative of the local community (Article 200(2)).

---

[52] At time of writing, this appeared to be Government Regulation 78 of 2007 on Procedures for the Establishment, Removal and Merging of Regions.

Ultimately, splitting and merging regions requires endorsement by statute (Articles 4(1) and 7(1)). The statute must set out the region's name, geographic area, capital city, jurisdiction, regional head and DPRD membership, and must provide for the transfer of personnel and funding (Article 4(2)).

Constitutional Court Cases

The Constitutional Court has heard several challenges to the constitutionality of the creation of new regions. The *Tambrauw case*[53] was brought by heads of several ethnic groups and *adat* chiefs in Manokwari, West Papua, who had pushed for the establishment of Tambrauw County in West Papua. Through consultative community *adat* processes, it had been agreed that 10 pre-existing districts – four from the Manokwari County and six from the Sorong County – would comprise Tambrauw.[54] The executive governments and DPRDs of Sorong, Manokwari and West Papua agreed to the plan.[55] Without consultation, the Governor of West Papua and the Regent of Sorong withdrew their support, however, deciding that Tambrauw should consist of only the six districts from Sorong.[56] The DPR enacted Law 56 of 2008 to that effect.

The Constitutional Court decided that any political or other considerations underlying Law 56 of 2008 should not displace the aspirations to create Tambrauw: the *adat* communities of Sorong and Manokwari had a constitutional right to establish Tambrauw with 10 sub-districts. To support its decision, the Court pointed to Article 28C(2) of the Constitution ('Every person has the right to promote themselves and push for collective rights to develop the community, nation and state'), and Article 28D(1) ('Every person has the right to legal recognition,

[53] Constitutional Court Decision 127/PUU-VII/2009.

[54] According to press reports, there was some doubt as to the genuineness and unanimity of the agreement of the citizens of all 10 regions to form Tambrauw. The Court did not mention this in its decision. Some civil society actors and activists in the district argued that the decision to include all 10 sub-districts into Tambrauw represented the interests of local elites, and not the community at large. Hundreds of citizens apparently protested against the Constitutional Court decision at the Manokwari Bupati office (*Cahaya Papua*, 'Ratusan Warga Tambrauw Timur Datangi Kantor Bupati Tolak Ikut Pilkada Tambrauw', 14 March 2011).

[55] Constitutional Court Decision 127/PUU-VII/2009, p 67.

[56] Constitutional Court Decision 127/PUU-VII/2009, p 67.

guarantees, protection and certainty that is just, and to equal treatment before the law'). It found that ignoring the *adat* community aspirations also constituted a breach of Article 28I(3) ('Cultural identity and community rights are respected provided that they are consistent with the "times" and civilisation').[57] The Court held that Law 56 of 2008 would therefore be invalid unless the four districts from Manokwari – Amberbaken, Kebar, Senopi and Mubrani – were included as part of Tambrauw.[58] The Court noted:

> Regions are created to help improve the efficacy . . . of government and services to improve community welfare. Determination of the boundaries of a region and choosing a capital city is, therefore, something that should be left to the community that wishes to come together in the new region. The role of existing district and provincial governments is to agree to hand over part of the region, assets, and personnel and to be prepared to help initially fund the new region.[59]

In the *West and Central Irian Jaya case*,[60] John Ibo, head of the Papua DPRD, complained about provisions of a 1999 statute under which West Papua had been divided into two provinces: West and Central Irian Jaya.[61] In 2001, Law 21 on Special Autonomy for Papua was enacted but did not mention West or Central Irian Jaya and did not explicitly seek to revoke the 1999 Law.

According to the Constitutional Court, the 2001 and 1999 Laws were inconsistent and it was unclear which of the two statutes should be applied to the establishment of new provinces in Papua. This, the Court found, gave rise to legal uncertainty that was unconstitutional[62] (and

---

[57]   Constitutional Court Decision 127/PUU-VII/2009, pp 69–70.

[58]   The Court handed down its decision in January 2009. Though the decision was formally binding and immediately enforceable, the decision had still not been put into effect in September 2010. Representatives from the four Manokwari districts excluded from Tambrauw had asked the Coordinating Minister for Political, Legal and Security Affairs to 'provide them with certainty', seeking to vote in elections for the regional head of Tambrauw for 2010 (Ichwan and Wisnubrata A Susanto, 'Menko Polhukam Ditagih Revisi Pemekaran', *Kompas*, 30 September 2010).

[59]   Constitutional Court Decision 127/PUU-VII/2009, p 68.

[60]   Constitutional Court Decision 018/PUU-I/2003.

[61]   Law 45 of 1999 on the Establishment of the Provinces of Central Irian Jaya and West Irian Jaya, and the Counties of Paniai, Mimika and Puncak Jaya, and the city of Sorong, as amended by Law 5 of 2000.

[62]   In Chapter 5 of this volume, we discuss cases in which the Constitutional Court has considered the extent of the constitutional right to legal certainty.

which could also cause socio-political conflict within the community).[63] The Court therefore invalidated the 1999 statute.

West Irian government officials feared that the decision thus invalidated the creation of the new provinces.[64] In a meeting with these officials, the then-Chief Justice of the Constitutional Court, Professor Jimly Asshiddiqie, quelled these fears, explaining that the Constitutional Court's decisions operated only into the future.[65] Because the Court's decision was made after the provinces were formed under the 1999 statute, they remained intact. The main effect of the Court's decision was therefore that any new regions in Papua that sought to use the 1999 Law as the legal basis for their creation after the Court's decision would be invalid. New regions could only be established under the 2001 Autonomy Law.

In the *West Sulawesi case*,[66] the Constitutional Court reviewed Law 26 of 2004 on the Establishment of the Province of West Sulawesi. In this case, the Governor of the Province of South Sulawesi sought a review of Law 26 of 2004, which split the Province of South Sulawesi into two provinces – South and West Sulawesi. In Article 16(7) the Law also required the South to pay the new West at least Rp 16 billion over its first two years of existence and then to make further allocations from its budget into the future. If payment was not made, then the central government could withhold payments it would otherwise have given to the South Sulawesi government (Article 15(9)). The Governor argued that the Law was discriminatory because the DPR had not required other provinces to financially support similar 'offshoot' provinces.

The Court rejected this application, holding that the central legislature's differential treatment of regional governments was not unconstitutional. The Court also appeared to chide the Governor for his lack of willingness to assist the new province, saying, somewhat optimistically:

[I]n the spirit of the Unitary Republic of Indonesia, which is based upon Pancasila, all regional governments should feel bound by a feeling of togetherness to help each other.[67]

---

[63] Constitutional Court Decision 018/PUU-I/2003, p 134.

[64] *Hukumonline*, 'Pembentukan Irjabar Sah, Tapi Undang-Undangnya Tidak Berlaku Lagi', 17 November 2004.

[65] *Hukumonline*, 'Masyarakat Papua Pertanyakan Putusan Mahkamah Konstitusi', 12 December 2004. For a discussion about the Constitutional Court's decisions operating only into the future, see Chapter 5 of this volume.

[66] Constitutional Court Decision 070/PUU-II/2004.

[67] Constitutional Court Decision 070/PUU-II/2004, p 46.

Finally, we observe that the Constitutional Court has denied standing to applicants who have argued that having a new capital city – necessary when a region is created – causes them undue inconvenience. For example, in Constitutional Court Decision 16/PUU-III/2005, reviewing Law 12 of 2001 on the Establishment of the City of Singkawang, the applicants complained that their new capital city – Bengkayang – was 127 kilometres away (the previous capital, Singkawang, was only 45 kilometres away); and that carrying on business in Bengkayang was more costly, risky and difficult than in Singkawang. According to the Court, inconvenience was not 'damage' for the purposes of founding a constitutional challenge.[68]

SPECIAL AUTONOMY

Two provinces have long been categorised as 'special' (*istimewa*) regions for historical reasons: the City of Yogyakarta[69] and the Capital City of Jakarta.[70] As part of the post-Soeharto decentralisation reforms, two other provinces – Papua and Aceh – were granted 'special autonomy' (*otonomi khusus*) status under specific legislation, pursuant to Article 18B

[68]   See also Constitutional Court Decision 4/PUU-VI/2008, in which the Court refused to hear a review, on similar grounds, of Law 36 of 2003 on the Creation of the Counties of Samosir and Serdang in North Sumatra province.

[69]   Yogyakarta was formally granted 'special' (*istimewa*) status as a province through Law 3 of 1950 on the Establishment of the Special Region of Yogyakarta. The primary difference between Yogyakarta and other provinces is the position of the Sultan, who has traditionally also held office as governor of the province (Bayu Dardias Kurniadi, 'Yogyakarta in Decentralized Indonesia: Integrating Traditional Institutions into a Democratic Republic', *Indonesia Council Open Conference* (University of Sydney, 16 July 2009)).

[70]   Law 29 of 2007 on the Administration of the Special Province of Jakarta, the Capital City of Indonesia. Like other provinces, Jakarta has a directly-elected governor and deputy governor (Articles 10 and 11); a DPRD with legislative, monitoring and budgetary functions (Article 12(1)); and authority to administer the region, including by law-making, although foreign affairs, defence, security, justice, national monetary and fiscal matters, and religious affairs are matters reserved for the central government (Article 26(1)). The Law also grants the Jakarta government special duties, rights, obligations and responsibilities due to it being the capital city of Indonesia and a centre for international institutions (Article 5). For example, the government has special rights in respect of spatial planning (Article 29) and the creation of special areas (*kawasan khusus*) for particular government functions or events (Article 30).

of the Constitution.[71] Both Papua and Aceh have been relatively isolated from much of the rest of Indonesia in the past, and are notable for secessionist movements and frequent threats to split away from the Republic. Both also have strong local identities tied to ethnicity and history, including local traditions of independence and resistance to rule from the outside.

Papua

Papua is ethnically a mainly Melanesian region, and comprises the western half of the island of New Guinea. Although poorly-developed, it is rich in natural resources and has been the location of major mining activity. Known for much of modern Indonesian history as 'Irian', its name was changed post-Soeharto to reflect local preferences. As mentioned earlier, the *Organisasi Papua Merdeka* (OPM) has for decades led a local rebellion seeking independence from Indonesia.

The legal basis for Papua's special autonomy is Law 21 of 2001 on Special Autonomy for Papua Province. As mentioned above in our discussion of the *West and Central Irian Jaya case*, the 2001 Law does not mention West or Central Papua, referring only to the Province of Papua. We assume that its provisions apply to both West and Central Papua but, as shown below, this is a matter of great debate.

In some matters, the 2001 Papua Autonomy Law is similar to the 2004 Regional Government Law. Papuan regional governments are granted power over 'all aspects of government' (*seluruh bidang pemerintahan*), although, like the 2004 Regional Government Law, the Papua Autonomy Law reserves for the central government foreign affairs, defence and security, monetary and fiscal matters, religion and judicial affairs (Article 4(1)). Provincial governors in Papua are responsible to the Papua DPRD and act as the central government's representatives in Papua. The 2001 Papua Autonomy Law gives the central government authority to override provincial government laws, using processes similar to those provided in the 2004 Regional Government Law, if they contradict higher-level laws or the public interests of the Papuan community (Article 68 and its Elucidation).

---

[71] Law 21 of 2001, amended by Interim Emergency Law 1 of 2008, which was confirmed as a statute by Law 35 of 2008.

Papuan regional governments have legislatures and executive governments similar to those of other regions governed by the 2004 Regional Government Law, with one main exception.[72] The 2001 Papua Autonomy Law sets up the Papuan People's Assembly (*Majelis Rakyat Papua*, or MRP), made up of indigenous representatives of traditional (*adat*) communities, women and religious figures in equal number, selected by their respective constituencies (Article 19(1)). One of the Assembly's main functions is protecting the indigenous rights of Papuans and to this end it is empowered to advise the Papuan government on these rights to ensure that they are upheld in regional government policies and laws.[73]

The 2001 Papua Autonomy Law differs from the 2004 Regional Government Law in several other ways, three of which we mention here. First, acknowledging that previous central government policies on resource-sharing were not 'optimal', the 2001 Papua Autonomy Law requires that 70 per cent of oil and gas revenues be returned to Papua for 25 years, after which the allocation becomes 50 per cent (Article 34(3)). The Law requires Papuan governments to allocate specified portions of this revenue to education and health (Article 36). Second, the Law requires Papuan provincial governments to protect customary law and communal land rights recognised under existing laws (Chapter XI). Finally, Papuan provinces have the right to use their own symbols, including flags and anthems (Article 2(2)).

Papua legislature appointments case[74]

The 2001 Law was challenged in the *Papua legislature appointments case*. Article 6(2) of the 2001 Law requires that the Papuan legislature be made up of both elected and appointed members 'in accordance with law'. Article 6(4) stipulates that one-quarter of members should be appointees.

---

[72] Initially, the provincial Papua legislature was granted powers to elect the governor and vice-governor, but these powers were removed in 2008 (Interim Emergency Law 1 of 2008, which amended Law 21 of 2001).

[73] Some controversy emerged when the province of West Papua was split. The MRP was initially conceived when Papua comprised of one province. There has been disagreement about whether a single MRP should cover both provinces, one of the two provinces or simply be disbanded (Nethy Dharma Somba, 'Govt "not serious" in Applying Papuan Special Autonomy', *Jakarta Post*, 26 July 2010).

[74] Constitutional Court Decision 116/PUU-VII/2009.

The applicants, Papuan figures who had failed to obtain seats in the 2009 elections, argued that the reference to 'law' in Article 6(2) was problematic for several reasons. These included that Article 6(2) did not specify which 'law' was intended, thereby providing an avenue for the central government to pass laws to make appointments to the DPRD that it favoured.[75] They argued that Article 6(2) therefore breached several provisions of the Constitution, including Article 18(2) ('Provincial, county and city governments are to regulate and administer matters of government themselves under the principles of autonomy and assistance [to other tiers of government]') and Article 28H(2) ('Every person has the right to facilities and special treatment to obtain the same opportunities and benefits in order to achieve equality and justice'). The applicants also pointed out that Article 6(2) and (4) had been ignored when the Papuan legislature was reconstituted without any appointed members after the 2004 and 2009 local elections.

Strangely, the Constitutional Court did not address the obvious implications of legislative appointments for Indonesian democracy. Instead, it simply accepted that appointments were part of a permissible 'affirmative action policy' to allow traditional Papuan representatives to participate in the formulation of local policy, to determine development strategies and to protect the natural environment and Papuan customs.[76] This was constitutionally justifiable, it held, by reference to Articles 28H(2) and Article 18B(1) ('The State recognises and respects special (*khusus/istimewa*) regional governments, as regulated by statute'). The Court seemed to accept that these provisions allow for the 'special' treatment of some regional governments including by making such appointments. The Court found that, after the 2004 and 2009 elections, the Papuan legislature should, therefore, have included appointees.[77]

The Constitutional Court urged the Papua Governor and legislature to immediately enact a law on appointment procedures and to appoint sufficient members to the Papuan legislature so that one-quarter of its members became appointees. This, the Court ordered, needed to be done through the enactment of a Perda, rather than a central government law.[78]

---

[75] Constitutional Court Decision 116/PUU-VII/2009, p 55.

[76] Constitutional Court Decision 116/PUU-VII/2009, pp 53, 63.

[77] Constitutional Court Decision 116/PUU-VII/2009, p 64.

[78] Constitutional Court Decision 116/PUU-VII/2009, pp 64–66. Specifically, the Court required the enactment of a Special Perda (*Perda Khusus*), a type of Perda

Aceh

The basis of the special autonomy of Aceh[79] is Law 11 of 2006 on the Governing of Aceh, which in Article 272 repealed its predecessor, Law 18 of 2001 on the Special Autonomy of Aceh. Both statutes were part of a series of post-Soeharto concessions granted by the national government to prevent Aceh from breaking away from the Republic, as did East Timor in 1999.

Aceh is an under-developed and largely rural province at the western tip of Sumatra. It has a history of isolation and warfare. Since the 1970s, it was effectively cut off from the rest of Indonesia and was a 'military operations zone' (DOM – *Daerah Operasi Militer*) from 1989 until the end of the New Order in 1998, as the Indonesian military fought Acehnese rebels led by *Gerakan Aceh Merdeka* (GAM). Hostilities continued after Soeharto's fall but were halted by the devastating tsunami of 26 December 2004. This led to massive international intervention to rebuild areas destroyed by flooding and rehabilitate victims of the disaster. It also placed great pressure on both sides in the conflict to achieve peace. The Law on the Governing of Aceh was a result of the 2005 Helsinki Agreement by which conflict was formally brought to an end and Aceh agreed to remain part of the Republic.

Islam has historically been influential in the creation of a distinct Acehnese identity. A form of Islamic law was implemented by the

---

that the 2001 Papua Autonomy Law declares in Article 1(i) is to be used to implement its provisions. The Court's primary holding was that the phrase 'in accordance with law' in Article 6(2) was conditionally unconstitutional unless interpreted to mean 'in accordance with a Special Perda' that allowed 11 appointees. However, the Court did not provide a constitutional basis for its decision that appointments and appointment procedures must be implemented through *Perda Khusus*. Rather, it drew this conclusion by referring to provisions of the Papua Autonomy Law itself and Law 10 of 2004 on Law-making.

[79] The province was known as *Daerah Istimewa Aceh* (Aceh Special Region) from 1975 until the promulgation of Law 18 of 2001, when it became known as *Nanggroe Aceh Darussalam*. After the promulgation of the Law on the Governing of Aceh in 2006, it was usually just referred to as 'Aceh' (Article 25) and this was confirmed by Governor of Aceh Regulation 46 of 2009. This discussion of Aceh draws on T Lindsey, *Islam, Law and the State in Southeast Asia, Vol. I: Indonesia* (London, IB Tauris 2012), Chapters 9 and 11; and T Lindsey, MB Hooker, R Clarke and J Kingsley, 'Sharia Reform in Aceh: New Born or Still Born?', in RM Feener and ME Cammack (eds), *Islamic Law in Contemporary Indonesia: Ideas and Institutions* (Cambridge, Harvard University Press, 2007) 216–54.

Sultanate of Aceh in the late sixteenth and early seventeenth centuries,[80] and the period from then until the mid-nineteenth century is still imagined by the Acehnese as their 'golden age'. This strong local tradition has created a local identity in which Islam plays a central part. The powers of self-government granted to Aceh in the post-Soeharto era were a response to this and they authorised the provincial government, the DPRA (*Dewan Perwakilan Rakyat Aceh*, Aceh People's Representative Assembly), to issue *Qanun*. These are Regional Regulations or Perda but, unlike anywhere else in Indonesia, Acehnese Perda may deal expressly with religion, specifically 'Syariah Islam'.[81] Elsewhere in Indonesia, the religion power is, as mentioned earlier, reserved to the central government.[82]

The DPRA has now passed Qanun covering many areas of law, including *syakshiyah* (family law), *mu'amalah* (commercial law) and, most controversially, *jinayat* (criminal law).[83] Likewise, a series of institutions have been developed to regulate the application of Islamic law. These include the Syariah Court (*Mahkamah Syar'iyah*);[84] the Consultative Assembly of Ulama or religious scholars (*Majelis Permusyawaratan Ulama*, MPU);[85] the Governor's Syari'ah Office (*Dinas Syariat*);[86] and 'religious police' (*Wilayatul Hisbah*).[87] The result is the most ambitious attempt to formally apply Islamic law in modern Southeast Asia.

Aceh's new '*syar'iyah*' regime has generally functioned effectively but has attracted controversy and has been much criticised for discriminating against women. Its critics argue that many of the Islamic Qanun

[80] A Salim, 'Shari'a from Below in Aceh (1930s–1960s): Islamic Identity and the Right to Self-Determination with Comparative Reference to the Moro Islamic Liberation Front (MILF)' (2004) 32(92) *Indonesia and Malay World* 80–99; MB Hooker, 'The Law Texts of Muslim South East Asia' in MB Hooker (ed), *Law of South East Asia*, vol 1, 'Pre-Modern Texts' (Singapore, Butterworths, 1986) 394–405.

[81] Articles 1(15), 1(2), 16(2)(a), 17(2)(a), 125–128 of the Law on the Governing of Aceh. Many regional legislatures outside Aceh have also enacted Perda which have implications for religious practice: R Bush, 'Regional Sharia Regulations in Indonesia: Anomaly or Symptom?' in G Fealy and S White (eds), *Expressing Islam: Religious Life and Politics in Indonesia* (Singapore, ISEAS, 2008) 174–91.

[82] Article 10(3) of the 2004 Regional Government Law.

[83] Article 129 of the Law on the Governing of Aceh.

[84] Articles 1(15) and 128 of the Law on the Governing of Aceh; Qanun 10 of 2002.

[85] Qanun 3 of 2000 and 9 of 2003; Article 1 of the Law on the Governing of Aceh.

[86] Qanun 33 of 2001; Article 1(15) of the Law on the Governing of Aceh.

[87] Qanun 5 and 11 of 2000.

passed in Aceh breach human rights guarantees in Chapter XA of the Constitution, Indonesia's international treaty obligations and laws passed by the DPR to implement them. These claims have not yet been tested in the Supreme Court, which has power to review and invalidate Qanun.[88]

The Aceh Independents case

In 2010 the Constitutional Court was asked to consider the validity of Article 256 of the Law on the Governing of Aceh,[89] which allowed independent candidates to run for Gubernatorial, County and Mayoral positions in Aceh, but *only* in the first election held after the promulgation of the Law in 2006.[90]

In its decision, the Court recognised the special autonomy status of Aceh and the general constitutionality of the Law on the Governing of Aceh. It held, however, that banning independent candidates in any election breached guarantees of legal certainty and rights to citizenship in Article 28D(1) and (4) of the Constitution, and therefore struck down Article 256. The Court supported this argument by referring to its own decision in the *Independent Candidates case* of 2007,[91] in which it held that independent candidates may run in national elections. It also referred to the 2008 amendments to the 2004 Regional Government Law that allow independents to run for local elections and noted that Papua has 'special autonomy' status like Aceh but does not ban independent candidates.

This case had been brought to the Constitutional Court in anticipation of Aceh's gubernatorial elections scheduled for 14 November 2011. GAM's political party, Partai Aceh, was the dominant faction in the DPRA and hoped its candidate would replace the incumbent governor, Irwandi Yusuf. Yusuf is a former GAM leader who was running as an independent. He and GAM had come to be at loggerheads but it was

---

[88]   Article 235 of the Law on the Governing of Aceh.

[89]   Constitutional Court Decision 35/PUU-VIII/2010.

[90]   Article 256 of the Law on Governing Aceh says 'The provisions governing independent candidates in the election of governor/vice governor, regent head/vice regent head, or the mayor/deputy mayor, as referred to in Article 67(1)(d), are valid and to be implemented only for the first elections after the promulgation of this Law'. Article 67(1) of the same Law provides that only 'certain people' can run for elections but defines this to include political parties (national, sub-national and coalitions of political parties) (Article 67(1)(a)–(c)) and 'an individual' (Article 67(1)(d)).

[91]   Constitutional Court Decision 5/PUU-V/2007.

thought his personal popularity might make him hard to defeat.[92] Anxious to prevent Yusuf running, Partai Aceh argued that the DPRA still has power to prohibit independent candidates, notwithstanding the Constitutional Court decision. It pointed to Article 7 of the Law on the Governing of Aceh. This reiterates the division of powers between central and regional government in Article 10(3) of the 2004 Regional Government Law. Article 7 provides:

> The government of Aceh and its district governments have the authority to manage *governmental affairs in all public sectors* except those that are the authority of the central government . . . including those having the characteristics of national affairs, foreign affairs, defence, security, justice-sector matters, monetary, national fiscal, and certain affairs in the religious sector.[93]

Partai Aceh's position seemed to be that because the conduct of local elections is not a central government affair under Article 7 it remains a residual 'public sector' power of the government of Aceh. On this view, the DPRA can regulate local elections to prohibit independent candidates notwithstanding the invalidation of Article 256, although that would seem to fly in the face of the Constitutional Court's decision. On 28 June 2011, the Partai Aceh-controlled DPRA therefore passed a new Qanun in defiance of the Constitutional Court to prohibit independent candidates from running in the 2011 election.[94] This led to a standoff with Governor Yusuf, who refused to sign the Qanun, thus preventing it from becoming law[95] and thereby keeping open his right to run in the elections (which he lost when they were eventually held in 2012).

CONCLUSION

Decentralisation was motivated by overwhelming resentment towards the highly-centralised, predatory and corrupt Soeharto regime. Yet commentators question whether decentralisation has improved the lot of ordinary Indonesians. No doubt some parts of Indonesia have fared well under competent local governments who have taken seriously their

---

[92] International Crisis Group, 'Indonesia: GAM vs GAM in the Aceh Elections', *Asia Briefing No 123* (Jakarta/Brussels, 2011) 1.
[93] ibid, 4 (emphasis added).
[94] A Warsidi, 'Pilkada Aceh Dipastikan Tanpa Calon Independen', *Tempo*, 29 June 2011.
[95] P Nugraha, 'Tak Ada Lagi Calon Independen di Aceh', *Kompas*, 28 June 2011.

obligations to provide fundamental public services such as health care and education. Equally, however, many local governments have been criticised for corruption and incompetence. Some scholars even claim that corruption may well have worsened under decentralisation, with local officials relishing the opportunity to exploit their office for private gain.[96] Anti-corruption Commission (KPK, *Komisi Pemberantasan Korupsi*) case statistics seem to support these claims. In early March 2011, the Commission revealed that it was investigating 13 former and four serving governors and 158 regents and mayors for corruption, 90 per cent of which allegedly occurred in the procurement of government goods and services. Of Indonesia's 33 provinces, 28 had a governor, mayor or regent who had been charged or prosecuted for corruption.[97]

Theorists claim that decentralisation should enhance government responsiveness to the needs of citizens,[98] by bringing 'government closer to the people'.[99] In parts of Indonesia it appears, however, that decentralisation has simply brought *bad* governance closer to the people. In fact, from a legal perspective, decentralisation has been nothing short of a disaster. There appears to be little or no order to the laws issued by regional governments. Many are said to be poorly drafted and hence unclear, and most are enacted without consideration of pre-existing laws or the effect that they will have. The result is legal chaos, in which citizens and business find it difficult to obtain, let alone determine precisely, the laws with which they must comply. Complaints are often made about the content of these laws, many of which are not directed at improving public services but

---

[96] Pratikno, 'Exercising freedom: Local Autonomy and Democracy in Indonesia, 1999–2001' in P Sulistiyanto, M Erb and C Faucher (eds), *Regionalism in Post-Suharto Indonesia*, (New York, RoutledgeCurzon, 2005); VR Hadiz, 'Decentralization and Democracy in Indonesia: A Critique of Neo-Institutionlist Perspectives' (2004) 35(4) *Development and Change* 697–718; VR Hadiz and R Robison, 'Neo-liberal Reforms and Illiberal Consolidations: The Indonesian Paradox' (2005) 41(2) *The Journal of Development Studies* 220–41.

[97] 'Aceh sampai Papua Tersandera Korupsi', *Kompas*, 24 January 2011.

[98] B Pranab and D Mookherjee, 'Decentralization, Corruption and Government Accountability' in S Rose-Ackerman (ed), *International Handbook on the Economics of Corruption* (Cheltenham, Edward Elgar, 2006) 161; J Edgardo Campos and JS Hellman, 'Governance Gone Local: Does Decentralization Improve Accountability?' in World Bank, *East Asia Decentralizes: Making Local Government Work* (Washington, The World Bank, 2005) 237–52.

[99] V Tanzi, 'Fiscal Federalism and Decentralization: A Review of Some Efficiency and Macroeconomic Aspects' in M Bruno and B Pleskovic (eds), *Annual World Bank Conference on Development Economics* (Washington DC, The World Bank, 1995) 295.

rather exact taxes, impose religiously-derived norms in the name of 'public order' (*ketertiban umum*) or simply regulate the administration of the local government. Overregulation, misdirection and continual testing of the jurisdictional boundaries of regional government law-making powers are common criticisms. According to a senior official from the national Finance Ministry:

> Since regional autonomy was introduced, a phenomenon that has emerged is the tendency for regions to wish to regulate everything on the view that all objects and subjects within their territory fall within their jurisdiction and must, therefore, be subject to the wishes of the region as regulated in regional regulations. What happens next is a type of euphoria, where the region appears to no longer observe the applicable rules, including by enacting regulations which regulate issues outside of their jurisdiction.[100]

The central government seems uninterested in intervening to invalidate problematic Perda, except when local governments seek to impose excessive taxes and user charges that eat into the central government's own revenue streams. Citizens' constitutional rights are left vulnerable, because there is no judicial institution with authority to directly review the constitutionality of Perda as against the Constitution.[101] Given that the regional regulations issued since decentralisation number in the thousands – perhaps tens of thousands – this is a significant flaw in the legal framework for decentralisation. There is limited utility in the Constitutional Court's growing rights jurisprudence discussed in the next chapter, if it cannot be applied to what is fast becoming the bulk of Indonesian law.

---

[100] T Ismail, 'Kebijakan Pengawasan atas Perda Pajak Daerah dan Retribusi Daerah' (n 35 above) 87–88.
[101] L Arnold, 'Acting Locally, Thinking Globally? The Relationship between Decentralization in Indonesia and International Human Rights' (2009) 1 *Journal of East Asia and International Law* 177–203.

SELECTED READING

Butt, Simon, 'Regional Autonomy and the Proliferation of Perda in Indonesia: An Assessment of Bureaucratic and Judicial Review Mechanisms' (2010) 32(2) *Sydney Law Review* 177.

Crouch, Harold, *Political Reform in Indonesia after Soeharto* (Singapore, ISEAS, 2010).

Ray, David, 'Decentralization, Regulatory Reform, and the Business Climate', *Decentralization, Regulatory Reform, and the Business Climate* (Jakarta Indonesia, Partnership for Economic Growth, 2003).

7

Human Rights

Introduction – National Human Rights Commission (*Komnas HAM*) – Part I: Express Constitutional Rights – Part II: Implied Rights and the *Negara Hukum* – Part III: Obligations – Conclusion

INTRODUCTION

BEFORE ITS AMENDMENT, the 1945 Constitution had little to say on human rights. Citizens were accorded equality in law and government (Article 27(1)) and had the right to work and to a 'life befitting human beings' (Article 27(2)). Article 28, however, merely provided that freedom to associate, assemble and to express an opinion would be prescribed by statute. It therefore could not be said that it actually guaranteed these rights.[1] Instead, it left them entirely to the discretion of the legislature. Worse still, even if rights were prescribed by statute they were unenforceable. Under Soeharto no institution had power to hear challenges against legislation or government conduct that appeared to breach provisions of the Constitution.[2]

It was therefore not surprising that while he was in power human rights were routinely flouted. Citizens were unable to assemble freely or criticise the government, let alone demonstrate publicly, as is now common. Political parties – now many in number and diverse ideologically – were then limited to three and their affairs closely manipulated by the regime. The media was muzzled by a licensing system designed to encourage self-censorship that was only abolished after Soeharto had resigned. Observers had to become expert in 'reading between the lines' to find the news hidden in veiled allusions and hints. The few labour organisations tolerated were tightly controlled by the government and

---

[1] TM Lubis, *In Search of Human Rights: Legal-Political Dilemmas of Indonesia's New Order, 1966–1990* (Jakarta, Published by PT Gramedia Pustaka Utama in cooperation with SPES Foundation, 1993).

[2] On this, see Chapters 1, 4 and 5 of this volume.

used to ensure a ready supply of cheap labour for the New Order development programmes that quickly delivered massive wealth to the elite but raised general living standards much more slowly. There was little that could be done about any of this. The courts had become notorious for corruption and an almost complete lack of independence from the executive. Prosecutors rarely lost and judges sometimes didn't bother even listening to evidence.[3] As a result, citizens were vulnerable to arbitrary arrest, detention and torture at the hands of intelligence and security officials, who routinely enjoyed almost complete impunity.[4] In more remote provinces, particularly those with secessionist sympathies, brutality and lawlessness became institutionalised. This became the subject of international condemnation when atrocities in East Timor, Papua and Aceh became known but that led to little real change in Indonesia.

As a result the absence of recognition of, or protection for, basic human rights became one of the most common criticisms of the New Order, domestically and overseas. It was therefore one of the most important popular grievances that the legislators charged with building a new system found themselves forced to address after 1998. In fact, upholding basic human rights or HAM (*hak asasi manusia*) became central to post-Soeharto political legitimacy, even if only rhetorically. So, within two years of Soeharto's fall, the Constitution was amended to grant citizens human rights drawn from the Universal Declaration of Human Rights (UDHR) and the Constitutional Court began to play a pivotal role in their enforcement. As mentioned, this Court has exclusive judicial authority to ensure that the DPR respects constitutional rights in the statutes it enacts. It has upheld many such rights in numerous judicial review challenges since 2003 and has developed Indonesia's first significant body of human rights jurisprudence. It is this that forms the subject matter of this chapter.

The chapter has three parts. The first discusses Constitutional Court decisions interpreting and applying express constitutional rights. Here we focus on cases involving the rights upon which the Court has most regularly adjudicated: freedom of speech and information; prohibitions

---

[3] S Zifcak, 'But a Shadow of Justice: Political Trials in Indonesia' in T Lindsey (ed), *Indonesia: Law and Society*, 1st edn (Annandale, NSW, Federation Press, 1999) 355–66.

[4] TM Lubis, 'The *Rechsstaat* and Human Rights' in T Lindsey (ed), *Indonesia: Law and Society*, 1st edn (Annandale, NSW, Federation Press, 1999) 171–85.

against discrimination and retrospective prosecution; and the right to life. In previous and subsequent chapters, we discuss the Constitutional Court's treatment of other express rights, including those associated with religion and local government;[5] the right to legal certainty; and the provisions of Article 33 of the Constitution on the 'people's economy'.[6] In the second part of this chapter, we consider rights that the Court has 'found' in the Constitution, despite the fact they are not explicitly mentioned there. The Court has implied these rights, claiming that they are integral to the 'law state' (*negara hukum*) concept proclaimed in Article 1(3) of the Constitution (which we discuss in Chapter 1). In the third part of this chapter, we briefly consider obligations that the Constitution appears to impose on the state. The Constitution expressly imposes several obligations but, as with rights, the Court has implied additional obligations that are not explicitly mentioned in the Constitution.

NATIONAL HUMAN RIGHTS COMMISSION (*KOMNAS HAM*)

Before turning to the Constitutional Court's jurisprudence on human rights, we make brief mention of Indonesia's National Human Rights Commission (*Komisi Nasional Hak Asasi Manusia*, commonly referred to as *Komnas HAM*). Soeharto established the Commission in 1993 by Decree.[7] Initially, its mandate was modest: to disseminate information about human rights; make recommendations to the government about ratifying United Nations human rights instruments; investigate the 'implementation of human rights' and report its findings to the government; and engage in regional and international cooperation on human rights.[8]

Much scepticism surrounded the Commission's establishment, not least because its founding commissioners were Soeharto appointees and it lacked powers to formally investigate and prosecute human rights cases.[9] Established one week before the World Conference on Human Rights in Vienna, it was widely considered a 'public relations gimmick'

---

[5] See Chapters 6 and 8 of this volume.
[6] See Chapters 6 and 9 of this volume.
[7] Presidential Decree 50 of 1993.
[8] Article 5 of Presidential Decree 50 of 1993.
[9] I Hadiprayitno, 'Defensive Enforcement: Human Rights in Indonesia' (2010) 11 *Human Rights Review* 373, 389.

aimed at deflecting criticism of Indonesia's human rights record, which had been worsened by the 1991 Santa Cruz massacre in East Timor, just a few years earlier.[10] The Commission exceeded expectations, however, quickly developing a reputation for being 'independent, forthright and diligent . . . often criticising government policies, actions by the police and military, and highlighting human rights anomalies'.[11]

Laws enacted in 1999 and 2000 gave Komnas HAM a statutory basis and expanded its powers to conducting investigations into alleged human rights abuses, including gross human rights violations; calling witnesses and victims to give evidence; making formal submissions to government and the national legislature about human rights breaches; and helping to settle human rights disputes.[12] Despite these reforms, Komnas HAM's powers remain limited. If it identifies violations, it cannot initiate criminal action against perpetrators. For this, Komnas HAM relies upon ordinary police, to whom it must present the evidence it obtains. The police, however, are not obliged to pursue cases reported by Komnas HAM. Often they do nothing. Likewise, some military officers have simply ignored Komnas HAM's calls to present themselves for questioning, and the courts have refused to compel them to attend.

Komnas HAM has therefore proved to be largely toothless and has become more of an advocacy body. In this role, however, it now competes with a large range of very effective NGOs established for similar purposes since Soeharto's fall.[13] This has raised questions about the purpose and usefulness of Komnas HAM and whether it should be significantly reformed or perhaps even abolished.

---

[10]   S Linton, 'Accounting For Atrocities in Indonesia' (2006) 10 *Singapore Yearbook of International Law* 199, 206.

[11]   J Herbert, 'The legal framework of human rights in Indonesia' in T Lindsey (ed), *Indonesia: Law and Society*, 2nd edn (Annandale, NSW, Federation Press, 2008) 461; see also P Eldridge, 'Human Rights in Post-Soeharto Indonesia' (2001) IX(1) *Brown Journal of World Affairs* 127.

[12]   Chapter VII of Law 39 of 1999 on Human Rights and Articles 18–20 of Law 26 of 2000 on the Human Rights Courts.

[13]   Such as the Institute for Study and Community Advocacy (ELSAM) and the Commission for Disappearances and Victims of Violence (KONTRAS).

PART I: EXPRESS CONSTITUTIONAL RIGHTS

Chapter 10A of the Constitution now provides Indonesian citizens the rights to:

- life, to maintain their lives and to a livelihood (Article 28A);
- form a family and continue their lineage through a valid marriage (Article 28B(1));
- develop themselves by fulfilling their basic needs; obtain an education; and obtain benefits from science and technology, art, and culture so as to increase their quality of life and further the wellbeing of humankind (Article 28C(1));[14]
- advance themselves by collectively upholding their rights to develop the community, nation and state (Article 28C(2));
- legal recognition, guarantees, protection and certainty that is just, and to equal treatment before the law (Article 28D(1));
- employment and to receive just and appropriate reward and treatment, if in an employment relationship (Article 28D(2));
- equal opportunity in government (Article 28D(3));
- nationality status (Article 28D(4));
- embrace their respective religions and worship in accordance with their religion; to choose their education, teaching, employment and citizenship; to choose a residence within the territory of the state, to leave and return to the state (Article 28E(1));
- be convinced of their beliefs, and express an opinion and attitude, in accordance with their conscience (Article 28E(2));
- associate, assemble and express an opinion (Article 28E(3));
- communicate and obtain information to develop themselves and their social environment and to seek, obtain, possess, store, manage and convey information using all available means (Article 28F);
- protection for themselves and their families, honour, dignity and property rights, and to a feeling of security and protection from threats to do or to refrain from something which is a human right (Article 28G(1));
- be free from inhumane torture or treatment and seek asylum to obtain political protection from another country (Article 28G(2));

---

[14] Article 31(1) of the Constitution reiterates the right to education.

- physical and mental well-being, to a place of residence, to a good and healthy environment and to health care (Article 28H(1));
- special treatment to obtain the same opportunities and benefits to achieve equality and justice (Article 28H(2));
- social security which permits holistic self-development as befits human dignity (Article 28H(3));
- personal property rights that cannot be arbitrarily appropriated (Article 28H(4)); and
- protection against discriminatory treatment (Article 28I(2)).

Children, in particular, have the right to 'continuation of life' and to grow and develop, as well as the right to protection from violence and discrimination (Article 28B(2)).

A number of other rights exist outside Articles 28A–28I, including rights to participate in the defence of the state (Article 30(1)); to equality before the law and in government (Article 27(1)); and to cultivate and develop cultural values (Article 32(1)).

The rights set out above are, however, subject to Article 28J(2). This provision permits these rights to be limited by legislation directed at:

> protecting the rights and freedoms of others and which accords with moral considerations, religious values, security and public order in a democratic society.

In the majority of cases in which the Constitutional Court has applied Article 28J(2), the Court has treated this provision as having two limbs. The first is that the legislation under challenge seeks to protect the rights and freedoms of others. Presumably, this is reference only to the constitutional 'rights and freedoms of others' and not rights and freedoms granted by legislation or lower-level laws and regulations, although to our knowledge, the Court has not yet been asked to make this distinction. The second limb is that the legislation limiting rights must be directed to one of four purposes: moral considerations, religious values, security or public order in a democratic society.[15] Legislation that fails to meet either limb should, according to this formulation, not be permitted to contravene other human rights.

Article 28I(1) of the Constitution appears to establish higher-order, non-derogable rights to which Article 28J(2) cannot apply:

---

[15] Constitutional Court Decision 6-13-20/PUU-VIII/2010, p 242.

The right to life, the right to not be tortured, the right to freedom of thought and conscience, the right to religion, the right to not be enslaved, the right to be recognised as an individual before the law, and the right to not be prosecuted under a law of retrospective application are human rights that *cannot be limited under any circumstances* (emphasis added).

As will be seen later in this chapter, the Court has eschewed the plain meaning of Article 28I(1) by repeatedly reading down the apparent 'absoluteness' of these rights.

Observations About the Court's Decision-making in Human Rights Cases

Before turning to some of the cases in which the Constitutional Court has interpreted and applied express rights, we offer some general observations about the Court's decision-making in rights cases. In many of its decisions, the Court has not provided clear interpretations of specific rights nor precisely delineated their nature and scope. Indeed, the Court's references to rights are often very generally cast and do not always use the wording of the Constitution when describing the rights at issue in a particular case. Instead, the Court usually sets out selected facts drawn from the case before it in a few sentences near the end of the section headed 'legal opinion' (*pertimbangan hukum*), and simply declares that they constitute a breach of a constitutional right.

In some cases, the Court has even struck down legislation but without clearly specifing the constitutional provision or provisions that the legislation breached. It did this in the *Unions case*[16] discussed above in Chapter 5, for example. In that case, a group of Bank Central Asia (BCA) employees and union representatives challenged the constitutionality of Article 120 of the Labour Law.[17] Article 120(1) stipulated that if more than one union represented employees in a particular company, the union entitled to negotiate with the company was the one representing more than 50 per cent of the total number of workers in that company. Article 120(2) allowed unions to form coalitions to make up the 50 per cent. Article 120(3) provided that if no such coalition could be formed, then membership of the union negotiating team was determined proportionally by reference to the number of company employees in each trade union.

---

[16] Constitutional Court Decision 115/PUU-VII/2009.
[17] Law 13 of 2003.

The Constitutional Court invalidated Articles 120(1) and (2) but left Article 120(3) in force. Without citing any constitutional provisions, it declared that the case raised three constitutional issues: first, the removal of the right of unions to collectively struggle for the rights of workers; secondly, 'unjust treatment' for some unions; and thirdly, disregard of the right to legal protection of workers not represented by the majority union. From our reading of the decision, the Court judged the constitutionality of Article 120 on the basis of whether it granted 'proportional representation', although this is not itself an express constitutional principle. The Court decided that to:

> fulfil constitutional principles and avoid breaches of constitutional rights that are guaranteed and protected by the Constitution, that is, to fulfil the principle of proportional justice, to guarantee and protect the rights of unions and the rights of workers that are guaranteed and protected by the Constitution, all unions within a company have the right to be proportionally represented during negotiations with the company.[18]

The Constitutional Court's Interpretation and Application of Express Rights

We now turn to discuss some of the specific constitutional rights the Court has considered since its establishment. Our aim is to briefly describe, where possible, broad trends in the Court's jurisprudence on particular rights. We do not purport to assess the decisions' 'correctness', compliance with international law or congruence with jurisprudence of the constitutional courts of other countries.

Freedom of Speech

The Lese Majesté and Hate Sowing cases

In the *Lèse Majesté case*[19] a bare majority of Constitutional Court judges (5:4) invalidated Criminal Code provisions that prohibited insulting the president or vice-president – the so-called *lèse majesté* (injured majesty)

---

[18]   Constitutional Court Decision 115/PUU-VII/2009, p 52.
[19]   Constitutional Court Decision 013-022/PUU-IV/2006.

articles.[20] One applicant, Pandapotan Lubis, had been arrested at a rally for displaying a poster urging President Susilo Bambang Yudhoyono (SBY) and Vice-President Muhammad Jusuf Kalla to resign from office. The other applicant, Eggi Sudjana, had publicly alleged in a report to the Anti-corruption Commission that a businessman had given a car to one of President SBY's sons and to three of his advisors.[21] Both applicants were awaiting trial at the Central Jakarta District Court when the Constitutional Court heard their cases.

According to the Court, the *lèse majesté* provisions, conceived during Dutch colonialism and designed to protect the authority of the Netherlands monarchy, had no place in independent democratic Indonesia. The provisions breached a number of constitutional rights, including the right to freedom of expression in Articles 28, 28E(2) and (3) and rights to legal certainty and equality (Article 27(1)) and to communicate and obtain information (Article 28F). The Court provided scant reasoning to substantiate these findings, however, declaring merely that the Code's provisions

> could impede the freedom to express opinions verbally and in writing. These three criminal provisions are always used by the legal apparatus to stem the momentum of demonstrations in the field.[22]

In the *Hate Sowing case*,[23] the Constitutional Court unanimously invalidated the so-called 'hate-sowing' provisions (*hatzai artikelen*) of the Criminal Code[24] that prohibited expressions of hostility, hatred or contempt towards the Indonesian government and the dissemination of those expressions.[25] The applicant in this case was Panji Utomo, who staged a rally at the Aceh Rehabilitation and Reconstruction Agency to protest against the Indonesian government's tardiness in assisting victims of the tsunami in Aceh and earthquake in Nias. He had been convicted and sentenced to three months' imprisonment by the Banda Aceh District Court. The provisions, the Court decided, were particularly egregious because they had been used against Indonesians who resisted Dutch colonialism

---

[20]   Articles 134, 136 and 137 of the Criminal Code.

[21]   N Royan, 'Increasing Press Freedom in Indonesia: The Abolition of the Lese Majeste and "Hate-sowing" Provisions' (2008) 10(2) *Australian Journal of Asian Law* 90.

[22]   Constitutional Court Decision 013-022/PUU-IV/2006, p 60.

[23]   Constitutional Court Decision 6/PUU-V/2007.

[24]   Articles 154 and 155 of the Criminal Code.

[25]   Royan, 'Increasing Press Freedom in Indonesia' (above n 21) 290–91.

and 'disproportionately hindered' constitutional rights to freedom of association and freedom of expression.[26] The provisions could be subjectively interpreted so that constitutionally-protected opinions and criticisms could fall within their ambit. Worse still, to secure a conviction, prosecutors were not even required to prove whether the statement had, in fact, resulted in the spread of hatred or hostility.[27]

These cases were hailed as a step forward for democracy and press freedom in Indonesia.[28] But while they constitute the high-water mark for protection of the right to free speech in Constitutional Court jurisprudence, they should not be seen as the beginning of a trend towards greater constitutional protection for freedom of speech in general. Indeed, in the *Lèse Majesté case* itself, the majority noted that the Criminal Code's ordinary defamation provisions – including Articles 207, 310 and 311 – remained available to protect the personal reputations and the 'office' of president and vice-president from insult.

These were, in fact, the very provisions unsuccessfully challenged in the next batch of freedom of speech cases. Brought by journalists in 2008, these are discussed in the next section, and, as we shall see, in most the Court applied Article 28J(2) to uphold legislation that appeared to breach the right to free speech. In other words, in most decisions since the *Lèse Majesté* and *Hate Sowing cases*, the Court has identified a competing right that the legislation under challenge seeks to protect, as well as one of the purposes mentioned in Article 28J(2), namely, public order. The Court has repeatedly held that these trump the right to free speech.

The journalist cases

In 2008, the Constitutional Court heard three separate constitutional challenges to Indonesia's defamation laws brought by journalists and press organisations. In the *Wijaya and Lubis case*, the applicants were Risang Bima Wijaya, editor-in-chief of the *Radar Jogja* newspaper, and veteran journalist Bersihar Lubis. Wijaya had written about allegations, initially made at a public press conference, that the head of the *Kedaulatan*

---

[26] Constitutional Court Decision 6/PUU-V/2007, paras 3.18.7 and 4.1.

[27] Constitutional Court Decision 6/PUU-V/2007, pp 77–78.

[28] Freedom House, 'Indonesia', *Freedom in the World Series* (Washington DC, 2008); Royan, 'Increasing Press Freedom in Indonesia' (above n 21); '2010 Country Reports on Human Rights Practices' (Washington DC, US Department of State, Bureau of Democracy, Human Rights, and Labor, 2011) 14.

Rakyat newspaper had sexually harassed a female employee. Before publishing, he had sought a response from the alleged perpetrator, who refused to comment and reported Wijaya to police.

Wijaya was charged under Articles 310(1) and 311(1) of the Criminal Code for defamation and was sentenced to six months' imprisonment.[29] Article 310 prohibits defamation: 'attacking the honour or good name of a person by accusing him or her of something with the clear intention that it will become publicly known'. The penalty for this criminal defamation offence is a maximum of nine months' imprisonment (Article 310(1)). Higher penalties apply if the 'attack' is in written or pictorial form and is broadcast, performed or publicly displayed (Article 310(2)). Under Article 311, if the person who committed the defamation attempts to 'prove the truth of the allegation but fails to do so and the accusation is contrary to what is known [to be true], that person faces a maximum of four years in jail for aggravated defamation'.

The second applicant in the *Wijaya and Lubis case*, Bersihar Lubis, had been convicted of defamation for writing a column in the *Koran Tempo* newspaper in which he called the Attorney General's Office a 'fool' (*dungu*) for banning school history books which, according to the Office, did not reveal the 'truth' about the coup of 30 September 1965, which the Office said had been led by the Communist Party (PKI, *Partai Komunis Indonesia*). Lubis was issued with a suspended sentence of one month's imprisonment for contravening Article 207 of the Criminal Code. Article 207 imposes a maximum of 18 months' imprisonment for publicly insulting, orally or in writing, a public body or authority.

In the second case, the *Piliang case*,[30] the applicant was journalist Narliswandi Piliang. In 2008, the DPR investigated coal-mining company PT Adaro Energy for impropriety in its initial public offering of shares. In June 2008, Piliang alleged on his Internet blog that the company had bribed DPR member Alvin Lie from the National Mandate Party (PAN) to influence the investigation in its favour. Police charged and detained Piliang under Article 27(3) of Law 11 of 2008 on Information and Electronic Transactions, which prohibits making available electronic information and documents that contain insults or defile the good name of another person. Article 45 of the Law imposes a maximum penalty of six years' imprisonment and a Rp 1 billion fine.

---

[29] Constitutional Court Decision 14/PUU-VI/2008, pp 11–12.
[30] Constitutional Court Decision 50/PUU-VI/2008, p 11.

The Court decided against the applicants in both the *Wijaya and Lubis* and *Piliang cases,* finding that limits on free speech were justifiable to protect the reputations of citizens. In both cases, the Court noted that freedom of expression (Article 28E(2) of the Constitution), the right to freely express an opinion (Article 28D(3)) and the right to communicate freely (Article 28F) must, by virtue of Article 28J(2), be balanced against the protection of other rights. In particular, the state must balance these rights with the constitutional right to protection of one's honour and reputation (Article 28G). The Court emphasised that this principle is reflected in Article 12 of the United Declaration of Human Rights and Articles 17 and 19 of the International Covenant on Cultural and Political Rights, and Indonesia's 1999 Human Rights Law.

Although the Court accepted that a free press is critical to a functioning democracy, it decided that when exercising their rights to free speech and communication, citizens, including journalists, should not disregard the constitutionally-protected reputations of others.[31] In fact, the Court claimed that without the right to honour and dignity that Article 28G provides, democracy would disintegrate,[32] although it did not specify how this might happen. Even so, the Court held that the Information and Electronic Transactions Law did not entirely neglect the right to freedom of expression. Rather, it struck an acceptable balance between the right to reputation and freedom of speech, because it required the insult or defamation to be 'deliberate' and 'without right' for a conviction to result.

The Blogger's case

In 2009, several bloggers and NGOs made a second attempt to challenge Article 27(3) of the Information and Electronic Transactions Law.[33] The Court threw the case out, pointing to Article 60 of the Constitutional Court Law, which prevents it from hearing a challenge to the same legislative provisions based on the same constitutional provisions it heard in a previous case. Nevertheless, the Court reiterated many of its arguments in the *Piliang* and *Wijaya and Lubis cases* about the need

---

[31] Constitutional Court Decision 14/PUU-VI/2008, pp 274–75; Constitutional Court Decision 50/PUU-VI/2008, p 11.

[32] Constitutional Court Decision 50/PUU-VI/2008, pp 99–101.

[33] Constitutional Court Decision 2/PUU-VII/2009.

to prevent freedom of expression being used to attack self-respect and honour.[34] The Court also noted that:

> The protection of human rights in the context of the Indonesian community is primarily directed towards the relationship between citizens and the government with the normative-traditional assumption that the interaction will be harmonious and balanced. In other words, the protection of human rights in Indonesia – including freedom of expression and opinion – is particularly directed towards the achievement of harmony and balance within the community.[35]

The Court specified no legal basis for its emphasis upon 'harmony and balance'. They are not explicit constitutional principles and do not fit within any of the purposes of Article 28J(2). Harmony and balance may well be desirable but if this statement is taken to its logical conclusion the Court appears to be sanctioning the legislative breach of human rights if those rights would endanger harmony and balance. The problem with this, of course, is that 'harmony' and 'balance' are highly subjective terms that could evolve into justifications for intolerance – particularly to override the rights of minorities that the government might find it inconvenient to protect. Indeed, terms like these, together with others like 'stability' and 'order', were routinely used by Soeharto's government to legitimise its brutal repression of dissent. The Constitutional Court's test thus leaves open the possibility that many of Chapter XA's human rights could become illusory in the hands of a future government that did not consider them important.

The Pornography Law and Book Banning Law cases

The recent high-profile *Pornography Law case*[36] highlights the Court's willingness to marginalise free speech in the face of competing interests. In this case, a large number of individuals and organisations argued that the Pornography Law[37] – which banned the production, reproduction and distribution of pornography (widely defined) – breached the freedom of expression in Articles 28E(2) and (3), among other constitutional rights and freedoms. A majority (6:3) of the Court rejected this

---

[34] Constitutional Court Decision 2/PUU-VII/2009, p 143.
[35] Constitutional Court Decision 2/PUU-VII/2009, p 133–34.
[36] Constitutional Court Decision 10-17-23/PUU-VII/2009.
[37] Law 44 of 2008 on Pornography.

argument, pointing to Article 28J(2) which, as mentioned, allows the state to restrict human rights (including freedom of expression) in order to guarantee the 'recognition and protection of the human rights of others, and moral considerations, religious values, security or public order in a democratic society'.

The Court's application of Article 28J(2) in the *Pornography Law case* was questionable for two main reasons. First, it claimed that provisions of the Pornography Law took into account Indonesia-wide community 'values of propriety' (*nilai-nilai kesusilaan*).[38] Yet these are not listed in Article 28J(2) as a purpose for which legislation contrary to constitutional rights can be enacted – the closest is 'moral considerations' (*pertimbangan moral*). The Court did not clarify whether *nilai kesusilaan* or *pertimbangan moral* were equivalents, nor did it explain why it did not adopt the Article 28J(2) terminology. Secondly, the Court did not identify the 'human right of others' that it believed should prevail over the freedom of expression.

In the *Book Banning Law case*, discussed below in the context of 'due process', the Court decided that provisions of a 1963 Law that gave unfettered power to the Attorney General to ban and seize books without judicial oversight breached the freedom of expression in Article 28E(2) of the Constitution.[39] However, the importance of this case to the Court's freedom of expression jurisprudence should not be overstated. In fact, the Constitutional Court's main objection to the impugned statute in this case was that it permitted seizure of property without due process. The majority even said that constitutionally-valid legislation could be formulated that authorised book banning – hence contravening freedom of expression – provided it was subject to judicial oversight.[40]

---

[38] Constitutional Court Decision 10-17-23/PUU-VII/2009, p 387.

[39] Constitutional Court Decision 6-13-20/PUU-VIII/2010, para 3.13.2.

[40] Justice Ahmad Fadlil Sumadi (dissenting) declared that he would have allowed the statute to remain in force on the condition that judicial oversight was required: Constitutional Court Decision 6-13-20/PUU-VIII/2010, p 255. For a discussion of 'conditional constitutionality', see Chapter 5 of this volume.

Freedom of Information Cases

In the *General Election Poll*[41] and *Presidential Poll cases*,[42] the Court provided its fullest discussion yet about the right to freedom of information.[43] In these cases, applicants who ran public policy research organisations that conduct political polling challenged provisions in the General Elections Law (2008) and Presidential and Vice-Presidential Elections Law (2008).[44] These established two criminal offences. The first was announcing survey or poll results in the days immediately preceding a presidential or general election.[45] If the announcement 'could influence' or is 'aimed at influencing' voters, then a prison sentence of between three and 12 months and a fine of between three and 12 million Rupiah applied.[46] The second offence was to announce exit polls 'earlier than the day after the election'.[47] This offence attracted between six and 18 months' imprisonment and a fine of between six and 18 million Rupiah.[48]

In both cases the Court invalidated these provisions by 6:3 majority, holding that they breached Article 28F of the Constitution, which provides a right to obtain, manage and distribute information, including scientific data such as this.[49] Although not a constitutional argument, the

[41] Constitutional Court Decision 9/PUU-VII/2009.

[42] Constitutional Court Decision 98/PUU-VII/2009.

[43] The Court had also upheld Article 28F in the *Lèse Majesté case*, discussed above, though its finding was accompanied by very little reasoning. The Court found that Criminal Code provisions prohibiting insulting the president could impede efforts at communication and obtaining information. This was because the provisions were vulnerable to subjective interpretation, such as whether a protest, declaration or thought constituted criticism or insult to the president or vice-president. The provisions, therefore, breached Article 28F (Constitutional Court Decision 013-022/PUU-IV/2006, p 60).

[44] Law 10 of 2008 on General Elections of the DPR, MPR, DPD, and DPRD (General Elections law); Law 42 of 2008 on the General Elections of the President and Vice-President.

[45] Article 245 of the 2008 General Elections Law; Article 188(5) of the 2008 Presidential and Vice-Presidential Elections Law.

[46] Article 282 of the 2008 General Elections Law; Article 228 of the 2008 Presidential and Vice-Presidential Elections Law.

[47] Article 245 of the 2008 General Elections Law; Article 188(5) of the 2008 Presidential and Vice-Presidential Elections Law.

[48] Article 307 of the 2008 General Elections Law; Article 255 of the 2008 Presidential and Vice-Presidential Elections Law.

[49] Constitutional Court Decision 9/PUU-VII/2009, p 60.

Court found that the provisions also hampered 'academic freedom', which, according to the Court, had become a principle of Indonesian law. The Court rejected the government's argument that the publication of such surveys might cause unrest or otherwise compromise public order. In the Court's view, polls were important to Indonesia's democracy. They helped educate the public about electoral processes and to 'monitor and balance electoral processes'.[50] Accordingly, the Court held that the exit polls were permissible and that pre-election surveys could be published.

This was not the end of the matter, however. In its decisions in these cases, the Court also pointed out provisions of the General and Presidential Election Laws that the applicants had neglected to challenge. These prohibited print media organisations from publishing, and broadcasters from broadcasting, any news, advertisements or track record assessments relating to the campaign that advantaged or disadvantaged candidates within three days of a general or presidential election.[51] Despite the invalidation of provisions prohibiting polls and surveys that 'could influence' or were 'aimed at influencing' voters, these remaining provisions would, in any event, have prevented the publication of the types of polls and survey results the applicants produced.

The remaining provisions were challenged by press and media figures in the *General Election Campaign Advertising case* and *Presidential Campaign Advertising case*.[52] Although the Court's decisions in these two cases focused on the legal uncertainty created by the provisions, the Court found that Article 47(5) of the 2008 Presidential Election Law[53] and Articles 98 and 99 of the 2008 General Election Law[54] breached Article 28F. In the *General Election Campaign Advertising case*, the Court provided virtually no reasoning for reaching this conclusion[55] but in the *Presidential*

---

[50]   Constitutional Court Decision 9/PUU-VII/2009, p 61.

[51]   Article 47(5) of the Presidential Election Law; Article 89(5) of the General Election Law.

[52]   Constitutional Court Decisions 32/PUU-VI/2008 and 99/PUU-VII/2009.

[53]   Law 42 of 2008 on the General Election of the President and Vice-President.

[54]   Law 10 of 2008 on the General Election of Members of the People's Legislative Assembly.

[55]   See Constitutional Court Decision 32/PUU-VI/2008, p 77. Article 47(5) of the 2008 Presidential Election Law is not replicated in the 2008 General Election Law. Articles 98 and 99 of the General Election Law allowed the Press Council and Broadcasting Commission to issue sanctions for breach of various provisions of the Law, including those concerning election advertising. Nevertheless, the Court

Campaign Advertising case it indicated why Article 47(5) breached Article 28F. The Court seemed to endorse the applicants' arguments that because the provisions established a subjective standard (they allowed the candidates themselves to determine whether a press report negatively affected their campaign) candidates could, in effect, limit information available to the public, which was a breach. The Court stated:

> According to the Constitutional Court, broadcasting the news is a part of the constitutionally-protected human rights of every person to seek, obtain, possess, store, manage and convey information using all available channels. News broadcasts about the candidates for the presidential and vice-presidential team will in fact assist in providing information as broadly as possible about the track record and quality of the pair to potential voters who will of course subjectively evaluate it . . . This will, in turn, improve the quality of the party of democracy that is the right of the people. In other words, obtaining news about the candidates is [part of] the right of every person or citizen to obtain and convey information.[56]

'Absolute' Human Rights Cases

As mentioned, Article 28I(1) of the Constitution states:

> The right to life, the right to not be tortured, the right to freedom of thought and conscience, the right to religion, the right to not be enslaved, the right to be recognised as an individual before the law, and the right to not be prosecuted under a law of retrospective application are human rights that cannot be limited *under any circumstances* (emphasis added).

On a plain reading, this provision seems designed to establish rights that are non-derogable, that is, rights to which Article 28J(2) does not apply. In other words, legislation that limits Article 28I(1) rights should be invalid, even if it seeks to pursue the higher-order goals of upholding the rights of others and achieving one of the purposes listed in Article 28J(2).

In a number of cases, the Court has been asked to consider whether the freedom from prosecution under retrospective laws, the freedom from torture and the right to life are, in fact, absolute. Contrary to the

---

decided that they unconstitutionally hampered the right to information, presumably because they provided a disincentive to the media to report on candidates.

[56] Constitutional Court Decision 99/PUU-VII/2009, p 33.

plain reading of Article 28I(1), in some of these cases, a Constitutional Court majority has held that such rights can be set aside if the interest to be protected is particularly important or serious or those rights have been set aside in comparable circumstances at the international level.

The Retrospectivity Cases

The right to be free from prosecution under a retrospective law has been the basis for constitutional challenge in two high-profile cases, which led to decisions that are hard to reconcile. We begin by outlining the facts of both cases before turning to the Constitutional Court's consideration of the freedom.

In the first case, *Bali Bombing*, a slim majority of the Constitutional Court invalidated a statute that sought to permit the investigation and prosecution of those involved in the 2002 Bali bombings using an anti-terrorism law that was enacted six days after the bombings took place.[57] The anti-terrorism law contains broad definitions of terrorism, provides substantial penalties for terrorists or those who help or fund them, and introduces procedures designed to make investigating, prosecuting and convicting terrorists easier.[58] The Court held these could not be applied to events that occurred before the law came into force.

The second retrospectivity case to attract significant public attention was the *Soares case*.[59] The applicant was Abilio Jose Osorio Soares, the last pre-independence East Timor Governor, who had been convicted under the 2000 Human Rights Court Law for gross human rights abuses in East Timor (now Timor Leste) in 1999. The Central Jakarta Ad Hoc

---

[57] Constitutional Court Decision 013/PUU-I/2003. In the majority: Asshiddiqie, Marzuki, Fadjar, Rustandi, and Soedarso. In the minority: Siahaan, Palguna, Natabaya, and Harjono. See S Butt and D Hansell, 'The Masykur Abdul Kadir Case: Indonesian Constitutional Court Decision No 013/PUU-I/2003' (2004) 6(2) *Australian Journal of Asian Law* 176–96; R Clarke, 'Retrospectivity and the Constitutional Validity of the Bali Bombing and East Timor Trials' (2003) 5(2) *Australian Journal of Asian Law* 1–32.

[58] S Butt, 'Indonesian Terrorism Law and Criminal Process' (*Islam, Syari'ah and Governance Background Paper Series*, Centre for Islamic Law and Society, University of Melbourne, 2008).

[59] Constitutional Court Decision 065/PUU-II/2004. In the majority: Asshiddiqie, Harjono, Natabaya, Palguna, Siahaan, Soedarsono. In the minority: Fadjar, Marzuki and Roestandi.

Human Rights Court had sentenced him to three years' imprisonment. At the time he made his application to the Constitutional Court, his conviction had been upheld on appeal by the Jakarta Ad Hoc Human Rights High Court and the Supreme Court.[60] Soares challenged the constitutionality of Article 43 of Law 26 of 2000 on the Human Rights Courts. This Law created Indonesia's human rights courts as a branch of Indonesia's general courts but Article 43 also allowed an ad hoc human rights tribunal to be constituted to hear cases involving gross violations of human rights that occurred before the 2000 Law itself was enacted. A majority of the Court refused to invalidate the statute despite its apparent retrospective operation.

The *Bali Bombing* majority and the *Soares* minority interpreted the prohibition on prosecutions using retrospective laws relatively strictly, emphasising that Article 28I(1) states that the right 'cannot be diminished under any circumstances'. The *Bali Bombing* majority did, however, leave open the possibility of the prohibition being set aside, but only in cases of gross violation of human rights:

> The application of the retroactivity principle in criminal law is an exception permitted . . . only in cases of gross violations of human rights . . . According to the Rome Statute of 1998, gross human rights violations include genocide, crimes against humanity, war crimes, and crimes of aggression. Article 7 of [Indonesia's] Law 39 of 1999 on Human Rights classifies only genocide and crimes against humanity as gross human rights violations. Therefore . . . the Bali bombing . . . cannot be categorised as an extraordinary crime for which the [prohibition can be set aside] but rather as an ordinary crime which was very cruel but which can still be dealt with under existing criminal law.[61]

By contrast, the *Soares* majority and *Bali Bombing* minority decided that although the right to be free from retrospective prosecution was 'textually formulated' as an absolute right, the right should not be read in isolation but rather in conjunction with Article 28J(2). Accordingly, they found that within the framework of 'fulfilling just demands in accordance with moral, religious, security and public order considerations', the right could be set aside.[62] The *Soares* majority found that the right could

---

[60] The Supreme Court ultimately acquitted Soares when it reviewed his case under the *peninjauan kembali* procedure, outlined in Chapter 4 of this volume.

[61] Constitutional Court Decision 013/PUU-I/2003, pp 43–44.

[62] Constitutional Court Decision 013/PUU-I/2003, pp 48–49; Constitutional Court Decision 065/PUU-II/2004, p 51.

be ceded in cases of alleged crimes against humanity, emphasising Article 28J(2). This, the majority pointed out, was consistent with international practice. International tribunals had been established to apply retrospective laws, including the International Criminal Tribunal for the Former Yugoslavia and the International Criminal Tribunal for Rwanda. The minority in *Bali Bombing* recognised that the Bali Bombings were not war crimes and did not satisfy the legal definition of crimes against humanity, but found that the right could be overridden because

> [of] the great number of victims, that the acts were directed towards particular races or groups, the extensive and organised network and trans-national preparations, the extraordinary social, economic and political consequences . . . and the public interest which needs to be protected, outweigh the individual Basic Rights of the applicant.[63] . . . [Even] without mentioning these figures and statistics, and by merely watching the television broadcast that captured the cruelty of the event, we believe . . . that the bombings in Kuta, Bali were crimes that satisfy the . . . arguments [which justify] the principle of non-retroactivity being set aside.[64]

Right to Life

In the *Death Penalty case*,[65] the applicants were death row prisoners, including some Australian members of the so-called 'Bali 9' convicted of attempting to smuggle heroin out of Indonesia. They asked the Court to consider whether Law 22 of 1997 on Narcotics, which allowed the imposition of the death penalty in some narcotics cases, contradicted Article 28I(1)'s right to life.

A 5:4 majority upheld the Law,[66] finding that narcotics offences were so serious that they could displace the right to life in Article 28I(1). The majority pointed out that the International Covenant on Civil and Political Rights permitted the death penalty being imposed by member states for the 'most serious crimes', like genocide and crimes against humanity, and noted that in Indonesia, narcotics offences were classified as such crimes. The majority also observed that drug offences were

---

[63]   Constitutional Court Decision 013/PUU-I/2003, p 51.

[64]   Constitutional Court Decision 013/PUU-I/2003, p 59.

[65]   Constitutional Court Decision 2-3/PUU-V/2007.

[66]   In the majority: Asshiddiqie, Fadjar, Natabaya, Palguna, Soedarso. In the minority: Harjono, Roestandi, Marzuki and Siahaan.

among the crimes considered 'most serious' under international law, in particular under the United Nations Convention Against Illicit Traffic in Narcotic Drugs and Psychotropic Substances of 1988, which Indonesia ratified in 1997 by enacting the very statute under review. Several parts of the UN Narcotics Convention emphasised the 'particularly serious' nature of drug offences. According to the majority, there was little difference between the 'particularly serious' crimes referred to in the UN Narcotics Convention and the ICCPR's 'most serious crimes' because both affected the 'economic, cultural and political foundations of society' and carried 'danger of incalculable gravity'.

The minority, in separate judgments, found the death penalty to be unconstitutional on the simple basis that Article 28I(1)'s right to life is one that cannot be diminished under any circumstances.

Freedom from Torture

In the *Firing Squad case*, some of the Bali bombers asked the Constitutional Court to assess whether the way the death penalty is carried out in Indonesia – by firing squad – constituted 'torture' and cruel and inhumane punishment, which are prohibited under the Constitution.[67] In this case, it was unnecessary for the Court to determine whether the right to be free from torture was absolute, because the Court found that execution by firing squad was, in fact, not torture:

> Pain that constitutes torture is not something that occurs naturally or ordinarily, but rather is something that is done deliberately, and in breach of the law, for a particular purpose outside the wishes of the person tortured. The naturally-caused pain experienced by every woman who gives birth and by a person who undergoes an operation for medical reasons is not torture. Moreover, the pain that arises and attaches to execution is unavoidable . . . Pain occurs, not because of the execution method; it occurs regardless of the method.[68]

We offer two brief observations about these Article 28I(1) cases. The first is that interpretation of the 'absoluteness' of Article 28I(1) rights is far from settled. The Court has been narrowly split in all cases in which

---

[67] Constitutional Court Decision 21/PUU-VI/2008. The statute under review was Law 2/PNPS/1964 on the Procedures for Carrying Out the Death Penalty.

[68] Constitutional Court Decision 21/PUU-VI/2008, pp 71–72.

the absoluteness of Article 28I(1) rights has been a critical issue and the Court's views may well shift as the composition of the bench changes with retirements and new appointments. Secondly, even the Constitutional Court judges who have held that Article 28I(1) rights are subject to Article 28J(2) appear to consider that Article 28I(1) rights are of a higher order than other constitutional rights. The judgments that set aside Article 28I(1) rights generally contain far more discussion about the seriousness or importance of the end the law under review seeks to achieve than the cases in which the Court sets aside non-Article 28I(1) constitutional rights.

PART II: IMPLIED RIGHTS AND THE *NEGARA HUKUM*

As mentioned, the Constitutional Court has been prepared to find rights within the Constitution that are not explicitly mentioned there. We label these 'implied rights', because the Court has held that these rights are necessary implications of concepts that the Constitution does mention. In the cases decided thus far, the main source of these implied rights has been the notion of *Negara Hukum*. As discussed in Chapter 1, this term literally means 'law state', and is often described as Indonesia's equivalent of the common law notion of 'rule of law'.[69] The Court regularly mentions the concept in its judgments and emphasises its importance. In *Bali Bombing*, for example, the majority stated that:

> the essence of the Constitutional Court's existence . . . to guard the Constitution and to uphold the principle of the supremacy of the law in the Indonesian state system after the *Reformasi* era, is nothing other than an effort to strengthen the realisation of the ideas of the *Negara Hukum*.[70]

From the *Negara Hukum*, the Court appears to have implied the rights to legal aid, due process and a fair trial, and the presumption of innocence. We now discuss some of the cases in which the Constitutional Court has implied these rights before considering the implications of implying rights.

---

[69] Lubis, 'The *Rechsstaat* and Human Rights' (n 4 above).
[70] Constitutional Court Decision 013/PUU-I/2003, p 46.

Right to Legal Aid

In the *Advocates Law case*,[71] applicants sought a review of Article 31 of Law 18 of 2003 on Advocates, which prohibited non-advocates from providing legal advice or services. The applicants were involved in a university-run community legal clinic in Malang, East Java and were concerned that Article 31 would prevent them from providing legal services to the community.[72]

The Constitutional Court's immediate focus was Article 1(3) of the Constitution, although neither party had referred to it in their applications or submissions to the Court. The Court nonetheless declared that Indonesia was a *Negara Hukum*, with the necessary implication that:

> the right to legal assistance, as a part of human rights, must be considered a constitutional right of citizens, even though the Constitution does not explicitly regulate or mention it. The state must, therefore, guarantee the fulfilment [of this right].[73]

Applying this principle to the case before it, the Court noted that non-profit institutions, such as the legal clinic, were important to fulfilling the right to legal aid. They provided a critical service for members of the community who could not afford to pay for legal advice.[74] The Court decided to strike down Article 31 because it could cause

> injustice for many members of the community who needed legal services and assistance . . . Article 31 could prevent many poor people from using the services of advocates for financial reasons or because they live in an area in which there are no practicing advocates. This would further restrict or close off the community's access to justice. However, access to justice is an inseparable part of another feature of the *Negara Hukum* – that the law must be transparent and accessible to all, as is recognised in developments in modern thinking on *Negara Hukum*. If, for financial reasons, a citizen does not have this access, then it is the obligation of the state [to provide it], and it is truly also the obligation of advocates to facilitate [that access,] not to close it.[75]

---

[71] Constitutional Court Decision 006/PUU-II/2004.
[72] Constitutional Court Decision 006/PUU-II/2004, p 28.
[73] Constitutional Court Decision 006/PUU-II/2004, p 29.
[74] Constitutional Court Decision 006/PUU-II/2004, p 29.
[75] Constitutional Court Decision 006/PUU-II/2004, p 32.

Right to a Fair Trial

In the *Bali Bombing case*, the Constitutional Court majority explained that a fair trial was an essential element of the 'rule of law' and that, in turn, a fair trial had five prerequisites.

> The minimum [requirements] of procedural justice include: the presumption of innocence; equality of opportunity for the parties; announcement of the decision [which is] open to the public; *ne bis in idem* [the 'double jeopardy' rule]; the application of less serious laws for pending cases and the prohibition against retrospectivity.[76]

In the *Advocates Law case*, discussed above in the context of the implied right to legal aid, the Court appeared to associate the right to a fair trial with access to justice:

> Article 31 is . . . excessive and . . . impedes . . . the community's access to justice, which in turn, can prevent the fulfilment of the right to a fair trial, particularly for those who are indigent. Article 31 is, therefore, contradictory to the ideal of the *Negara Hukum*, which is clearly formulated in Article 1(3) of the Constitution.[77]

Due Process and Presumption of Innocence

In a series of cases, the Court has struck down legislation that imposes a punishment or breaches a constitutional right without providing 'due process of law'. The Court appears to have drawn this due process right from the presumption of innocence. The presumption is not itself expressly mentioned in the Constitution but, as mentioned above, in the *Bali Bombing case* the majority declared it to be one of the five elements of a fair trial, which, in turn, is an aspect of the *Negara Hukum*. As the following cases show, the Court clearly considers that due process and the presumption of innocence are closely related: those who are not given an opportunity to defend themselves or their rights are effectively presumed guilty.

---

[76] Constitutional Court Decision 013/PUU-I/2003, p 38. Dissenting in the *Soares case*, Justice Roestandi listed the same minimum standards for a fair trial and confirmed that fair trials are 'a mainstay of the rule of law' (Constitutional Court Decision 065/PUU-II/2004, pp 62–63).

[77] Constitutional Court Decision 006/PUU-II/2004, p 33.

The Broadcasting Law case (2003)

The *Broadcasting Law case*[78] was the first in which the Constitutional Court referred to the due process right. The applicants objected to a provision of Law 32 of 2002 on Broadcasting that required broadcasters to 'correct' broadcasts or news about which a complaint was made, regardless of whether the complaint had any foundation. The Court upheld the objection, deciding that a piece of news or broadcast is not proven to be untrue or mistaken merely because a complaint is made about it.[79] It declared that no correction would be necessary if the broadcaster simply publishes the objection:

> In accordance with the principle '*cover both sides*', if there is an objection or complaint against a piece of news or a broadcast, then broadcasting the objection or protest itself is sufficient to fulfil the principle of '*cover both sides*', unless there is other strong supporting evidence that accords with the principle of '*due process of law*'.[80]

The Court stated that

> it would be extraordinary if a correction was made in response to an objection or complaint, indicating that the objection or protest was correct, but in court it was proven that the objection or protest was incorrect.[81]

The Court concluded that to find otherwise would be inconsistent with the *Negara Hukum*:

> the obligation to make a correction based on an objection or complaint sets aside the presumption of innocence . . . because it suggests that if a complaint or objection is made, the broadcast or piece of news is definitely wrong and that a correction must be made, and it is insufficient only to broadcast the objection or protest. The infringement of the presumption of innocence means a breach of the '*due process of law*' and, therefore, is contrary to Article 1(3) of the Constitution, which states that Indonesia is a *Negara Hukum*.[82]

---

[78] Constitutional Court Decision 005/PUU-I/2003.
[79] Constitutional Court Decision 005/PUU-I/2003, p 83.
[80] Constitutional Court Decision 005/PUU-I/2003, pp 83–84.
[81] Constitutional Court Decision 005/PUU-I/2003, p 84.
[82] Constitutional Court Decision 005/PUU-I/2003, p 84. Italics in English as in the original.

The PKI case

In another early case, the *PKI case*, an 8:1 majority of the Court over-turned legislation that barred former members of the Indonesian Communist Party (PKI), other prohibited organisations and people involved in the coup attempt of 30 September 1965, from being nominated for candidature in regional and national elections.[83] The Court held that this breached the applicants' rights to participate in government and to be free from discrimination.[84] However, the Court also held that prohibiting a group of citizens from nominating themselves for election clearly 'had a nuance of political punishment for the group'.[85] The Court stated that

> as a rule of law state, prohibitions that relate directly to the rights and freedoms of citizens must be based on a binding court decision.[86]

The Book Banning Law case

In this case,[87] a large coalition of NGOs supporting individual authors and journalists challenged statutes under which the Attorney General could ban books and then confiscate them. The impugned provisions were Articles 1 and 6 of Law 4/PNPS/1963 on Securing Printed Materials that Impede Public Order, and Article 30(3)(c) of Law 16 of 2004 on Public Prosecution. One applicant was Darmawan MM, whose book '*Enam Jalan Menuju Tuhan*' (Six Roads to God) was one of nine banned in 2009. The Court held that these Laws breached several constitutional protections, including freedom of expression, the right to not have property arbitrarily seized and freedom of information.

The Court was, however, primarily concerned that the Laws gave unfettered power to the Attorney General to ban and seize books without judicial oversight. The majority even declared that book seizure would not necessarily breach these rights and freedoms if obtaining judicial permission was a prerequisite to seizure. The Court declared that:

---

[83] Constitutional Court Decision 011-017/PUU-I/2003. In the majority: Asshiddiqie, Marzuki, Natabaya, Harjono, Palguna, Fajar, Siahaan, and Soedarso. In the minority: Roestandi. The provision in question was Article 60(g) of Law 12 of 2003 on General Elections for Members of the DPR, DPD and DPRD.

[84] Constitutional Court Decision 011-017/PUU-I/2003.

[85] Constitutional Court Decision 011-017/PUU-I/2003, p 36.

[86] Constitutional Court Decision 011-017/PUU-I/2003, p 36.

[87] Constitutional Court Decision 6-13-20/PUU-VIII/2010.

In a *Negara Hukum* like Indonesia, due process – that is, law enforcement through a judicial system – is imperative. If an act is to be characterised as illegal, it must be [declared as such] by judicial decision. Banning the distribution of items, such as printed materials, because they may breach public order cannot be simply left to a government agency without a judicial decision. The Attorney General's power to prohibit the distribution of written materials . . . without judicial process is something an authoritarian state [would do], not a *Negara Hukum* like Indonesia.[88]

Although the Attorney General's decision could be challenged in the administrative courts, the administrative courts:

> would base their decisions on the impugned law which indeed gives the Attorney General authority to prohibit the distribution of a book and to seize written materials the contents of which could disrupt public order.[89]

Bibit and Chandra case

The Court's most high-profile case thus far has been the *Bibit and Chandra case*.[90] The applicants were two embattled Commissioners of the Anti-corruption Commission (*Komisi Pemberantasan Korupsi*, or KPK), Chandra Muhammad Hamzah and Bibit Samad Rianto. They had been charged with criminally misusing their authority as Commissioners by issuing and revoking travel bans. With overwhelming public support they argued that senior law enforcement officials were trying to remove them from their positions and had framed them for concocted offences.[91] By the time they lodged their case with the Constitutional Court, they had already been suspended and feared their dismissal was imminent.

Bibit and Chandra challenged the validity of Article 32(1)(c) of Law 30 of 2002 on the Anti-corruption Commission, which states:

> Anti-corruption Commission leaders are to leave their position or be removed from their positions if they become a defendant (*terdakwa*) in a criminal case.

---

[88] Constitutional Court Decision 6-13-20/PUU-VIII/2010, para 3.15.

[89] Constitutional Court Decision 6-13-20/PUU-VIII/2010, para 3.13.4.

[90] Constitutional Court Decision 133/PUU-VII/2009.

[91] These claims were proved true when the Constitutional Court, during its first hearing of the case, allowed KPK-recorded taped conversations between suspects the KPK was investigating and senior prosecutors and police to be played in open court. These conversations revealed a plot to frame Bibit and Chandra (Simon Butt, *Corruption and Law in Indonesia* (London, Routledge, 2011) pp 90–117).

One of their arguments was that the Constitution gave citizens the right to be presumed innocent until proven guilty, despite the Constitution not expressly stating this presumption. Article 32(1)(c) breached that right, they said.

The Court affirmed that the due process of law is a fundamental constitutional guarantee. It requires that all legal processes are fair: people must be informed of legal processes against them and have the right to be heard before their rights, freedoms or property are taken away.[92] In particular, the Court argued, due process of law and the presumption of innocence are primary principles of Indonesia's democratic *Negara Hukum*. It agreed that Article 32(1)(c) contravened the presumption of innocence because it imposed a sanction without trial. As the applicants had argued, they could be dismissed before being found guilty of an offence – indeed, even if they were never found guilty of an offence.

Is the *Negara Hukum* a Source of Stand-Alone Rights?

The Court appears to have used the *Negara Hukum* concept to imply 'new' constitutional rights in some of the cases mentioned above. In other decisions, however, the Court has preferred using *Negara Hukum* in conjunction with other constitutional rights to support its rulings. In these other decisions, the Court could have reached the same decision by applying only the express constitutional rights provisions, without recourse to the *Negara Hukum* concept. For example, in the *Bibit and Chandra case*, the applicants had argued that the presumption of innocence was also encompassed within Article 28D(1) of the Constitution ('Every person has the right to legal recognition, guarantees, protection and certainty that is just, and to equal treatment before the law'). The Court agreed, holding that the presumption of innocence was a universal principle, citing various international instruments and Indonesia's 1999 Human Rights Law.[93] It held that the presumption was, therefore,

> recognised and can be constructed as a part of human rights and constitutional rights . . . and must, therefore, be respected, protected and effectively fulfilled.[94]

---

[92] Constitutional Court Decision 6-13-20/PUU-VIII/2010, para 3.18.
[93] Law 39 of 1999.
[94] For more discussion of this case, see Butt, n 91 above.

In a more recent case, however, the Constitutional Court has indicated that it might no longer treat the *Negara Hukum* as a source of stand-alone rights. In the *Peninjuauan Kembali case*,[95] the applicant – a party in a long-standing dispute over land in central Jakarta – objected to statutory provisions that prohibited litigants from seeking a second *peninjauan kembali* request with the Supreme Court.[96] He argued that this restriction breached the *Negara Hukum* concept and several express constitutional rights in Articles 27(1), 28D(1), 28H(2) and 28I(2). In particular, he claimed that if new evidence was found but no avenue of appeal remained, justice would be compromised.[97] The Court turned down the application, holding that the limitation promoted legal certainty and, because it applied to all, was not discriminatory.[98] Nevertheless, the Court made the following statement about the *Negara Hukum*:

> the *Negara Hukum* is a state which adheres to principles including supremacy of law, equality of law and due process of law which are constitutionally guaranteed. The *Negara Hukum* principle is a general principle adhered to in the administration of the state of Indonesia and in its implementation must be connected with other provisions in the Constitution. Therefore, whether the provisions put forward for review by the applicants breached Article 1(3) will be considered interrelated with the other constitutional provisions put forward by the Applicant.[99]

Implying Rights and Obligations

While the rights the Constitutional Court appears to have implied may well be desirable, the way it has implied them is, in our view, highly problematic. For the most part, the Court has simply proclaimed the existence

---

[95] Constitutional Court Decision 16/PUU-VIII/2010. In Constitutional Court Decision 10/PUU-IX/2011 the applicant had been sentenced to life imprisonment for drug possession by the Supreme Court, and had exhausted both *kasasi* and PK rights. Claiming that she had uncovered new decisive evidence in her case, she sought to lodge a second PK but the Supreme Court refused to accept it. She argued that limiting her PK rights breached Articles 1(3) and 28D(1) of the Constitution. Her application was rejected on the basis that the Court had already decided the issue in Constitutional Court Decision 16/PUU-VIII/2010 (*Hukumonline*, 'Terpidana Seumur Hidup Uji Aturan Pembatasan PK', 27 January 2011).

[96] The *peninjauan kembali* concept is discussed above in Chapter 4 of this volume.

[97] Constitutional Court Decision 16/PUU-VIII/2010, p 67.

[98] Constitutional Court Decision 16/PUU-VIII/2010, p 67.

[99] Constitutional Court Decision 16/PUU-VIII/2010, p 66.

of these rights as though their coming into being, nature and requirements are self-explanatory. In reality, they are not. Just as there is no universally accepted definition of the 'rule of law',[100] the components of Indonesia's *Negara Hukum* are not agreed (as explained in Chapter 1). The Constitution does not define 'Negara Hukum' and no other law explains the concept in significant detail. Although the Constitutional Court has identified it as a key constitutional principle and emphasised the Court's role in upholding it, a majority of the Court has not, to our knowledge, clearly formulated its elements.[101]

The need for a clear and well-reasoned description of what the *Negara Hukum* entails in post-Soeharto Indonesia is highly desirable, particularly given previous misuse of the concept. As mentioned in Chapter 1, for most of Indonesia's post-colonial history the concept was manipulated as a tool of political rhetoric. It was part of the ideological arsenals exploited by both Soekarno and Soeharto to bolster their legitimacy and claims to sweeping power – and, perversely, to justify authoritarianism.[102] While appealing to the virtues of the *Negara Hukum* and declaring their governments to be adhering to the values it embodies, both presidents largely disregarded limits the law sought to impose on the

---

[100]   D Clark, 'The Many Meanings of the Rule of Law Law' in K Jayasuriya (ed), *Capitalism and Power in Asia* (London and New York, Routledge, 1999).

[101]   Individual judges have attempted to do so, however. In his dissent in the *KPK case*, for example, Siahaan set out a formulation of *Negara Hukum*: recognition and protection of human rights; the principle of legality, meaning that all state bodies and institutions and citizens must base their actions on legal rules; and an independent and impartial judiciary. In the same case, Siahaan explained further that the *negara hukum*'s principle of legality requires law-makers to obey the hierarchy of laws when lawmaking – that is, lower-level laws must be based on higher-level laws, with the Constitution at the apex. He noted that every lower-level law that is inconsistent or conflicts with a higher-level law breaches the principle of legality: Constitutional Court Decision 006/PUU-I/2003, p 111. In this case, Soedarsono also confirmed that 'The purpose of the *negara hukum* . . . is to protect human rights': Constitutional Court Decision 006/PUU-I/2003, p 125.

[102]   DS Lev, 'Judicial Authority and The Struggle for An Indonesian Rechsstaat' (1978) 13 *Law and Society Review* 37 44–49; DS Lev, 'Between State and Society: Professional Lawyers and Reform in Indonesia' in DS Lev and R McVey (eds), *Making Indonesia* (Ithaca, NY, Cornell Univeristy, 1996) 152; Lubis, *In Search of Human Rights* (above n 1) 88; Lubis, 'The *Rechsstaat* and Human Rights' (above n 4); P Burns, 'Crime Wave in Indonesia: Negara hukum Tidak Jadi' (1984) 15 *Kabar Sebarang* 51, 52; D Ramage, 'Ideological Discourse in the Indonesian New order: State Ideology and the Beliefs of an Elite, 1985–1993' (University of South Carolina, 1993) 76–77.

state. In particular, the New Order appeared to be the antithesis of a law state, however defined.[103]

The Court has also ignored debate on the wider issue of the propriety of implying rights. In many countries, the implication of constitutional rights has been extremely controversial, with some theorists arguing that it can undermine the legitimacy of judicial review as a whole. For them, judicial review is only democratically justifiable if judges strictly interpret the Constitution, rather than add to or reduce it according to their personal preferences.[104] After all, most judges are not elected and judicial review allows them to overrule laws made by a democratically-elected legislature.[105] Most countries, however, consider judicial review legitimate when it is permitted by the Constitution – the 'highest law' or the ultimate source of legal legitimacy, assumed to express the will of the people.[106] Yet arguably when the Court implies rights that are not expressly stated in the Constitution, it breaches the very Constitution that empowers it.

The Court has also not addressed compelling arguments against implying rights. If the Constitution intended to provide rights, then why did it not clearly express them, instead of leaving them open to supposition? After all, the Constitution was only recently amended. Why did the MPR not insert specific provisions on *Negara Hukum* rights if it wanted the Court to enforce them? And if the rights flowing from the *Negara Hukum* are so fundamental that they do not need to be expressed, then why is the right to protection from retrospective prosecution – one of

---

[103] Asia Watch, Human Rights Concerns in India and East Timor' (USA, Asia Watsch Committee, 1988); International Crisis Group, 'Indonesia's Presidential Crisis', *Indonesia Briefing* (Jakarta/Brussels, 2001); Lubis, 'The *Rechsstaat* and Human Rights' (above n 4); H Thoolen, *Indonesia and the rule of law: twenty years of 'New Order' Government* (London, Frances Pinter Publishers, 1987).

[104] J Kirk, 'Rights, Review and Reasons for Restraint' (2001) 23(1) *Sydney Law Review* 19, 46; LG Jacobs, 'Even More Honest Than Ever Before: Abandoning Pretense and Recreating Legitimacy in Constitutional Interpretation' (1995) *University of Illinois Law Review* 363, 365, 369.

[105] B Friedman, 'The History of the Countermajoritarian Difficulty, Part One: The Road to Judicial Supremacy' (1998) 73 *New York University Law Review* 333; I Somin, 'Political Ignorance and the Countermajoritarian Difficulty: A New Perspective on the Central Obsession of Constitutional Theory' (2004) 89(4) *Iowa Law Review* 1287–372; L Hilbink, 'Beyond Manicheanism: Assessing the New Constitutionalism' (2006) 65(1) *Maryland Law Review* 15, 15.

[106] LG Jacobs, 'Even More Honest Than Ever Before' (above n 104) 364; AS Sweet, *Governing with Judges: Constitutional Politics in Europe* (Oxford, Oxford University Press, 2000).

the five pillars of a fair trial, which itself formed part of the rule of law as identified by the Court – included in the Constitution?

PART III: OBLIGATIONS

As mentioned, the Constitution imposes a number of express obligations upon citizens. Every person must respect the human rights of others (Article 28J(1)); participate in the defence of the state (Article 30(1)); obey the law and the government (Article 27(1)); and take part in basic education (Article 31(2)).

The Constitution also imposes obligations upon the Indonesian government, providing that the cultural identity of traditional communities, including communal land rights, is to be protected in accordance with 'progression and civilisation' (Article 28I(3)); and 'protection, promotion, enforcement and fulfilment of human rights are principally the government's responsibility' (Article 28I(4)). The state must also run and fund basic education and a national education system that increases faith, piety and morality within the framework of enlightening the nation (Articles 31(2) and (3)); care for the poor and for abandoned children (Article 34(1)); develop a social security system for all and to empower the weak and impoverished as befits human dignity (Article 34(2)); and provide appropriate health care and public service facilities (Article 34(3)).

The Court has, to our knowledge, decided very few cases involving constitutional obligations. One example is the *Education Entity cases*,[107] in which legislation concerning the structure of the national education system was challenged. In both cases, the issue in dispute was whether the government could, by statute, require providers of formal education to incorporate. The applicants were students, lecturers, teachers, parents, private sector bodies, educational institutes and study centres. They were concerned that requiring incorporation might reduce access to high-quality education for the Indonesian community. In the 2009 case, the Court agreed. It held that the requirement that educators form a legal entity was unconstitutional, largely because it involved the government shirking its constitutional obligations concerning education. The Court emphasised that the Constitution required the state to provide education in Articles 28C(1) and (2), 28E(1) and 31.[108]

---

[107] Constitutional Court Decisions 021/PUU-IV/2006 and 11-14-21-126-136/PUU-VII/2009.

[108] Constitutional Court Decision 11-14-21-126-136/PUU-VII/2009, p 374.

Implied State Obligations

The Constitutional Court might in future imply obligations of the state from the Constitution's Preamble (which is discussed in Chapter 1). This is particularly true of the statement in the Preamble that the Indonesian state was established to protect:

> all Indonesians and their native land, and to further public welfare, the intellectual life of the people, and to contribute to the world order of freedom, peace and social justice.

So far, however, the Court has used the Preamble primarily as an aid to support its application of other constitutional rights and obligations rather than as a source to imply 'new' obligations not expressly mentioned in the Constitution.[109]

CONCLUSION

The rapid development of a sophisticated public human rights discourse in post-New Order Indonesia has been remarkable. Under Soeharto, frank discussions about human rights were mainly conducted by reformist dissidents. Usually behind closed doors and in fear of military reprisal, but sometimes (and with considerable courage) in protests and in courts, they complained about the parlous disregard for fundamental democratic rights and freedoms that prevailed. Less than a decade after Soeharto's fall, however, human rights had become an integral aspect of public discourse about the Constitution and the running of the state. The focus of attention has now moved from fundamental political rights – most of which are now effectively respected, if not always protected – to a vast array of so-called 'second generation' socio-economic rights.

The contribution of the Constitutional Court to the development of rights consciousness in Indonesia cannot be overstated. Not only has the Court upheld many rights, it has also provided an important forum

---

[109] See for example, Constitutional Court Decision 013/PUU-I/2003, pp 63–64; Constitutional Court Decision 005/PUU-I/2003, pp 84–85; Constitutional Court Decision 065/PUU-II/2004; Constitutional Court Decision 021/PUU-IV/2006; and Constitutional Court Decision 11-14-21-126-136/PUU-VII/2009.

in which human rights discourses can be openly aired without fear of reprisal. Its proceedings are public – often shown on live television and streamed over the Internet – and the Court usually allows applicants to put their arguments unimpeded.

Although the Court has developed a jurisprudence of rights that had never previously existed in Indonesia, thus filling a longstanding and significant gap in Indonesian constitutional thought, it has also often read down those rights to allow the state broad powers to restrict them. It has done this even to those rights that seem on a plain reading of the Constitution to be non-derogable, apparently intended by their drafters to be absolute guarantees beyond the reach of government. And, despite the importance of the *Negara Hukum* concept to the Court's constitutional interpretation, the Court has yet to properly explain exactly how it understands that crucially important concept. Unfortunately, this leaves the basic jurisprudential foundation underpinning the whole emerging jurisprudence of human rights in Indonesia uncertain, perhaps even hollow. It is thus vulnerable to repudiation should a regime less accepting of such rights one day come to power.

SELECTED READING

Eldridge, P, 'Human Rights in Post-Soeharto Indonesia' (2001) 9(1) *Brown Journal of World Affairs* 127.

Herbert, J, 'The legal framework of human rights in Indonesia' in T Lindsey (ed), *Law and Society in Indonesia* (NSW, Federation Press, 2008).

Lubis, Todung Mulya, *In Search of Human Rights: Legal-Political Dilemmas of Indonesia's New Order, 1966–1990* (Jakarta, PT Gramedia Pustaka Utama in cooperation with SPES Foundation, 1993).

Royan, Naomita, 'Increasing Press Freedom in Indonesia: The Abolition of the Lese Majeste and "Hate-sowing" Provisions' (2008) 10(2) *Australian Journal of Asian Law* 290.

8

Religion, Pluralism and Pancasila

━━⋙◦⋘━━

Introduction – The *Religious Courts case* – *Polygamy case* – The
Preamble: Islam, The Pancasila and The Jakarta Charter –
Guarantees of Religious Freedom: Articles 29, 28E and 28I –
Article 28J: Restrictions on Freedom of Religion – Recognition of
Beliefs (Kepercayaan) – Conclusion

INTRODUCTION

INDONESIA HAS THE world's largest Muslim population, comprising at least 80 per cent of its estimated 245 million citizens.[1]
Indonesia might therefore be an overwhelmingly Muslim society
but, as shown in Chapter 1, it is not an Islamic state in a constitutional
sense, even if it does enforce some Islamic legal norms. This was confirmed in 2008 by the Constitutional Court in the *Religious Courts case*,
which directly addressed the question of the place of Islamic law in the
republic. This is an issue that has been repeatedly raised since Islam and
shar'iah (Islamic law) were deliberately excluded from the Constitution in
1945, as also shown in Chapter 1.

RELIGIOUS COURTS CASE

Suryani, a young madrasah graduate from Banten, challenged the constitutionality of Article 49(1) of Law 7 of 1989 on the Religious Courts.

---

[1] CIA, 'Indonesia', *The World Fact Book* (2011): www.cia.gov/library/publications/
the-world-factbook/geos/id.html, accessed 20 July 2011. This chapter draws on
T Lindsey, *Islam, Law and the State in Southeast Asia, Vol. I* (London, IB Tauris 2012),
Chapters 1, 2 and 12; and S Butt, 'Islam, the State and the Constitutional Court in
Indonesia' (2010) 19(2) *Pacific Rim Law and Policy Journal* 279–302.

The religious courts (*pengadilan agama*) are Indonesia's shari'ah courts. Article 49(1) sets out the limited areas of Islamic law over which they have jurisdiction, which are chiefly personal law matters: marriage (*perkawinan*); succession (*waris*); gifts (*hibah*); bequests (*wakaf*); ritual payment of alms (*zakat*); charitable gifts (*infaq*); gifts to the needy (*shadaqah*); and shari'ah economy (*ekonomi syari'ah*).

Suryani argued that Islam required Muslims to follow Islamic law in its entirety, not just as regards the limited matters listed in Article 49(1). Muslims, he said, should be subject to the full scope of Islamic criminal law, including, for example, hand amputation for theft.[2] He argued that restricting the matters of Islamic law that Indonesia's religious courts could apply breached his rights to religious freedom under Articles 28 and 29 of the Constitution (discussed below) and, indeed, those of the entire Indonesian Muslim community.[3]

In reply, the Court declared:

> the Applicant's argument does not accord with the understanding of the relationship between religion and the state [in Indonesia]. Indonesia is not a religious state that is based only on one religion; but Indonesia is also not a secular state that does not consider religion at all. It does not hand over all religious affairs entirely to individuals and the community. Indonesia is a state that is based on Almighty God. The state protects [the right of] all religious adherents to carry out the teachings of their respective religions . . . If the issue [in contention is whether] Islamic law is . . . a source of law, it can be said that Islamic law is indeed a source of national law. But it is not the only source of national law, because in addition to Islamic law, customary law, western law and other sources of legal tradition are sources of national law. Therefore, Islamic law can be one of the sources of material for law as part of formal government laws. Islamic law, as a source of law, can be used together with other sources of law, and, in this way, can be the material for the creation of government laws that are in force as national law.[4]

A statement made by Justice Muhammad Alim during case hearings made the Constitutional Court's position clearer still:

> You must understand that in this Republic of Indonesia, the highest law is the 1945 Constitution, not the Qur'an. As Muslims, we consider the Qur'an

[2] Constitutional Court Decision 16/PUU-VI/2008, para 2.1.
[3] Constitutional Court Decision 16/PUU-VI/2008, para 2.1.
[4] Constitutional Court Decision 16/PUU-VI/2008, para 3.18.

to be the highest law but . . . the national consensus is that the Constitution is the highest law.[5]

POLYGAMY CASE

In its judgment in the *Religious Courts case* the Constitutional Court followed a position that it had adopted a year earlier in the *Polygamy case*, namely that the state is not bound by Islamic law but rather has the power to interpret and restrict it, more or less as it sees fit. The applicant in the *Polygamy case*, a man named M Insa, objected to provisions in Law 1 of 1974 on Marriage that he claimed prevented him from engaging in polygamy.[6] He had gone to the Religious Affairs Office expecting to be able to marry polygamously but officials rejected his request because he had not obtained judicial consent as required by the Marriage Law. Dissatisfied, he applied to the Constitutional Court for a review of the Law.

Insa argued that several aspects of the Marriage Law contradicted Islamic law, including the provisions declaring that marriages should, in principle, be monogamous (Article 3(1)). He also objected to provisions fixing the various requirements that men must meet in order to obtain judicial consent for polygamy, as well as those invalidating polygamous marriages not approved by the courts. Insa's two main constitutional arguments were first, that Article 28B(1) of the Constitution states that every person has the right to create a family and to continue their lineage through a valid marriage. He claimed that restricting polygamy impeded the exercise of this right. Second, Insa argued that Article 28E(1) of the Constitution guarantees citizens freedom to embrace a religion and to worship in accordance with that religion. Insa argued that restricting polygamy was tantamount to breaching Islamic law, thus denying him that freedom.

The then Minister for Religious Affairs, HM Maftuh Basyuni, responded to Insa's arguments. He began by observing that Article 28J(2) of the Constitution (discussed further below) allows the state to impose limits on the human rights guaranteed by the Constitution and that, while

---

[5] Constitutional Court Decision Transcript 16/PUU-VI/2008, 31 July 2008, p 7.

[6] In fact, 'polygamy' refers to the taking of multiple spouses by either a man or a woman. 'Polygyny' refers to a man taking multiple wives. In Indonesia, however, *poligami* is the term used for polygyny and we follow that usage.

the Constitution contains a right to marriage, it contains no right to polygamous marriage. In any event, he pointed out, the Marriage Law does not
prohibit polygamy but merely restricts it.[7] The Court seems to have
adopted Minister Basyuni's views in its judgment. It found, first, that the
Marriage Law did not prohibit Muslims from marrying, and even allowed
them to marry polygamously, provided preconditions to ensure that the
purposes of marriage were met had been fulfilled in the view of the religious courts.[8] Secondly, the Court found that according to the *ulama* (religious scholars), matters of Islamic law may legitimately be determined by
statute and, through courts, by the state:[9]

> [T]he state, as the highest organisation in a community, created on the basis
> of agreement, not only has the authority to regulate (*bevoeg te regel*) but also
> the obligation to regulate (*verplicht te regel*), to guarantee the realisation of
> justice, through laws that fall within its jurisdiction and which are upheld
> through the courts. This accords with the *fiqh* [Islamic jurisprudence] cited
> by the expert Prof. Dr. Hj. Huzaemah T. Yanggo . . . The state (*ulil amri*) has
> the authority to determine the requirements which must be fulfilled by citi-
> zens who wish to enter into a polygamous marriage in the interests of the
> public benefit, particularly to achieve the goals of marriage – that is, to cre-
> ate a happy and everlasting family (household) based on the Almighty God.[10]

THE PREAMBLE: ISLAM, THE PANCASILA AND THE JAKARTA CHARTER

The decisions of the Constitutional Court in the *Religious Courts* and
Polygamy cases were not surprising. They reflect well-established views as
to the limited constitutional place of religion – and, in particular, Islam
– in the Indonesian state, and the broad power of that state to regulate
and restrict religious practice. These views have been shared by every
government since Independence was declared in 1945, and the arguments put by the applicants in both cases have been used with equal
consistency to challenge governments on this issue. In fact, argument
about the legal status of Islam has been constant since well before
Independence. As in these two cases, the debate has most often been

---

[7] Constitutional Court Decision 12/PUU-VI/2007, para 2.2.1.
[8] Constitutional Court Decision 12/PUU-VI/2007, para 3.18.2.
[9] Constitutional Court Decision 12/PUU-VI/2007, paras 3.15.3–3.15.4.
[10] Constitutional Court Decision 12/PUU-VI/2007, para 3.15.4.

expressed in terms of whether Muslims in Indonesia should be required to comply with conservative understandings of shari'ah by way of a legal obligation imposed and enforced by the state.

The argument in favour of the enforcement of *shari'ah* was led in the decades before World War II by Mohammad Natsir, later Prime Minister of Indonesia (1950–51). He called for Islam to be the *dasar negara* (basis of the state, *Grundnorm*) of a future independent Indonesia. In 1939, Natsir said, with considerable prescience, that the nationalist movement

> would achieve its goal with the attainment of Independence, but Muslims
> . . . would not stop at that and would continue their struggle as long as the
> country continued not to be based on, or administered according to, the
> laws and regulations of Islam.[11]

The question of whether Islam would be the basis of their proposed republic was therefore a very important one for the drafters who met in 1945 to prepare Indonesia's first Constitution. As discussed in Chapter 1, they answered it in the Preamble to that Constitution by rejecting Islam as the *Grundnorm* in favour of an uneasy compromise patched together by Soekarno from the competing ideologies and beliefs represented among nationalist leaders. These were diverse and included, among others, Socialism, Fascism and liberal democracy, as well as Islam.[12]

The Preamble identified five norms as the *dasar negara*: 'Belief in Almighty God' (*Ketuhanan yang Maha Esa*), 'Just and Civilised Humanitarianism', 'the Unity of Indonesia', 'Democracy Guided by Deliberations amongst Representatives' and 'Social Justice'. Together these formed the state philosophy, the *Pancasila* or 'five Principles'. While the Preamble referred to belief in God in the first *sila*, or principle, it did

[11] MB Pranowo, 'Which Islam and Which Pancasila? Islam and the State in Indonesia' in A Budiman (ed), *State and Civil Society in Indonesia* (Clayton, Victoria, Monash University, 1990) 479, 483, citing D Noer, *The Modernist Muslim movement in Indonesia, 1900–1942* (East Asian historical monographs; Kuala Lumpur, Oxford University Press, 1973) 276. See also MB Hooker, *Indonesian Islam: Social Change Through Contemporary Fatawa* (Crows Nest, NSW, Asian Studies Association of Australia in Association with Allen and Unwin and University of Hawaii Press Honolulu, 2003) 30–3, for the debates between Natsir and Soekarno.

[12] AB Nasution, *The Aspiration for Constitutional Government in Indonesia: A Socio-Legal Study of the Indonesian Konstituante, 1956–1959* (Jakarta, Pustaka Sinar Harapan, 1992); HM Yamin, *Naskah Persiapan Undang-Undang Dasar 1945* (Jakarta, Yayasan Prapanca, 1959–60). The full text of the Preamble appears in Chapter 1 of this volume, at note 36.

not establish Islam as the basis of the state. In fact, Islam was not mentioned at all in the Preamble or anywhere else in the Constitution.

There has since been great disagreement regarding the first *sila*. This is because in its original formulation it included additional words proposed by a 'Committee of Nine' appointed specifically to consider the *dasar negara* issue by the Investigatory Body for Preparatory Work for Indonesian Independence (*Badan Penyelidik Usaha-usaha Persiapan Kemerdekaan Indonesia*, BPUPKI). These words were: 'with the obligation to carry out Islamic shari'ah for its adherents' (*dengan kewajiban menjalankan syariat Islam bagi pemeluk-pemeluknya*). The 'seven words' (*tujuh kata*), as they became known,[13] were not included in the final draft of the Constitution when it was promulgated in August 1945. They had been deleted at the insistence of Soekarno and his future Vice-President, Mohammad Hatta, as the Constitution was being finalised. This happened pursuant to what Soekarno claimed had been an out-of-session 'Gentlemen's Agreement' between delegates.[14] The deletion was motivated by fears that Christians in Eastern Indonesia would abandon the new Republic in favour of the returning Dutch colonial forces. It was also supported by objections from nationalist and other leaders who were ideologically opposed to the imposition of Islamic law.[15]

The first draft of the Preamble – with the 'seven words' included – is now commonly referred to as the 'Jakarta Charter' *(Piagam Jakarta)*. It has long stood as a symbol of aspirations for an alternative Indonesian state based on Islamic law. Different conservative Muslim groups have persistently called for reinstatement of the 'seven words'.

---

[13] M Feener, 'Indonesian Movements for the Creation of a "National Maddhab"' (2001) 9(1) *Islamic Law and Society* 86.

[14] Yamin, n 12 above, 145; Endang Saifuddin Anshari, *Piagam Jakarta 22 Juni 1945: sebuah konsensus nasional tentang dasar negara Republik Indonesia (1945–1949)* (Jakarta, Gema Insani Press, 1996); A Salim, *Challenging the Secular State: the Islamization of Law in Modern Indonesia* (Honolulu, University of Hawaii Press, 2008) 64–69; BJ Boland, *The Struggle of Islam in Modern Indonesia* (The Hague, Martinus Nijhoff, 1982) 243.

[15] MC Ricklefs, *A History Of Modern Indonesia Since C. 1300*, 4th edn (Stanford CA, Stanford University Press, 2008) 249; Z Adnan, 'Islamic Religion: Yes, Islamic Ideology: No! Islam and the State in Indonesia' in A Budiman (ed), *State and Civil Society in Indonesia* (Clayton, Victoria, Centre of Southeast Asian Studies, Monash University, 1990) 441, 447; D Noer, 'Bung Hatta yang Taqwa' in CLM Penders (ed), *Mohammad Hatta, Indonesian Patriot: Memoirs* (Singapore, Gunung Agung, 1981) 617–22.

The debate about Islam as the basis of the state arose again in the mid-1950s, when it led to deadlock in the Constituent Assembly (*Konstituante*). As mentioned in Chapter 1, this was an elected body charged with writing a new Constitution.[16] Influenced by Natsir's ideas, 43.1 per cent of the members of the *Konstituante* supported reinstating the Jakarta Charter. This was unacceptable to most delegates but its supporters refused to give ground, despite the fact that any resolution of the *Konstituante* required a two-thirds majority. Their insistence that any new constitution establish a republic grounded on Islam, and the deadlock this created, were among the reasons used by Soekarno in 1959 to legitimise his dissolution of the *Konstituante* and the reinstatement of the wartime 1945 Constitution – which, of course, included the Pancasila as the *dasar negara*. As discussed in Chapter 1, Soekarno then ruled directly until overthrow by the army in 1966 ended his Guided Democracy (*Demokrasi Terpimpin*) dictatorship.

After the collapse of Soekarno's Old Order in 1966, Soeharto's New Order systematically elevated the Pancasila from official ideological formula to a status approaching that of an institutionalised secular state 'religion';[17] and it was used to repress aspirations for the implementation of shar'iah and an Islamic state. The peak of the political subordination of Indonesian Islam by the New Order state was achieved with the passing of Laws 3 and 8 of 1985 on Social Organisations, known as the *Azas Tunggal* (Sole Foundation) Laws. These statutes required all political and social organisations (including major Islamic mass organisations such as *Nahdlatul Ulama* and *Muhammadiyah*) to adopt the Pancasila as their sole philosophical base. Refusal to do so – for example, by insisting that only Islam could be the philosophical basis of a Muslim religious organisation – was seditious, as was any questioning of the Pancasila. Soeharto made this very clear:

> The Pancasila as *perjanjian luhur* (noble agreement) of the Indonesian Nation should be honoured forever. And those who betray Pancasila will end with destruction.[18]

[16] Pranowo, 'Which Islam and Which Pancasila?' (n 11 above); Adnan, 'Islamic Religion: Yes, Islamic Ideology: No! Islam and the State in Indonesia' (n 15 above); Nasution, *The Aspiration for Constitutional Government in Indonesia* (n 12 above).

[17] M van Langenburg, 'The New Order State: Language, Ideology, Hegemony' in A Budiman (ed), *State and Civil Society in Indonesia* (Clayton, Victoria, Centre of Southeast Asian Studies, Monash University, 1990).

[18] Adnan, 'Islamic Religion: Yes, Islamic Ideology: No! Islam and the State in Indonesia' (n 15 above) 453, citing Krissantono, *Pandangan Presiden Tentang Pancasila* (Jakarta, CSIS, 1976) 10, 11.

Most major Islamic organisations eventually complied with the Azas Tunggal Law acknowledging, nominally at least, that Pancasila was their 'sole foundation' on the grounds that it embraced and was 'inspired' by Islam. Some developed sophisticated arguments from *fiqh* (Islamic jurisprudence) to legitimise their concession.[19] Others, however, maintained defiance, even characterising the Pancasila as un-Islamic, polytheistic and heretical.[20] This opposition was seen by the state as political dissent and subversion, and was often treated as a security issue, with state responses including intimidation, detention and sometimes killings.[21]

The New Order's use of the Pancasila as legitimiser was far more comprehensive than this brief account of the Azas Tunggal Law suggests. It was directed more widely than just at Muslim organisations. The requirement of a belief in God was used, for example, to demonise Communists as atheists and thus un-Indonesian, a view that is still widely held and which generally renders atheism unacceptable (although most true atheists adopt a nominal religion for convenience). In fact, under Soeharto, Pancasila became the medium for a remarkably effective sweeping de-politicisation of the public, to create a 'floating mass' of individuals who could be deployed as units in the New Order's remarkably successful corporatist and developmentalist strategies. The Pancasila became the vehicle for a massive saturation indoctrination programme aimed at creating 'development-oriented persons' (*manusia pembangunan*) who would contribute to achieving the regime's national development plans.[22] Famously tedious but also overwhelming in its scope, this programme left very little room for Islamic critiques of the New Order system and none for the Jakarta Charter discourse.

By the mid-1990s, the New Order government began to realise its ideological programme was losing traction and needed re-thinking, but it was engulfed in economic and political crisis sparked by the floating of the Rupiah in 1997 and the 'Asian Economic Crisis'. By the time Soeharto resigned in 1998, the Pancasila had become discredited by its extensive and programmatic exploitation as a political tool to legitimise

---

[19]   Adnan, 'Islamic Religion: Yes, Islamic Ideology: No! Islam and the State in Indonesia' (n 15 above); Pranowo, 'Which Islam and Which Pancasila?' (n 11 above).

[20]   A Qadir Djaelani, cited in Adnan, ibid, 465.

[21]   Van Langenburg, 'The New Order State: Language, Ideology, Hegemony' (n 17 above) 123, 133–34, fn 43.

[22]   S Nishimura, 'The Development of Pancasila Moral Education' (1995) 33(3) *Southeast Asian Studies* 303–16.

a regime that had now collapsed. In fact, the Pancasila even seemed for a while to be headed for irrelevance.[23] The close association of the five principles with the New Order policies of repressing its critics and, in particular, marginalising Islamic legal and political traditions, had tainted them. Likewise, as Indonesia gradually democratised, moving to a genuine and open multi-party system, the Soeharto-era restrictions that had constrained Islamic political activity were removed. The administrations that followed Soeharto needed coalitions to govern and often relied on Islamic parties to pass legislation. These administrations were also unable to assert the tight control that Soeharto once enjoyed over public debate, the flow of information and religious politics. This meant that the New Order interpretation of Pancasila as a tool to counter dissent and, in particular, Muslim political activity, was much harder to assert.

This 'fading'[24] of the Pancasila was twice formally acknowledged by the MPR: first, in 1998, directly after Soeharto's resignation, when it formally suspended Pancasila indoctrination courses; and again, in 2000, when it stated that the Pancasila had been 'misused' to support the New Order and it should become a national ideology that is 'open to discussion for the future of Indonesia'.[25]

The 'fading' of the Pancasila was accompanied by a renewal of the ambitions of the proponents of an Islamist *dasar negara*. Calls by Islamic groups for rights of political expression seemed, at first, to sit well with the liberalising and democratising rhetoric shared by both the governments that succeeded Soeharto and the reform movement that helped topple him. They also seemed to fit well with a popular human rights discourse directed at reining in the military, which had been active in repressing political Islam. The result was a resurgence of the Islamic identity and ideological expression that inevitably took political form. This resulted in political pressure for legal Islamisation and even reinstatement of the Jakarta Charter aim of imposing an enforceable obligation on Muslims to observe shari'ah.

---

[23] R Cribb, '"The Incredible Shrinking Pancasila": Nationalist Propaganda and The Missing Ideological Legacy of Soeharto' in T Reuter (ed), *The Return of Constitutional Democracy in Indonesia* (Annual Indonesia lecture series; Caulfield, Victoria, Monash Asia Institute, 2010) 65–76.

[24] This term is Sarah Waddell's: 'The Role of the 'Legal Rule' in Indonesian Law Reform: The Reformasi of Water Resources Management in Indonesia' (Sydney, University of Sydney, 2002).

[25] Decree V/MPR/2000 on the Implementation of National Unity and Unification. Waddell, n 24 above, 79.

GUARANTEES OF RELIGIOUS FREEDOM:
ARTICLES 29, 28E AND 28I

During the final constitutional amendment session in 2002, the Jakarta
Charter issue was raised again. A formal proposal to amend Article 29
of the Constitution was put to the MPR by Islamic parties PBB (*Partai
Bulan Bintang* – Moon Star Party), the political successor of Natsir's
Masyumi party, and PDU (*Partai Daulat Ummah* – Ummah Sovereignty
Party).[26] Article 29 originally read:

(a) The State shall be based upon Belief in Almighty God.
(b) The State guarantees all persons the freedom of worship, each according
to their own beliefs.

The proposal sought to add a provision that would make the practice of
shari'ah an obligation for Muslims. In a strict sense, this was not an
attempt to reinstate the Jakarta Charter, as it would not have led to the
amendment of the Pancasila, which survived the amendment process
unchanged. Inserting the 'seven words' requirement in Article 29(1)
would, however, have had precisely the same effect and this was obvious
to all involved in debate.[27]

By an overwhelming majority, the MPR – the first democratically-
elected assembly since the 1950s – adopted Soekarno's position 57 years
earlier and rejected the proposal.[28] It did this despite initial support for the
amendments from then-Vice-President, Hamzah Haz, and his party,
PPP.[29] One reason was the same fear that had occupied politicians' minds
in 1945: fear of dividing largely Christian Eastern Indonesia from the

[26] N Hosen, *Shari'a and Constitutional Reform in Indonesia* (Singapore, ISEAS, 2007)
4; T Reuter, 'Winning Hearts and Minds? Religion and Politics in post-Suharto
Indonesia' in T Reuter (ed), *The Return of Constitutional Democracy in Indonesia* (Caulfield,
Monash Asia Institute, 2010) 77, 83.

[27] For accounts of the amendment debates in the MPR and the politics surround-
ing them, see D Indrayana, *Indonesian Constitutional Reform, 1999–2002: An Evaluation
of Constitution-Making in Transition* (Jakarta, Kompas Book Publishing, 2008);
N Hosen, *Shari'a and Constitutional Reform in Indonesia* (n 26 above); Hosen, 'Human
Rights Provisions in the Second Amendment to the Indonesian Constitution from
Shari'ah Perspective' (2007) 9(2) *The Muslim World* 200–224.

[28] Hosen, *Shari'a and Constitutional Reform in Indonesia* (n 26 above) 59; Indrayana,
Indonesian Constitutional Reform, 1999–2002 (n 27 above).

[29] Reuter, 'Winning Hearts and Minds? Religion and Politics in post-Suharto
Indonesia' (n 26 above) 83.

overwhelming majority in Muslim central and western Indonesia. In 2002, the recent loss of Christian East Timor and secessionist demands in parts of Eastern Indonesia, including Papua (which is predominantly Christian), made this a real concern for many MPR members.

Just as significant, however, was the question put by Pranowo:[30] 'Which Islam, which Pancasila?' If shari'ah became a constitutional obligation for Indonesian Muslims, the question would arise as to whose selection from Indonesia's diverse and contested Islamic legal traditions would the state enforce. Influential leaders of mainstream Muslim organisations, such as Nahdlatul Ulama and Muhammadiyah, have long been concerned that implementing shari'ah would hand a political weapon to their main competitors – each other – or even to smaller, more conservative islamist organisations. Both PKB (created by leading members of Nahdlatul Ulama) and PAN (which has links to Muhammadiyah) therefore opposed the amendments.[31]

New provisions on religious freedom were, however, inserted during the second round of constitutional amendments in 2000. Article 28E echoes the second paragraph of Article 29 ('The State guarantees all persons the freedom of worship, each according to their own beliefs'), and appears to strengthen that guarantee. It reads:

> Each person is free to profess their religion and to worship in accordance with their religion . . . Each person has the freedom to possess convictions and beliefs, and to express their thoughts and attitudes in accordance with their conscience.

In addition, Article 28I(1) lists a number of basic human rights that may not be limited under any circumstances.[32] Among these is the right to have a religion (*hak beragama*).

ARTICLE 28J: RESTRICTIONS ON FREEDOM OF RELIGION

Despite their plain terms, the religious freedoms guaranteed by Articles 28E, 28I and 29 are highly qualified. This is chiefly because Article

---

[30] Pranowo, 'Which Islam and Which Pancasila?' (n 11 above).

[31] J McBeth, 'Islam and Society: The Case for Islamic Law', *Straits Times*, 22 August 2002.

[32] Although, as discussed in Chapter 7 of this volume, the Constitutional Court has held that these rights are, in fact, not absolute in all circumstances.

28J(2) of the Constitution, also inserted by the post-Soeharto amendments, allows for restriction of rights granted elsewhere in the Constitution. It provides:

> In carrying out his or her rights and freedom, every citizen has the responsibility to abide by the restrictions set out by legislation protecting the rights and freedoms of others and which accords *with moral considerations, religious values, security and public order in a democratic society* (emphasis added).

As shown in detail in Chapter 7, the Constitutional Court has relied on this provision to allow the government to legislate in ways that limit citizens' freedoms to follow their religious beliefs, as Minister Basyuni argued in the *Polygamy case*. This the Court did most notably in its April 2010 decision upholding Law 1/PNPS/1965 on Preventing the Abuse and Dishonouring of Religion,[33] commonly referred to as the 'Blasphemy Law'. This decision constitutes the Court's fullest discussion yet about the scope of the constitutional right to freedom of religion.

The Blasphemy Law Case

In October 2009, dozens of NGOs and individuals, including former president Abdurrahman Wahid, asked the Constitutional Court to review the Blasphemy Law. Among other things, this statute permits the government, by Joint Ministerial Decree, to order religious groups whose beliefs diverge from the fundamental tenets of Indonesia's recognised religions, to refrain from particular activities and, ultimately, to disband those groups if they disobey the order.

The applicants argued that the Blasphemy Law breached their rights to freedom of religion in Articles 29 and 28E and asked the Court to strike it down. In an 8:1 majority decision[34] handed down in April 2010 the Court refused the application.

---

[33] Constitutional Court Decision 140/PUU-VII/2009.

[34] The sole dissenter, Justice Maria Farida Indrati, accepted the distinction proposed by the majority between 'internal freedoms' (*kebebasan internal*), peoples' spiritual beliefs that cannot be regulated by the state, and 'external freedoms' (*kebebasan eksternal*), the way that people express or spread those beliefs (p 316). Farida decided that the inclusion in the Elucidation to Article 1 of the phrase 'the government attempts to channel them in the healthy direction of belief in Almighty God', demonstrates that the Law seeks to authorise the state to attempt to interfere with this internal freedom of religion (at least with respect to those whose beliefs do not

The Blasphemy Law contains only four substantive provisions. Article 1 provides that:

> Every person is prohibited from deliberately and publicly talking about, advocating, or seeking public support for the interpretation[35] of a religion adhered to in Indonesia, or performing religious activities resembling the religious activities of [a religion adhered to in Indonesia], if that interpretation or activity deviates from the basic tenets of that religion.

The Elucidation to Article 1 explains that the religions adhered to in Indonesia are Islam, Protestantism, Catholicism, Hinduism, Buddhism and Confucianism. Others, such as Judaism, Zoroastrianism, Shintoism and Taoism are not prohibited, it adds, because Article 29 of the Constitution provides citizens with freedom to adhere to a religion and to worship in accordance with that religion. These other faiths are allowed to exist, provided they do not breach the Blasphemy Law or other laws. 'Religious activities' include 'calling a school of belief a religion, using religious terms when following the tenets of the belief, worshiping, etc'. As for mystical sects (*kebathinan*), the Elucidation exhorts the government to 'channel them in the healthy direction of belief in almighty God'.

Article 2(1) provides that:

> Any person who breaches Article 1 is to be ordered and strongly warned to cease their acts, by Joint Decree of the Religious Affairs Minister, the Attorney General and the Home Affairs Minister.

Article 2(2) adds that:

> If a breach referred to in Article 2(1) is perpetrated by an organisation or a school of belief, the President can disband that organisation and declare the

fall within the six recognised religions). Accordingly, she decided that Article 1 was inconsistent with freedom of religion (p 317). Farida also agreed with the applicants that Article 3 had often been misused to discriminate against religions outside the six recognised by the state. Although the Law did not explicitly state that only six religions were recognised, in practice, she said, only these six religions have enjoyed legal guarantees, protections and state assistance, such as in the issuance of identity cards, death certificates and in marriage.

[35] The significance of the word 'interpretation' here is discussed further below. Briefly, it is intended to allow the state effectively to enforce orthodox understandings of any of the recognised religions by legally restricting the propogation of unorthodox doctrine, as opposed to ritual behaviour (which is caught by the phrase 'religious activities').

organisation or school to be a prohibited organisation/school after obtaining advice from the Religious Affairs Minister, Attorney General and Home Affairs Minister.

Article 3 adds that if the organisation or school continues its activities after being warned by Joint Decree, adherents and members of the organisation or school face a maximum of five years' imprisonment.

Article 4 inserts a provision in the Criminal Code. This is Article 156a, which threatens with a maximum of five years' imprisonment any person who deliberately and publicly makes a statement or performs an act:

a. that, in essence, constitutes animosity towards, or misuse or 'dishonouring' (*penodaan*)[36] of, a religion adhered to in Indonesia; or
b. intended [to make] people not to adhere to any religion based on the Almighty God.

Article 156a has been used to convict and jail members of minority religious groups and so-called 'deviant sects' (*aliran sesat*), that is, unorthodox religious groups, and such prosecutions have increased significantly in the post-Soeharto period.

In the *Blasphemy Law case*, the applicants argued that Article 1 of the Blasphemy Law undermines the right to freedom of belief, expression and thought, because it allows the government to identify religious interpretations as deviant. Article 2, they said, likewise constitutes a breach of freedom of religion, association and opinion because it authorises the government to prohibit and disband religious 'deviant' religious activities and sects. They also argued that the Blasphemy Law gives the state power to determine which interpretation of religious beliefs are 'correct' or 'wrong', even though the Constitution allows the state to restrict only the behaviour of citizens, not their beliefs. It similarly does not protect freedom of religion because it allows people who hold different beliefs or religious interpretations to be punished, and discriminates against those whose religions fall outside the six state-recognised religions.

The DPR and the government argued in their submission that the Law's purpose was, in fact, not to criminalise a person's interpretation or practise of a religion but rather to criminalise the intentional encourage-

---

[36] *Penodaan* literally means 'staining' or 'soiling', and can also be translated as 'besmirching' or 'disgracing'.

ment of public support for a religious act or interpretation that deviates from the primary religions adhered to in Indonesia. Rather than limiting freedom of religion, the Law, they said, protects religious freedom by protecting believers against humiliation and the desecration of their religion. In their view, the Law was designed to ensure harmony, religious tolerance, public order and security. It gives law enforcers power to handle religious desecration cases to prevent conflict and vigilantism.

The Court again essentially accepted the government's submissions. The majority held that Indonesia is a religious country, not a secular one. They significantly restricted the term 'religious country', however, by defining it by reference to a wide range of regulatory features of the state. These included, of course, the Pancasila, which the Court said was the *Grundnorm* or *Dasar Negara*. Echoing New Order rhetoric, the Court said that the Pancasila – including the first *sila*: Belief in Almighty God – must be accepted by all citizens, in full.

The other religious regulatory features identified by the Court include the Constitutional provisions that recognise religious rights, described above; the fact that courts issue their decisions 'in the name of almighty God'; the existence of a Religious Affairs Ministry; that religious holidays are celebrated; that some (limited) rules of Islamic law have been adopted in state law for Muslims; and that the role of religion was specifically discussed when the Constitution was drafted and the decision to include religious freedom came out of this discussion as a compromise.

Having established that Indonesia is a 'religious state' – albeit a limited one, and not one that was necessarily Islamic in nature – the Court next found that it must therefore take religious values into account when reviewing the constitutional validity of statutes:

> The Indonesian Constitution does not allow campaigns pushing for freedom to have no religion, to promote 'anti-religion', or to offend or discredit religious teachings or texts which are the source of religious beliefs, or which sully the name of God. This is one thing that sets Indonesia's *Negara Hukum* [rule of law] apart from the Western rule of law. In the administration of government and the judiciary, and in law-making, religiosity and religious teaching and values are yardsticks to determine whether the statute is good or bad – even for determining whether law is constitutional or unconstitutional.[37]

---

[37] Constitutional Court Decision 140/PUU-VII/2009, p 275.

According to the majority, the right to freedom of religion is a private right to hold a religious belief (*forum internum*). This is a human right that the state has the responsibility to protect, advance, enforce and fulfill. Belief is a private experience influenced by social environment, teachings, preaching and parenting. It is therefore not possible for freedom of belief to be changed through 'coercive' measures or by law.

On the other hand, the majority held, the state can place limitations on the right to express one's beliefs.[38] The right to manifest one's religion (*forum externum*), including expressing beliefs to others, relates to community life, the public interest, and the interests of the state. The Court then emphasised that none of the rights contained in Articles 28A to 28I are absolute. All rights are subject to the fundamental responsibilities set down in Article 28J.[39] As discussed in Chapter 7, rights can be limited under this provision in order to guarantee 'recognition and respect of rights and freedoms of others in fulfillment of just demands in accordance with moral considerations, religious values, security and public order in a democratic community'.[40]

The majority also held that Article 1 of the Law did not prohibit people from interpreting religious teachings or performing among themselves religious activities diverging from those of an official religion adhered to in Indonesia. Rather, it prohibited deliberately and publicly speaking about, or seeking public support for, interpretations or activities that diverge from the fundamental teachings of a religion that resembles a religion officially adhered to in Indonesia. Faiths that fall within the Pancasila 'Belief in Almighty God' are a personal matter, but (and this a significant qualification) they must be consistent with fundamental religious teachings that use 'appropriate methodology' based on 'relevant holy books' in order to be recognised as legitimate by the state.[41] The Blasphemy Law was, therefore, a justifiable restriction of religious freedoms under Article 28J(2). In fact, the Court even held that the Law protected the right to religion by preventing blasphemy and misuse of religion.[42] Islamic scholars (*ulama*), it held, had become the 'face' of the Islamic community and had intellectual authority in interpreting the teachings of Islam. If others promote teachings that diverge

---

[38] Constitutional Court Decision 140/PUU-VII/2009, p 288.
[39] Constitutional Court Decision 140/PUU-VII/2009, p 292.
[40] Constitutional Court Decision 140/PUU-VII/2009, p 293.
[41] Constitutional Court Decision 140/PUU-VII/2009, para 3.52.
[42] Constitutional Court Decision 140/PUU-VII/2009, p 295.

from those the ulama espouse, followers of the teachings of ulama will be 'offended'.[43] Without Article 1, there would be conflict, unrest, disintegration and animosity in the community.[44] If the state allowed this to occur, it would have failed to meet its obligation to create security and order in the community.

Article 2(1) of the Blasphemy Law was held to not breach the right to religion for similar reasons. The state, the Court found, needs power to order people who contravene Article 1 to refrain from their acts. If the state could not do so, law and order would likely break down.[45] Article 2(2), which allowed the president to disband organisations that breached Article 2(1), was also valid simply because it enforced Article 2(1).[46] Again, the Court found that any breaches of the applicants' right to freedom of association could be justified by reference to Article 28J(2).[47]

As for Article 3, the Court pointed to specific examples the applicants had highlighted in an attempt to prove that the Blasphemy Law was discriminatory. The Court decided that these examples merely demonstrated a misapplication of the Blasphemy Law, not problems with the Law itself.[48] The Court followed its usual path of emphasising that it lacked jurisdiction to assess the constitutionality of the application of a statute, and could review only of the contents of the statute itself.[49]

The *Blasphemy Law case*, like the *Religious Courts case* and the *Polygamy case*, thus upheld the state's broad right to legislate to deal with religious issues as it sees fit, so as to ensure public order. The *Religious Courts case* confirmed that the first principle of the Pancasila (minus the 'seven words') still marks the outer limits of religious obligation for Indonesians, Muslim or otherwise, at least for the purposes of the state. This is because this case, with the *Polygamy case*, confirmed the state's right to limit formally enforceable shari'ah to a narrow field, largely family law, and to interpret and restrict it. On this view, the Pancasila is the ideological antithesis of the Islamic state implicit in the Jakarta Charter, and a brake on efforts to apply a wider form of shari'ah in Indonesia.

---

[43] Constitutional Court Decision 140/PUU-VII/2009, p 291–92.

[44] Constitutional Court Decision 140/PUU-VII/2009, p 287.

[45] Constitutional Court Decision 140/PUU-VII/2009, p 297.

[46] Constitutional Court Decision 140/PUU-VII/2009, p 298.

[47] Constitutional Court Decision 140/PUU-VII/2009, p 299.

[48] Constitutional Court Decision 140/PUU-VII/2009, p 290–91.

[49] See Chapter 5 of this volume for further discussion of cases in which the Court has confined itself to reviewing the words of statutes, rather than their implementation.

The *Blasphemy Law case* also confirmed that the first *sila* marks the outer limits of religious protection for Indonesians, which is restricted to beliefs officially constructed by the state as having 'belief in almighty God'. The religious freedoms in Articles 28E and 29 are thus restricted to these state-endorsed religions, the theological content of which is determined by recognised orthodox religious leaders and their organisations. This has very significant implications for followers of beliefs that do not fit within this narrow official framework. A plethora of mystical spiritual traditions found in Indonesia are usually seen as falling outside this framework, including those linked to Javanese traditions and known as *kebathinan* ('inwardness', spirituality) and others that include aspects of the recognised religions but do not fully accept orthodox interpretations of them.

RECOGNITION OF 'BELIEFS' (*KEPERCAYAAN*)

As indicated above, Soeharto's New Order came to recognise six religions as 'monotheistic' (in the sense of worshipping an 'almighty God') and thus encompassed by the Pancasila: Islam, Protestant Christianity (*Kristen*), Roman Catholic Christianity (*Katolik*),[50] Hinduism, Buddhism and Confucianism (*Khonghucu*), although the state was inconsistent in its attitude towards the latter.[51] These remain the officially recognised 'religions' today. Recasting Hindu polytheism as 'belief in an almighty God' presented challenges for bureaucratic creativity, as did Buddhism, which in some forms does not necessarily involve belief in a god. Confucianism was problematic too. In its different manifestations in Indonesia it is sometimes more like a philosophy or an amalgam of folk beliefs and Chinese religious traditions than a single formal, institutionalised

[50] For an account of Muslim-Christian relations under the New Order, see F Husein, *Muslim-Christian Relations in the New Order Indonesia* (Bandung, Mizan, 2005).

[51] On changing state attitudes to Confucianism in Indonesia and a discussion of the complex and ambiguous legal status of Confucianism, see T Lindsey, 'Reconstituting the Ethnic Chinese in Post-Suharto Indonesia: Law, Racial Discrimination, and Reform' in T Lindsey and H Pausacker (eds), *Chinese Indonesians: Remembering, Distorting, Forgetting – A Festschrift for Charles A. Coppel* (Singapore/Clayton, ISEAS, 2005) 41–76; JD Howell, '"Spirituality" vs "Religion" Indonesian Style: Framing and Re-framing Experiential Religiosity in Contemporary Indonesian Islam', *Paper presented to the 15th Biennial conference of the Asian Studies Association of Australia* (Canberra, ACT, 29 June–2 July 2004 (on file with authors) 4.

religious tradition. The state's solution was to fit the non-monotheistic religions into the Abrahamic mould of Islam and Christianity by identifying a single godhead, a messiah figure and a holy book. In the case of Confucianism, these were, respectively, *Tien* (heaven), Confucius and his Analects.[52]

The result of this contrived exercise has been that while religious beliefs or *kepercayaan* other than the official six are not illegal, they have not received the same level of state recognition, support and protection – particularly from the Ministry of Religion, which has Directorates General for each of the 'official' religions, except Confusianism. As was made clear in the *Blasphemy Law case*, followers of officially unrecognised 'beliefs' cannot easily avail themselves of the state protection available to the 'religions'. While not illegal per se, 'beliefs' risk being considered to be heretical or 'deviant' (*sesat*) versions of a recognised religion if they publicly express their faith. This exposes them to persecution or even prosecution, for example under the Criminal Code's 'blasphemy' provisions, including Article 156a.

The state's position on 'beliefs' has changed over time, usually in response to the political needs of the government of the day. In the 1960s, for example, Indonesians with beliefs that did not fit the approved 'orthodox' religions were designated as followers of beliefs (*kepercayaan*) and were officially encouraged to 'return' to one of the official 'religions'.[53] By the 1970s, however, the Soeharto government was keen to attract support for its political vehicle, Golkar (*Golongan Karya*), from Indonesians whose spiritual beliefs did not fit easily within any of the official religions and, in particular, those uncomfortable with Islam. It therefore upgraded the official status of 'beliefs' by MPR Decree, including in the Broad Outlines of State Policy, a document that was then central to government planning.[54] Referring to Article 29 of the Constitution, the Decrees still did not recognise 'beliefs' as 'religions'

[52] Presidential Decision 6 of 2000 formally allowed the open practice of Chinese religious activities, overruling Presidential Decision 14 of 1967: T Lindsey, 'Reconstituting the Ethnic Chinese in Post-Suharto Indonesia, Law, Racial Discrimination, and Reform' (above n 51) 41–76; Howell, '"Spirituality" vs "Religion" Indonesian Style' (n 51 above) 4; C Coppel, *Indonesian Chinese in crisis* (Kuala Lumpur and Melbourne, Oxford University Press, 1983).

[53] Howell, '"Spirituality" vs "Religion" Indonesian Style' (n 51 above) 2.

[54] MPR Decrees II/MPR/1973 (which incorporated this recognition in the Broad Outlines of State Policy) and IV/MPR/1978: ibid, 2.

but did formally accept them as legitimate expressions of the constitutional right to religion and the Pancasila 'Belief in Almighty God'.

Some Muslim politicians strongly opposed the recognition of 'beliefs', arguing that it supported heresy. Some walked out of the MPR session in protest when the issue was put to the vote.[55] Despite these objections, 'beliefs' received state bureaucratic representation and a budget under the New Order, although responsibility for them was given to the Department of Education and Culture, not the Department of Religion. Soon after, however, the government decided to make some concession to Islamic opposition and mention was not made of 'beliefs' in the Broad Outlines of State Policy for the next five years.[56]

'Beliefs' were thus still recognised by the state but only as a second-class form of compliance with the Pancasila requirement of 'belief in Almighty God.' Few followers of 'beliefs' were, for example, willing to conduct marriages or take oaths according to their beliefs or identify as followers of 'beliefs' in censuses. Instead, they tended to opt for one of the recognised six orthodoxies on these occasions, and when choosing the religious affiliation that appeared on their identity cards.[57]

In the late 1980s, official support for 'beliefs' had begun to decline further, hastened by the New Order's concern to improve relations with Muslim groups in the last decade of its rule. After Soeharto's fall in 1998, Soeharto's own association with various *kebathinan* beliefs[58] added to their official marginalisation. Beliefs were again downgraded, relegated to a new and relatively less important Department, Culture and Tourism, which has shown little interest in supporting them and no longer requires 'belief' groups even to register.[59]

---

[55] Adnan, 'Islamic Religion: Yes, Islamic Ideology: No! Islam and the State in Indonesia' (n 15 above); Pranowo, 'Which Islam and Which Pancasila?' (n 11 above) 454.

[56] MC Ricklefs, *A History Of Modern Indonesia Since C. 1300* (n 15 above) 351.

[57] Howell, '"Spirituality" vs "Religion" Indonesian Style' (n 51 above) 5; Adnan, 'Islamic Religion: Yes, Islamic Ideology: No! Islam and the State in Indonesia' (n 15 above) 448.

[58] See, for example, D Bourchier, *Dynamics of Dissent in Indonesia: Sawito and the Phantom Coup* (Ithaca, NY, Cornell University, 1984) and D Bourchier and VR Hadiz, *Indonesian Politics and Society: a Reader* (New York, Routledge, 2003) 103–09.

[59] Howell, '"Spirituality" vs "Religion" Indonesian Style' (n 15 above) 6 suggests this may be a result of government embarrassment in an era of increasing public orthodoxy. Certainly, the 'faiths' office now has a substantially reduced budget, reflecting a declining interest on the part of the state in supporting alternatives to the six official religions (ibid).

'Beliefs' are, however, still officially recognised on paper. In theory, a citizen could argue membership of a 'belief' to justify state protection for beliefs that conservative groups label 'deviant'. In practice, however, 'beliefs' have little political weight and attract little protection. The state's vestigial formal recognition of unorthodox mystical beliefs has not, for example, prevented increasing use of a mixture of gang violence from Muslim vigilantes, condemnatory *fatawa* (opinions on Islamic law) from *ulama* organisations, and prosecution under the Criminal Code, to close down unorthodox religious groups. More often, Indonesian police, prosecutors and courts view these groups as deviancies within one of the official religions (and not protected by the Constitution), rather than legitimate spiritual beliefs outside, and independent of, the six official religions (and thus protected).

When one of these groups is attacked – politically, legally or physically – the state now frequently stands to one side, allowing religious vigilantes to operate with relative impunity, often characterising these as 'horizontal' conflicts and not 'vertical' ones that require state intervention. Sometimes, the state even offers support for the attackers by prosecuting unorthodox groups and imprisoning their leaders, by failing to act against attackers, or even by seeming to tacitly approve violence. The latter can be seen, for example, in the case of the Ahmadiyah sect.

Ahmadiyah

On 1 June 2008, Pancasila Day, a violent, public attack was launched on pro-Pancasila demonstrators holding a peaceful rally at the Monas (National Monument) in Jakarta to celebrate the Pancasila. The rally had aimed to show that people from a wide variety of religions, races and ethnicities 'could walk together in harmony'. It was endorsed by more than 60 organisations from across the archipelago including well-respected human rights, Christian, Hindu and Islamic organisations and groups involved in inter-religious dialogue. A particular aim of the rally was to defend the Ahmadiyah sect from persecution.

Ahmadiyah was founded in the 1880s, in what is now Pakistan, by Mirza Ghulam Ahmad, and has been active in Indonesia since the 1920s. Ahmad is believed by many to have claimed to be a successor prophet to Muhammad – a claim Sunni Muslims find offensive. The sect had earlier been deemed deviant by the Indonesian Ulama Council (*Majelis Ulama*

Indonesia, MUI) and other leading Muslim organisations.[60] Its members faced persecution in many parts of Indonesia. At the time of the rally, the government was publicly discussing whether it should be banned outright.

The rally was attacked by a group, *Komando Laskar Islam* (KLI, Islamic Militia Command). This vigilante gang included many members of *Front Pembela Islam* (FPI, Islamic Defender's Front), who beat demonstrators with sticks. Up to 34 men, women and children of various religious affiliations, including Muslims, were injured. Also hurt were senior leaders of moderate Islamic groups.[61] Although arrests were later made and several of the attackers, including some leaders, were later imprisoned, the thousand or so police in attendance at the rally did little to stop the violence.[62]

A week later, on 9 June 2008, the Minister of Religion, the Attorney General and the Minister for Home Affairs issued a Joint Decision, pursuant to the Blasphemy Law.[63] Although the text of the Decision is open to different interpretations,[64] it has been widely seen as prohibiting Ahmadis from publicly practising their beliefs and has prompted regional governments, particularly in Java, to enact regional laws (Perda, *peraturan daerah*) with similar effect.[65]

---

[60] MUI Fatwa 11/MUNAS VII/MUI/15/2005, confirming MUI Fatwa MUNAS/II/MUI/1980. See also Persis Statement on Ahmadiyah of 12 January 2008.

[61] Those injured included Syafi'i Anwar, Director of International Centre for Islam and Pluralism (ICIP); Kiai Maman Imanuhaq, leader of the Pesantren Azzaman; Ahmad Suaedi, Director of the Wahid Institute; and Mohamad Guntur Romli of the Utan Kayu Community and *Jurnal Perempuan* (M Crouch, 'Indonesia, Militant Islam and Ahmadiyah: Origins and Implications', *Islam, Shari'ah and Governance Background Paper Series* (Centre for Islamic Law and Society, Melbourne Law School, University of Melbourne, 2009)).

[62] Human Rights Watch, 'Indonesia: Reverse Ban on Ahmadiyah Sect: Government Should Protect Religious Minority, Not Threaten Prison for Beliefs', 9 June 2008: www.hrw.org/en/news/2008/06/09/indonesia-reverse-ban-ahmadiyah-sect (accessed 26 May 2011).

[63] Decisions of the Minister for Home Affairs 3 of 2008, KEP-033/A/JA/6/2008 and 199 of 2008: www.legalitas.org/database/lain/nasional/SKB%20ahmadiyah.pdf (17 September 2008).

[64] It provides, in Point 2, that 'the organisers of Jemaat Ahmadiyah Indonesia (JAI) for as long as they call themselves Muslims, must cease the spreading of interpretations and activities that deviate from the main teachings of Islam, that is spreading the belief that acknowledges a prophet, with a variety of teachings, after the Prophet Muhammad'.

[65] For a discussion of regional law-making, see Chapter 6 of this volume.

Point 4 of the Joint Decision prohibits the community from carrying out undefined 'illegal action' against Ahmadiyah and declares that sanctions apply to those who violate Points 2 and 4 of the Decision. The inaction of police does not, however, inspire confidence that these provisions will have much effect. Police have done little to prevent earlier attacks, for example in Tasikmalaya, West Java in 2007 or subsequent ones, for example, in July 2010, when the An-Nur Ahamdiyah mosque in Manislor, Kuningan, was closed following continued aggressive protests against the 2,000 or so Ahmadis living in the area.

On 28 August 2010, the Minister for Home Affairs, obviously concerned by the continuing conflict, issued Decision 450/3457/Sj. This reiterates the main provisions of the Joint Decision and states that it 'is a form of supervision and law enforcement for any violation of the law by either the Ahmadi or members of the public who conduct an act of violence'. Nevertheless, in October 2010, the Ahmadiyah mosque in Ciampea, Bogor, was burnt along with Ahmadi houses in the area[66] and violence continued in early 2011 with attacks in Makassar, South Sulawesi, in January. In February, five Ahmadi followers were injured and three killed during an attack in Cikeusik, Banten. Gruesome footage of the violent attack was made widely available through the Internet.[67]

Local governments in at least four provinces (West Java, East Kalimantan, South Sumatera and East Java) and at least eight districts (Depok, Garut, Tasikmalaya, Bogor, Samarinda, West Lombok, East Lombok and Pandeglang) have relied on Decision 450/3457/Sj to issue new regulations targeting the Ahmadis. In 2011, for example, the West Java Governor issued a regulation prohibiting the spreading of teachings of Ahmadiyah in written, oral or electronic form and banning use of the name 'Jemaat Ahmadiyah Indonesia' on public signage or on mosques or educational institutions, to prevent 'social unrest or conflict in the community'.[68] A 2011 East Java Governor's Regulation adopts these provisions. It also creates an investigation team to monitor Ahmadis in the province and authorises local police, government, community leaders and MUI to 'inform and educate' the public about the Decision.[69]

---

[66] M Crouch, 'Indonesia, Militant Islam and Ahmadiyah: Origins and Implications'(n 62 above) 56.

[67] ibid, 56.

[68] Regulation of the Governor of West Java 12 of 2011, 3 March 2011.

[69] Decision of the Governor of East Java 188/94/KPTS/013/2011, 28 February 2011.

These regulations are, in fact, not a new development in Indonesia. They follow dozens of similar bans issued since the 1970s by around 30 or so local governments across Indonesia.[70] By reiterating the prohibitions, however, local laws help create an atmosphere of de facto legitimacy for persecution of the Ahmadis. There can be no doubt that they are interpreted locally as bans on all Ahmadi activities and tacit permission for vigilante attacks, which were continuing at time of writing.

The state's treatment of Ahmadiyah reflects deep divisions within the government about how to deal with unorthodox religious groups. Yudhoyono's government seems ultimately, however, to have opted to treat the Ahmadiyah not as a 'belief' within the ambit of Pancasila and Constitutional protection, but rather as a heretical 'deviant' branch of Islam and thus, it would seem, unable to avail itself of state protection.

CONCLUSION

Soekarno always claimed that he merely 'excavated' (*menggali*) the Pancasila from Indonesian tradition[71] and that it embodied his nation's innate diversity and pluralism, as embodied in the republic's motto, *Bhineka Tunggal Ika*, 'the many are one' or 'unity in diversity'. This understanding of Pancasila as guarantor of a traditional social and religious pluralism has proved as persistent as the efforts to impose Islamic law that it was designed to combat.

Within a decade of Soeharto's fall in 1998, Pancasila had partially recovered from its post-Soeharto 'fading' and was no longer marginalised in national political discourse. Speaking at Pancasila Day celebrations in June 2006, President Yudhoyono stated, for example, that:

> [a]bandoning the Pancasila state ideology for narrow religious or ethnic-based doctrine will only jeopardise Indonesia's unity and diversity . . . We should end the debate on alternatives to Pancasila as our ideology . . . We

---

[70] See, for example, Decision of BAKORPAKEM and the High Prosecutor of Subang Kep.01/1.2 JPKI 312/PAKEM/3/1976 on the prohibition of the spreading of the teachings of Ahmadiyah Qadiani; and Decision of the High Prosecutor of South Sulawesi 02/K.1.1/3/1977 on Ahamdiyah.

[71] On this, see R Cribb, '"The Incredible Shrinking Pancasila" (above n 23) 67, citing H Antlov, 'The Social Construction of Power and Authority in Java' in H Antlöv and J Hellman (eds), *The Java that Never Was: Academic Theories and Political Practices* (Münster, Lit Verlag, 2005) 56–57.

should keep on with efforts to increase the people's welfare and to uphold justice based on the ideology that we have (Ministry of Culture and Tourism 2006).

A year later, Yudhoyono reiterated these ideas in his August 2007 'state of the nation' address to the DPR, again seeking to revive the Pancasila. He stressed that it was one of the four basic, non-negotiable pillars of the state, alongside the 1945 Constitution, the unitary state (NKRI, *Negara Kesatuan Republik Indonesia*) and pluralism:

> The 'unity in diversity' principle must be constantly interpreted and applied in our daily lives to safeguard the ideology of pluralism in relation to the nation's different ethnic groups, religions, languages and cultures . . . Let us revive, implement and maintain it as our state ideology.[72]

Yudhoyono's remarks came amidst a growing number complaints that his previous lack of concrete support for Pancasila principles of pluralism had 'opened the door' for hard-line Islamist groups' ideas, allowing the spread of intolerant ideologies that made women and minority religious groups vulnerable. This, it was said, had already begun with local governments passing regional regulations imposing socially-conservative aspects of shari'ah, including obligatory dress codes and curfews for women. His critics pointed also to the fatwa issued a year earlier by the influential, and increasingly conservative, state-endorsed MUI, opposing pluralism, liberalism and secularism. In that fatwa (7 of 2005), MUI stated that 'religious teachings influenced by pluralism, liberalism and secularism are against Islam' and Muslims must consider all other faiths to be wrong. At the time, the anti-pornography bill was also being discussed in the DPR. This bill sought to impose similar morally-conservative restrictions on clothing, sexuality and behaviour. Opponents of the bill feared it would criminalise aspects of traditional cultures and the arts. They criticised it as another attempt by Muslim conservatives to undermine the principles of diversity and pluralism they saw as enshrined in the Pancasila.

Accordingly, while Pancasila had lost the central place in state rhetoric it had enjoyed under Soeharto, it had regained a symbolic role in public debate as a state-endorsed symbol of religious and social pluralism and even of resistance to a 'formal link between Islamic ideology

[72] Sijabat, RM , 'Pancasila Ideology Absolute: President', *Jakarta Post*, 18 August 2007.

and the state'.[73] It is, once again, a rhetorical tool that can be wielded against the Jakarta Charter agenda and used with implicit state endorsement to formally oppose the 'legal Islamisation' efforts of Islamist conservatives. This was confirmed by the Constitutional Court's use of the Pancasila and the constitutional provisions on religious freedom in the cases described above as authority for the state's right to legislate to restrict the application of Islamic law.

Just how effective the Pancasila and Constitution are as a means of ensuring religious freedom for religious minorities remains much less certain, however. In the *Blasphemy Law case*, the Constitutional Court also confirmed that the constitutional power to regulate religion enables the state to restrict the 'expression' of beliefs outside the formal orthodoxy of the six officially-recognised beliefs. It remains an open question as to how effective the revival of the Pancasila in its original role as ideological alternative to the application of shari'ah – 'as code for the rejection of an Islamic state'[74] – will be.

SELECTED READING

Adnan, Zirfirdaus, 'Islamic Religion: Yes, Islamic Ideology: No! Islam and the State in Indonesia' in Arief Budiman (ed), *State and Civil Society in Indonesia* (Clayton, Victoria, Centre of Southeast Asian Studies, Monash University, 1990) 441–78.

Butt, Simon, 'Islam, the State and the Constitutional Court in Indonesia' (2010) 19(2) *Pacific Rim Law and Policy Journal* 279–302.

Cribb, Robert, '"The Incredible Shrinking Pancasila": Nationalist Propaganda and The Missing Ideological Legacy of Soeharto' in Thomas Reuter (ed), *The Return of Constitutional Democracy in Indonesia* (Annual Indonesia lecture series; Caulfield, Victoria, Monash Asia Institute, 2010) 65–76.

Hosen, Nadirsyah *Shari'a and Constitutional Reform in Indonesia* (Singapore, ISEAS, 2007).

---

[73] Adnan, 'Islamic Religion: Yes, Islamic Ideology: No! Islam and the State in Indonesia' (n 15 above) 470.

[74] R Cribb, '"The Incredible Shrinking Pancasila" (n 23 above) 72.

Howell, Julia Day '"Spirituality" vs "Religion" Indonesian Style: Framing and Re-framing Experiential Religiosity in Contemporary Indonesian Islam', *Paper presented to the 15th Biennial conference of the Asian Studies Association of Australia* (Canberra, ACT, 29 June–2 July 2004 (on file with authors)).

9

Article 33 and Economic Democracy

Introduction – 'State Control' – Article 33(4): Principles of the National Economy – Conclusion

INTRODUCTION

THIS CHAPTER DEALS with one of the most contested provisions of the Indonesian Constitution. Article 33 reflects long-standing anxiety about control of the economy that can be traced back to nationalist analyses of the Dutch colonial economic system and suspicion of economic 'liberalism' tied to ideas about colonial domination.[1] 'This discourse has bedevilled Indonesian economic policy since the 1950s with questions about the role of markets versus constitutional "anti-liberalism"'.[2] These are frequently expressed by reference to the notion of *ekonomi rakyat* or the 'People's Economy'.

The economic nationalism and anti-liberalism so often associated with Article 33 are clear from its text. Before the Fourth Amendment in 2002, Article 33 of the Constitution read:

(1) The economy shall be structured as a common endeavour based upon the family principle.

---

[1] D Linnan, 'Bankruptcy Policy & Reform: Reconciling Efficiency and Economic Nationalism' in T Lindsey (ed), *Law Reform and the Commercial Court in Indonesia* (Sydney, Federation Press, 1999) 94–112; M Pabottingi, 'Konteks Ekonomi Nationalisme Indonesia' in Alfian and N Sjamsuddin (eds), *Profil Budaya Politik Indonesia* (Jakarta, Pustaka Utama Grafiti, 1991) 87–123. Earlier versions of parts of this chapter appear in S Butt and T Lindsey, 'Economic Reform when the Constitution Matters: Indonesia's Constitutional Court and Article 33' (2008) 44(2) *Bulletin of Indonesia Economic Studies* 239–62.

[2] Linnan, 'Bankruptcy Policy & Reform' (n 1 above) 109.

(2) Branches of production that are important to the state, and that affect the public's necessities of life, are to be controlled by the state.

(3) The earth and water and the natural resources contained within them are to be controlled by the state and used for the greatest possible prosperity of the people.

The following two paragraphs were added to Article 33 by the Fourth Amendment:

(4) The national economy is to be run on the basis of economic democracy, and the principles of togetherness, just efficiency, sustainability, environmentalism, and independence, maintaining a balance between advancement and national economic unity.

(5) Further provisions to implement [Article 33] will be provided in legislation.

The political content of these provisions reflects the origins of Article 33. Conceived in the lead-up to the declaration of Indonesia's independence on 17 August 1945, it was inspired by socialist and nationalist ideals of the kind common to many of the anti-colonial Asian Independence movements of the period. These are clear from the formal Elucidation to Article 33 that was originally included in 1945 but removed in the post-Soeharto amendments. It reads:

> Article 33 embraces economic democracy under which production is carried out by all, and for all, under the leadership or supervision of members of the community. The main priority is the prosperity of the community, not the prosperity of individuals.
>
> This is because the economy is structured as a collective endeavour based on the family principle. A business entity along these lines is a cooperative. The economy is based on economic democracy, prosperity for all people!
>
> Branches of production that are important for the state and which affect the lives of most people must, therefore, be controlled by the state. If not, control of production might fall into the hands of individuals, who might exploit the people. Only businesses that are not important for the lives of many people may be left in private hands.
>
> The land and water and natural resources in the earth are the fundamentals of community prosperity. For this reason, they must be controlled by the state and used for the greatest prosperity of the people.

Article 33 survived the various shifts of the Indonesian state that followed Independence – from the Left under Soekarno to the Right under Soeharto. It has remained in place during the democratic post-Soeharto era despite the annihilation of organised socialist groups in the killings and jailings of the mid-to-late 1960s. The decision in 2002 to retain Article 33 in the amended Constitution, and even expand it, nonetheless led to significant and often heated argument in the People's Consultative Council (*Majelis Permusyawaratan Rakyat* or MPR), the state body responsible for the amendments.

Supporters of economic liberalism sought the removal of Article 33 altogether, or at least its overhaul to limit state intervention.[3] Some saw it as an archaic ideological leftover. The so-called 'neo-liberals', for example, argued that excessive government economic control was partly responsible for Indonesia's economic collapse in 1997. They believed that the world economic order required Indonesia to open itself up, liberalise and become competitive in global markets. After all, Indonesia was a member of the World Trade Organization, the main purpose of which is to break down barriers to free trade. Other members of the MPR sought middle ground in a 'socialist market' system – a socialist economy with enough liberalism to enable participation in global markets. As one member who appeared to support this system stated, 'it is ok to go to the left, ok to go to the right, but not ok to go too far either way'.[4]

Notwithstanding these ideological differences, most MPR members ultimately supported the retention of the principle of the 'people's economy' (*ekonomi kerakyatan*), commonly translated as 'Indonesian Socialism', embodied in Article 33. For them, state protectionism was required to prevent the evils of the free market harming the people and their prosperity. As one prominent advocate of the people's economy argued during the debates: 'I say that competition is good if we win. If competition is the way that we are re-colonised, then competition is bad'.[5]

According to these members, protection could take two forms. First, the state must ensure that Indonesians – particularly cooperatives and small-medium enterprises – have the opportunity to participate in the economy, including the exploitation of natural resources, and to share in

[3] B Susanti, 'Neo-liberalism and its Resistance in Indonesia's Constitutional Reform 1999–2002' (Masters Dissertation, University of Warwick, 2002) 66.

[4] Submission by Ir Ahmad Hafiz Zawawi, MSc (F-PG), *Risalah PAH I Rapat Ke 20*, 27 March 2002, at 31–32, available at: www.mpr.go.id.

[5] Submission by Adi Sasono (CIDES), *Risalah PAH I Rapat Ke 8*, 28 February 2002, at 22–23, available at: www.mpr.go.id.

its spoils. Secondly, the state should protect the economically weak from excessive domestic and international competition:

> In an *asas kekeluargaan* [family principle] house, we have [several] children. We want all of them to advance; they must compete with each other to advance. But they cannot kill each other. The disabled and disadvantaged must be looked after. If the father allows the strong to win, the strong will eat more . . . The weak will die because they cannot take back their food.[6]

In this chapter, we show that this protectionist view of the 'people's economy' has largely prevailed, at least in the MPR and in the Constitutional Court, with the Court generally interpreting Article 33 in line with this view. In some cases, the Court has appeared to enforce even greater state intervention and control over important branches of production and natural resources than Article 33 appears to require. We analyse Constitutional Court decisions that have cast light on the meaning of 'controlled by the state' and the branches of production that are 'important'. We then assess the extent to which the Court is willing to consider whether legislation dealing with these branches and resources does in fact result in the 'greatest possible prosperity of the people'. Finally, we briefly discuss cases in which the Court has described and applied the Article 33(4) national economic principles of 'economic democracy' and 'efficiency in justice'.

'STATE CONTROL'

In the years after Soeharto's fall, the DPR enacted several laws intended to break down state monopolies over important sectors, such as electricity, water, oil and natural gas. Many state-owned enterprises holding these monopolies were notoriously inefficient, unreliable and corrupt. Run for the 'benefit of individuals and special interest groups', they caused a 'major drag' on Indonesia's overall economic performance.[7] During the Asian Economic Crisis that began in 1997, the International Monetary Fund (IMF) and other multilateral donors made large financial bailouts for Indonesia contingent on breaking down these monopolies. They demanded that the government introduce a range of new

---

[6] Submission by Ir AM Luthfi (F-Reformasi), *Risalah PAH I Rapat Ke 20*, 27 March 2002, at 35, available at: www.mpr.go.id.

[7] Government of Indonesia Letter of Intent, 13 December 2001, point 29, available at: www.imf.org.

policies, from restructuring, to opening up to private-sector competition, and even privatisation.[8] For example, the Indonesian government made the following pledge in a 1999 Letter of Intent:

> With the support of the World Bank and ADB (Asian Development Bank), the government will (i) establish the legal and regulatory framework to create a competitive electricity market; (ii) restructure the organisation of PLN [*Perusahan Listrik Negara* – the State Owned Electricity company]; (iii) adjust electricity tariffs; and (iv) rationalise power purchases from private sector power projects. The government has commenced renegotiations with independent power producers; will initiate the organisational restructuring of PLN by June 1999; and will enact a new Electricity Law by December 1999.[9]

In its first three years, the Constitutional Court heard several cases in which applicants objected to many of these very reforms – including government attempts at privatising important 'branches of production' and natural resource exploitation, or allowing greater private-sector involvement in them. Applicants argued that the state had, through the impugned statutes, relinquished its 'control' over these sectors and had, therefore, breached either Article 33(2) or (3). These cases included the *Electricity Law case*,[10] the *Oil and Natural Gas (Migas) Law case*,[11] and the *Water Law case*.[12] Before providing a brief outline of the Court's decisions in these three cases we consider the Court's interpretation of 'controlled by the state' in Article 33.

The Court provided its leading discussion on the meaning of 'controlled by the state' in the *Electricity Law case* and endorsed this discussion in the other Article 33 cases. In the *Electricity Law case*, the government had argued that the state would control a branch of production if it merely 'regulated' it; and expert witnesses claimed that 'controlled'

---

[8]   S Butt and T Lindsey, 'Unfinished Business: Law Reform, Governance and the Courts in Post-Soeharto Indonesia' in M Kunkler and A Stepan (eds), *Indonesia, Islam and Democratic Consolidation* (New York, Columbia University Press, 2012).

[9]   IMF website: www.imf.org/external/NP/LOI/1999/031699.htm.

[10]   Constitutional Court Decision 001-021-022/PUU-I/2003. The Court was also asked to review a new Electricity Law – 30 of 2009 (Constitutional Court Decision 149/PUU-VII/2009). The Court found that the 2009 Law did not breach the Constitution because it did not relinquish state control over the electricity sector as had the 2002 Law (Constitutional Court Decision 149/PUU-VII/2009, p 96).

[11]   Constitutional Court Decision 002/PUU-I/2003.

[12]   Constitutional Court Decision 058-059-060-063/PUU-II/2004 and 008/PUU-III/2005.

was synonymous with 'ownership'.[13] The Court rejected these arguments, reasoning that although ownership was required, it was insufficient in itself, because it did not necessarily guarantee the welfare of the people or social justice, as is required in the Constitution's Preamble.[14] Similarly, the government's power to 'regulate' was necessary, but was not sufficient in itself to constitute 'control'. According to the Court, the government would have inherent power to regulate, even in the absence of the phrase 'controlled by the state' in Article 33.[15]

In addition to ownership and regulation, the state needed to be able to manage the enterprise, for example by having sufficient shares to control decision and policy-making. The state would also exercise managerial control if the entity engaged in the sector was a State-Owned Legal Enterprise (*Badan Usaha Milik Negara*).[16] The state likewise needed administrative control, such as the power to issue and revoke permits, licences and concessions to participate in the industry. Overarching all other considerations was the state's obligation to supervise and monitor the sector to ensure that the branches of production and natural resources were, in fact, exercised for the greatest prosperity of the people.[17]

For the Court, Article 33 does not close off all private-sector involvement in important branches of production, however. The government may still allow private sector involvement, provided that it does not in so doing extinguish these elements of its own control.[18]

We now briefly consider how the Court applied this interpretation of 'controlled by the state' in the *Electricity*, *Migas* and *Water Law cases*. In the *Electricity Law case*,[19] three applicants requested that the Court review the constitutional validity of Law 20 of 2002 on Electricity, including on grounds that it breached Article 33. Before the Law's enactment in 2002, the state electricity company (*Perusahaan Listrik Negara*, PLN) had enjoyed a monopoly over the generation, distribution, transmission and

---

[13] Constitutional Court Decision 001-021-022/PUU-I/2003, p 332.

[14] Constitutional Court Decision 001-021-022/PUU-I/2003, pp 332–33.

[15] Constitutional Court Decision 001-021-022/PUU-I/2003, p 333.

[16] Constitutional Court Decision 001-021-022/PUU-I/2003, pp 334–36; Constitutional Court Decision 002/PUU-I/2003, pp 210–11.

[17] Constitutional Court Decision 001-021-022/PUU-I/2003, p 334; Constitutional Court Decision 002/PUU-I/2003, pp 208–9; Constitutional Court Decision 21-22/PUU-V/2007, pp 231–32.

[18] Constitutional Court Decision 001-021-022/PUU-I/2003, p 336.

[19] Constitutional Court Decision 001-021-022/PUU-I/2003.

sale of electricity.[20] Provisions of the Law prohibited government monopolies in areas in which competition would be viable (*wilayah kompetisi*). The Law also divided or 'unbundled' the provision of electricity into seven activities – including generation, transmission, distribution and sale – and allowed different entities, including the private sector, to directly perform them.[21] Only in areas 'not ready for competition', could the state retain its monopoly. PLN was left to compete, on an equal footing, with other operators. These provisions, the Court held, relinquished state control and therefore breached Article 33(2).[22]

The Court decided that competition and unbundling were at the 'heart' of the Law and for that reason decided to invalidate the entire statute. The Court claimed that it had no choice because, in its view, the invalidity of only a small part of the statute would 'cause chaos that would lead to legal uncertainty' in the Law's application.[23] The Court reinstated the previous Electricity Law (Law 15 of 1985) on the basis that Article 70 of the 2002 Electricity Law – which declared the 1985 Law to be no longer in force – was, itself, no longer valid.

In the *Oil and Natural Gas (Migas) Law case*,[24] applicants sought a review of Law 22 of 2001 on Oil and Natural Gas. The Law established a Mining Authority to control upstream commercial activities in oil and natural gas, including exploration and exploitation, using profit sharing and other cooperative contracts, with proportions of profits required to be used for 'the greatest prosperity of the people'.[25] Management, transportation, storage and commercial activities all required permits.[26]

The Court decided that, in essence, the Migas Law did not relinquish state control over oil and natural gas: 'all aspects of "controlled by the state" – regulation (*regelen*), administration (*bestuuren*), management

---

[20] While private power companies existed in Indonesia before 2002, most had exclusive power purchase agreements with PLN (D Hall and E Lobina, 'Private and Public Interests in Water and Energy' (2004) 28(4) *Natural Resources Forum* 268–77).

[21] See Articles 8(2), 16 and 17 of the 2002 Electricity Law.

[22] Constitutional Court Decision 001-021-022/PUU-I/2003, pp 349–50.

[23] Constitutional Court Decision 001-021-022/PUU-I/2003, pp 349–50. However, in the interests of legal certainty, the Court did not invalidate contracts or licences signed or issued under the Law but allowed them to continue until they expired.

[24] Constitutional Court Decision 002/PUU-I/2003.

[25] Article 1(19) and (23) of Law 22 of 2001 on Oil and Natural Gas.

[26] Constitutional Court Decision 002/PUU-I/2003, pp 223–24.

(*beheeren*) and supervision (*toezichthouden*) – remain in the hands of the government . . . or bodies established for that purpose'.[27]

Finally, in the *Water Law case*,[28] almost 3,000 individuals and several NGOs requested that the Constitutional Court review Law 7 of 2004 on Water Resources. The Water Law, which replaced Law 11 of 1974 on Irrigation, purported to allow the private sector to 'play a role' (*berperan*) in, and impose a fee for, the provision and management of some types of water resources, such as drinking water and water for irrigation.[29] The Water Law also sought to introduce a new 'right to exploit' water resources (*hak guna usaha*).[30] A majority found that the Water Law did not, in fact, divest the government of control over water resources. The Law merely made it possible for the state to grant to the private sector a right to exploit water. The government retained power to make policy and regulations, manage water resources and grant permits for water exploitation.[31]

Land Rights

The Constitutional Court has held that land rights – including ownership rights, exploitation and usage rights – can also be limited by reference to Article 33. In the *Investment Law case*,[32] to which we return below, the majority made the following statement:

> The interest to be protected by [Article 33(3)] of the Constitution is the welfare of the people in relation to the exploitation of the land, water and resources contained therein. In relation to land, this interest was translated into national land policy intended to achieve the welfare of the people, including by redistributing ownership of land and limiting the permissible amount of owned land, so that land control and ownership is not concentrated in the

---

[27] Constitutional Court Decision 002/PUU-I/2003, p 224. The Court did, however, make slight alterations to the Law (*Hukumonline*, 'MK "Koreksi" Sebagian Materi Undang-Undang Migas', 21 December 2004).

[28] Constitutional Court Decisions 058-059-060-063/2004 and 008/2005.

[29] See for example Articles 7, 8 and 80 of Law 7 of 2004.

[30] *Hukumonline*, 'Ini dia, kelemahan RUU SDA versi LSM', 18 March 2004.

[31] Constitutional Court Decision 058-059-060-063/PUU-II/2004 and 008/PUU-III/2005, pp 496–99. See further, *Hukumonline*, 'Mukhti dan Maruarar, Dua Hakim yang Ajukan Dissenting Opinion UU SDA', 17 August 2005; *Hukumonline*, 'Mahkamah Konstitusi Ogah Membatalkan UU Sumber Daya Air', 19 August 2005.

[32] Constitutional Court Decision 21-22/PUU-V/2007.

hands of a group of people. This was among the things achieved through the Agrarian Law (Law 5 of 1960) and Law 56 of 1960 on Restriction of Agricultural Land Holdings. This restriction and distribution means that economic sources are spread more evenly and, ultimately, that the goals of people's prosperity will be achieved equitably. Further, for land that is controlled by the state, the even distribution of land rights is achieved through a policy of equal opportunity to obtain various land rights . . . for a limited and not excessive period.[33]

In the *Excess land case*,[34] the applicant, a farmer, contested provisions of Law 56 of 1960 on the Restriction of Agricultural Land Holdings, mentioned above in the extract from the *Investment Law case*. These provisions prohibited individuals, families or legal entitles from owning more than 20 hectares of agricultural land. Land exceeding this limit could be appropriated and redistributed to others.[35] After referring to its discussions about the meaning of 'controlled by the state' in previous cases, a majority of the Court declared that the state's 'control' gave it power to grant land rights but also to take them away if the state thought that the public interest so demanded.[36]

In 2007 the DPR enacted an Investment Law that sought to make Indonesia more regionally competitive in attracting investment capital.[37] One of the Law's incentives was making it easier for foreigners to obtain various, limited land rights – including to cultivate (*hak guna usaha*), build (*hak guna bangunan*) and use (*hak pakai*) – for the maximum term permissible.[38] Pre-existing law had allowed these rights to be extended, at the absolute discretion of the government, for 20 to 30 years (depending on the right) after the initial grant of between 25 and 35 years had expired. The 2007 Law purported to allow the upfront extension of those rights, if the investment met particular requirements. These included improving the competitiveness of Indonesia's economy, being high-risk, not

---

[33] Constitutional Court Decision 21-22/PUU-V/2007, p 256.

[34] Constitutional Court Decision 11/PUU-V/2007.

[35] The Government had argued that land had a social function under Article 6 of the 1960 Agrarian Law and that, therefore, ownership, use and exploitation of land is subject to both the interests of the community and public order.

[36] Constitutional Court Decision 11/PUU-V/2007, p 62. In the Majority: Asshiddiqie, Natabaya, Marzuki, Harjono and Roestandi. In the minority: Siahaan, Fadjar, Soedarsono.

[37] Law 25 of 2007 on Investment.

[38] Foreigners remain unable to obtain freehold title (*hak milik*).

offending society's sense of justice and not damaging the public interest (Article 22). Article 22(4) allowed the government to revoke the grant if the recipient neglects the land, uses land contrary to the purposes of its grant or otherwise damages public interests.

In the *Investment Law case*,[39] several applicants, including the Indonesian Chamber of Commerce, challenged the constitutionality of these upfront extensions on several grounds, including that they breached Article 33(3). The Court found that land was clearly a natural resource within Article 33(3) and that the state was therefore required to 'control' it and the rights associated with it. The Court decided that allowing extensions to various land rights in itself did not breach Article 33(3): the state retained power to 'regulate' the land because the state could determine the term of the right and could attach conditions to it; the state continued to 'manage' the land because it could continue to exploit the land; and supervisory control was maintained because the state could impose sanctions for misuse of the land.[40] Additionally, the land rights would automatically revert to the state once the grants expired.

Upfront extensions were another matter, however, because, according to the Constitutional Court, they had the potential to 'reduce or remove' state control. The Court seemed concerned that upfront extension left the state without absolute discretion to revoke or refuse to extend these rights – discretion that it had enjoyed under the pre-existing law. In this context, Article 22(4), which limited the state's power to revoke the grant to particular circumstances only, impeded – perhaps even relinquished – the state's right of absolute control.[41] In particular, the Court pointed to Article 32, which allows foreign investors to bring disputes with the government before international arbitration. Such disputes would include investors' objections to the application of Article 22(4) against them. If the state were to lose, its 'control' would likely cease – at least for the remainder of the term of the land right. Accordingly, the Court invalidated these upfront extensions.[42]

---

[39] Constitutional Court Decision 21-22/PUU-V/2007.
[40] Constitutional Court Decision 21-22/PUU-V/2007, p 257.
[41] Constitutional Court Decision 21-22/PUU-V/2007, p 258.
[42] Constitutional Court Decision 21-22/PUU-V/2007, p 263.

'Important' Sectors

The categorisation of branches of production as 'important' within the meaning of Article 33, thereby triggering the state's obligation to 'control' them, has not, to our knowledge, been contentious in the Article 33 cases brought before the Court thus far. This is because in all these cases the relevant sector's importance has been clear.

The Court has appeared content to let the legislature decide whether a branch of production is 'important', rather than outlining criteria for determining what 'important' amounts to.[43] For example, in the *Electricity Law case*, the Court accepted that electricity was sufficiently 'important' merely because the Law under review itself emphasised the importance of the electricity sector in its Preamble.[44] The Court has also made it clear that the 'importance' of branches of production is not static. If, for example, the government believed that a particular industry – such as electricity – was no longer a public necessity, then the state could relinquish its control over the sector and leave policy, management, supervision and regulation to the market.[45]

It remains to be seen how the Court might respond if the legislature attempts to evade its scrutiny by legislatively re-categorising a branch as no longer being 'important'. If this occurs, the Court might need to establish objective criteria by which to identify important branches of production to prevent the state from circumventing Article 33(2).

Evaluating Policy?

In its Article 33 cases, the Court has not discussed in detail the boundaries of its judicial review jurisdiction. Nevertheless, Article 33(3) obliges the legislature to enact laws that use natural resources to maximise the people's welfare, and confers a constitutional right that citizens and legal entities can seek to enforce. It seems to be an open question whether Article 33(3) requires the Court to consider competing alternative poli-

---

[43] Constitutional Court Decision 21-22/PUU-V/2007, p 215.
[44] Constitutional Court Decision 001-021-022/PUU-I/2003, p 345.
[45] Constitutional Court Decision 002/PUU-I/2003, pp 209–10.

cies to determine whether the policy the government chooses provides the maximum potential 'prosperity'.[46]

The text of Article 33(2) does not require state control over important sectors to achieve any particular purpose such as maximising public welfare. It merely requires state control. Nevertheless, in the *Electricity Law case* the Court decided that under Article 33(2) state control needed to be exercised to ensure the availability, even distribution and affordability of important branches of production.[47] According to the Court, Article 33(2) needed to be read together with the Preamble to the Constitution, which required the state to 'protect the entire Indonesian nation . . . to advance public welfare [and] to create social justice for the people of Indonesia'. This interpretation seems to require the state to exercise its 'control' under Article 33(2) for a very similar, if not identical, purpose to that of Article 33(3): to advance public welfare or prosperity.

The Court then decided that privatisation of the electricity sector was unlikely to fulfil these purposes. The Constitutional Court expressed doubts that privatisation would, as the government argued, necessarily improve electricity capacity, quality and price, and considered 'far from realistic' the suggestion that the market would naturally provide readily-available, evenly-distributed and affordable electricity.[48] In any event, the Court said, the government could attract private-sector involvement without privatisation: PLN, for example, could seek financial assistance from, or partner with, domestic or foreign investors.[49] The Court also feared that competition would not guarantee the supply of electricity to all parts of Indonesia. It expected the private sector would prioritise its own profits and concentrate on established markets – primarily in Java,

---

[46] In the *Migas* and *Water Law cases*, for example, the Court's primary concern appeared to be whether state control was sufficient, rather than whether the statutes provided the greatest possible prosperity to the people. In the *Migas Law case*, the Court merely expressed the view that the greatest possible prosperity was not just a matter of cheap prices or high quality but also involved the availability of fuel to all members of the community (Constitutional Court Decision 2/PUU-I/2003 p 230).

[47] Constitutional Court Decision 001-021-022/PUU-I/2003, p 330.

[48] Constitutional Court Decision 001-021-022/PUU-I/2003, p 331. To support this view, the Court referred to both the testimony of a British expert (David Hall, Director of Public Services, International Research Unit, University of Greenwich, London) and Joseph E Stiglitz, in his *Globalisation and its Discontents*, p XII: 001-021-022/PUU-I/2003, pp 332, 342.

[49] Constitutional Court Decision 001-021-022/PUU-I/2003, p 348.

Madura and Bali – rather than 'less competitive' parts of Indonesia in dire need of electrification.[50]

The *Electricity Law case* raises questions about the capacity of Constitutional Court judges, many of whom are former judges and academics, to handle complex social, economic and political issues. The Electricity Law was part of a $900 million power-sector restructuring programme funded by the Asian Development Bank (ADB) and others. The Court did not take into account that state control over electricity had failed to guarantee supply for decades. At the time its decision was made, 75 million Indonesians did not have access to power, and coverage extended to only 65 per cent of Indonesia.[51] The government had pledged to extend coverage to 90 per cent by 2020 but PLN itself had admitted that it lacked the capacity to meet this target, which would require it to establish one million new connections per year.[52] To meet demand, Indonesia needed an estimated US$ 27 billion of investment, much of which would have to come from the private sector due to lack of government funds.[53]

The Court also did not consider the potential of its decisions to obstruct compliance with undertakings the Indonesian government had made to the IMF, World Bank and ADB, which, as mentioned, made bail-out loans contingent upon Indonesia's attempts at deregulation and liberalisation, including in the electricity, oil and gas, and water industries.[54]

---

[50] Constitutional Court Decision 001-021-022/PUU-I/2003, p 347.

[51] P Venning, 'Determination of Economic, Social and Cultural Rights by the Indonesian Constitutional Court' (2008) 10(1) *Australian Journal of Asian Law* 100, 117; World Bank, *Lighting up Indonesia: Options for Increasing Access to Electricity* (Washington DC, World Bank, 2005).

[52] Venning, ibid, 117.

[53] 'In Financial Difficulties, PLN Searches for Investors in Coal Power Plant', *Harian Ekonomi Negara*, 14 October 2005; 'PLN shall increase by one million customers', *Republika*, 26 October 2005.

[54] *Hukumonline*, 'AGI: RUU Sumber Daya Air Kurang Perhatikan Isu Pemanfaatan Air Tanah', 21 October 2003; *Wahli*, 'Kontroversi RUU Air (1) Terjebak', 6 February 2004; *Wahli*, 'Mendukung Mahkamah Konstitusi Menjaga UU 1945: Air Tidak untuk Diprivatisasi', 10 May 2004; *Wahli*, 'Privatisasi air melanggar prinsip air sebagai hak asasi rakyat', 21 September 2003; *Wahli*, 'Kampayne menolak privatisasi dan komersialisasi sumberdaya air', 14 April 2005.

Protectionism

The *Livestock culling case*[55] deserves special note as the high-water mark of the Constitutional Court's economic and welfare protectionism. In this case, individuals, farmers and organisations challenged several provisions of Law 18 of 2009 on Livestock and Animal Health. Two provisions are relevant to the present discussion.[56] The first was Article 59(2), which required live animals imported in Indonesia to come from a country, or 'a zone within a country', that fulfils international health standards. The second was Article 68(4), which gave the Minister discretion to delegate authority over animal health to veterinary authorities.

The applicants argued that Article 59(2) was not effective in preventing animal diseases entering Indonesia and spreading, thereby threatening the health of humans, animals, the environment and the economy.[57] The Court agreed, finding that it was imprudent for the government to allow imports from only one 'safe' zone in a country. To be safe, the entire importing country needed to meet the standards, because disease may have spread into the zone from unsafe parts of that country, particularly if airborne.[58] The Court decided that the phrase 'a zone within a country' was, therefore, unconstitutional and deleted it from Article 59(2). The Court also found Article 68(4) unconstitutional, holding that giving the Minister discretion to delegate authority over animal

---

[55] Constitutional Court Decision 137/PUU-VII/2009.

[56] The applicants also challenged Article 59(4), which set the requirements and procedures for allowing livestock imports into Indonesia by reference to 'international norms based on a risk analysis involving animal health, health of veterinarians and prioritising the national interest'. The Court decided that this reference to international norms' did not provide legal certainty and perhaps even breached the people's sovereignty because it was not clear which international norms were being referred to and whether those norms had been approved by the national legislature as the Constitution required. The applicants also challenged Article 44(3) of the Law, which allowed for the culling of livestock without compensation. The Court decided that Article 44(3) was not unconstitutional. The provision aimed to protect humans and other livestock. Failing to destroy them would not help their owners because the animals would die anyway and they would infect other animals and people. And if healthy livestock were put down as a precautionary measure, under Article 44(4), owners were, in fact, entitled to compensation (Constitutional Court Decision 137/PUU-VII/2009, pp 132–35).

[57] Constitutional Court Decision 137/PUU-VII/2009, pp 110–11.

[58] Constitutional Court Decision 137/PUU-VII/2009, p 134.

health to non-veterinary experts jeopardised community protection and welfare.[59]

Although the Constitutional Court did not specify which constitutional provisions or principles were breached by Articles 59(2) and 68(4), the following extract suggests it is reasonable to speculate that it had in mind Article 33, the Preamble, or both:

> In a welfare state, the government must participate in running the economy, including by establishing protectionist regulations and encouraging the protection of the public good. The government should regulate to protect the public against potential economic losses.[60]

ARTICLE 33(4): PRINCIPLES OF THE NATIONAL ECONOMY

To our knowledge, the Court has considered the somewhat unclear economic principles mentioned in Article 33(4) in only two cases. In the *Tobacco excise case*, the Court considered the meaning of 'economic democracy'. In the *CSR case*, it considered 'efficiency in justice'.

'Economic democracy': the *Tobacco excise case*[61]

In the *Tobacco excise case*, the applicant – the provincial government of West Nusa Tenggara – sought a review of Law 39 of 2007, which amended Law 11 of 1995 on Excise Tax. Article 66A(1) of Law 39 required the allocation of two per cent of central government tobacco excise revenue to 'tobacco-producing regions'. According to Article 66A(1), this was to be used to improve the quality of raw materials, develop the industry and the social environment, promote excise laws and eradicate illegal tobacco products.

The central government had interpreted 'tobacco producing regions' to be 'regions in which there were cigarette factories'.[62] The applicant complained that, although West Nusa Tenggara was Indonesia's biggest grower of tobacco, it did not receive a proportion of the excise because

---

[59] Constitutional Court Decision 137/PUU-VII/2009, p 136.
[60] Constitutional Court Decision 137/PUU-VII/2009, p 132.
[61] Constitutional Court Decision 54/PUU-VI/2008.
[62] Constitutional Court Decision 54/PUU-VI/2008, p 4.

it did not have cigarette factories.[63] This, the applicants argued, contravened the principle of 'economic democracy' required by Article 33.[64]

The Constitutional Court agreed, deciding that provinces in which tobacco was grown should also receive the allocation. This, the Court noted, was required by Article 33(4):

> From the perspective of economic democracy and the principle of togetherness, efficiency in justice, balanced advancement and national economic unity as regulated in Article 33(4) . . . two per cent of tobacco excise obtained under Article 66A that is not implemented to include tobacco-growing provinces does not accord with the purpose, spirit and ideals of Article 33(4) of the Constitution. The Court, therefore, believes that Article 66A(1) is unconstitutional if interpreted without including provinces that grow tobacco amongst those who receive the tobacco excise.[65]

'Efficiency in justice': the *CSR case*[66]

In the *CSR case*, several companies and a number of institutions, including KADIN (*Kamar Dagang dan Industri Indonesia*), the Indonesian Chamber of Commerce, challenged the constitutionality of Article 74 of the 2007 Corporations Law.[67] Article 74 makes corporate social and environmental responsibility (CSER) mandatory for those engaged in industries with operations related to natural resources.[68] One of the applicants' constitutional arguments was that Article 74 failed to achieve 'efficiency in justice', one of the principles on which the national economy must be based under Article 33(4).

A 6:3 majority found that Article 74 did not breach the Constitution.[69] In response to the applicant's Article 33 argument, the court said:

> Economic individualism and liberalism is certainly not consistent with, and perhaps even contradicts, the economic democracy adhered to by the

---

[63] WSA Wulan, 'MK: Provinsi Penghasil Tembakau Peroleh Cukai Tembakau', *Kompas,* 14 April 2009; *Hukumonline*, 'Gubernur NTB Persoalkan UU Cukai Ke MK', 18 December 2008.

[64] Constitutional Court Decision 54/PUU-VI/2008, p 48.

[65] Constitutional Court Decision 54/PUU-VI/2008, p 59.

[66] Constitutional Court Decision 53/PUU-VI/2008.

[67] Law 40 of 2007 on Limited Liability Companies.

[68] Article 74 makes Indonesia one of very few countries to have mandatory CSR.

[69] In the majority: Alim, Fadjar, Mahfud, Mochtar, Harjono and Sodiki. In the minority: Farida, Siahaan and Sanusi.

Indonesian nation . . . The economy, as a collective endeavour, is not merely a matter between businesspersons and the state, but also [involves] cooperation between businesspersons and the community, particularly the surrounding community. Sincere concern from businesses about the social environment will provide a safe business environment because the surrounding community will feel that companies are paying attention to them. This will strengthen the ties between the company and the community.[70]

The Court went further, stating, somewhat idealistically, that community participation is, in fact, the very basis of the Indonesian economy. Imposing CSR as a legal responsibility is thus 'one way that the Government pushes companies to participate in the economic development of the community'. Therefore, making CSR a mandatory legal obligation, it held, was 'consistent with, and does not contradict, Article 33(4) of the Constitution, particularly the phrase "efficiency in justice" '.[71]

CONCLUSION

Article 33 remains one of the Constitution's core provisions – rhetorically at least. For many Indonesians, it is a potent symbol of economic justice and fairness: all citizens should benefit from Indonesia's natural resources; the government should help smaller enterprises in the face of competition; and citizens should have access to the basic necessities of life, such as electricity and fuel. However, Article 33 also sometimes seems to be an ideological left-over from another era, one that conflicts with many post-*Reformasi* attempts by the Indonesian legislature and executive to liberalise Indonesia's economy. Accordingly, the Constitutional Court has become the site of significant political contestation over the shape of the economy in Indonesia's new democracy.

In many of the Article 33 cases described in this chapter the Constitutional Court has emphasised notions of justice and fairness to assess whether statutes – and, we argue, the government policy they contain – comply with the Constitution. By so doing, the Court has required that the Indonesian government maintain a strong presence within the economy and, in particular, high levels of control over, and protection of, important industries. The Court's conservative interpreta-

---

[70] Constitutional Court Decision 53/PUU-VI/2008, p 99.
[71] Constitutional Court Decision 53/PUU-VI/2008, p 99.

tion of Article 33 has thus impeded legal reforms aimed at improving the efficiency of the Indonesian economy and, critically, attracting much-needed high levels of foreign investment in key industries. Whether the Court's interpretation and application of Article 33 does, in fact, maximise the welfare of the Indonesian people, therefore, remains an open – and much debated – question.

SELECTED READING

Butt, Simon and Lindsey, Tim, 'Economic Reform when the Constitution Matters: Indonesia's Constitutional Court and Article 33' (2008) 44(2) *Bulletin of Indonesia Economic Studies* 239–62.

Susanti, Bivitri, 'Neo-liberalism and its Resistance in Indonesia's Constitutional Reform 1999–2002' (Masters Dissertation, University of Warwick, 2002).

Venning, Philippa, 'Determination of Economic, Social and Cultural Rights by the Indonesian Constitutional Court' (2008) 10(1) *Australian Journal of Asian Law* 100–32.

Bibliography

Adnan, Zirfirdaus, 'Islamic Religion: Yes, Islamic Ideology: No! Islam and the State in Indonesia' in Arief Budiman (ed), *State and Civil Society in Indonesia* (Clayton, Victoria, Centre of Southeast Asian Studies, Monash University, 1990) 441–78.

Anshari, Endang Saifuddin, *Piagam Jakarta 22 Juni 1945: sebuah konsensus nasional tentang dasar negara Republik Indonesia (1945–1949)* (Jakarta, Gema Insani Press, 1996).

Antara News, 'Proses Politik Century Belum Tentu Berujung Pemakzulan', 2 March 2010.

Antlöv, Hans, 'The Social Construction of Power and Authority in Java' in Hans Antlöv and Jörgen Hellman (eds), *The Java that Never Was: Academic Theories and Political Practices* (Münster, Lit Verlag, 2005) 43–66.

Arnold, Luke Lazarus, 'Acting Locally, Thinking Globally? The Relationship between Decentralization in Indonesia and International Human Rights' (2009) 1 *Journal of East Asia and International Law* 177–203.

Asia Watch, 'Human Rights Concerns in Indonesia and East Timor' (USA, Asia Watch Committee, 1988).

Aspandi, Ali, *Menggugat Sistem Hukum Peradilan Indonesia Yang Penuh Ketidakpastian* (Surabaya, LeKSHI and Lutfansah, 2002).

Aspinall, Edward and Fealy, Greg, 'Introduction' in Edward Aspinall and Greg Fealy (eds), *Local Power and Politics in Indonesia: Decentralisation and Democratisation* (Singapore, ISEAS, 2003).

Assegaf, Rifqi S, 'Judicial Reform in Indonesia, 1998–2006' in Naoyuki Sakumoto and Hikmahanto Juwana (eds), *Reforming Laws and Institutions in Indonesia: An Assessment* (Ciba, Japan, Institute of Developing Economies (IDE) / Japan External Trade Organization (JETRO), 2007).

Asshiddiqie, Jimly, 'Creating a Constitutional Court for a New Democracy', *Centre for Comparative Constitutional Studies and Asian Law Centre Public Lecture* (Melbourne, Melbourne Law School, 2009).

—— *The Constitutional Law of Indonesia: A Comprehensive Overview* (Selangor, Malaysia, Sweet and Maxwell Asia, 2009).

Autheman, Violaine, 'Global Lessons Learned: Constitutional Courts, Judicial Independence and the Rule of Law', *IFES Rule of Law White Paper Series* (International Foundation of Electoral Systems (IFES), 2004).

Bahar, Saafroedin, Sinaga, Nannie Hudawati, and Kusuma, Ananda, *Risalah Sidang Badan Penyelidik Usaha-usaha Persiapan Kemerdekaan Indonesia (BPUPKI), dan Panitia Persiapan Kemerdekaan Indonesia (PPKI)*, *28 Mei 1945–22 Agustus 1945* (Jakarta, Sekretariat Negara Republik Indonesia, 1992).

Barton, Greg, *Abdurrahman Wahid: Muslim Democrat, Indonesian President; a View from Inside* (Honolulu, University of Hawaii Press, 2002).

Bedner, Adriaan, "'Shopping forums'": Indonesia's administrative courts' in Andrew Harding and Penelope Nicholson (eds), *New courts in Asia* (London/ New York, Routledge, 2010).

Bjornlund, Eric, 'Indonesia's Change of President and Prospects for Constitutional Reform: A Report on the July 2001 Special Session of the People's Consultative Assembly and the Presidential Impeachment Process' (Jakarta/Washington, National Democratic Institute for International Affairs, 2001).

Boland, BJ, *The Struggle of Islam in Modern Indonesia* (The Hague, Martinus Nijhoff, 1982).

Booth, Anne, 'Splitting, Splitting and Splitting Again: A Brief History of the Development of Regional Government in Indonesia Since Independence' (2011) 167(1) *Bijdragen tot de Taal-, Land- en Volkenkunde* 31–59.

Bourchier, David, *Dynamics of Dissent in Indonesia: Sawito and the Phantom Coup* (Ithaca NY, Cornell University, 1984).

—— 'The 1950s in New Order Ideology and Politics' in JD Legge and David Bourchier (eds), *Democracy in Indonesia, 1950s and 1990s* (Monash papers on Southeast Asia; Clayton, Victoria, Centre of Southeast Asian Studies, Monash University, 1994) 50–60.

—— 'Positivism and Romanticism in Indonesian Legal Thought' in Tim Lindsey (ed), *Indonesia: Law and Society*, 2nd edn (Annandale, NSW, Federation Press, 2008).

Bourchier, David and Hadiz, Vedi R, *Indonesian Politics and Society: a Reader* (New York, Routledge, 2003).

Burns, Peter, 'Crime Wave in Indonesia: Negara hukum Tidak Jadi' (1984) 15 *Kabar Sebarang* 51.

—— 'The Myth of Adat' (1989) 28 *Journal of Legal Pluralism and Unofficial Law* 1.

——*The Leiden Legacy: Concepts of Law in Indonesia* (Jakarta, PT Pradnya Paramita, 1999).

Bush, Robin, 'Regional Sharia Regulations in Indonesia: Anomaly or Symptom?' in Greg Fealy and Sally White (eds), *Expressing Islam: Religious Life and Politics in Indonesia* (Singapore, ISEAS, 2008) 174–91.

Butt, Simon, 'The Constitutional Court's Decision in the Dispute Between the Supreme Court and the Judicial Commission: Banishing Judicial Accountability?' in Ross H McLeod and Andrew J MacIntyre (eds), *Indonesia: Democracy and the Promise of Good Governance* (Singapore, ISEAS, 2007).

—— 'Judicial Review in Indonesia: Between Civil Law and Accountability? A Study of Constitutional Court Decisions 2003–2005' (Law Faculty, Melbourne University, 2007).

—— 'Surat sakti: The Decline of the Authority of Judicial Decisions in Indonesia' in Tim Lindsey (ed), *Indonesia: Law and Society*, 2nd edn (Annandale, NSW, Federation Press, 2008).

—— 'Polygamy and Mixed Marriage in Indonesia: Islam and the Marriage Law in the Courts' in Tim Lindsey (ed), *Indonesia: Law and Society*, 2nd edn (Annandale, NSW, Federation Press, 2008).

—— 'Indonesian Terrorism Law and Criminal Process' (*Islam, Syari'ah and Governance Background Paper Series*, Centre for Islamic Law and Society, University of Melbourne, 2008).

—— '"Unlawfulness" and Corruption under Indonesian Law' (2009) 45(2) *Bulletin of Indonesian Economic Studies* 179–98.

—— 'Two at the Top: the Constitutional Court and the Supreme Court' (2009) XI(8) *Van Zorge Report on Indonesia* 12–20.

—— 'Regional Autonomy and the Proliferation of Perda in Indonesia: An Assessment of Bureaucratic and Judicial Review Mechanisms' (2010) 32(2) *Sydney Law Review* 177.

—— 'Islam, the State and the Constitutional Court in Indonesia' (2010) 19(2) *Pacific Rim Law and Policy Journal* 279–302.

—— *Corruption and Law in Indonesia* (London, Routledge, 2011).

—— 'Anti-corruption Reform in Indonesia: an Obituary?' (2011) 47(3) *Bulletin of Indonesian Economic Studies* 381–94.

Butt, Simon and Hansell, David, 'The Masykur Abdul Kadir Case: Indonesian Constitutional Court Decision No 013/PUU-I/2003' (2004) 6(2) *Australian Journal of Asian Law* 176–96.

Butt, Simon and Lindsey, Tim, 'Indonesian Judiciary in Crisis (parts 1 and 2)', *Jakarta Post*, 6–7 August 2004.

—— 'Economic Reform when the Constitution Matters: Indonesia's Constitutional Court and Article 33' (2008) 44(2) *Bulletin of Indonesia Economic Studies* 239–62.

—— 'Who Owns the Economy? Privatisation, Property Rights and the Indonesian Constitution' in Aileen McHarg, et al (eds), *Property and the Law in Energy and Natural Resources* (Oxford, Oxford University Press, 2010).

—— 'Unfinished Business: Law Reform, Governance and the Courts in Post-Soeharto Indonesia' in Mirjam Kunkler and Alfred Stepan (eds), *Indonesia, Islam and Democratic Consolidation* (New York, Columbia University Press, 2012).

—— 'Judicial Mafia: Corruption and the Courts in Indonesia' in E Aspinall and G Van Klinken (eds), *The State and Illegality in Indonesia* (The Netherlands, KITLV Press, 2011) 189–216.

Cahaya Papua, 'Ratusan Warga Tambrauw Timur Datangi Kantor Bupati Tolak Ikut Pilkada Tambrauw', 14 March 2011.

Cammack, Mark, 'Islamic Law in Indonesia's New Order' (1989) 38(1) *International and Comparative Law Quarterly* 53–73.

Campos, Jose Edgardo and Joel S Hellman, 'Governance Gone Local: Does Decentralization Improve Accountability?' in *World Bank, East Asia Decentralizes: Making Local Government Work* (Washington, The World Bank, 2005) 237–52.

CIA, 'Indonesia', *The World Fact Book* www.cia.gov/library/publications/the-world-factbook/geos/id.html, accessed 20 July 2011.

Clark, David, 'The Many Meanings of the Rule of Law Law' in K Jayasuriya (ed), *Capitalism and Power in Asia* (London and New York, Routledge, 1999).

Clarke, Ross, 'Retrospectivity and the Constitutional Validity of the Bali Bombing and East Timor Trials' (2003) 5(2) *Australian Journal of Asian Law* 1–32.

Cohen, David, *Intended to Fail: the Trials before the Ad Hoc Human Rights Court in Jakarta* (New York, International Center for Transitional Justice, 2003).

Coppel, Charles, *Indonesian Chinese in crisis* (Kuala Lumpur and Melbourne, Oxford University Press, 1983).

Cribb, Robert, *The Indonesian Killings of 1965–1966: Studies from Java and Bali* (Clayton, Centre of Southeast Asian Studies Monash University, 1991).

—— '"The Incredible Shrinking Pancasila": Nationalist Propaganda and The Missing Ideological Legacy of Soeharto' in Thomas Reuter (ed), *The Return of Constitutional Democracy in Indonesia* (Annual Indonesia lecture series; Caulfield, Victoria, Monash Asia Institute, 2010) 65–76.

Crouch, Harold, *Political Reform in Indonesia after Soeharto* (Singapore, ISEAS, 2010).

Crouch, Melissa, 'Indonesia's National and Local Ombudsman Reforms: Salvaging a Failed Experiment?' in T Lindsey (ed), *Indonesia: Law and Society* (Annandale, NSW, Federation Press, 2008).

—— 'Indonesia, Militant Islam and Ahmadiyah: Origins and Implications', *Islam, Shari'ah and Governance Background Paper Series* (Centre for Islamic Law and Society, Melbourne Law School, University of Melbourne, 2009).

Eldridge, P, 'Human Rights in Post-Soeharto Indonesia' (2001) IX(1) *Brown Journal of World Affairs* 127.

Ellis, Andrew, 'The Indonesian Constitutional Transition: Conservatism or Fundamental Change?' (2002) 6(1) *Singapore Journal of International and Comparative Law* 116–53.

Emmerson, Donald K, *Indonesia beyond Suharto: Polity, Economy, Society, Transition* (Armonk, NY, ME Sharpe Inc, 1999).

Fadil, Iqbal, 'Cegah Konflik Baru, SBY Diminta Jawab Langsung Interpelasi', *Detik News*, 5 June 2007.

Faiq, Mohammad Hilmi, 'Hak Angket Masih Jauh dari Pemakzulan', *Kompas*, 26 June 2008.

Feener, M, 'Indonesian Movements for the Creation of a "National Maddhab"' (2001) 9(1) *Islamic Law and Society* 86.

Feith, Herbert, *The Indonesian Elections of 1955* (Ithaca, NY, Modern Indonesia Project, Dept of Far Eastern Studies, Southeast Asia Program, Cornell University, 1957).

—— *The Decline of Constitutional Democracy in Indonesia* (Ithaca, NY, Cornell University Press, 1962).

Feith, Herbert and Castles Lance, *Indonesian Political Thinking, 1945–1965* (Ithaca, NY, Cornell University Press, 1970).

Fenwick, Stewart, 'Measuring Up? Indonesia's Anti-Corruption Commission and the New Corruption Agenda' in Timothy Lindsey (ed), *Indonesia: Law and Society*, 2nd edn (Annandale, NSW, Federation Press, 2008).

Ferrazzi, Gabriele, 'Using the "F" Word: Federalism in Indonesia's Decentralization Discourse' (2000) 30(2) *Publius: The journal of federalism.*

Fitrani, Fitria, Hofman, Bert, and Kaiser, Kai, 'Unity in Diversity? The Creation of New Local Governments in a Decentralising Indonesia' (2005) 41(1) *Bulletin of Indonesian Economic Studies* 57–79.

Frankenburg, Gunter, 'Critical Comparisons: Re-thinking Comparative Law' (1985) 26 *Harvard International Law Journal* 411–55.

Freedom House, 'Indonesia', *Freedom in the World Series* (Washington DC, 2008).

Friedman, Barry, 'The History of the Countermajoritarian Difficulty, Part One: The Road to Judicial Supremacy' (1998) 73 *New York University Law Review* 333.

Friend, Theodore, '*The Asian Miracle, The Asian Contagion, and the USA*' (Speech to the Foreign Policy Research Institute, 16 November 1998, copy in possession of the authors).

Gale, Bruce, 'For DPR Members, Life's a trip', *Jakarta Globe*, 16 April 2011.

Hadiprayitno, Irene Istiningsih, 'Defensive Enforcement: Human Rights in Indonesia' (2010) 11 *Human Rights Review* 373–99.

Hadiz, Vedi R, 'Decentralization and Democracy in Indonesia: A Critique of Neo-Institutionalist Perspectives' (2004) 35(4) *Development and Change* 697–718.

Hadiz, Vedi R and Richard Robison, 'Neo-liberal Reforms and Illiberal Consolidations: The Indonesian Paradox' (2005) 41(2) *The Journal of Development Studies* 220–41.

Hall, David and Lobina, Emanuele, 'Private and Public Interests in Water and Energy' *Natural Resources Forum* 268–77.

Hamzah, Andi, *Kamus Hukum* (Jakarta, Ghalia, 1986).

Hapsari, Arghea Desafti, 'Court Ruling Won't Affect Education Budget', *Jakarta Post*, 4 March 2010.

Harian Ekonomi Negara, 'In Financial Difficulties, PLN Searches for Investors in Coal Power Plant', 14 October 2005.

Harijanti, Susi and Lindsey, Tim, 'Indonesia: General elections test the amended Constitution and the new Constitutional Court' (2006) 4(1) *International Journal of Constitutional Law* 138–50.

Harman, Benny K, 'Peranan Mahkamah Konstitusi dalam Mewujudkan Reformasi Hukum' in R Harun, ZAM Husein, and Bisariyadi (eds), *Menjaga Denyut Konstitusi: Refleksi satu tahun Mahkamah Konstitusi* (Jakarta, Konstitusi Press, 2004).

Hartwig, Matthias, 'The Institutionalization of the Rule of Law: The Establishment of Constitutional Courts in the Eastern European Countries' (1991) 7 *American University Journal of International Law and Policy* 449.

Harun, Refly, 'MK Masih Bersih?', *Kompas*, 25 October, 2010.

Harutyunyan, G and Mavcic, A, *Constitutional Review and its Development in the Modern World (a Comparative Constitutional Analysis)* [online text], Armenian Constitutional Court, 2009 www.concourt.am/Books/harutunyan/monogr3/book.htm.

Herbert, Jeff, 'The legal framework of human rights in Indonesia' in Tim Lindsey (ed), *Indonesia: Law and Society*, 2nd edn (Annandale, NSW, Federation Press, 2008).

Hilbink, Lisa, 'Beyond Manicheanism: Assessing the New Constitutionalism' (2006) 65(1) *Maryland Law Review* 15–31.

Holland, Peter, 'Regional Government and Central Authority in Indonesia' in Tim Lindsey (ed), *Indonesia: Law and Society*, 1st edn (Annandale, NSW, Federation Press, 1999) 200–20.

Hofman, Bert and Kaiser, Kai, 'The Making of the Big Bang and its Aftermath: A Political Economy Perspective', *Paper presented at conference 'Can Decentralization Help Rebuild Indonesia'* (Georgia State University, 1–3 May 2002).

Hooker, MB, *Indonesian Islam: Social Change Through Contemporary Fatawa* (Crows Nest, NSW, Asian Studies Association of Australia in Association with Allen and Unwin and University of Hawai'i Press Honolulu, 2003).

—— 'The Law Texts of Muslim South East Asia' in MB Hooker (ed), *Law of South East Asia*, vol 1, 'Pre-Modern Texts' (Singapore, Butterworths, 1986).

Hooker, MB and Lindsey, Tim, 'Toward a New Mazhab? The Public Faces of Syariah in Indonesia' (2003) 10(1) *Studia Islamika* 23–64.

Hosen, Nadirsyah, 'Human Rights Provisions in the Second Amendment to the Indonesian Constitution from Shari'ah Perspective' (2007) 9(2) *The Muslim World* 200–24.

—— *Shari'a and Constitutional Reform in Indonesia* (Singapore, ISEAS, 2007).

Howell, Julia Day, '"Spirituality" vs "Religion" Indonesian Style: Framing and Re-framing Experiential Religiosity in Contemporary Indonesian Islam',

Paper presented to the 15th Biennial conference of the Asian Studies Association of Australia (Canberra, ACT, 29 June–2 July 2004 (on file with authors)).

Hukumonline, 'AGI: RUU Sumber Daya Air Kurang Perhatikan Isu Pemanfaatan Air Tanah', 21 October 2003.

—— 'Ini dia, kelemahan RUU SDA versi LSM', 18 March 2004.

—— 'Masyarakat Papua Pertanyakan Putusan Mahkamah Konstitusi', 12 December 2004.

—— 'Mengupas "Itjihad" Kontroversial Mahkamah Konstitusi', 6 January 2004.

—— 'MK "Koreksi" Sebagian Materi Undang-Undang Migas', 21 December 2004.

—— 'Pembentukan Irjabar Sah, Tapi Undang-Undangnya Tidak Berlaku Lagi', 17 November 2004.

—— 'DPR Tanggapi Serius Implikasi Perluasan Kewenangan MK', 3 May 2005.

—— 'Mahkamah Konstitusi Ogah Membatalkan UU Sumber Daya Air', 19 August 2005.

—— 'Mukhti dan Maruarar, Dua Hakim yang Ajukan Dissenting Opinion UU SDA', 17 August 2005.

—— 'PP Listrik Swasta Diajukan Uji Materiil', 17 July 2005.

—— 'Gubernur NTB Persoalkan UU Cukai Ke MK', 18 December 2008.

—— 'Hakim Agung Mangkir, KY Akan "Vonis" secara in absentia', 24 May 2010.

—— 'Hendarman Supandji Harus Berhenti', 22 September 2010.

—— 'MK: Masa Jabatan Jaksa Agung Konstitusional Bersyarat', 22 September 2010.

—— 'MK Legowo Sambut UU Baru', 22 June 2011.

—— 'MK Tegaskan Peninjauan Kembali Hanya Sekali', 18 April 2011.

—— 'PERMA Hak Uji Materiil Perlu Direvisi', 25 March 2011.

—— 'Putusan Majelis Kehormatan MK Bakal Digugat', 14 February 2011.

—— 'Telah Terbit PERMA Hak Uji Materiil 2011', 20 June 2011.

—— 'Terpidana Seumur Hidup Uji Aturan Pembatasan PK', 27 January 2011.

Human Rights Watch, 'Indonesia: Reverse Ban on Ahmadiyah Sect: Government Should Protect Religious Minority, Not Threaten Prison for Beliefs', 9 June 2008. Available www.hrw.org/en/news/2008/06/09/indonesia-reverse-ban-ahmadiyah-sect (accessed 26 May 2011).

Husein, Fatimah, *Muslim-Christian Relations in the New Order Indonesia* (Bandung, Mizan, 2005).

Indra, Muhammad Ridhwan, *The President's Position under the 1945 Constitution* (Jakarta, Trisula, 1998).

Indrayana, Denny, *Indonesian Constitutional Reform, 1999–2002: An Evaluation of Constitution-Making in Transition* (Jakarta, Kompas Book Publishing, 2008).

International Crisis Group, 'Indonesia's Presidential Crisis', *Indonesia Briefing* (Jakarta/Brussels, 2001).

—— *Indonesia: Impunity versus Accountability for Gross Human Rights Violations* (Jakarta, International Crisis Group, 2001).

—— 'Indonesia: GAM vs GAM in the Aceh Elections', *Asia Briefing No 123* (Jakarta/Brussels, 2011).

Ismail, Tjip, 'Kebijakan Pengawasan atas Perda Pajak Daerah dan Retribusi Daerah' in *Decentralization, regulatory reform, and the Business Climate* (Jakarta Indonesia, Partnership for Economic Growth, 2003).

Jacobs, Leslie Gielow, 'Even More Honest Than Ever Before: Abandoning Pretense and Recreating Legitimacy in Constitutional Interpretation' (1995) *University of Illinois Law Review* 363.

Jakarta Post, 'SBY urges end to debate on Pancasila's merits', 2 June 2006.

—— 'Honor council for justice Akil: MK chief', 22 December 2006.

—— 'Papuans protest en masse against Council, "special autonomy"', 26 January 2011.

Kahin, George, *Nationalism and Revolution in Indonesia* (Ithaca NY, Cornell University Press, 1952).

Kartoyo, DS, 'Konflik Pilkada: Gafur Gugat Pelantikan Thaib ke MK', *Surakarya*, 7 October 2008.

Katz, June S and Katz, Ronald S, 'The New Indonesian Marriage Law: A Mirror of Indonesia's Political, Cultural, and Legal Systems' (1975) 23(4) *American Journal of Comparative Law* 653–81.

Kirk, Jeremy, 'Rights, Review and Reasons for Restraint' (2001) 23(1) *Sydney Law Review* 19.

Komisi Yudisial, *Laporan Tahunan* 2010 (Jakarta, Komisis Yudisial, 2011).

—— *Menemukan Substansi Dalam Keadilan Prosedural: Laporan Penelitian Putusan Kasus Pidana Pengadilan Negeri* (Jakarta, Komisis Yudisial, 2009).

—— *Potret Profesionalisme Hakim Dalam Putusan: Laporan Putusan Pengadilan Negeri* (Jakarta, Komisis Yudisial, 2008).

Kompas 'Aceh sampai Papua Tersandera Korupsi', 24 January.

Koopmans, Thijmen, 'Retrospectivity Reconsidered' (1989) 39(2) *Cambridge Law Journal* 287.

KPU, 'Profil Komisi Pemilihan Umum', www.kpu.go.id/index.php?option=com_content&task=view&id=32&Itemid=50, accessed 20 July 2011.

Krissantono, *Pandangan Presiden Tentang Pancasila* (Jakarta, CSIS, 1976).

Kurniadi, Bayu Dardias, 'Yogyakarta in Decentralized Indonesia: Integrating Traditional Institutions into a Democratic Republic', *Indonesia Council Open Conference* (University of Sydney, 16 July 2009).

Lev, Daniel S, *The Transition to Guided Democracy: Indonesian Politics, 1957–1959* (Ithaca, NY, Cornell University, 1966).

—— 'Judicial Institutions and Legal Culture in Indonesia' in Claire Holt (ed), *Culture and Politics in Indonesia* (Ithaca, NY, Cornell University Press, 1972).

—— 'Judicial Authority and The Struggle for An Indonesian Rechsstaat' (1978) 13 *Law and Society Review* 37–37.

—— 'Social Movements, Constitutionalism and Human Rights: Comments from the Malaysian and Indonesian Experiences' in Douglas Greenberg et al (eds), *Constitutionalism and Democracy: Transitions in the Contemporary World* (Oxford, Oxford University Press, 1993).

—— 'Between State and Society: Professional Lawyers and Reform in Indonesia' in Daniel Lev and R McVey (eds), *Making Indonesia* (Ithaca, NY, Cornell University Press, 1996).

—— 'Between State and Society: Professional Lawyers and Reform in Indonesia' in Tim Lindsey (ed), *Indonesia: Law and Society*, 1st edn (Annandale, NSW, Federation Press, 1999) 227–46.

—— 'Comments on the judicial reform program in Indonesia' (paper presented at Seminar on Current Developments in Monetary and Financial Law, International Monetary Fund, Washington, DC, 3 June 2004) http:// www. imf.org/external/np/leg/sem/2004/cdmfl/eng/lev.pdf. p 2.

Lewis, Blane D, 'Tax and Charge Creation by Regional Governments under Fiscal Decentralization: Estimates and Explanations' (2003) 39(2) *Bulletin Of Indonesian Economic Studies.*

Liddle, William, 'Indonesia's Democratic Transition: Playing by the Rules' in Andrew Reynolds (ed), *The Architecture of Democracy: Constitutional Design, Conflict Management, and Democracy* (Oxford UK/New York, Oxford University Press, 2002).

Lindsey, Tim, 'Indonesia's Negara Hukum: Walking the Tightrope to the Rule of Law' in Arief Budiman, Barbara Hatley and Damien Kingsbury (eds), *Reformasi: Crisis and Change in Indonesia* (Clayton, Monash Asia Institute/ Centre for Southeast Asian Studies, 1999) 363–83.

—— 'History Always Repeats? Corruption, Culture and "Asian Values"' in Timothy Lindsey and Howard Dick (eds), *Corruption in Asia: rethinking the governance paradigm*, 2nd edn (Sydney, Federation Press, 2002) 1–23.

—— 'Indonesia: Devaluing Asian Values, Rewriting Rule of Law' in Randall Peerenboom (ed), *Asian Discourses of Rule of Law* (London and New York, Routledge, 2004) 286–323.

—— 'Reconstituting the Ethnic Chinese in Post-Suharto Indonesia: Law, Racial Discrimination, and Reform' in Timothy Lindsey and Helen Pausacker (eds), *Chinese Indonesians: Remembering, Distorting, Forgetting – A Festschrift for Charles A Coppel* (Singapore/Clayton, Victoria, ISEAS, 2005) 41–76.

—— 'Constitutional Reform in Indonesia: Muddling towards Democracy' in Tim Lindsey (ed), *Indonesia: Law and Society* (Sydney, Federation Press, 2008) 2347.

Lindsey, Tim, (forthcoming) *Islam, Law and the State in Indonesia* (London, IB Tauris, 2012 forthcoming).

Lindsey, Tim and Butt, Simon, 'Unfinished Business: Law Reform, Governance and the Courts in Post-Soeharto Indonesia' in Mirjam Künkler and Alfred Stepan (eds), *Indonesia, Islam and Democratic Consolidation* (New York, Columbia University Press, 2010).

Lindsey, Tim and Santosa, MA, 'The Trajectory of Law Reform in Indonesia: A Short Overview of Legal Systems and Change in Indonesia' in Lindsey, T (ed), *Indonesia: Law and Society*, 2nd edn (Sydney, Federation Press, 2008) 2–22.

Linnan, David, 'Bankruptcy Policy & Reform: Reconciling Efficiency and Economic Nationalism' in T Lindsey (ed), *Law Reform and the Commercial Court in Indonesia* (Sydney, Federation Press, 1999) 94–112.

Linton, Suzannah, 'Accounting For Atrocities in Indonesia' (2006) 10 *Singapore Yearbook of International Law* 199–231.

Lotulung, Paulus, 'Judicial Review in Indonesia' in Y Zhang (ed), *Comparative Studies on the Judicial Review System in East and Southeast Asia* (The Hague, Kluwer Law International, 1997).

Lubis, Todung Mulya, *In Search of Human Rights: Legal-Political Dilemmas of Indonesia's New Order, 1966–1990* (Jakarta, Published by PT Gramedia Pustaka Utama in cooperation with SPES Foundation, 1993).

—— 'The *Rechsstaat* and Human Rights' in Tim Lindsey (ed), *Indonesia: Law and Society*, 1st edn (Annandale, NSW, Federation Press, 1999) 171–85.

Mahfud, Mohammad, 'The Role of the Constitutional Court in the Development of Democracy in Indonesia' (Cape Town, South Africa, 2009).

Mahkamah Agung, *Laporan Tahunan 2007 Mahkamah Agung Republik Indonesia* (Jakarta, Mahkamah Agung, 2008).

—— *Cetak Biru Pembaruan Peradilan 2010–2035* (Jakarta, Mahkamah Agung, 2010).

—— *Laporan Tahun 2010* (Jakarta, Mahkamah Agung, 2011).

McBeth, John, 'Islam and Society: The Case for Islamic Law', *The Straits Times*, 22 August 2002.

McLeod, Ross H, 'Soeharto's Indonesia: A Better Class of Corruption' (2000) 7(2) *Agenda*.

Merryman, John, *The Civil Law Tradition: an Introduction to the Legal Systems of Western Europe and Latin America* (Stanford CA, Stanford University Press, 1984).

Mietzner, Marcus, 'Political Conflict Resolution and Democratic Consolidation in Indonesia: The Role of the Constitutional Court' (2010) 10(3) *Journal of East Asian Studies* 397–424.

Millie, J, 'The *Tempo* Case: Indonesia's Press Law, the *Pengadilan Tata Usaha Negara* and the Indonesian *Negara Hukum*' in T Lindsey (ed), *Indonesia: Law and Society* (Sydney, Federation Press, 1999).

Nasution, Adnan Buyung, *The Aspiration for Constitutional Government in Indonesia: A Socio-Legal Study of the Indonesian Konstituante, 1956–1959* (Jakarta, Pustaka Sinar Harapan, 1992).

—— 'Towards Constitutional Democracy in Indonesia', *Adnan Buyung Nasution Papers on Southeast Asian Constitutionalism* (Asian Law Centre, The University of Melbourne, 2011).

Nishimura, Shigeo, 'The Development of Pancasila Moral Education' (1995) 33(3) *Southeast Asian Studies* 303–16.

Noer, Deliar, *The Modernist Muslim movement in Indonesia, 1900–1942* (East Asian historical monographs; Kuala Lumpur, Oxford University Press, 1973).

—— 'Bung Hatta yang Taqwa' in CLM Penders (ed), *Mohammad Hatta, Indonesian Patriot: Memoirs* (Singapore, Gunung Agung, 1981) 617–22.

Nordholt, Henk Schulte and Klinken, Geert Arend van (eds), *Renegotiating Boundaries: Local Politics in Post-Suharto Indonesia* (Verhandelingen van het Koninklijk Instituut voor Taal-, Land- en Volkenkunde, Leiden, KITLV Press, 2007).

Nugraha, Pepih, 'Tak Ada Lagi Calon Independen di Aceh', *Kompas*, 28 June 2011.

Ombudsman Republik Indonesia, *Laporan Tahunan 2009: Ombudsman Republik Indonesia* (Jakarta, Ombudsman Republik Indonesia, 2010).

Pabottingi, Mochtar, 'Konteks Ekonomi Nasionalisme Indonesia, in Alfian and Nazaruddin Sjamsuddin, (eds), *Profil Budaya Politik Indonesia* (Jakarta, Pustaka Utama Grafiti, 1991) 87–123.

Pasandaran, Camelia, 'Judges Slap Back at Constitutional Court Corruption Probe', *Jakarta Globe*, 11 December 2010.

Patrono, Mario, 'The Protection of Fundamental Rights by Constitutional Courts – A Comparative Perspective' (2000) 2 *Victoria University of Wellington Law Review* 24.

Permana, Sugeng, 'Not your Local Member' in Tim Lindsey (ed), *Indonesia: Law and Society*, 1st edn (Sydney, Federation Press, 1999) 197–99.

Pollicino, Oreste, 'Legal Reasoning of the Court of Justice in the Context of Principle of Equality between Judicial Activism and Self-Restraint' (2004) 5(3) *German Law Journal* 283–317.

Pompe, Sebastian, *The Indonesian Supreme Court: A Study of Institutional Collapse* (Ithaca, NY, Cornell University, 2005).

Pranab, Bardhan and Dilip Mookherjee, 'Decentralization, Corruption and Government Accountability' in Susan Rose-Ackerman (ed), *International Handbook on the Economics of Corruption* (Cheltenham, Edward Elgar, 2006).

Pranowo, M Bambang, 'Which Islam and Which Pancasila? Islam and the State in Indonesia' in Arief Budiman (ed), *State and Civil Society in Indonesia* (Clayton, Victoria, Monash University, 1990) 479–502.

Pratikno, 'Exercising freedom: Local Autonomy and Democracy in Indonesia, 1999–2001' in Priyambudi Sulistiyanto, Maribeth Erb, and Caroline Faucher (eds), *Regionalism in Post-Suharto Indonesia* (New York, RoutledgeCurzon, 2005).

Price Waterhouse Coopers (PWC), 'Summary of Electricity Law no 15/1985 and Government Regulation no 3 /2005' (Available at: www.pwcglobal.com/ Extweb/pwcpublications.nsf/4bd5f76b48e282738525662b00739e22/f9c5d fb9ed11c524ca25703e0025e3c6/$FILE/Energy_Utilities_Mining_ NewsFlash_2005-_23.pdf).

Quinn, B, *The Administrative Review Act of 1986: Implications for Legal and Bureaucratic Culture* (Honours thesis, Faculty of Asian Studies, Australian National University, 1994).

Rahardjo, Satjipto, 'Between Two Worlds: Modern State and Traditional Society in Indonesia' (1994) 28(3) *Law and Society Review* 493–502.

Ramage, Douglas, 'Ideological Discourse in the Indonesian New order: State Ideology and the Beliefs of an Elite, 1985–1993' (University of South Carolina, 1993).

Ray, David, 'Decentralization, Regulatory Reform, and the Business Climate', *Decentralization, Regulatory Reform, and the Business Climate* (Jakarta Indonesia, Partnership for Economic Growth, 2003).

Republika, 'PLN shall increase by one million customers', 26 October 2005.

Reuter, Thomas, 'Winning Hearts and Minds? Religion and Politics in post-Suharto Indonesia' in Thomas Reuter (ed), *The Return of Constitutional Democracy in Indonesia* (Caulfield, Monash Asia Institute, 2010) 77–88.

Ricklefs, MC, *A History Of Modern Indonesia Since C. 1300*, 4th edn (Stanford CA, Stanford University Press, 2008).

—— 'Religion, Politics and Social Dynamics in Java: Historical and Contemporary Rhymes' in Greg Fealy and Sally White (eds), *Expressing Islam: Religious Life and Politics in Indonesia* (Singapore, ISEAS, 2008) 115–36.

Rosdianasari, Eko Susi, Anggriani, Novi, and Mulyani, Basri, *Dinamika Penyusunan, Substansi dan Implementasi Perda Pelayanan Publik* (Jakarta, World Bank Justice for the Poor Project, 2009).

Royan, Naomita, 'Increasing Press Freedom in Indonesia: The Abolition of the Lese Majeste and "Hate-sowing" Provisions' (2008) 10(2) *Australian Journal of Asian Law* 290.

Sagita, Dessy, 'Constitutional Court Justice Steps Down Over Kin's Alleged Bribery', *Jakarta Globe*, 12 February 2011.

Salim, Arskal, 'Shari'a from Below in Aceh (1930s–1960s): Islamic Identity and the Right to Self-Determination with Comparative Reference to the Moro Islamic Liberation Front (MILF)' (2004) 32(92) *Indonesia and Malay World* 80–99.

—— *Challenging the Secular State: the Islamization of Law in Modern Indonesia* (Honolulu, University of Hawaii Press, 2008).

Saragih, Bagus BT and Christanto, Dicky, 'Boediono Brushes Off Threat of Impeachment', *Jakarta Post*, 15 January 2011.

Savitri, Isma, 'Akil Mochtar: Tudingan Refly Bisa Bunuh Karakter Hakim', *Tempo*, 12 December 2010.

Schmidt, Adam 'Indonesia's 2009 elections: Performance Challenges and Negative Precedents' in Edward Aspinall and Marcus Mietzner (eds), *Problems of Democratisation in Indonesia: Elections, Institutions and Society* (Singapore, ISEAS, 2004).

Schwarz, Adam, *A Nation in Waiting: Indonesia's Search for Stability* (Boulder CO, Westview Press, 2004).

Sherlock, Stephen, 'Combating Corruption in Indonesia? The Ombudsman and the Assets Auditing Commission' (2002) 38(3) *Bulletin of Indonesian Economic Studies* 367.

—— 'The Indonesian Parliament after Two Elections: What has Really Changed?', *CDI Policy Papers on Political Governance* (Canberra, Centre for Democratic Insitutions (CDI), 2007).

Sihaloho, Markus Junianto, 'Court Ruling Fails to Kill Impeachment Petition', *Jakarta Globe*, 3 May 2010.

Sijabat, Ridwan Max, 'Pancasila Ideology Absolute: President' *Jakarta Post*, 18 August 2007.

Simanjuntak, Marsillam, *Pandangan Negara Integralistik: Sumber, Unsur, dan Riwayatnya dalam Persiapan UUD 1945* (Jakarta, Pustaka Utama Grafiti, 1994).

Simanjuntak, PNH, *Kabinet-kabinet Republik Indonesia: dari awal kemerdekaan sampai reformasi* (Jakarta, Djambatan, 2003).

Sjadzali, H Munawir, *Islam and Governmental System* (Jakarta, INIS, 1991).

Smoke, Paul, 'The Rules of the Intergovernmental Game in East Asia: Decentralisation Frameworks and Processes' in World Bank (ed), *East Asia Decentralizes: Making Local Government Work* (Washington DC, World Bank, 2005).

Soedijarto, 'Some Notes on the Ideals and Goals of Indonesia's National Education System and the Inconsistency of its Implementation: A Comparative Analysis' (2009) 2 *Journal of Indonesian Social Sciences and Humanities* 1–11.

Soemantri, Sri, *Prosedur dan Sistem Perubahan Konstitusi* (Bandung, Alumni, 1979).

Somba, Nethy Dharma, 'Govt "not serious" in Applying Papuan Special Autonomy', *Jakarta Post*, 26 July 2011.

Somin, Ilya, 'Political Ignorance and the Countermajoritarian Difficulty: A New Perspective on the Central Obsession of Constitutional Theory' (2004) 89(4) *Iowa Law Review* 1287–372.

Strange, Paul, ' "Legitimate" Mystical Groups in Indonesia' (1986) 2(20) *RIMA* 76–117.

Subekti, Raden, *Law in Indonesia* (Jakarta, Center for Strategic and International Studies, 1982).

Sukma, Rizal, 'Indonesian Politics in 2009: Defective Elections, Resilient Democracy' (2009) 45(3) *Bulletin of Indonesian Economic Studies* 317.

Sumner, Cate and Lindsey, Tim, *Courting Reform: Indonesia's Islamic courts and justice for the poor*, Lowy Paper no 31 (Double Bay, Lowy Institute for International Policy, 2010).

Susan, Novri, 'The DPR's Politics of Ignorance', *Jakarta Globe*, 16 April 2011.

Susanti, Bivitri, 'Neo-liberalism and its Resistance in Indonesia's Constitutional Reform 1999–2002' (Masters Dissertation, University of Warwick, 2002).

Susanto, Ichwan and Wisnubrata, A, 'Menko Polhukam Ditagih Revisi Pemekaran', *Kompas*, 30 September 2010.

Sutarmi, 'Pemakzulan SBY-JK, Golkar Belum Tentukan Sikap', *Okezone*, 6 October 2008.

Swamurti, Aqida, 'Komnas Perempuan Desak 154 Perda Diskriminatif Dibatalkan', *Tempo*, 29 January 2010.

Sweet, AS, 2000, *Governing with judges: constitutional politics in Europe* (Oxford, Oxford University Press, 2000).

Tampubolon, Hans David, 'Impeachment initiative starts rolling', *Jakarta Post*, 13 March 2010.

Tanzi, Vito, 'Fiscal Federalism and Decentralization: A Review of Some Efficiency and Macroeconomic Aspects' in Michael Bruno and Boris Pleskovic (eds) *Annual World Bank Conference on Development Economics* (Washington DC, The World Bank, 1995) 295.

Tempo, 'Old Hand at the Helm', 7 December 2010.

Thoolen, Hans, *Indonesia and the rule of law: twenty years of 'New Order' Government* (London, Frances Pinter Publishers, 1987).

US Department of State, '2010 Country Reports on Human Rights Practices' (Washington DC, US Department of State, Bureau of Democracy, Human Rights, and Labor, 2011).

van Langenburg, Michael, 'The New Order State: Language, Ideology, Hegemony' in Arief Budiman (ed), *State and Civil Society in Indonesia* (Clayton, Victoria, Centre of Southeast Asian Studies, Monash University, 1990).

Venning, Philippa, 'Determination of Economic, Social and Cultural Rights by the Indonesian Constitutional Court' (2008) 10(1) *Australian Journal of Asian Law* 100–32.

Waddell, Sarah, 'The Role of the "Legal Rule" in Indonesian Law Reform: The Reformasi of Water Resources Management in Indonesia' (University of Sydney, 2002).

—— 'Shifting Visions of the Social and Legal Order in Indonesia: Implications for Legislative Style and Form' (2005) 7(1) *Australian Journal of Asian Law* 43–59.

Wahli, 'Privatisasi air melanggar prinsip air sebagai hak asasi rakyat', (updated 21 September 2003) www.walhi.or.id/kampanye/air/privatisasi/030921_privairhak_sp/.

—— 'Kontroversi RUU Air (1) Terjebak' (updated 6 February 2004) www.walhi.or.id/kampanye/air/privatisasi/air_kntrvrsi_ruu_060204/.

—— 'Mendukung Mahkamah Konstitusi Menjaga UU 1945: Air Tidak untuk Diprivatisasi' (updated 10 May 2004) www.walhi.or.id/kampanye/air/privatisasi/050510_privair_sp/.

—— 'Kampayne menolak privatisasi dan komersialisasi sumberdaya air' (updated 14 April 2005) www.walhi.or.id/kampanye/air/privatisasi/kamp_tolak_priv_air_info/.

—— 'Pemerintah harus ubah PP Air Minum yang Mendorong Privatisasi' (updated 20 October 2005) www.walhi.or.id/kampanye/air/privatisasi/kamp_tolak_priv_air_info/.

—— 'PP Air Minum Muluskan Privatisasi' (updated 15 July 2005) www.walhi.or.id/kampanye/air/privatisasi/kamp_tolak_priv_air_info/.

Warsidi, Adi, 'Pilkada Aceh Dipastikan Tanpa Calon Independen', *Tempo*, 29 June 2011.

World Bank, *Decentralizing Indonesia: a Regional Public Expenditure Review Overview Report* (Washington, DC, World Bank, 2003).

—— *Combating corruption in Indonesia: enhancing accountability for development* (Jakarta, World Bank Office Jakarta, 2004).

—— *Lighting up Indonesia: Options for Increasing Access to Electricity* (Washington DC, World Bank, 2005).

Wulan, Wahyu Satriani Ari, 'MK: Provinsi Penghasil Tembakau Peroleh Cukai Tembakau', *Kompas*, 14 April 2009.

Yamin, H Muhammad, *Naskah Persiapan Undang-Undang Dasar 1945* (Jakarta, Yayasan Prapanca, 1959).

Ziegenhain, Patrick, *The Indonesian Parliament and Democratization* (Singapore, ISEAS, 2008).

Zifcak, Spencer, 'But a Shadow of Justice: Political Trials in Indonesia', in Tim Lindsey (ed), *Indonesia: Law and Society*, 1st edn (Annandale, NSW, Federation Press, 1999) 355–66.

Index